THE STORYTELLER'S SHADOWS

Published by Reed Independent, Melbourne, 2018

Printed by IngramSpark, Ingram Content Group

This composite volume is available as a paperback or as an ebook from most major bookshops or online stores worldwide under:
paperback   9780648175698
ebook   9780648175643

All of these scripts have been individually selected for inclusion in the Australian playwriting depository, the Australian Script Centre, and can be purchased individually as play scripts through its website australianplays.org.

Front cover illustration courtesy of Google Images

National Library of Australia Cataloguing-in-Publication entry
Creator: Reed, Bill - author.
Title: The Storyteller's Shadows/Bill Reed
ISBN: 9780648175698 (paperback)
ISBN: 9780648175643 (ebook)
Subjects: Contemporary Australian Drama -- Shadow Plays – Drama/Anthology.
Dewey Number: A822.3

Live-acted Shadow Plays for Today

THE STORYTELLER'S SHADOWS

BILL REED

R

also by Bill Reed

novels
Dogod
The Pipwink Papers\
Me, the Old Man
Stigmata
Ihe
Crooks
Tusk
Wi
Throw her back
The Wild Waves Whist
Reveal
Tasker Tusker Tasker

nonfiction
Water Workout

staged and published plays
Burke's Company
Truganinni
The Pecking Order
Mr Siggie Morrison with his Comb
and Paper
Jack Charles is Up and Fighting
Just Out of Your Ground
You Want It, Don't You, Billy?
I Don't Know What to Do with You.
Paddlesteamer
Cass Butcher Bunting
Bullsh/More Bullsh
Talking to a Mirror
Mirror, Mirror
Auntie and the Girl
Daddy the 8th
Truganinni Inside Out
Living on Mars
Spouting Black Holes
Shorts
The Storyteller's Shadows

The Shadow Plays
A Mind of Its Own
Box and Cox
Dimmer
Gogol's The Nose (adaption)
Last of Her Tribe
Monkey and Half-goddess
Nosey Parker
Tanzir's Fifth
Tears and the Mozzies
Top Knot Down
Two Shiny Beacons
Way of the Tilt

Runyon's The Brain Goes Home
Meeta Jarred-a-lot

award-winning short stories; also
published under 'Passing Strange'
Messman on the C.E. Altar
English Expression
The 200-year Old Feet
The Case Inside
Blind Freddie's Pickle Jars
The Old Ex-serviceman
Mahood on the Thin Beach
The Shades of You Dandenong

'commended' short stories
The Rotten Sea
The Quiet Torment
Goofiest Thing of All
Runs in the Veins

To Aubrey Mellor and the play of shadows upon the wall of all our wonderments

Contents

TODAY'S LIVE-ACTED SHADOW PLAY 1

The Plays:

GOGOL'S THE NOSE   11

WAY OF THE TILT   46

LAST OF HER TRIBE   73

RUNYON'S THE BRAIN GOES HOME   104

NOSEY PARKER   128

TWO SHINY BEACONS   152

THE TOP KNOT DOWN   179

BOX AND COX   209

TANZIR'S FIFTH   255

MONKEY AND HALF-GODDESS   289

A MIND OF ITS OWN   310

TEARS AND THE TAIL LIGHT   336

DIMMER   356

MEETA JARRED-A-LOT   384

Today's Live-acted Shadow Play

Today's live-acted shadow play is a performance which employs live actors behind a scrim screen, performing at a pace enough to at least keep pace with a substantial story being read by a storyteller upfront.

It combines natural stage acting with the stylizations of traditional shadow-play techniques to give a poetically-synchronized and real-time and ongoing substance of the story in a way that a storyteller's shadows do so in, say, a candle-lit room or by firelight on a rock wall

As such, a modern live-acted shadow play, at least conceptually, requires a separate director to manage the shadow-action... one who can distill the storyteller's tale into a shadowed performance that reflects the essence of the story, rather than trying to illustrate every nuance of it. It is very really an echoing play-within-a-play... a poetic or balletic metaphor of what is being read, but doing so in cadence with the narration.

Again at least in theory, this requires two directors – one to look after the behind-the-scrim, and the other to give fact to the theatrical impact of the voice of the storyteller *and* the overall 'look' of the play as a whole. Alternatively, these are the two essential creative parts for a single director.

We should note, though, this shadow-action – or 'inner background' play -- can only ever keep 'pace' with the reading, not keep *up* with it. It does not try to illustrate every twist and turn, nor every nuance, of the plot. It complements visually what is vocally heard.

Because of this, the actual behind-the-screen shadow show is a distillation of the storyteller's tale – almost like a series of scenes make up a play in conventional theatre, but with the added dreamlike wonderment that only shadow-playing can bring. To this purpose, the directions given in the scripts printed in this book are deliberately excessive to what the shadow-play director may need to realize his individual vision of this distillation. They are not given here as do-this-do-that; they are given as a type of storyboard captions, in excess only

1

to modestly suggest how a fusion of the storyline into the 'shadowing' shadow-play might be realised. They are, yes, overelaborated. But they are merely signposts to an end result.

Nonetheless, the live-acted shadow play of today renders its shadow action faster than what we are used to in traditional shadow 'presentations' or puppet plays. The actors use lively passing movements – that is, are acting in the shadows in a much more lively manner than traditionally thought possible or 'allowed' – and interact with each other almost on a conventional stage-acting basis. They certainly do not endeavour to perform projecting their bodies as quirky body shapes, or what almost all other shadow companies call, and pursue as, human architecture – as in three or four of them contorting themselves to form the shape of an elephant etcetera. This sort of shadow acting can move no story along, nor illustrate any normally-moving story. The flexibility possible to live actors of today's shadow plays comes from assistants manipulating simple and lightweight movable props that are quickly manoeuvred moved on an off from outside the back-lighting's areas. For example, a desk is a real desk (or a lightweight outline version of one); it does not have to be clod-hopped onto the lit areas and clomped down; nor is that desk slowly conjured by a couple of shadow actors twisting themselves along a spotlight's parallax and remaining static while the narration sails on.

This prop-aiding makes scene setting, scene giving and scene changing almost as fast as conventional stage acting of set props, but adds the magic of shadow acting to reality by allowing a cadence that moves with what the storyteller is relating to the audience.

In the past and well up to now, the shadow play hasn't been live-acted, in the sense that shadow players have been human counterparts to traditional puppetry, as in the Wayang Orang of Indonesia and some contemporary aspects of Kabuki. That is not to say that these human-puppet performers are anything less than spectacular and less than wonderful actors. Yet their art, in other nonreligious forms, has been somewhat restricted to the entertainment vignettes, like short-form and simple morality tales or song-lyric illustrations, or even magical-show cameos that are there to show the wonder of the shadow techniques, not the wonder of the story.

A modern live-acted shadow play presents the staging of a full-blown playscript, presenting every-day plots with modern visual and sound effects, while maintaining all the wonder of shadows which extends stage-bound reality into the magical and the fantastical.

The storyteller

For most of the modern live-acted shadow play, the storyteller remains in front of the scrim screen, in an area that is his or hers and probably under individual spotlight. He or she will read from a script quite openly and generally makes a virtue of his reading being unapologetically ill-rehearsed. In a sense – if we settle here for a he! -- he is more of a story reader than a story teller.

Additionally, for the purpose of workshopping and/or training amongst groups, having a virtue of even an unrehearsed reading of the script allows the whole group to participate virtually immediately from the beginning of the staging (or pretend staging) preparations, since there is little learning of lines before things of overall rehearsal can be going.

We have untold number of examples that an actor reading a script, alone and unembellished, fully memorized or only partly so, is fascinating to audiences in itself -- in Kabuki and Wayang; in puppet theatre; in most children's stage literature; in the fine traditions of one-man shows, from Charles Dickens's often gaslight reading his own novels to, say, Malcolm Robertson in Melbourne needing only a single pine table to enthrall an audience for two hours dramatically reciting the Gospel According to St. Matthew.

What happens here is that the human voice becomes an instrument that lifts and falls, that lilts and tilts, that encaptures and enthralls audiences for what the human Voice is… the primary and first instrument of theatre; the very root cause of theatre itself, and, oftimes, more spell-binding than any visual effect riding along with it.

All this doesn't mean the storyteller has to be isolated on his own 'stool' in his own spotlight front-of-screen. As in the first play reproduced in this book, Gogol's 'The Nose', if need be, the storyteller can also be as animated and conducting proceedings as any traditional circus M.C. He can also project himself into the action, either going back behind the scrim to join in, or when the shadow actors and acting from time to time spill out front-of-screen to carry on front stage.

The plays

Each of these plays contain some major element of fantasy which lends itself to shadow acting over the staging limitations of three-dimensional acting of conventional theatre. Take, for example, the floating giantish nose in Gogol's 'The Nose'; how much more winning, more convincing and amusing is it than, say, a 'live' actor strutting the stage dressed in some type of sandwich-board costume? Or the flighted wheelchair odyssey of Tru and Flo over all that is their Austral-land in 'The Last of the Tribe'?

Shadow action underpinning tales requiring some fantasy adds a magic that is difficult to achieve in conventional staging, and certainly difficult to compete with. Using a shadow-play in the staging extends reality into wonder, blends the imagined with, but over-and-beyond, the stage/earth-bound.

The resulting shadowed representation of the storyteller's reading is so in-everyway-possible that, again, it relies much more on the imagination of the director and his aides than any direction given in the playscript. No script can give definitive stage directions for all the possible shadow-action elements a director will think of. No shadow playscript can be the be-all and end-all. It is why, at the start of each play, I add the (same old) reminder that the directions given in this printed-page playscript are 'over supplied', and deliberately so. They are only suggestions, guidelines. They only indicate what might be considered by the director when he or she is conceiving what needs to go toward the 'inner, background' shadow play itself.

On the 'reality' side, the storyteller will anchor the actuality of the story. The shadow director need not be hamstrung by trying to represent every story nuance, every plot twist and turn from behind the scrim curtain. His or her job is to provide a concurrently-flowing shadowed distillation of the story.

The shadow play and fantasy-with-realism

A conventional play suffers when its plot calls for some para-realism. It tends to be awkward when a stage standard play tries to suddenly inject a bit of surrealism into the proceedings with, say, a belch of camouflaging smoke and ghost-quavering voices.

Fantasy-magic is where the shadow play comes into its own. For the modern live-acted shadow play, the fantastical is blended into the plot naturally. By employing quickly-mobile props and shadow-perspectives behind the scrim screen, surreal and dream-like sequences become integrated in practical staging effects, in which the unseeable and the realistic side of the story can offer up a seamless performance.

If one remembers that the modern live-acted shadow play need not be only played out behind the scrim screen in shadows, but allows the live actors to come front-screen to play parts of their roles in full audience view, then the juxtaposition of fact and fantasy in staging these live-acted shadow plays becomes such a major difference over presenting the storyteller's tale over conventional theatre ways. For example, with a little creativity, the present could be acted front screen and the past enacted behind the curtain, with the storyteller linking them both. Flashbacks and flashforwards and character repercussions etcetera can come to the production and *naturally* explained by naturally integrated voice and sights.

The origins of shadow storytelling within all of us
However, many theories there are on this, it seems undeniable that we all have a shared memory of having been rivetted by a cherished (think bedtime and father) storyteller's voice, especially when it is accompanied by shadows, whether these be on the yurt's tent side or the cave wall or by cottage candlelight or along with sparks flying into the night from a campfire -- or just from your father's finger-figure shapes on a bedroom wall. That dear-to-heart voice somehow goes heightened by that 'shadow-illustrating', with both voice and shadow show simultaneously playing on our (audience) senses. The magic is piled on.

What's past has been going past
Whether shadows on the cave wall or the walls of the candlelit hovel or torchlit home or gaslit theatre, live-acted shadow plays are as old as the hills... as old as human beings developed speech in order to better communicate with one another. The shadow play is the first theatre of all.

Yet, to date, shadow plays using real actors acting naturally have been used rarely, if at all, to present modern plays as we know a full-blown play to be. There have of course been the traditional presentations of Buddhist/Hindu/Zen Wayang and Kabuki, but few, if any, attempting full-length stories presented in the modern everyday theatre other than short novelty pieces, however admirable. To date, all have been stylisations.

It would seem only rarely have shadow plays for the large stage even been attempted. In 1998 the company 'Shadows of Bali' was set up by Larry Reed, an American Wayang devotee out of the US Peace Corps of the day. He toured the US and played in Bali quite successfully using real actors instead of puppets, but only remained true to the Wayang traditional themes. Still, Mr Reed (no relation) was the pioneer in attempting to attempt to fit full stories, however 'mannered', into the acting possibilities of the modern Western theatre. He went on to found the famous ShadowLight Production company in the US; it remains at the cutting edge of shadow theatre, although, perhaps, not attempting fully-scripted plays as offered in this book.

Other companies around the world, such as Verba of Hungary. El Gamma Penumbra of the Philippines, OpenEye Theatre of the US, have all performed many prize-winning shows using the human-figure as parts of shape-architecture presentations without attempting to use a full playscript narrative before a regular theatre-going audience.

In workshopping and course studies
All across any country, courses and classes are being conducted by theatre companies high and low, dramatic-arts schools high and low, community groups high and low – in all the wonderful aspects of theatre: acting, stagecraft, design, dramaturgy, cultural aspects.

But where are the classes in that neglected, yet vast, landscape that lies between mime and the mainstream theatre?

It seems they are hard to be seen. It hardly need to be said that, between the mime and conventional theatre sides of things, in modern live-acted shadow plays, there are extra challenges when it comes to shadow action, prop management, stylization blending into realism, stage

6

blockings and so forth. These new requirements are not only for actors themselves but for all involved in presentation from stage-and-costume designers through to dramaturgy and directors. But, however new as requirements they are, they are not new in themselves; they are theatre techniques that are as old as theatre itself and they lie untaught. This surely needs to be corrected in our theatre-arts institutions and companies, which should be teaching the full gamut of the theatrical arts, surely.

The amazing thing to me is that, in their wide appeal, such shadow plays can be a delight to teach and to learn – from the young of age to the hoariest of professionals. The extra and extending techniques they require give freer participation for all dramatic-arts communities, if for nothing else than the once-conventional back-stage work becomes part of the upfront (that is 'audience seen') action in a way that all or more people, including the hammer-and-nails technicians, can participate in and feel part of the larger staging or watching experience. After all, here is a medium that extends conventional theatre into mime arts on the one hand, and pushes stagecraft into exciting lighting and stage-management areas on the other hand. And they do so in fun ways that are far more inclusive of age or talent or intention or hobby-horse.

It's not as though the actors in live-acted shadow plays have to play dumb to their art, either. They can have as much spoken dialogue as deemed supportive of the story and/or the storyteller. They can interact with the storyteller or each other with dialogue either behind the screen or by coming out momentarily front stage to appear three-dimensionally… for example, in a chase sequence where the chase proceeds around and around the screen itself, as well as many instances in the plays given in this book. As natural extensions, these new acting skills alone are not hard to incorporate and therefore no burden to add to teaching or to acting courses or to rehearsals.

The play scripts in this book
Included in this book are two specially-adapted classic short stories by Gogol and Damon Runyon, the famous Morton's farce 'Box and Cox', a specially-written shadow play for children ('Meeta Jarred-a-lot'), plus nine other specially-written one-act shadow plays which I have included not so much out of any overly self-regard, but because -- and sad to say – any director or educator looking for new shadow works or

just to pick'n'pluck workshop passages will undoubtedly find a dearth of writing for the live-acted shadow play.

This is a shame. Hopefully, it won't be too long before the live-acted shadow play, with its garrulous storyteller, will have a full body of literature behind it. It deserves a tradition of its own.

Live-Acted Shadow Plays for Today

THE PLAYS

10

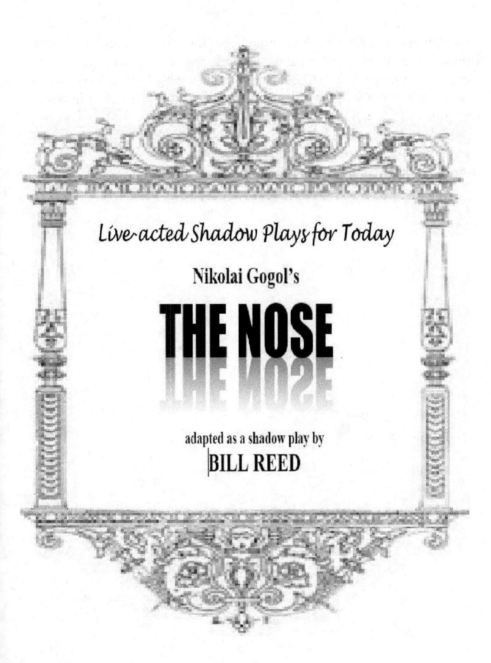

Live-acted Shadow Plays for Today

Nikolai Gogol's

THE NOSE

adapted as a shadow play by

BILL REED

The behind-the-screen shadow action – or 'inner background' play --
can only ever keep 'pace' with the reading, not *keep up* with it.
Because of the resultant and necessary shadow-play distillation of the
storyteller's tale, the extensive stage directions given in this script are
only intended to be indicators as to what *might* be used for the shadow-
play side of things. They deliberately go beyond what the director
would employ and are given merely as a range of possible shadow-
actions he or she might want to use in the 'distillation'.

The Characters

STORYTELLER
Reads his lines from a script, and quite openly. He sits off-centre but front stage on his own reading 'stool', although he moves around a lot. He blusters in and out of play, and is over-bullish in trying to maintain control of the shadow acting/illustration when he feels it justified. It mostly never will be justified. His manner of reading rises and falls to keep the attention on the shadow players from stealing the scenes from him.

THE NOSE
a stuck-up, beery, lumpy snotter of a floating sticky beak that ever looked down its nose at more-fleshed-out Mankind.

IVAN JAKOVLEVITCH SHADOW PLAYER

KOVALOFF SHADOW PLAYER

DOCTOR SHADOW PLAYER

THE SHADOW PLAYERS
A cast of, say, three or four to shadow play the daughter, the newspaper clerk, the doctor, the police inspector, strollers along the mall and so forth.

The Nose

1.

*(There is only one thing shadowed on the screen and it is the
nose... a huge nose... a giantish nose. It is, yes, 'a stuck-up,
beery, lumpy snotter of a floating sticky beak that ever looked
down its nose at more-fleshed-out Mankind'.*

*It hangs arrogantly, looking down its nose at the audience from a
lofty height, then from a peering nose-to-nose impertinent close-
up, then turning contemptuously away at what it sees, then
spinning around on its axis in mid-air as if it was showing off.
Which it is.*

*Finally, it steadies and remains defiantly in mid-air as the
STORYTELLER comes into his front-of-screen spotlight with
script in hand.*

*With such a presence behind him, the STORYTELLER isn't
exactly brimming with confidence.*

*Indeed, the first thing he does is come forward to rather
quakingly whisper to the audience while cocking his thumb back
in the direction of the giantish NOSE...)*

STORYTELLER: I have to tell you we think its behaviour... and
therefore things in general... will continue to deteriorate over the
course of the evening.

> *(The NOSE gives a great snort of disdain – which almost blows
> him over -- presses itself impolitely up against the scrim curtain)*

STORYTELLER: If the worst happens, and it starts going right off, we
can only hope you remember to block your ears or latch onto the person
next to you so you're not thrown from your seat... and remember of
course the management doesn't bear any responsibility in the way of
risks of bodily injury.

> *(While the NOSE flits menacingly around, the screen*

14

acting/lighting/prop/backdrop preparations for the show come to light.

The STORYTELLER starts the proper play by clearing his throat and formally reading the script, as an old St Petersburg skyline comes up in backdrop to the shadow area behind him:)

STORYTELLER: So…
  (reads)
'On the exact day of the 25th of March, 1836 or thereabouts, give or take a year or two, a very strange occurrence took place in St Petersburg. On the Ascension Avenue, there lived a barber of the name of Ivan Jakovlevitch. He seemed to have lost his family name because it wasn't on his sign board, only the words, 'Blood-letting done here'.

(One of the shadow players emerges from behind the screen holding aloft a sign saying 'Blood-letting down here!', moves across the STORYTELLER's front stage and returns back screen on the other side. The STORYTELLER continues after a long-suffering pause:)

STORYTELLER: On this particular morning Ivan J. awoke pretty early to the delicious smell of his wife baking fresh bread. He was very partial to fresh loaves with onions… so partial that, hung over as he was, he positively jumped out of bed and made for the breakfast table.
                    (as a breakfast scene proceeds…)
Where he shook out some salt for himself, prepared two onions, assumed a serious expression, and began to cut the bread.

(As he does this, the NOSE floats down to be above, casting a very long shadow and looking down closely at him with an air of curiosity, and:)

STORYTELLER: (whisper to audience) It's best we keep getting prepared to ignore it.
  (goes back on script)
After he had cut the loaf in two halves, he looked, and to his great astonishment saw something whitish sticking out. He carefully poked round the thing with his knife, and felt the whole shape of it tentatively with his finger, murmuring into his beard, 'What can it be?'

15

IVAN SHADOW PLAYER: (shout out to be heard) What can it be?

(The NOSE gives the first of its rude interruptions. It is a snort of derision of such volume that it feels like the whole theatre is rocked, stopping everything.

There follows a hiatus while everyone and everything take time to recover enough to carry on.

The NOSE takes great 'jiggling' satisfaction at its disruptive effect and its own self-importance.

Note: this will happen throughout with similar stunning results.

Finally, the STORYTELLER intrepidly feels able to proceed by repeating:)

STORYTELLER: Eventually, as revolted as he felt, Ivan Jakovlevitch dug the thing out and drew out -- a nose! He did. A nose!
  (and, while following the shadow action for...)
An actual nose! And, moreover, it seemed to be the nose of an acquaintance! Alarm and terror were depicted in Ivan's face, if it wasn't so shadowy; but these feelings were slight in comparison with the disgust which took possession of his wife, the wife of a barber, after all, and she shouted, 'Whose nose have you cut off, you monster?'

WIFE SHADOW PLAYER: (fit to be heard) You monster! You scoundrel! Whose nose have you cut off and left lying around the kitchen to invade my dough!

STORYTELLER: ... her face red with anger, and that wasn't all, going: 'You drunk! You dirty guzzler! I'll report you to the police! Can't get your head out of a bottle!
  (while the WIFE mimes her abuse and other shadow players enact the barbershop scene of...)
Many customers have told me that while you were shaving them, you hold them so tight they're sure you're trying to get to their nose! Now look what you've done! Drunk, you. Guzzler!

CUSTOMER SHADOW PLAYER: Hey, easy on the old honker there, Jakovlevitch!

STORYTELLER: But, never mind all that; right then, at breakfast and what he had found in the bread, Ivan Jakovlevitch looked more dead than alive.

(IVAN J. holds up the bread nose and roundly inspects it... the giantish nose hovers above out of curiosity, too...)

He saw at once that this nose could belong to no other than to Kovaloff, a member of the Municipal Committee whom he shaved every Sunday and Wednesday. There was a nose you couldn't forget! And so he shouted, 'Stop your mouth, wife! I'll wrap this thing up safely and you put it out of sight in the corner. Since you never clean there, you won't notice it anymore. I'll take it away later if no one claims it in the meantime.'

(As the WIFE shadow player removes it with tongs from the table and IVAN paces up and down to:)

STORYTELLER: Well, poor old Ivan Jakovlevitch had to think hard, and quickly. This was a pretty pass! We can only guess what he was thinking but it had to be something like: 'Whether I came home drunk last night or not, I'm still a bit too under the weather to remember; but I can shake all I like: there's no doubt about it that this is a quite extraordinary occurrence, for a loaf is something baked and a nose is something different not usually undergoing baking'. That was Ivan Jakovlevitch's opinion anyway. In agitation, and to avoid his wife wielding those tongs in his direction in her proven deft way, he rose and went to dress.

(Scene behind changes to his sitting at his dressing table, with the giantish NOSE 'smirking' above him...)

STORYTELLER: In front of his dressing table he felt something was laughing at him, something was wrong over and above the fierce ringing in his head. But he just couldn't figure out what or why.

(The giantish NOSE above gives him a derisive snort, which stops him, but, try as he might, he can't see where it came from. Anyway, the STORYTELLER is moving on...)

17

STORYTELLER: So, our barber finished his dressing and finished powdering his face and then had a brain wave. He rose shakily and shakily went back down to the kitchen, used the tongs to get the nose out of the corner and wrapped it in a cloth. Put on his hat and coat and left the house.

(A street scene, with IVAN J. skulking along the street, parcel under his arm...)

STORYTELLER: However shakily, what he intended to do was lose the nose somewhere—either on someone's doorstep, or in a public square, or in a narrow alley... anywhere he could get rid of it without being seen. But, as the luck of great hangover always has it, down this street or that, in that park or this, he kept running into his customers who normally would never be seen dead outside in the street before noon much less want to stop and chat, especially about what he had in his hands. He even tried to let the nose just slip out of his grasp as he slipped on by, but a watcher fellow appeared out of nowhere calling out to him, 'Hoi, sir! You've dropped something!'

WATCHER SHADOW PLAYER: Hey, no littering unless that's a litter and that only makes it worse, mate!

STORYTELLER: You can see how a feeling of despair soon began to take possession of poor Ivan Jakovlevitch... even loosening the hold that hangover had on him, which shows you how desperate that despair was! Until Ivan J. shakily had the shaky idea of just throwing it into the river... a fate, anyway, almost too good for a nose that poked its nose into his bread in the morning.

(As IVAN shadow player comes 'forward' a la a police mug shot to present his shadowy profile for closer inspection....)

STORYTELLER: But...
   (waves script)
it says here I am not minding my manners. All might be shadowy to you and me but apparently, I haven't properly introduced you to Ivan Jakovlevitch, an estimable man in many barber-pole ways.
   (and)

18

Like every honest Russian tradesman, he was a terrible drunkard and terribly honest over vodka with it, and...
(turns script over in inspection)
Well, that appears all you need to know about him.

(At least he can point to behind where IVAN is now standing on a bridge, looking furtively left and right, ready to throw the nose into the river:)

STORYTELLER: After all, in hangover time, there is nothing so much as a lot of fuss over nothing, don't you think? And so, there our Ivan J. is, on the bridge there, wavering in hungover body and nose-flickered mind, wanting just one small opening of an opportunity of getting rid of this thing into the river. Leaning over the rail, pretending to count the dead fishes as against those just floating stunned from their own heavy night-before... until that nose just slipped from his grasp so suddenly that he could cunningly pretend later he had dropped it and all its bread crumbs into the water deliberately.
(as this is shadowedly done with a loud plop over and to IVAN's great relief...)
After which, he felt as though a ton weight had been lifted off him, and laughed fit to lift his thumping head. But, when he went to push off and scuttle back home, he felt this tap on his shoulder and there was none other than a police inspector of, as they used to say, imposing exterior, with long whiskers, three-cornered hat, and sword hanging at his side, which was imposing on Ivan J.'s quivering interior even more than his imposing exterior.

(The INSPECTOR appears, hoists IVAN by the collar, etc, as...)

STORYTELLER: And to make any hangover feel worse... even worse than finding a nose in you breakfast bread... the Inspector had him by the collar and was going:

INSPECTOR SHADOW PLAYER: (loud enough) Rightio then, why are you acting suspiciously on this bridge? Confess the truth or you'll get this long arm of the law up you!'

STORYTELLER: Oh, Ivan Jakovlevitch nearly fainted so much he wouldn't have even been able to blame his hangover even if he tried. 'I am willing', he cried out, 'to shave your beard, Your Grace, two or even three times a week free of charge!'. To which he only got the gruff back tugging at his collar…

INSPECTOR SHADOW PLAYER: Fellow, I've already got three barbers daily digging in there seeing what they can find. It takes three of them too! Now then, out with it! What were you doing just now?!

(*But here, just as the action between IVAN and the INSPECTOR could well heat up, the shadow area freezes for:*)

STORYTELLER: But here the strange episode vanishes in mist, and what further happened is not known to us or to anyone alive today. Not even any little bit of Ivan Jakovlevitch's hangover survived to say, and that seemed to have settled in for the long haul.

(*Blackout*)

2.

(*When the lighting returns, the giantish NOSE snorts with great contempt that converts into overwhelming thunder, followed by blowing its own nose monstrously – or makes an even more terrifying sound, such that it takes a moment for the STORYTELLER, if not the audience, to recover*)

STORYTELLER: (to include audience) Everybody okay? We've put band-aids on sale out in the foyer. Follow the first-aid lines.
    (*pointing openly back to floating giantish NOSE*)
My advice is continue to ignore it.

(*He gathers himself to get back on script. As he does so, it is the turn of KOVALOFF to emerge as the principal shadow player…*)

STORYTELLER: Now, here's somebody we'll certainly get to know… His name is Kovaloff. I don't think it need shortening. Kovaloff. Not a bad ring to it. Eg, might cough-a-lot and what have you.
    (*that falls flat. He gets back on script*)

We can give you some information. Kovaloff was a typical committee-men of the local Municipal Committee who was addedly typical by refusing to call himself 'committee-man' but 'Major', in order to make himself feel more important... than just being a mere committee man, if you see what it means here... which he desperately needed to think he was. Major, that is, not committee man.

(In the shadow area, it is now a simple bedroom scene, with KOVALOFF just waking up while his servant enters with warm water, and:)

STORYTELLER: So, finally, here's Kovaloff waking up early that morning, and going: 'Brr!, brr!' understandably-enough through his lips, as he always did, though he could not say why. He might have asked his lips, ha ha.
  (that falls flat too; he continues)
Kovaloff stretched himself, and told his servant to pass him the hand mirror which was on the dressing table. He wished to look at the small boil which had appeared on his nose the previous evening; but to his great astonishment, he saw that, instead of his nose, he had a perfectly smooth vacancy in his face. He did! Or rather, it was! Or rather, there it was! Or rather, there his nose wasn't! Somebody should have put up a sign on it saying...

(From around the side of the scrim curtain a shadow player holds up a sign saying 'Vacancy. To let' in plain view. Gets waved back.)

STORYTELLER: Oh, you can imagine it if it's still a bit shadowy! There was poor old Kovaloff, just awakened from a good sleep on an ordinary morning and late-night mosquitoes and early-morning flies are using the front of his face as a skating rink.

(He pauses to allow KOVALOFF shadow player to go through his shock-horror routine again...)

STORYTELLER: Thoroughly alarmed, Kovaloff threw himself at the wash basin, dashed water over his disbelief – that was throbbing away even more than the head of a certain barber we know -- then rubbed his

21

eyes with a towel. He dashed to his dressing mirror and dared open his eyes one more time!

(pause for dramatic effect)

Sure enough, he had no nose any longer! He still had no nose any longer! He no longer had any nose still! Hells bells! Godsbold! Nose equals nothing! He threw himself back into bed, then he sprang out of bed, dressed himself and went at once to...

(The scene shifts to a sergeant's desk, where KOVALOFF staggers towards the SERGEANT...)

STORYTELLER: ... the police station where its Inspector... the same one on the bridge who had the three barbers a day to toil away in and amongst his beard... was known to most likely be on the couch in his office.

SERGEANT SHADOW PLAYER: He'd most likely be on the couch in 'is office.

INSPECTOR SHADOW PLAYER; ('off') I am not. If I am, I am not *up*!

(KOVALOFF leaves the police station dejectedly. He proceeds 'along' the backdrop of the old St Petersburg skyline and along the street, sauntering aimlessly, shoulders slumped...)

STORYTELLER: What we can say about Kovaloff's state-of-mind, other than he couldn't even remember having a drop last night? Apart from the lack of a nose, was he was not so much a confirmed bachelor that he was in great demand as a suitor who was nowhere near inclined to marry any lady who couldn't bring with her a dowry of at least two hundred thousand roubles? A vast sum that still held a psychological hold on him even without a nose.

(turns script over and over examining it again; gives up, carries on)

Now, as the discerning audience that you are...

(He gets another show-stopping blow-out of disdain from the giantish NOSE which threatens to shake everything loose and bust a few eardrums. Eventually its shattering interruption tempers itself. The STORYTELLER bravely carries on, while,

behind, KOVALOFF equally bravely braves the streets)
… We were saying, as a discerning audience, you can judge for yourselves what our poor not-altogether-whole Kovaloff was feeling when he found in his face, instead of a fairly symmetrical nose, that broad, flat vacancy, even yet starting to be pestered by advertising-board agencies. To increase his misery, not a single droshky… whether you knew that was a sort of taxi or not… was to be seen, or even a taxi of a droshky, if you knew that was the same thing, and he was obliged to walk openly in the streets where normal people would be expected to have something on between their eyes and upper lip, especially if you're holding out for a dowry of two hundred thousand on the marriageable nose.

(as KOVALOFF forges on…)
He wrapped himself up in his cloak, and held his handkerchief to his face as though he had a nose bleed. The more he walked the more hopeful of passing muster he became. 'Perhaps', he thought…

KOVALOFF SHADOW PLAYER: Perhaps it's all only my imagination It's just impossible that a nose should drop off in such a silly way! Or be so irresponsible!

(He moves into a coffee house…)

STORYTELLER: … he thought, yes, as far as we can tell, as he stepped into his favourite coffee shop, in order to look again into the wall mirror he knew it had there, not knowing or realising that wall mirrors in comforting warm and friendly environments can still get as shocked as the next wall mirror around town. Despite its efforts to shy again, he stepped gingerly up to, putting his face right into its face.
(as the giantish NOSE jiggles with delight above…)
Horror! Still, no nose! Not even a sign saying 'gone fishing'! Not even a 'Post No Bills' or 'Advertising Hoarding Going Cheap' sign! Just a plain old unexplained no nose!
(pause while KOVALOFF has to force the wall mirror to face squarely up to him)
What else was our man to do but make his escape back to the streets, neither looking nor smiling to the left or to the right, his handkerchief covering a pretend cold, but he not able to even make a sniffle or two because…of course!... a sniffle requires at least one nasal passage, two sniffles, two.

(By now KOVALOFF is well into getting through the streets, averting his face to passers-by, muttering, if he has to, muffled greetings in return...)

STORYTELLER: But yet... if it was possible, even more horror was awaiting him! For there, right in front of his nose where his nose should have been ...
(as one – a grand government one – does...)
a carriage drew up in front of a government building up ahead; a grand affair; a high-official's affair; the carriage door opened; a high-born gentleman in a general's uniform emerged to hurry up the steps as though being seen in a public street was far too low-class. At first, like all were and would have been, Kovaloff was impressed. But then his eyes started telling him he shouldn't believe them; rather he should start thinking about what he was seeing from the standpoint of what had gone missing beneath them.
(KOVALOFF starts to peer closer...)
As soon as he took his eyes' advice, Kovaloff could see that this high'n'mighty government official in that-there glittering general's uniform wasn't all he seemed! No sirree!

(He cues, and gets, an introductory drum roll and trombone fanfare.)

STORYTELLER: And yes indeedee! How great was Kovaloff's astonishment when he saw that it was none of the high-born getting out of that carriage – but it was, in fact, his own nose! Yes sirree and nose indeedee!
(gets another drum roll)
Oh, you can remain skeptical, good people, but there was no mistake once you looked with the clarity of eyes that were missing their nose! A nose that twitches never lies!

(KOVALOFF staggers about in growing realization, as the giantish NOSE returns over all to thunder out another disturbing snort of derision before disappearing just as suddenly...)

STORYTELLER: By Gods Gobness! Poor old Kovaloff felt as though he wouldn't be able to stay standing upright. (It's the ballast a normal

24

nose gives, you know, that we all tend to take for granted.) Yet, brave soul!, though trembling all over as though with fever from the cold he was pretending to have, he resolved to wait till his nose came back out of the building, rather than make a scene inside. So, he hid in the shadows and held his breath that he now was only just getting used to getting through his mouth, just to make things feel even more strange hiding there. If you can see what I mean.

> *(The shadow action holds itself in suspense as KOVALOFF melts into the shadows of the shadows.*
>
> *It doesn't take long before the giantish NOSE re-appears pompously, emerging from the government building in grand style and state. It is indeed decked out in a splendid braidful general's uniform with Napoleon hat and thigh length boots.*
>
> *For a moment, it preens itself in the showcase mirror of an adjacent shops before climbing, shows great pleasure as, below, a lesser shadow of itself – decked out similarly magnificently – climbs in and out of the carriage, posing on its threshold for any admiring glances, while…)*

STORYTELLER: It was unbelievable! Kovaloff's eyes were so right! His own nose as a high-ranking government official and in a general's uniform full of medals, when there he was having to call himself a mere Major just to avoid being called a mere committee-man. And that was when he had a nose attached to his face! It wasn't even an ordinary high-falutin' general's uniform with medals, either, but it was gold-embroidered with a stiff, high collar, trousers of chamois leather, and a sword hung at its side… something Kovaloff had only dreamed of ever being able to wear! The hat, adorned with a plume, showed that it held the rank of a State Councillor.

(and)

It was too much! If it was only paying a brief visit, that might be excusable, but it was obvious that nose of his was paying a State visit, one of those 'duty-calls but I mustn't dally for I have to get on with the affairs of State' type of visits.

(and)

It was so shocking that poor Kovaloff was just glued to the spot. He wanted to rush out from his cover and give his nose a good old talking

25

to, but he *couldn't*. Why wouldn't his feet move, if his nose could go off gallivanting everywhere like that?

(and as it is enacted in the shadow area...)
He couldn't even move a muscle when his nose had enough of posing, looked around on both sides, motioned royally to the coachman 'drive on'...

THE NOSE: (in imperious, nose-twangy voice) Drive on, fellow!

(KOVALOFF has to watch the carriage drive away)

STORYTELLER: Poor Kovaloff nearly lost his reason then and there. If he could let go the handkerchief that he was covering his shame with, he would have cried out and tried to tear his hair out on the spot if he had had enough hair to try to pull out. How was it possible that his nose, which only yesterday he had on his face, and which could neither walk nor drive... and, as far as he was concerned, had very few wits of its own.... should now be wearing a uniform of such magnificent high rank even if you didn't have the social standing to do so? I mean, if it was your beak, even beacon-like, wouldn't you have run after the carriage waving your arms that weren't holding the cloth over the vacant space spread all over your face?... a state that was continuing because you didn't have the nerve or the social standing to chase after and confront the drop-out?

(He watches KOVALOFF mope off, thoroughly dejected under a burst of mournful music...)

STORYTELLER: Losing your nose and then coming across it so far above you in life that they might throw you in jail if you were a trouble-maker enough to chase after it...?

(and while KOVALOFF mopes along unwanted and unloved...)
All through the Grand Bazaar of Moscow wandered poor Kovaloff... through society waking up, taking the airs, all better than he suddenly... all more whole-some!... wending his way in the shadows with the beggars with their faces covered up and he no better than they since they at least had poverty and leprosy to justify the state of their protuberances with all those vacant looks!...

(KOVALOFF stops suddenly on seeing something up ahead)

26

STORYTELLER: But what can be miracles can still stick their beaks into things when all seems to be lost, you know. For, there, suddenly up ahead, he saw, almost by some miracle sticking its beak into things, was the carriage -- and it was stopped before the Grand Palace shopping mall… parked where ordinary people wouldn't dream of leaving their nose parked. He ran, he stumbled forward… a cry of joy almost coming out of his lips if it wasn't so ashamed to show its face in a face like that… but… oh, yes, one of those *buts*… where was his errant nose? It was not to be seen!

(KOVALOFF casts around wildly in a sea of shoppers pushing by…)

STORYTELLER: … running around like a mad man waylaying people, backing them up against wall, had they seen his nose… big plumed hat, wellington boots, in an outfit all generals worth their salt should never be seen out of… until… until…

(He points and motions for a musical flourish on the sudden appearance of the giantish NOSE so elegantly posing before its own reflection in a shop window and so snorting snuff that it is making the shop window shake:)

STORYTELLER: … there! There it was in the snozulated flesh, half-buried in that oh-I'm-so-much-better-than-you stiff archy collar, standing looking at itself in a shop window so fashionable it was an honour for it that the Nose had stopped to window-shop by it… pretending to be sooo-oo engrossed in the display of a porcelain loaf of fresh-baked bread that it didn't notice poor Kovaloff managing to creep up to be standing right next to it…
(and as they stand man shoulder to nose shoulder – the one very awkwardly, the other loudly snorting on such social impertinence…)
And if you've never had the occasion to sneak up and stand shoulder-to-shoulder with your own nose, looking in on a display model of a loaf of fresh-baked bread for some weird reason, you mightn't wonder so much at how strange our poor Kovaloff felt. Also, it wouldn't surprise you the conversation went something like this when our whole man plucked up the courage for:

(He conducts back into the shadow area for:)

KOVALOFF: Honourable sir…honourable sir…

THE NOSE (giantish boom but still wheezily) WHAT, WHAT?!

KOVALOFF: Oh, I know that sniff of a snort, you know.

THE NOSE: (even more disdain) WHAT, WHAT?!

(and gives off a snort of derision that almost rocks the house down. The STORYTELLER hangs on while it passes)

STORYTELLER: Yes, yes, 'what, what?', would you believe? Caught red-handed out in the open and that's all it has to say to your face? And so rudely, you know… you saw, you heard!… that it wasn't even putting itself out of joint to turn around, as you'd expect any nose with any sort of breeding in bleeding to do. And poor Kovaloff had given it a whole lifetime of bleeding, too! But no, casting a simple sideling glance would have been too beneath it, wouldn't it? And for all of his innate breeding, our man Kovaloff was getting a bit miffed. He was going, at least trying to get off on the right foot:

KOVALOFF: (cued and loud enough) It seems to me strange, most respected sir, that you do not know where you belong. Judge yourself, man!

STORYTELLER: … he cried, presuming he meant to say 'nose' not 'man' there, but too late to make the correction.

THE NOSE: (even more thunderously) WHAT, WHAT?!

STORYTELLER: There's that 'What, what' oh so haughty again! As if a nose belonging to you had any right to say somesuch viz'n'suchlike!
   (and)
'Pardon me', retorted his nose, 'I do not understand what you are talking about. You, sir, are addressing a General of the most majorest of Generalships, without, I may bother to add, being asked to. Explain yourself more distinctly or away with you, fellow!'. 'Look,' pleaded

28

Kovaloff, 'You must admit it is not befitting that I should go about without a nose. It might be all right for some old apple-cart woman on the bridge to carry on her stewed business without a pot to pee in, but I am on the lookout for a suitable posting and more importantly a suitably-endowed lady of means for my long-lasting dowry support, sir... nothing less than two hundred thousand roubles, don't you know?, and it is very low class of you to depart from me without as much as a by-your-leave, especially while I was sleeping and could not defend a punch in the nose!'

(and)

'I understand nothing,' answered the Nose, but now in a distinct thrall of a nervous wheeze, if not outright sneeze. 'I repeat, please explain yourself more distinctly'. 'Honourable sir,' replied Kovaloff with a dignity he always just seemed to miss out on and which pretty much always pushed his luck, 'I do not know how I am to make it any clearer. Honourable sir, you are after all my own nose! Those veins run through your nostrils, run through my nostrils!' His nose, though, by now had seemingly recovered its bearing and finally deigned to turn and look down its nose at him very deignfully, going: 'I can see from you lowly uniform, that it is beneath my shoulders-back bearing...

KOVALOFF: You haven't got any shoulders!

THE NOSE: I say again, beneath me even being seen talking in public with you, fellow. Your nose, indeed, when I have one of my own! Be gone, fellow! Blow your trumpet somewhere else or put up your blow-hard right here and now and get cleared out by my men!

KOV ALOFF: I say, put 'em up!

THE NOSE: And when my men return, they will to your detriment!

> *(Their confrontation is interrupted by the mall-orchestra striking up 'Easter Parade' to herald the march along the mall of the eligible young ladies and their chaperones...)*

STORYTELLER: Ah, how unfortunate was this as well? The time of the parade of the eligible ladies and there at the head of it was the rustling and the bustling of the crinolines of the not-so-young lady who was leading in his affections of winning the dowry race for him. At least she was the highest bidder – at ten thousand roubles to his demand of two hundred thousand.

(The lady and her mother swan into view, stand 'loitering' around, expecting him to come up to them, pay courtesies, but he is very displaced...)

STORYTELLER: Desperately, he tried to hide himself by pretending to concentrate on the display model of the loaf of bread in the shop window, but it was to no avail. There she was, standing in proximity looking at him out of the corner of her eye, with her mother... this graceful daughter in a white dress which set off her slender figure to advantage – which it needed to! -- and wearing a light straw hat which had money written all over it, with too many zeros for his liking if the truth be known. Too late! The graceful young thing fluttered her dancing eyes in his direction him and dropped her kerchief in his path with a giddy giggle. Oh, here goes!, it's on tonight!, he thought. But... of course!... he remembered that he had nothing but an absolute blank in place of a nose, and tears started to his eyes. Shame! Ruination! Shame and ruination!

(While the young lady and her mother mill around waiting for his approach as the parade of the eligible ladies reaches its peak:)

STORYTELLER: What was poor Kovaloff to do now? Go to the police? But what did the wicked departure of his nose have to do with the constabulary? As for demanding any explanation from the high-up Government department to which his nose now claimed to belong, it would, he felt, be useless. By the answers his nose had given him, it showed itself quite capable of even denying it had even ever known a Kovaloff, let alone been some integral part of him! How was he ever born with such a rascal of a thing? Oh, woe!

(From 'off'... even of the shadow area or at least only the tip of its giantish nose showing... the NOSE gives an earth-shaking snuffle of triumph, during which all is suspended while everyone grabs hold of the nearest solid thing.

By the time everything is reasonably restored, KOVALOFF has taken off from the women and is miserably trudging the streets again, until he comes across...)

STORYTELLER: There he goes, poor Kovaloff. Have you ever seen anything more trudging along in the shadow of such misery? How sad? How would you feel without a hooter to pioneer your way with? To poke into your lighted way? Without a nostril nor hair to it to catch, to filter debris of the air from entering your brain? With just a flat smooth space that no even a fly would feel safe to get a grip to land on, not without skates on? Without a nose left, he couldn't even find his way back home!
(and as it is enacted...)
Finally, Kovaloff saw he had stopped by a newspaper office. Of course! He would advertise the loss of his nose, giving all its distinctive characteristics in detail... its nobility and its home-bodiedness!... so that anyone who found a stray nose would know on whom it belonged and so where to bring it. A newspaper advertisement. Again, of course!

(He cues KOVALOFF to come around one side of the screen to stand in full audience view, and the newspaper CLERK to do likewise on the other side of the scrim.

They stand, shyly in 'full light', waiting for his cues to begin.

STORYTELLER: (introducing) Kovaloff, as almost, now, just a shadow of himself, and the clerk of the newspaper office who was so worn down by now he was always only a shadow of himself. And they may begin...
(cueing)

KOVALOFF: (from his side of the stage) Who takes in the advertisements here?

CLERK: At your service, sir!
(but mumbles about an advertisement he's doing)
Would you believe them 'ouses of nobility? This 'ere dog I wouldn't give a farthing for, but some countess is quite gone on it, and offers a reward of a full 'undred to anyone what finds it. For that money, I'd find the bleeder! The things people ask to be found, you wouldn't credit, you wouldn't, sir.

31

KOVALOFF: I wish to…

CLERK: 'Ere's one wanting to sell a four-'orse carriage with only three 'orses… here's one wants to sell a wart cure that don't work except in coffee 'ouses. Who wants to only cure your wart in a coffee 'ouse?

KOVALOFF: (again) I wish to place an advertisement for a missing nose!

CLERK: What sort of nose?

KOVALOFF: A good, lively… spirited… kind of nose. Romanesque, not-always-appreciated sort of nose, really. Patrician, one might say. Which you can say in your advertisement.

CLERK: (a sage) Ah, an' you want to take that-there kerchief off your face and replace it with the said errant nose. Replace the sniffles with a sniffer, like…?

KOVALOFF: That is so.

CLERK: Any proof of ownership?

KOVALOFF: It possesses more than a passing semblance of me.

CLERK: An' fair enough too. Name, sir?

KOVALOFF: The nose's?

CLERK: Yours, sir.

KOVALOFF: I have many lady friends of the highest bank balance. Just put down 'Major or higher'.

CLERK: An' the man what run off with your nose, sir?

KOVALOFF: There was no man. It dispossessed itself itself. Just a nose.

32

CLERK: Rummy sort of name for a man, 'Mr A. Nose'. So, this A. Nose fellow has stolen from you a considerable sum, is it?

KOVALOFF: There is no 'Mr A. Nose'! The nose dispatched itself into the come-hither by itself, fellow... my own nose... and there's going to be hell to play!

CLERK: Oh, then sorry, sir. No can do.

KOVALOFF: Why not?

CLERK: 'Cors it might compromise the rep o' the paper, sir. Suppose everyone could just come in an' advertise his or her nose's gone lost. People would accuse this paper of printing nothing but nonsense. Noses are not dogs, like.

KOVALOFF: But this is anything but nonsense!

CLERK: 'Ere, last week there was a case very like it, I'll grant 'ee. An official came, just as you have done, bringing an advertisement for the insertion of which he paid two roubles, sixty-three kopecks; and this advertisement simply announced the loss of a black-haired poodle. There did not seem to be anything out of the way in it, but it was really what them smart-arses call a satire; by the poodle was meant the loss of his salary to a cashier of a flashy establishment with a lot of garters, if you see what I mean. And the next thing his wife's around her shouting it's all nonsense an' pointing to us in public from outside this very door.

KOVALOFF: But I am not talking of a poodle. I'm talking about my own nose!

CLERK: Calm yourself, sir. 'Ere, join me in a bit of snuff, calm your nerves?

KOVALOFF: Don't you see that I lack precisely the essential feature for taking snuff?

CLERK: Fortunately, I've been blessed in not being able to see that far, sir. To the end of me own nose is about as far as I go, m'self.

KOVALOFF: The devil take your snuff-box! I don't want to look at snuff now, not even the best, certainly not your vile snuff stuff!

CLERK: Well, when you find your nose, sir, bring it around an' we might give it a little interview. 'Runny nose returns' an' the like.

(The STORYTELLER can wave them to go back to the shadow area behind the screen, which they do with a visible relief...)

STORYTELLER: So saying, our poor Kovaloff left the newspaper office in a state of profound irritation, hoping some shadow would swallow him up.

(The KOVALOFF shadow returns to the street, returns to trudging along and avoiding people looking strangely at him... until he arrives back at the police station, enters and enacts:)

STORYTELLER: Next stop our poor blower-less man went to the police as a last resort. He arrived just as our Inspector was forcing himself to recline in a more comfortable position on his couch after the third of his daily shaves, which, inevitably, made our poor Kovaloff's visit quite inopportune. Accordingly, this visit ended up with the Inspector calling all his troops together and telling him in front of them that respectable people did not have their noses stolen and that even the greatest rogue known to Man did not have a nose that would take leave of him without a damnably good reason.
  (There is a general police agreement)
The Inspector got his Sergeant to advise Kovaloff to develop a funny walk, in order to prepare himself for the way laughter would follow him out of the police station.

(Shadow acting goes back to street scenes and KOVALOFF trudging back the way home. He is trailed by gross snorts of ridiculing laughter from the giantish NOSE with just the giantish peak of its nose poking out from the side.

When all can recover from this unusual sight on an ordinary street, the STORYTELLER proceeds to draw attention to himself:)

STORYTELLER: Ladies and genials, perhaps, it says here, that last allusion by the Inspector as to only rogues losing their noses was too direct. We must remember that Kovaloff was a very sensitive man, hurt easily. After all, the collar of his shirt was always remarkably clean and stiff which often says a lot about one being sensitive and hurt easily, although that's news to me. He wore the same style of whiskers as those that are worn by district governors, architects without their sleeves rolled up, and regimental doctors; in short, all those who have full red cheeks and play a good game of whist while being able to look their fellow man in the face. Furthermore, his whiskers grew straight across the cheek towards the nose, which should tell us what sort of bruisability our poor Kovaloff had to live with, especially when he wasn't getting promoted as much as he would like. Which is to say no promotion and a lot of like.

(By now KOVALOFF is wearily entering his bedroom)

STORYTELLER: Well, be that as it sadly may, our man reached his house quite wearied out. It was already growing dark. After all his fruitless search, his room seemed to him melancholy and even ugly the way it lacked a nose, or even any sniff of a semblance of a nose. What is a room without a sniff of a whiff?

(KOVALOFF sits on his bed to think with head in hands…)

STORYTELLER: Depressed, he walked slowly over to the looking-glass and at first closed his eyes, hoping to see his nose suddenly back in its proper place; but on opening them, he had nothing but disappointment again. 'What a hideous sight!', he cried out.

KOVALOFF: HOW HIDEOUS!

STORYTELLER: And who wouldn't cry out so? One could imagine losing a button, a silver spoon from one's mouth, a watch when they were invented, or something; but a loss like this, and between one's own walls! Between one's own ears! Reduced to the status of even being lower than a child's toy… at least with a child's toy, one could

35

sew a button back on to cover up the tragedy of it all! What a slap in the face! Oh!
　　(urging)
Think, man, think!

　　　　(In response, KOVALOFF does his best to. Eventually...
　　　　thinking... he rises from the bed and imagines himself back in the
　　　　Ivan Jakovlevitch barber's chair and being shaved...)

STORYTELLER: One thing, the barber Ivan Jakovlevitch had shaved him the day before, he remembered, and during that whole day he was almost positive his nose had been there. If it hadn't, surely he would have felt some pain... or, if not, at least some sort of itch? The wound wouldn't have healed so quickly, nor would the surface of where-the-nose-had-been have been as flat as a pancake, as smooth as a billiard ball, mostly of the red variety. And so forth. And so on.
　　(as KOVALOFF falls back on the bed from thinking-exhaustion...)
With the result of all that thinking... the worst kind, as I have said, without any nose to let the thoughts out to run free and do minimal damage... he fell asleep. Or at least he made a good passing imitation of it since he wasn't used to drifting off without snoring through his nose and being lullabied to bye-byes. Despite what you might say, here a mouth has nothing on a nose.

　　(quick blackout)

3.

(After short interval, in the gloaming of the lighting, the giantish NOSE has once more fully appeared and is obviously at it again.

Emanating from its growing outline is a brontiferous 'snah-snah-snah' of it having difficulty clearing its sinuses, but it is obvious it is doing this deliberately to disrupt things, which it is highly successful at.

The STORYTELLER, as all others, cannot control his panic anymore...)

STORYTELLER: ('timber!') SNOT! BOGIES AT TWELVE
O'CLOCK!

(but the 'danger' passes)

STORYTELLER: Was that close or was that close?!

*(The shadow area has returned to KOVALOFF's bedroom and
he being asleep. He is awakened by a knock on the door and a
small packet obviously being left at the foot of it. He gets up, has
to open the door to retrieve it. As he does so, as if by holy
revenge, a large prop of a handwritten note pops out of the
package and slaps against the giantish NOSE, entrapping it for
all its struggles)*

STORYTELLER: What is this Righter of Wrongs, good people? It is
none other than a handwritten note... and he unable to write; so's you
what a miracle!... from the same Inspector of Police from the bridge so
early on and who was too busy back at the station getting more
comfortable on his couch to deliver it himself. And it reads if you must
know, as, indeed, we all must!...

*(as he reads, a musical bouncing ball dances over the note's
letters, with the NOSE, still not able to escape its clutches,
coming to rather nicely rise and fall with it all...)*

STORYTELLER: 'Hoi, Kovaloff, have you lost this nose? Well, it's
just been found. It was taken into custody floating down the river trying
to get over the border with a false passport and, what is still more
strange, I myself took it at first for a gentleman. Fortunately, I had my
just polished my boots and could see at once in their reflections that it
was a nose. At least I'm better than my mother-in-law. She hardly puts
polish to hobnail boot at all. I must say it's not the bravest nose I've
come across. One twist of it between the knuckles of the first and
second fingers and it confessed to everything... that it was sick of
going around on a face only pretending to be the nose of a real Major...
meaning your face, Kovaloff... so it decided to masquerade as a
General on its own. Cheeky fellow, this nose of yours, Kovaloff. The
other villain of the piece is a scoundrel of a barber living not far from
you and who is now locked up as my fourth daily barber studying the

37

wildlife living in my beard… without payment of course, or he'll get
the book thrown at him. Despite all this and as you can see, your nose
is quite uninjured, though by the crumbs of it, it looks like it has been
fooling around in some hot spot with some saucy fresh-baked bread.
PS: don't invite me for tea; I can hardly say no if I'm not there.'

> *(KOVALOFF unwraps his nose and joyfully holds it up, and
> celebrates. As he does so, the giantish NOSE gnashingly
> withdraws. The accompanying music is all sweetness and light)*

STORYTELLER: The truth be known our hero soon swooned with
relief and remained for some time plunged in a kind of vague reverie,
so great was the effect of this unexpected good news.

> *(KOVALOFF, with joy, enacts the following…)*

STORYTELLER: He placed the recovered nose carefully in the palm
of his hand, and examined it again with the greatest attention. 'Yes, this
is it! There can be no doubt about it!' he cried, 'Here is the boil on the
left side, which was ready to be squeezed even as long ago as
yesterday!'
> *(as a bit of sombreness returns to shadow area…)*
But many of us understands how nothing is permanent in this world of
noses. Even through his joy, our man began to see his problems weren't
over yet; his nose had been recovered, but one of the next steps…
certainly one with some priority… was to join it on his face again and
in its proper place preferably.
> *(KOVALOFF anxiously sit in from of his dressing table mirror,
> and…)*
But suppose it could not? Suppose, having made it on its own to the
rank of five-star General, it's whole outlook had changed and brought
with it a new outline?
> *(pause as he watches KOVALOFF's dread…)*
With a feeling of utter dread, he sat there before his dressing table
mirror in order that he might not place his nose back on crookedly.
That would be the final insult! And so, with trembling hands, he tried
to place it where he calculated it had been before, which is not as easy
as a lot of people think.
> *(and, as the action relates…)*

Having got it where he thought was right, he then pulled out the glue, and… and…
(waits while the nose keeps falling from K's face)
Horror! More than that! Horror of horrors! The nose wouldn't stick! Each time he tried, it slowly peeled off again, slowly slid down his face, and did a slow parabola to drop down plop on the dressing table below him! Desperately, he blew on it to breathe some life into it and tried again… but it would not hold! Slurp, slip, whee parabola slide! It was as if it was made of wood, and fell back on the table with a soft thud, as though it had been a cork in the bottle of Failure only waiting to go pop! Horror, oh yes!

KOVALOFF: CALL THE DOCTOR!

> *(Immediately, 'chase' music rises and falls, while KOVALOFF and the DOCTOR's shadow march purposely to either end of the screen, where this time they are the pair standing in full view at either side of the scrim curtain. They conduct their dialogue blandly across the stage, as with the CLERK earlier:)*

KOVALOFF: Doctor, do you have clean hands?!

DOCTOR: I live in a flat better than this. I have magnificently pointed elbows and a healthy wife I have never had to use them on. I eat a fresh apple every morning, and clean my teeth with extreme care, using five different tooth-brushes for three-quarters of an hour daily. That's each. My hands will stand up against any doctor's squint you care to bear upon me.

KOVALOFF: Never mind the clean hands.

DOCTOR: I wouldn't go as far as saying that.

KOVALOFF: Forget the hands! Just look at this vacant place on my face and this nose that won't go back on it!

DOCTOR: Mind if I use my binoculars?
(doesn't wait for permission)
Hmm! Hmmm! Hmmmm!

KOVALOFF: *What?*

DOCTOR: (smoothly) And what would you like done?

KOVALOFF: Put it back!

DOCTOR: I see. Well, terribly sorry and all that, but no, it cannot be done. My advice is remain as you are, lest you shake something else loose.

KOVALOFF: Doctor, I beg of you! There are a goodly number of ladies in polite society to need my strength to carry their purses over the two hundred thousand roubles mark!

DOCTOR: (impressed) Two hundred thousand roubles. Is that with or without a nose?

KOVALOFF: And who will give you a better fee than I'm going to, providing you keep your wits about you and don't do something silly like putting it back on upside down? Find some way of sticking it back on, I beg you. And please don't go saying I can keep it in place by employing my fingertip. I wouldn't be able to go dancing.

DOCTOR: Kovaloff, my dear man, believe me, there is nothing I would like better than your record-breaking fee, but that would be contrary to my principles and to my art. It is true that I accept fees, but that is only not to hurt my patients' feelings by refusing them. You have no nose, so you don't count. Now, dear chap, take my advice. Better let Nature do her work. Wash the place often with soap and cold water, and I assure you'll feel just as well as if you had a nose, if not only to smell better. As to the nose itself, I advise you to have it preserved in a bottle of spirits, or, still better, of warm vinegar mixed with two spoonfuls of brandy, and then you can sell it at a good price. I would be willing to take it off your fingertip myself, provided you do not ask too much. I've been thinking of trading mine in for a better one.

KOVALOFF: No, no! I will never sell it until it returns to where it properly belongs and then I'd only consider it by way of swap with one of clearer sinuses.

40

DOCTOR: Pity. Still, think on the bright side. If you can lose a nose, perhaps you can grow eyelashes that grow down long enough to take its place, or lose your mouth so that nobody notices about the nose.

(Without ceremony, the two shadows turn back into the shadow area. KOVALOFF takes to his bed to groaning over...)

STORYTELLER: Yes, poor Kovaloff took to his bed. It was hours, if not days and weeks before he was heard of again. He even tried to lift his spirits by returning in his dreams to the clerk in the newspaper office to show him how, despite the old boy's skepticism, noses can be returned.

(the CLERK shadow needs no invitation to re-appear around the side of the screen again. He has KOVALOFF's nose in hand and is examining it closely through a printer's glass and:)

CLERK: Call that a valuable snorter? It can't fold, collate, get a page number, trim. Dab a dob of the finest printer's ink on it and it's stuffed. I told you why bother, sir. 'Ere, you bring it back one day and we might give it a quote or two on page two or three.

(disappears, making bedridden KOVALOFF groan even more)

STORYTELLER: Yes, poor old Kovaloff still! Even his heating had gone off. Even the tip of his nose felt icy... almost as frosty as the rest of his life seemed to be.
(pause to let a soulful strain of music rise and fall)
But our man was still young, let's not forget that. And, down in the dumps, with only a beak in his hand not worth two in the bush, he wasn't in the best position to know how rumours of the extraordinary nose peradventure started spreading far and wide in the society he desperately wanted to succeed in, and why wouldn't they?

(The scene changes to the city's main concourse and milling crowds huddling, breaking off, huddling again etc...)

STORYTELLER: Just look at that. Soon it was nothing astonishing in hearing that Major Kovaloff's nose was to be seen walking every day at

41

three o'clock on the Neffsky Avenue, sometimes on and sometimes off. The crowd of curious spectators which gathered there daily was enormous. On one occasion, someone spread a report that the nose was in Junker's stores and immediately the place was besieged by such a crowd that the police had to interfere and establish order. A certain speculator had benches placed before the shop window, but no matter how many roubles he took hiring them out, nothing would make the nose come out from behind the ordinary flannel waistcoat hanging crookedly on a half dressmaker's dummy in that shop window there. One man, a retired colonel, so said, paid for a bench, waited two hours and then stormed off, grumbling, 'How can the fools let themselves be fooled by such idiotic stories?'

(and)

Then another rumour got abroad, to the effect that the nose was in the habit of sometimes marching, sometimes jogging, in the Tauris Gardens. Some students of the Academy of Surgery went there with needles and threads with thoughts of helping, but only came away with poison ivy stings that they had to wait in line at their own emergency department with.

(and)

Oh, these and many more! There were so many supposed sightings of now-said His Excellency Kovaloff's nose that could well have been collected into a book, if, here, the course of events didn't again get shrouded by a veil of obscurity and has left us in the dark...

(He orchestrates a slow fade of lighting)

4.

(When lighting returns, the shadow area is back to a happy, sun-shining world of the old St Petersburg's skyline again, with a dawn full of promise coming over the city's roof tops. The STORYTELLER is likewise chirpy...)

STORYTELLER: We can say what we like, but strange things happen in this world. That nose... yes, the very same nose we have been speaking of... that nose which had masqueraded as a five-star General simply because it didn't believe its owner was ever going to make

Major... was found one morning in its proper place... namely, between the cheeks of our hero Kovaloff, as if nothing had happened!

(waves script)

Oh, you should see the exclamation marks here!

(The scene by now has changed back to KOVALOFF's bedroom, where he is waking up, then tentatively feeling his face, then sitting bolt upright, then dashing to his dressing table and looking in the mirror, and...)

STORYTELLER: We're not quite sure at what time of night this miracle actually occurred but we know it came about precisely on 7th of April of some precise year, the precision of which is yet to be decided. Upon waking, Kovaloff looked by chance into a mirror and perceived a nose. He quickly put his hand to it; a nose was there beyond a doubt! 'Oh, no, the nose!' he exclaimed. And if nothing else much is, that much is recorded... and of course

(waves hand to shadow area)

clearly shown.

(and)

And when he had finished admiring himself, he still could not believe it not only returned but was remaining in place no matter how much he blew it. He dressed, ran out into the street, took a taxi cab into town and drove straight to the newspaper office.

(As the shadow scenes shift back to the main city concourse and happy milling crowds...)

STORYTELLER: There, he found the Clerk doing a brisk business taking advertisements for lost-and-found body parts, especially toes and fingernail parings and errant gold fillings making nuisances of themselves other than where they should be making nuisances of themselves. The old fellow had such a packed-up body-parts lost'n'found department that he had no time to marvel with Kovaloff about the return of his nose. 'I told yer, I told yer' was pretty much all the old fellow would mumble on the matter.

(and)

But still, our man Kovaloff was not discouraged. No matter how many times, he glanced at himself in windows and mirrors, his nose still remained above his upper lip, where Fate had first put it in the first place, even if his nose didn't like it!

(and)

And so, he hurried excitedly to the coffee house and had a cup of chocolate which normally made his nose want to jump right off his face, but nothing. Stuck there! Cemented back in place! Well and truly, tamed!

(and)

Back at his own office, he applied for the post of vice-governor of a province or government bailiff – one of the other -- and they accepted his applications as if nothing had happened to him, and even as if he had not the slightest chance of succeeding. They did not even as much as glance at his nose when they promoted him to start immediately as the vice-governor of a certain province or, if he wished, as the government bailiff in a certain other province. It was all on the basis of his new medical report which stated he was 'A man who could hold it all together. With a nose for working with his betters. No better profile.'

SHADOW PLAYERS CHORUS: 'A man who could hold it all together. With a nose for working with his betters. No better profile.'

STORYTELLER: And, as if the sun wasn't shining on him enough, even as he strolled along one evening in the blessing light, he perchanced upon the same the lovely daughter and her mother who would have shunned him if they saw he didn't have a nose then, although they did now live on the story that they saw he didn't have a nose yet still didn't shun him.

(as they converse...)

He made his presence known to them, and even introduced himself by name, and then lingered over passing pleasantries for the longest of time of at least a minute and a quarter before he divulged to them his decision that any vice-governor of a province or a government bailiff would decisively make, 'No, you haven't caught me in your trap. You both look old enough to be the mother, so I will say to you both, "As to your daughter, madam, I shan't marry her at all".'

(as he resumes promenading, strutting...)

After that, our hero resumed his walks on the Neffsky Avenue following his nose and even appeared in the theatre where his face with his appendage could be seen between Acts Two and Three. Yet, still, his nose remained in its place as if it had never quitted it. No even vigorously nodding to just about everyone who passed and wanted to greet him would shake it off! 'Why, how the man has kept his features over the years!', is what he most heard. Oh, and the other thing he often heard was the upping of dowry offers – under his minimum demand of two hundred thousand roubles, the bidding around town had climbed to as high as twelve-and-a-half thousand roubles.

(By now the lighting has dimmed to deep evening. KOVALOFF enters his room and takes to his bed.

Sleepy slow fade-out, while the STORYTELLER winds up to wind down...)

STORYTELLER: Such was the occurrence which took place in the northern capital of Russia's then-vast empire. On considering the account carefully, we can see that there is a good deal which looks a bit improbable about it. For example, how could Kovaloff not understand you really can't go around advertising for a lost nose? I don't mean about the cost of it – that's a mere trifle compared to it not being either a proper or befitting thing to do. The newspaper Clerk was quite right.
    (and)
I don't know about you, but another difficulty I have is how was the nose found in the baked loaf, and how did the barber Ivan Jakovlevitch himself not know about what he'd supposedly done straight off the razor strop? But what gets me the most is how authors, even mad old Russian ones, can choose such subjects for their stories. In the first place, no advantage results from it for the country; and in the second place, no harm results either. So what's the point? All the same, they tell me such cases do occur in reality -- rarely, you'd have to admit, but enough to make us all realize that when it comes to nose jobs, try very hard not to rub them up the wrong way.
                    (and then, re script)
That's what it's got down here, anyway.

(Fade out)

---000---

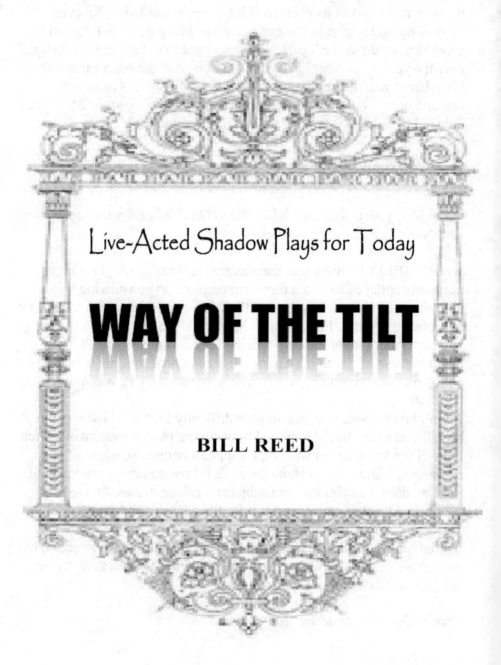

Live-Acted Shadow Plays for Today

WAY OF THE TILT

BILL REED

The behind-the-screen shadow action – or 'inner background' play --
can only ever keep 'pace' with the reading, not *keep up* with it.
Because of the resultant and necessary shadow-play distillation of the
storyteller's tale, the extensive stage directions given in this script are
only intended to be indicators as to what *might* be used for the shadow-
play side of things. They deliberately go beyond what the director
would employ and are given merely as a range of possible shadow-
actions he or she might want to use in the 'distillation'.

The Characters

STORYTELLER
He comes and goes in the action. When or if needed, he has his own
shadow player:

STORYTELLER SHADOW PLAYER
represents the STORYTELLER in the shadow play behind the scrim; is
pretty impassive as an action character, but plays his part.

CREEPY MANNY SHADOW PLAYER
As the main shadow-acting character, he will be adept at moving from
one walkway platform to the other without damaging himself – and this
applies to moving between the behind-scrim shadow area to front stage
and full-viewed. Is very often dictated to by the over-arching winged
moustache prop, which, whenever he bids, he points 'biddingly' up to
as to how it, by gesture, indicates his thinking.

SHADOW PLAYERS
4 or 5 as necessary to illustrate the narrated incidents. The occasional
'huddled masses' etc can be achieved by props-plus-lighting-plus-
sounds.

Production note

Behind the scrim curtain, at the very basic, should be an acting walk-way from one side of the stage to the other sloping, say, 10 degrees, plus at least one 'flat' walk-way, positioned such that a shadow player can step from one to the other without much discernible difference.

Down or up the slope, people and 'things' will slide along one way or the other -- either mechanically or free-wheeling or clinging desperately to a lifeline. Or they can comprise a whole scene – say, a prehistoric group sitting around a fire – as they slide by.

The moustache and the pince-nez are 'giantish' props… either stringed or hand/pole-held… that float above the action at stage level with amusing artificial intelligence. The moustache in particular evokes a large open-winged creature, very lopsided and does a lot of curling-the-old-mo etc.

Way of the Tilt

1.

(The scrim curtain divides the stage into two lateral areas – the shadow-playing behind-the-curtain area; and the front stage where the STORYTELLER is positioned.

When lighting comes up, it does so firstly behind the scrim where it seems that perhaps child-like figures seem to be playing... some are sliding downhill; some are pulling themselves uphill (perhaps hauling on lifelines); some are running left-to-right, right-to-left on the flat.

Then general light emerges to show the STORYTELLER, who rather gently stands with back to audience and, using conductor's hands, motions for all the movement behind the scrim to slow down, then to stop. Satisfied with his 'place' having been established, he turns back to audience)

STORYTELLER: It's the tilt, don't you know. It's what we do, being tilted. Including you, I dare say.
   (obligatory wave of his script)
Doesn't it happen to all of us? There was one time I was at an important interview for a job and they asked me when I was born, and for the life of me, I couldn't remember. My own birthday! See?, it had just slipped on by. Even the year of it!
   (waves script)
No wonder I... or any of you would... need this.

(Behind the scrim curtain, there comes, on the flat, CREEPY MANNY and the STORYTELLER shadow players. They carefully manipulate each other into position, while the props and the other shadows... live and inanimate... come into view to re-enact as many of the narrated episodes to come as possible:)

STORYTELLER: His name was Creepy Manny. What's sure was he wasn't called that in any putting-down way. It was just what he did. Not crime-related or anything; just 'Creepy' around *where he was placed in the world.*

50

(He pauses while CREEPY shadow player wobbles on his feet)

STORYTELLER: And that where-he-was wasn't where he was as an antique buyer – in that, it says here, he was unfailing. No, don't let appearances fool you; apparently he was this unfailing antique buyer who just was never in the right place at the right time and blamed the wind for this, not his pathological inability to make up his mind about where he was from one moment to the next.

(He points out the CREEPY shadow player who is turning circles on the spot, needing steadying by the STORYTELLER's shadow player)

STORYTELLER: Something like that, you see. And there he is, not lost or anything, but right in the middle of an auction. I mean, which way's the auctioneer and which way's not where the bidding is? Don't ask him, Creepy Manny, it looks like.
(calls back stage)
Stop that, okay?

(CREEPY shadow player does so, waits for the next narrative cue)

STORYTELLER: (goes back to script) What we are looking at here is a gentleman from Cairns, of once Anglo-Indian stock, or certainly looks it, who was this pretty good antique buyer who was a serious human being committed to going to see no other doctor than consulting his own mind because he could give himself free advice and doctors couldn't. Creepy Manny, yes, a bit unfair, sound-wise, a bit over-familiar. He wore a pince-nez, possibly the only one left in being borne aloft in any everyday-way in Australia in this present...

(CREEPY has bowed flourishing with his pince-nez, while the giantish pince-nez prop comes over like a cloud and is not shy to 'introduce' itself with an impertinent wiggle and a waggle)

STORYTELLER: ... day, which made him a walking antique in itself, when you think of it.
(and)

51

Creepy Manny had this way of looking over his pince-nez at you -- or any auctioneer -- that suggested he might have been better in a profession in which one didn't need to make up one's mind on anything at all concerning where you might be at any one time... say, maybe... I don't know... acting behind curtain or some other thing, right?. And perhaps those nose-job glasses not only gave him the look of an undertaker but also make him sound like one if you ever got a word out of him that made sense when it wasn't a bid from the auction floor.

(CREEPY disappears as a shadow for a moment and then re-appears from around the edge of the scrim curtain to stand front stage in full view... on seeming very slippery ground... and waits patiently, ready to converse with the STORYTELLER.

The STORYTELLER ignores his presence. CREEPY has to shrug 'don't ask me' to the audience, then continues waiting)

STORYTELLER: It was like he simply considered you had to be dead to want to talk to him and if you did get to talk to him you simply hadn't noticed you were dead, so out of not wanting to hurt your feelings, he would go on talking to you as though you were in a normal alive state. But not talking when you were, if you see what I mean. Or *he* wasn't talking when he was, because how could be when he didn't know if he was there or not, or wherever. It was just disconcerting that he would continuously interrupt you or himself in the middle of a sentence to suddenly pop up with questions concerning your deadness-as-he-saw-it like: 'What's it like over there?'

CREEPY: ('about time too') What's it like over there?

STORYTELLER: (answering back) I don't know. What's it like over on your side?

CREEPY: Not bad.

STORYTELLER: A bit shadowy?

CREEPY: (nodding) A bit shadowy.
   (then peers more closely at STORYTELLER)

Say, what did it?… a particularly bad divorce, the ravages of chemotherapy, or just walking down the street one day and bang! before you know it?

STORYTELLER: (sudden outcry) What's wrong with me?

CREEPY: Nothing really. It's just… sad to see.

STORYTELLER: *What is?*

> *(But CREEPY just turns around and slip'n'slides back to being the shadow conversing with the STORYTELLER shadow player behind the screen)*

STORYTELLER: That's what I mean. How can you talk to the man?
(then)
Worse than that, but, it was the way Creepy Manny couldn't stay still but didn't not stay still either…

> *(He can indicate behind him as an illustration where CREEPY is slowly sliding away from the STORYTELLER shadow player even as they are obviously conversing…)*

STORYTELLER: He just kept creeping creepily along in front of you, halfway between standing still and not standing still. You'd be talking to him and before you knew it he'd have crept away from you, as though you weren't making word sounds but was blowing on him -- or he might be creeping off on one or other side of you or creeping on past you to behind you…

> *(Behind, CREEPY reverses the creep and starts creeping the other way past the STORYTELLER shadow player…)*

STORYTELLER: …so if you wanted to talk to him face-to-face you'd have to creep-swivel sideways with him at first, until you ended up going in a slow circle as he went, providing you were able to see him creeping in the first place and not find you were suddenly talking to nothing in front of you because he had crept by you.

> *(Pauses for breath as, now, the STORYTELLER shadow player is*

53

turning circles trying to keep up with him...)

STORYTELLER: Who wanted to stop and talk to him? And as if that was all...

(and he gestures back to the shadow-playing area to get ready for something big, and:)

STORYTELLER: ...when we come to the troubles of Creepy Manny, you ain't seen nothing yet. We have to first address the rumour that, despite what you could see with your own two eyes, his feet never touched the ground, not together at one time, they didn't... but were always slip-sliding all over the place. Other rumours maintained all that slip-sliding – often leading to downright *swirling* about -- was due to his father trying to throw him out of the house at birth and onto the footpath outside, but missing his aim by a long shot. In fact, the feet weren't Creepy's base problem. Oh, no. His moustache was.

(He 'conducts' back into the shadow-acting area for yet another major construct coming... a life-size moustache 'coming by', which CREEPY now attaches to his upper lip, while its giantish winged prop counterpart comes floating over, nudging out the giantish pince-nez, and:)

STORYTELLER: That-there Creepy moustache was a vital part of the family heritage, especially because it was a long line of antique buyers and because it was the inviolate family tradition to do one's bidding at auction by the tipping upwards of the right side of that moustache by virtue of a tip of the right side of the mouth which the Creepy Manny family could only conquer, so it seems... which over the antique-buying ages made the family moustaches all grow longer on the right-hand side than the left-hand side, just like weight-lifting does, say, to your biceps.

(The giantish moustache, and CREEPY as well, demonstrate bidding by tipping the right sides)

STORYTELLER: You see how it goes. And there's no doubt about it Creepy Manny was the best antique buyer in the family for generations.

It was just his fiddling around with *his* right-side, lop-sided mo which let the family pith down – and not just a bit, but a real lot.

(Behind, both the prop moustache and CREEPY show a lot of agitation, a lot of twitching in discomfort, in 'no-no')

STORYTELLER: You see, without any warning, one day, what happened was he had his down-the-ages moustache surgically trimmed simply on a whim of wanting to look a bit more dapper as an antique buyer than any of his antique-buying forebears and their kind-of military-style right side of the old mo. Oh, he might have gotten away with that if he had left it as trimmed equally on the right and left sides. But did he? Of course, he didn't! You have to know where you are to stop there at logic. No, Creepy had to gone on with it and have that nostril-tickler of his shortened to make its left side shorter than its right… in direct contradiction of, or because of it, the family tradition.
   (and)
How can any of us wonder there was chaos from then on?

(Over, there is electric barber-snipping sounds and the giantish moustache panicking in the air as its left side gets the chop:)

STORYTELLER: No, I'm not kidding, or so it says here. Prior to that, things in the family were rock-solid; each and every Creepy Manny before him lived to the age of fifty-nine if the wind never changed in his or her lifetime. But *our* Creepy Manny just had to go and think, didn't he?, that shortening that moustache on the other side would lengthen his life span or, if not, he would go out more dapperly than those who had come before. Who were a pretty scruffy lot, by all accounts. And when, a few seconds after doing having it trimmed, he saw that it hadn't changed the length of his lifeline on the palm of his hand one iota, he tried to get the moustache put surgically back to what it had been given to him heritage-wise… that is, with the right side the longer by half on the strength of being built up all that muscle toning through making all those bids down through the ages.
   (then)
Needless to say, such recklessness dictated that his moustachio would never grow back to be the right-side military-style lopsidedness it should be. Of course, it wouldn't. That left side of his moustachio stayed half a length longer than the right side and would not grow back

55

nor would submit to any hair supplement or even an electric razor of industrial strength.

(waving hands around wildly)

What a flaunting of the family's strictest taboo! What a rejection of his heritage, of his very identity! Lop-sided to the left! Good God! Golly Goddy! So twisted, therefore, in bidding that any auctioneer would be looking towards his mo's right side and not seeing a thing, while the left side was going crazy trying to attract attention before the bidding ran out! No wonder Creepy Manny suddenly had no idea where he was in the world! No auctioneer taking any notice of you had to mean you couldn't even be there!

(The moustache finally manages to stop twitching, droops badly and sadly.

It and the pince-nez prop begin a mortified danse macabre around each other like planets. They both start to wobble, start to become disorientated. Some sound track music-of-the-stars underline this.

The AUCTIONEER shadow player comes into view, together with a sound over of a hectic bidding war going on… until, the sound over suddenly stops and the AUCTIONEER shadow player waits with his 'gavel' expectantly in the air… as the left side of the moustache rises and lowers itself wildly and CREEPY become very agitated to attract his attention).

STORYTELLER: It got so there wasn't an auctioneer in the whole of North Queensland who could tell when Creepy Manny was making a bid or not… or, if so, whether it was a final bid or just a passing bid watch-this-space, or wasn't a bid at all but just a twitch of the old mo coming from the left. Or if he was still making up his mind, or what. It had gotten to the stage that, even if he was the last bidder standing, auctions with him could go on for hours, but only if Creepy protested long and hard enough on the assumption that he might know where he was, but it was best to be sure than sorry.

(nods sadly at what is going on behind him)

It wasn't that he didn't know this himself, so no wonder he started to doubt even doubting where he was. In any bidding war, it got to the stage he started to feel he wasn't in the right place or the right time for

56

whatever it was he was bidding on and so was only really and truly bidding against himself. If he didn't know where in the world he was all of a sudden, why would he ever want to make any bid at all, let alone a final one?

(Behind, all sag to near-defeat, especially the AUCTIONEER, whose bidding voice cracks then stops altogether)

STORYTELLER: Wasn't that when he started to do the slipping and sliding all over the place? …When he became sure he didn't not only know where on earth he was but where he was going without knowing it?

(Again, the shadow players come back to life with the STORYTELLER shadow player trying to talk to CREEPY while the latter keeps sliding one way (downhill) past him, then sliding the other way (uphill) past him, while the former is having a hard time keeping his 'conversational' eyes on him)

STORYTELLER: Slip, slide. Slip, slop. As he goes. As it all started to go.
   (and)
Finally, even Creepy Manny realised the something he knew was up inside him was not showing as really 'off' on the outside of him. He needed a good old think.
   (and)
It's not quite known how, with all that sudden slipping and sliding, how he managed to stay still longer enough to sit down for a good old think when he didn't know where he was. Still… sit down to think, he did.

(shrugs as, behind, CREEPY get down to a good old think, 'The Thinker' style)

STORYTELLER: What was on the thinking menu was this: Moustache apart, there had to be a reason for a man not being able to put his foot down without going on the down slide or the up slide or just the plain old slide along.
   (pausing for effect)
And I'm down here to pause for effect here which I now do so…

57

(gets back on script)

… for pretty much no reason whatsoever, it looks like. So sorry about that.

(back on script)

Fortunately, Creepy Manny was at core a thinking man and so, even not knowing where he was, he sat there thinking right up his alley. And whatever he was holding onto to keep him at it, he kept hold off, until all the thinking was done. Firstly, it seems, the good thing to come out of it was to make him look into what it was about down-lop and up-lop. And here, the National Geographic channel was there to help, just going to show it was more of a good old watch as much as a good old think.

(and)

Creepy Manny's thinking discovered it all had nothing to do… not really; at least not on a global scale… with any left-hand-down lop-sidedness or any right-hand-side lop-sidedness of his, or any, moustache or military-style soup-strainer. No, it wasn't the moustache at all!

> *(Behind, the moustache jiggles with joy of good revelation and CREEPY goes from the Thinking Man to one bravely demonstrating fighting against the wind… to hurricane sights and sounds)*

STORYTELLER: He came to see clearly how, like most of his fellow man, he believed Man was feckless as he was by nature. And yet it became even more clear as the thinking went on and the TV stayed on that Mankind wasn't just being blown along where it didn't want to go by winds like the monsoons. No, the winds were only part of the story and a small part whose importance the National Geographic channel quickly blew out of the water by showing him the real culprit was not the winds themselves but what *made* the winds. And what made the winds was the tilt of the earth.

> *(Now, behind, CREEPY's against-the-wind equilibrium starts to waver)*

STORYTELLER: If the winds couldn't resist it, how could mere Man be expected to resist the tilt of the earth towards the sun? Of course Mankind couldn't, which is why Mankind almost always found itself, like him, in the wrong place at the wrong time, not knowing where the hell on the planet he was or it was. And little wonder!

(and)

Mankind just didn't know it yet.

(and)

Creepy Manny couldn't believe how obvious it was. For one thing, how many times have people found themselves in the wrong place at the wrong time, not knowing where they were, when there wasn't a breath of wind blowing, not a breeze, not a zephyr? Millions! Down the ages? Trillions! How many times has the human species stopped in its track, shake its head totally confused, and raise a quizzical eyebrow at Evolution, thinking it's fishing in the gene pool and finding it's being phished in some murder trial?

(and)

So, you can see what was left, can't you? That left only the one culprit exposed for what it was. The tilt of the earth! Was that obvious, or what?

> *(Now, behind, the down- and up-slope possibilities really come into play. CREEPY has to dig his heels in to stop sliding down or being pulled up from where he wants to be. The STORYTELLER shadow player helps out by holding his arm.*
>
> *Also, while the following 'episodes' are narrated, the cast shadow players come into their own... either as Mankind's groups or as individuals fighting against the 'tide'/grain... they begin by shivering and sweating, by opening and closing umbrellas and parasols under – by background soundtrack – seasons which come and go or don't come at all or pass too quickly...)*

STORYTELLER: And when he thought of it, what purpose did tilt have, apart from the seasons? What are the seasons to come home to anyway; do or do they not just come and go?   If you live in the tropics like Cairns, they don't even bother to come and go, and you don't even bother to write home about them. So, tilt regarding the seasons, in Creepy's mind, should be totally disregarded when it came to finding yourself in the wrong place at the wrong time or finding where on earth you were. Tilt when it comes to seasons, he saw, was no reason one didn't know where one was.

(then)

His new clear thinking went further than that. He could see how tilt really was deep down when it came to the seasons. Oh, it was very different to what you think you know – the tilt of the planet versus the spinning of the earth which affected people, aka Mankind, so much by simply refusing to let Mankind, aka people, *be*, oh yes.

> *(All over, behind, now, shadow players are starting to hold onto each other to stop themselves from sliding off one way or the other. CREEPY is now on his knees, holding onto the STORYTELLER shadow player's legs for dear life. As the full-view STORYTELLER has to raise his voice considerably:)*

STORYTELLER: Creepy would ask, and did in a fine old shout: how many people do you see going around like tops, spinning like crazy?

CREEPY: (shout out) HOW MANY PEOPLE DO YOU SEE GOING AROUND LIKE TOPS, SPINNING LIKE CRAZY?

STORYTELLER: Very, very few and very, very rarely, he would argue.

CREEPY: VERY, VERY FEW AND VERY, VERY RARELY! SO THERE!

STORYTELLER: (now riding over all sight and sounds) Exactly!
(then)
No, this invidious tilting caper wasn't engineered into the human make-up like the spin was and the fact was that if you were mad enough not to apply traction… if you didn't take measures to dig your heels in and keep things down to a manageable creep… you, aka Mankind-stroke-people-stroke-humanity, could be totally swept off your feet and end up unable to stop the tilt of the Earth from sliding you into where *it* wanted you to be, not where *you* needed to be. Which, if it wasn't the very definition of not knowing where on earth you are, you could have fooled Creepy Manny.
(pause for emphasis)
Or where you knew you were to be, even, since how can you tell for sure? How did you know *anything*?
(and)

60

So, as Creepy came to explain it, and often did… and, it has here, that it was to no less that yours truly in that time of tilt, as you may have noticed…

(has pointed out the shadows)

… one, aka *you*, only had to look at the place human beings had been impelled to settle down over human history.

> *(Behind now, the cast shadow players and props have specific 'dioramas' that can re-enact, settling into groups or breaking away into individual extemporised routines)*

STORYTELLER: What we have here is no less than Creepy Manny's theory that much of the theories of voluntary human migration, aka *us* on the hoof all over, had to be all bunkum. No man in his right mind who knew exactly where he was, would volunteer to land up anywhere near the polar caps…

(the frozen-waste sights and sounds…)

let alone in Iceland or Australia, before the tilt of the Earth got at him too… not if he, aka *they*, had a right mind in the right place and time they or he wouldn't. No, it was a total myth to say early humans followed…

(valley-birds and surf sights and sounds…)

the valleys or followed the coastlines, following the green grapes or the great migrating herds.

(snorting and herd-hooves-thundering sights and sounds…)

No, there was only sliding down the tilt. Or, see how they…

(pointing to slidings up behind)

… up. Knowing where you are, that is.

> *(Now CREEPY, still holding on for dear life to the legs of the STORYTELLER's shadow player, is being pulled by the tilt uphill and is crying out:)*

CREEPY: NO, THERE'S ONLY SLIDING DOWN THE TILT! OR UP! KNOWING WHERE YOU ARE!

STORYTELLER: 'You' there being aka you.

(and)

All there was, was ending up where the tilt put you, not having a clue where you are or were. And that would, without doubt, be at the wrong time at the wrong place, as didn't Creepy keep saying over and over?

(Somehow, CREEPY shadow player has got 'away' and not appears front stage at edge of scrim curtain, where he coolly repeats to audience:)

CREEPY: And that would, without doubt, be at the wrong place at the wrong time, as don't I keep saying to you?
            (peers at audience, shakes his head in sympathy)
What was it?... a devastating divorce, the ravages of chemo-therapy, or just walking down the street one day and *bang!* before you know it? Sad to see.

(In a blink of an eye... and lighting... he is hurrying back to re-take his place in the shadow acting of the tilt of things, where large props etc show huge stencilled hands on cave wall, igloos, climbing trees, Stone Age scenes... all effects intermingling into a single Mankind diorama as much as possible...)

STORYTELLER: (almost hailing now) You only had to take those stencilled hands on early-man's caves. Those nail scratchings in Pleistocene clays? Those bones dug in around cave man's first eating sites, showing how burping rudely hasn't changed much down the ages? These had to be signs of some poor beggar fighting desperately to find some handhold to cling on for dear life against the tilt. Mean, who would want to build a town by the side of a glacier when man wasn't made with claws to use as crampons? Who'd live in the trees when you didn't have wings or tails, or on the flats when you were the slowest juiciest game for miles around and the drag of the offspring from your wife's last mate making things slower, worse?
(shadow players getting run down...)
Who'd want to go and live where they didn't know where they were living? Who in his right mind, aka common dog fuck, would want to settle his family at the sea's edge when babies didn't come out knowing how to swim?
(shadow players getting drowned or shark-fed)

Well, they did, but their parents didn't know that. And why didn't they know that? Because the tilt made them not have a clue where they were, that's why.

(shadow player goes down the third time)
That wasn't even the point, aka the goods. Creepy Manny could now see how it was far worse if you took the state of individual bidding on the auction floor, which who didn't have the need to?

(behind, traffic jams and honking sounds compete with auction-bidding sounds)
If you didn't execute your creep rights, then you would most likely end up sliding into one of tilt's so-common blockages, jam-ups, nobules-and-nodes – call them any aka that you will -- with a lot of very strange people you didn't know.

(behind, crowds getting unruly)
Like you, not one of them wants to be there, or even knew they were, in any real sense. None ever was, or is, likely to have *asked* to be there. You ask them and you get the knuckle sandwich, right? They do their blocks, their nanas… aka *do their tit*. They start fighting. Where did you think road rage came from?

> *(Now, to near rioting, behind-screen, cymbals clash and war clouds come over… which he waits for, and self-justifiably points to… then pitched battles starting up all over the shop. And:)*

STORYTELLER: Soon, too, all there is, is tilt-chaos -- a throng, a murderous crowd, a mob of berserkers, traffic-jam madness, commuter blockages, pockets of rape and brutality, rock and Molotov cocktail throwing, armies against armies flung together by tilt where they never wanted to be in the first place, wars and conflicts as populations collide. *Aka tile chaos!* Without a blessed one of them… aka one of the nut cases, all… knowing what they are, or were, doing because they've got barley's on where they are! Or were! That's tilt! It's tilt! Fault tilt!

(has to now shout to be heard)
What's God's, aka Send-Her-Down-Huey's, immeasurable design got to do with it? Either tilt shouldn't be on earth or Mankind shouldn't be on earth. Stands to reason, you can't have both. Either Mankind, aka nut cases all, or tilt is in the wrong place at the wrong time – and maybe, even, only one knows where it is and that one isn't saying, and little wonder because none of it makes sense.

(Finally, the melee and pitched battles die down in part to shadow players becoming more concerned with stopping themselves slipping down the tilt or slipping up the tilt... or simply sliding up or sliding down without a thought.

Soon these are displaced by the props-and-sounds of India/China and old butter knives and of an auction well underway. In this small interim, the 'real' STORYTELLER can gather himself and finally:)

STORYTELLER: All this left Creepy Manny with one big question in life: how could anyone think his mind was made up as to even where he was, if nobody had any say in where his mind might be thinking from, due to ongoing, ever-present tilt? You might be bidding on, say, a Chola-period butter knife from the 9th century but how can you take it to the final bid not knowing if the 9th century was really that butter knife's rightful place and time as it crosses your path? How could you be positive it wasn't actual Chola but some butter knife of the Tang dynasty in China slid out of its time by tilt from a time and place where butter knives were as common as dirt in their day and not worth a finger's-lick of bidding on by anyone knowing where he or she was? Or not?
    (and stresses urgently:)
Never mind about the left- or right-side lop-sidedness of your moustache, military-style or otherwise, how could you be sure about the butter bit?

(Again, CREEPY shadow player has amazingly gets to the edge of the scrim and to suddenly appear three-dimensionally before the audience:)

CREEPY: NEVER MIND ABOUT THE LEFT- OR RIGHT-SIDE LOP-SIDEDNESS OF YOUR LIP TICKLER, HOW'S ABOUT EVEN BEING SURE ABOUT THE BUTTER BIT?

(He peers once more at the audience, shakes his head at what he sees of them, and sadly:)

CREEPY: So very sad to see. Didn't you tell me what it was, or you did and I wasn't all there at the time?

(and, again, in a blink of the eye, returns to behind the scrim screen where there come candle-light shadows on, say, a yurt's side or a cottage wall...)

STORYTELLER: He meant, he was saying to you, even getting his lines screwed up more than a little bit... he could end up with their distance ancestors huddling together on some godforsaken waterless treeless plain or some godless auction room wanting to set up a tent or something... and you wouldn't know or even know where you were.
(and)
DA TILT'S GOT YA!
(manages to quieten down)
Ladies and gyros, don't panic. This theatre can take any tilt within the bounds of reason. If you feel any wind down your neck, it's not tilt, aka tilt, but probably only your neighbour, aka the hot breath down your neck.
(waves script)
Also, it says here there's a cure for all this.
(aside)
It doesn't say 'temporary', but it should. Even I know that.
(back to being on-script)
Sleep. It's sleep. A good old get-the-konk-down crash-out. That's what. Never mind about the lop-sidedness of any moustache you've got or trying to coax along -- aka: ladies, think metaphorically if you don't secretly have the mo -- or wondering where the hell you are, or why nobody's taking any notice of you or even your otherwise-winning bid on butter knives... those Cholas and Tangs were sly old sods at the best of time... or even about the butter bit.
(time to nod sagely)
Sleep. Put the lids down on it all. Sleep's Mankind's biological defence mechanism, aka big juicy gorby right smack in the gob, against tilt. Is it not?
(new aside)
Aha, I see some of you be nodding. Some of us have had the experience of hibernation, eh? Well, Creepy Manny's even got from the National Geographic a theory about who you lot are too, which we'll get to... if I can find it...

(shifts through script, finds the place he wants)
Here we are. For those lucky few sleepy-heads of you…
(reads)
You see, Natural Selection selected those who slept with their feet to
the tilt and with sides on their beds to stop rolling with the tilt before
they could get to realise where they were. That's why sides were on
beds that weren't tilted right, after all, he… oops!...

*(Behind, CREEPY nearly slides right away from the
STORYTELLER, but somehow manages to get himself righted,
even if he over-corrects and threatens to slid right off up-tilt)*

STORYTELLER: Close thing, that.
(back on script)
If that illustrates something, it illustrates you always know where you
stood with the dead. The dead are tilt-less when it comes to having no
clue as to where on earth they are. They tell no lies, just lie down. Too
late, maybe, but the dead at least can put their heads back long enough
to know exactly where they are just before the very moment they cease
to. That even applies to you, the survivor, in order for you to know
exactly where they are… or by consulting a reliable tilt table know
where they'll be at any one time. Laying flowers and digging in the
right place, and all that. That mightn't be any good for antique buyers
at auctions but historians love it or them, aka the dead, or whatever…
like you lucky few who can hibernate and make like dead. The tilt just
seems to go right around you! Remember the Bible's angel of death
and the lambs' blood on the front doors? And as Creepy Manny came
to say, since 'over there' seemed to be a favourite subject of his, the
dead are not a total waste of time; tilted right, each and every one of
them has a tale to tell of *what-was-it?*, ha ha.

*(Yet again, CREEPY almost miraculously appears at edge of
scrim on the front apron, and shouts full-frontally to audience:)*

CREEPY: THE DEAD AREN'T A TOTAL WASTE OF TIME!
GOOD TO BID AGAINST AT AUCTIONS!

*(He waits to get his own laugh… perhaps even repeats line… but
gets no encouragement from anywhere, much. He peers again at
the audience, shakes head sadly again)*

CREEPY: So how's it going on the other side? If you can hear this, it can't be as bad as you think, so that's something. Still… sad to see. No, really.

(Once more, he escapes back to behind the screen in a blink of the eye, as the giantish moustache and pince-nez take prominence again. They have to shoulder their ways to the fore. They are just as air-lively as before and greet the sights and sounds of the railway station and busy traffic openly…)

STORYTELLER: By this time, Creepy had been thinking so much that he was beginning to waste away, not had had a cup of tea or coffee for hours. Even his pince-nez was starting to slip down onto his lower lip as though it wanted to scrutinise his left-handed moustache a lot more closely in order to describe how he was starving it. Meaning the nose under it, of course.

(as those props fight over themselves accordingly, they are interrupted by large train whistling, and train-track sounds over)

STORYTELLER: (change coming) It was most fortunate, then, that the tilt had Cairns railway station coming on by just at that moment, aka whatever-moment-that-was… and that he – and I in attendance, I have to admit – found himself, aka ourselves, on the steps of the station just as that left-hand side of that moustache of his gave off the best upwards twitch it had ever managed, so said. Which, of course, meant it had just made a bid at auction which couldn't be denied, couldn't be topped, and couldn't be surpassed in a flourish to end all flourishes on any bidding floor.
(pauses to gather for climacteric)
Therefore, over milk with some tea and more sugar than the cup could hold from the Cairns station cafeteria, Creepy Manny found himself – *and knowing precisely where he was!* – in the right spot of tilt at the right time of tilt – *slid just right!* – and and and

(He spots off on raising suspense and plays on it:)

STORYTELLER: Wait, waitee. A little suspense never tilts anything that can't be mucked up, no? First, we can get back to who those of you who nodded when I asked about hibernation and whatnot are when they're sleeping. Remember? Well, Creepy would tell you, you are the special ones... the tilt-avoiders... who are always in the right place and the right time as the good things in life come sliding by. He'd say you're one of the few lucky ones belonging to one of those pockets of humans throughout history who knew exactly where they were and so had proven themselves to be immune to being slid to any wrong place at any wrong time by tilt.

(For the time being, the train whistles and train tracks rumblings die down to allow a golden band of shadow players show themselves beneath halos and rainbow, picking their teeth leisurely and lazing about without a care in the world...)

STORYTELLER: That's them all right. Special. Without, yep, a care in the world. The staunch people! The staunchies! And, down through history, this breed-apart... these unique as-good-as-dead stand-outs... had developed the ability to stand sideways to whatever tilt threw at them while they adjusted both eyebrows ... read moustache there if you will or aka it... to keep their balance and thereby could remain on an even keel. They settled where they liked; they went where they liked. They tended towards places that were the right places and the right time as well, but it was not known whether that was in spite of tilt or no tilt.
   (gay and careless, they play ring-around-the-rosies)
They tended to cluster around flatlands bordered on all sides by mountains or on mountain sides too steep for tilt to get at them, or not be able to slide them too far if it did. Places tilt-proof. For them, everything was knowing to be where they were; everything was a level auction field. All smooth running and tiltless.
   (and)
What a lesson that realisation about the staunch people... those staunchies like you!... gave him! Oh, you staunchies, you! He could see he was only a short moustache's non-military side away from being one of them. All he had to do was to *place himself where he knew he was*... and then... and then...

(As CREEPY takes back attention from the ideal groups of the staunch people and positions himself as the STORYTELLER describes:)

68

STORYTELLER: And now we can get back to Creepy and me on the railway station's steps and past all that '… and and and' suspense caper I bet I got you back there with. And then, and then… Creepy, starved by all this thinking, now honed to himself as to where he was or staunchie-could-be, and crystal clear, having had railway-cafeteria tea, or at least that part of the tea which hadn't done too much damage… well, our Creepy for the first time in his lifelong *suddenly knew how to place himself precisely where he was!*

(As the shadow area 'clearly' shows… CREEPY stands upright and sure of himself, his face to the wind, his chest breasting the tilt:)

STORYTELLER: And there on the steps of the Cairns railway station, he stood, did Creepy, tilt staunchied, allowing himself to turn sideways to tilt or any of its sneaky-windy minions, and let the outer side of his right-side eyebrow act as a balance to the lop-sidedness of the left non-military side of his moustache into the wind, into that tilt… and he braced himself with the sun over his right shoulder refusing by the sheer force of knowing just where the shit he was to budge an inch. Not one. Not a millimetre of an inch! Not a sixty-fourth of a metre, even!

(As if to prove it, he waits and shows how, now, CREEPY refuses to be budged by the tilt or its gales. He even lets go of everything but the tilt nor its windy minions can make him budge)

STORYTELLER: I mean, I was there. I saw it. Finally, it had boiled down to a bit of stopping'n'thinking and getting his right eyebrow coordinated with the left-side lop-sidedness of his moustache, and there… yes, right there'n'then!… to wait and wait… to wait again if necessary… for the Right Thing to come sliding-on-the-tilt along past his rightful place at his rightful time and for him to toss that eyebrow like his family-before that tossed the right side of their moustaches. And to *pluck* that Right Thing up in the delicious throes of knowing exactly where he was and how he was going to stay there when it came along the tilt of the world!

(Behind, now CREEPY is positive heroic. He is even lending one hand to the STORYTELLER's shadow player to stop him from

starting, now, to slide with the tilt, even to the extent of having to grimly hold onto CREEPY's legs himself)

STORYTELLER: What a waking-up to where he needed to wake up!

(The scene behind begins to quieten down with CREEPY fully victorious. Soon, rising in volume, the train whistling and the rumbling train tracks start to come back over)

STORYTELLER: But did he get over-excited, liable to slip back on the tilt's trolley? No sir! Not our new Creepy Manny. As cool as the cucumber that was part and parcel of the whole Cairns railway station shebang, Creepy finished his tea on a sour note like a normal being with tea that had gone on the tilt long, long ago, and hesitated not. He looked up the railway timetable for which way the tilt was on for, turned sideways to it – the tilt not the timetable -- kept his right eyebrow to the wind to give a float-balance to the left-hand lop-sidedness of his moustache... and let that now-beauteous hairy thing on his upper lip laden with railway froth so fittingly and guided by his non-military right eyebrow... I say again, let it make an unimpeachable, untoppable, undiminishable bid from the auction floor for...
(again milks the suspense)
... for the whole lock, stock and barrel of the whole Cairns railway station just as the final hammer came down for the last time!
(pauses for effect, before:)
And that included...

(As, behind, the Right-Thing 'it' reveals itself as a model of the railway station, followed by trains, and garnered by the sounds of railway announcements and props of trains pulling in and out etc... all now in full flight)

STORYTELLER: ...all its rolling stock on the tracks going as far back south all the way to Brisbane, plus all the road vehicles passing by tilt along Bunda Street at the time the hammer fell.

(CREEPY picks trains and cars up like toys, cradles them as mine, mine, while above him the moustache and pince-nez come back out to play, and:)

STORYTELLER: What made the new Creepy all the more brazen was that he had no money at the time… made even more brilliant because one of the vehicles passing along Bunda Street that was caught up in his winning bid was a rarest of rare 1920 Silver Ghost Rolls Royce tourer just dug up from where it lay buried in L'Auguillon-sur-Mer in France away from the Nazis, and just then as the hammer fell being hunted down by private detectives 100 years past their prime.

(as, behind, this shows)

It just went to show what a heck of a right time and a right place Creepy was able to pluck from out of all that tilt-slide slipping on by simply by knowing what stance to take up in order to know where he was, right time-and-place-wise.

(added to which)

The car financed his coming fortune in wind socks, and the railway station gave him a killing in the soon-to-be boom in auction sales of anything Victorian to do with railways which was just around the corner before the railway antique business tilted the other way. But that was well into the future. To the antique-buyer young hopefuls that came to sit at his feet, Creepy always advised… well, let's hear it from the horse's mouth…

(He motions CREEPY to come out from. It is an invitation that is now taken up boldly. {Noticeably, the STORYTELLER shadow player, has now shaken off from holding onto CREEPY's leg for dear life against the tilt and by now has slid off to oblivion.}

Front and centre, CREEPY is now a bold, new CREEPY:)

CREEPY: So I tell them there's a right time and place to do your bidding, sure, but the really clever ones know how to stand with their shoulders up against it. It's up to you to find out what 'it' is. You'll know 'it' if it nods to you okay m'man you're in the right time and place. It 'it' never does, then presume you're not in the right time and place. In that case, I wouldn't know what to say to you.

(The STORYTELLER taps him on the shoulder 'well done' and motions he can leave. This, CREEPY does happily, but stops to turn back a while nod his own 'well done' to the audience:)

71

CREEPY: You're looking pretty good, considering. Well done.

(and waves goodbye, making sure all can see how he sidles off sideways to avoid the slide – now very easily.

The STORYTELLER and takes over again, while, behind, the moustache and the pince-nez might even be seeming to be waving goodbye as they toggle away)

STORYTELLER: He never mentioned tilt to those who came to sit at his feet, not even needing grappling irons under the influence of his solidarity, his knowledge of precisely where he was. Nor did he mention anything about killer mustachios, or snazzy pince-nezs or the art of perfecting the bid. He never felt himself rich enough or silly enough to give away all his trade secrets. You don't give away trade secrets if you know where you are, where you stashed them and how you can go get back to 'em when you wanted to. Even if they're uphill and on the other side of the mountain from the tilt.

(He motions CREEPY to take a final bow. CREEPY does so. But he means not front stage, but back behind the scrim and openly indicates so. CREEPY doesn't mind; he pulls on as many cast shadows as he can to come with him, does a final-curtain bow, while…)

STORYTELLER: As to the tilt… I don't know whether it ever got back to being the same Earth's tilt that it used to be, given the beating Creepy Manny gave it. How would we know anyway? Don't the winds still blow you along the same as they once did? Or do they, covering up any hole let by any tilt whose cover is blown? Who knows, rightfully. I wouldn't, anyway; I keep magnet soles with grappling irons beneath my feet. You ever see many mountaineers go sliding on by you?
   (and)
Thought not.

(Blackout)

---oOo---

72

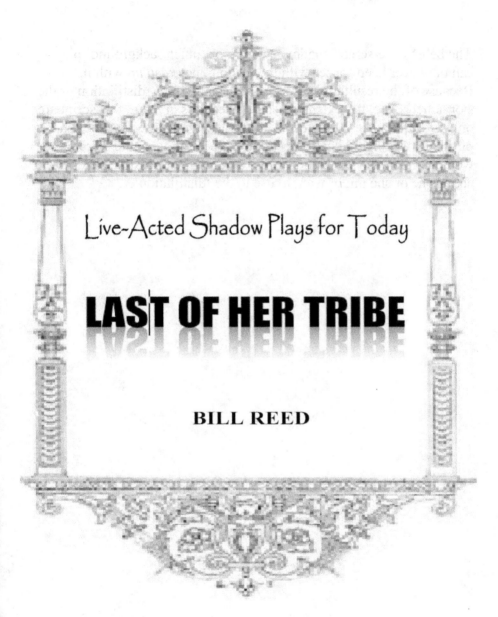

Live-Acted Shadow Plays for Today

LAST OF HER TRIBE

BILL REED

The behind-the-screen shadow action – or 'inner background' play --
can only ever keep 'pace' with the reading, not *keep up* with it.
Because of the resultant and necessary shadow-play distillation of the
storyteller's tale, the extensive stage directions given in this script are
only intended to be indicators as to what *might* be used for the shadow-
play side of things. They deliberately go beyond what the director
would employ and are given merely as a range of possible shadow-
actions he or she might want to use in the 'distillation'.

The Characters

STORYTELLER
He reads from a manuscript, Kindle, iphone, tablet or laptop; it doesn't matter. He need not do this rehearsed; in fact, the effect will be better if done unrehearsed after just a few read-throughs. He is not slow to point out 'himself' as an occasional shadow player in his own right.

JESSIE (2ND) STORYTELLER
As a younger Jessie comes back to life in the full flush of the great adventure of her life, and the saddest.

KING BILLY SHADOW PLAYER
a large goanna shadow that has complete freedom of the shadow area, both landed or in air. Is more of a Godzilla walker than a four-legger. He might be a shadow, but he's all purply technicolour all right.

TRUGANINNI/TRU SHADOW PLAYER

JESSIE SHADOW PLAYER

STORYTELLER SHADOW PLAYER

SHADOW PLAYERS
say, 4 or 5, called on to play as many characters as needed to illustrate the episodes on the run. A few of these will be:
Crowther
Manager
Seniors' Home residents

Last of Her Tribe

1.

(At first there is an 'unpeopled' stage showing the scrim curtain with a dim light behind and a softly-lit STORYTELLER's stool.

The audience 'waits' on this stillness, before the STORYTELLER comes on front stage, stands greeting the audience, then finally waves the script he or she will be reading from and:)

STORYTELLER: ('settles in') So, I've been told to start out telling you what you're going to see here is a metaphor mainly about Truganinni and King Billy. Or vikky versa.
   (pause)
Now, King Billy… the so-called last of the Tasmanian Aboriginal males… who wouldn't have heard of King Billy?...

(As he relates, the shadows come up – first King Billy and Truganinni and then the others – to enact the incidents which the STORYTELLER reads out:)

STORYTELLER: (starts the reading) If we follow Wikipedia – on the pathia to Wicki, ha ha -- it pretty much says this: 'King Billy (real name William Lanne) died in 1869 at the age of 34. As the 'last' male Tasmanian, his skeleton was valuable. He was captured along with his family in 1842 during a period known as the Black War. His native name is lost. In 1855, he joined a whaling ship and regularly visited Oyster Cove when he had time. Lanne died on 3 March 1869 from a combination of cholera and dysentery.
       (aside to let the shadow playing catch up…)
Now here comes the really disgusting part…
   (back on script, as the gruesome details are shadow-acted...)
In a maniac's rush to secure his scientifically-rare skeleton, a member of the English College of Surgeons named William Crowther broke into the morgue and decapitated Billy's corpse, removing the skin and inserted a skull from a recently-deceased white man. Another society, this time The Tasmanian Royal Society soon discovered what had

happened and rushed in to get its share of his bones by amputating the hands and feet.

(bitter aside)

Logical, right?

(gathers himself)

And so, King Billy was then buried… without hands, without feet, without skull, in a fine old bloody mangled assaulted mess. Later that night, his grave was robbed… you wouldn't have thought there was enough left to make it worth it… leaving, to be found next morning, a gaping hole and a trail of body leading out of the cemetery gate.

(disgusted pause before reading on)

Crowther later became Premier of Tasmania. Crowther claimed that, because Lanne had lived much of his life within the European community, his brain had exhibited physical changes, demonstrating 'the improvement that takes place in the lower race when subjected to the effects of education and civilisation.'

CROWTHER SHADOW PLAYER: (fit to be heard) The improvement that takes place in the lower race when subjected to the effects of education and civilisation!

STORYTELLER: (bitterly) Well, that was worth hearing a second time. *Jesus.*

(goes on)

The bones of King Billy were never found. His skull. His hands. His feet. For small mercies we have that the government hid them where it finally shovelled what was left of him in.

(He marks the end of King Billy's section by pausing to allow the shadow players to change over to illustrate his reading of what happened to TRUGANINNI…)

STORYTELLER: And now we have Truganinni, the so-called last Tasmanian, the Queen, full-stop… well, as Clive Turnbull says, she was what we'd call a princess, but her mother was stabbed to death by a European; her sister was carried off by sealers. When she was only a teenager, two white shithead timber men said they'd row her and her husband across to Bruni Island. In mid-channel, they threw him overboard, chopping off his hands when he tried to hang onto the gunwales; then they took her off to do what they pleased and to do what we'll never be able to take back.

(When the abuse of the girl is displayed adequately enough he is able to narrate the happier scenes of old TRUGANINNI swaggering along Hobart streets...)

STORYTELLER: And it has it here the most worthy Tess Lawrence writing: 'Seven years after King Billy's death, Truganinni stood alone, a living relic of her race. She would walk the streets of Hobart Town, resembling Queen Victoria in her voluminous skirts and headdress. Towards the end, she appeared to bear no malice towards her race's persecutors. Growing stoutish, she smoked a pipe and enjoyed a daily jug of beer. But she began to grow ill and as her death loomed, so did the memories of what happened to King Billy's body...'
 (pause)
'The fear obsessed her like a disease and repeatedly she begged and pleaded, "Don't let them cut me up! Bury me behind the mountain!"'

OLD TRUGANINNI SHADOW PLAYERS: (choking up) Don't let them cut m...!

(cannot finish. After a while, the STORYTELLER resumes and so can the episodic shadow enacting:)

STORYTELLER: On May 8th 1876, aged around 73, Truganinni died. She was buried in a secret grave in a plain wooden casket. But the promises made to her were false ones, yet again. Years after her death her body was exhumed and her skeleton was displayed in the Tasmanian Museum, alongside the skeletons of animals. And so, there it was: in a black casket in Hobart's Tasmanian Museum lay the broken bones of an aboriginal queen – and in her irreverent tomb are squashed the broken dreams of a race.' That, good people, is what Tess Lawrence wrote.

(Against the ominous shadow of a standing casket, rhythm sticks break out, then tribal chanting rises for a brief time, until both fade.

The STORYTELLER finds himself alone front stage again. He

takes up an impressive camcorder, slings it around his neck – a
professional -- then waits kindly for full attention, before
resuming reading. As he does so, the shadow area starts to come
to life. This starts with TRU and JESSIE wrapped in shawls in
the home for the aged, with the latter fidgeting about the former:)

STORYTELLER: Seems we've now popped into in the present time
in a hostel for the aged down King Billy's Avenue. That's the name of
the street. It says here it is. King Billy's Avenue. Because it's lined
with King Billy's pines. If you don't get confused, I won't be
confused.
  (aside with shrug)
I did remember to say this was all metaphor, didn't I?
  (back to reading script)
Don't blame me like for rubbing salt into the wounds of the Tasmanian
Aborigines. I'm only the mouth here.
  (and)
I'm already treated like snot back stage, so it's no big surprise when
they-who-pay go the fiction and make the play of lumbering me with
having to record these two good old-boners down the old-boners home
in King Billy's Avenue Street there, like I said, right?
  (as the old girls start slapping each other's hands away)
I think push-over job, but I soon start to think maybe pushover's a bit
premature. At least Nursie Nice-nough's nice enough to shunt me past
the old near-goners watching the box in what could be the morgue
waiting room and out through the back where old Tru and Jessie are
hunched over the Sun-Herald's giant crossword like they wouldn't care
if I'm from the UN''s refugee thingo, let alone out of a shadow play, so
I'm recording straight off, aren't I?

  (As he does so… remaining front stage… TRU and JESSIE, both
  in wheelchairs, come out from either side of the scrim curtain,
  shaking their fists at each other. When, though, and
  simultaneously, they notice they are out in full view of the
  audience, they jump with surprise and skid their wheelchairs
  back into the shadow area behind the scrim curtain.

  A relief to all.

  And there, they aggressively sit, wheelchair to wheelchair, back

79

doing the crossword, while the STORYTELLER handles the filming of them as well as the narration from his front-stage area:)

STORYTELLER: What I'm down here to go on about is: if you're like listening to what I'm taping here, old Tru's got the crotchety voice past gappy teeth and Jessie's the dentures with a life of their own. And right now apparently they've both got the shits with each other over that crosswords...

(to the shadow-illustration of the description:)

NARRATIVE: Old Tru's blowing her grey mop over old Jessie's dumb silence over some clue and suddenly screech-like going, 'What's the delay, what's the time lag?'

TRU: (fit to be heard) What's the delay, what's the time lag?

NARRATIVE: and, you have to laugh, old Jessie's mistaking as a separate clue thrown at her, and she's going, 'Time lag, eh? How many letters?'

JESSIE: (ditto) Time lag, eh? How many letters?

STORYTELLER: And now this gets old Tru really blowing her stack this time going, 'Ya dopey old moll!'

TRU: Ya dopey old moll!

JESSIE: Fuccough, who's a dopey old moll?'

STORYTELLER: Is what Jessie said. I recorded it. And it making Tru's hackles really come up, going, 'You, ya mug!'

TRU: You, ya mug.

JESSIE: Fuccough!

TRU: You fuccough, y'dopey old moll!

(They start 'head-butting' the foot-stands of their wheelchairs, glare across at each other, while his other-self appears as the STORYTELLER SHADOW PLAYER allowing him, in the meantime, to continue reading:)

STORYTELLER: I hadn't even got around to introducing myself, either. So I start to stick out my hand, when old Tru sort of mentally shoves it away, and she suddenly throws down her biro and pokes in me right in the ship's navel like follow-me-y'big-falooka, and, if that wheelchair of hers could spring to its feet, it would have been burning rubber if it had rubber the way she's already starting doing wheelies burning off down the creepy squelchy old corridor caper there.

> *(which TRU proceeds to do, whizzing around front stage like an enraged bull, while:)*

STORYTELLER: Making old Jessie go blurting out herself at being left behind or something, and taking off after old Tru, putting in her own burning of the old rubber. The trouble is it looks like…
   (waving script annoyingly)
and this thing looks like it changing back to past tense now…
   (carries on reading)
… she didn't have the joints to overcome gravity as easily as Tru. When she finally struggled to her feet, her Tru was already metres ahead and gaining speed. Panicking now, old Jessie, she Jessie shoved me out of the way and was going into wheelies of her own trying to keep up. You can hear on the tape even me doing my own best to keep up.

> *(Now both of the old ladies are doing wheelies around front stage, with mounted horns blazing. His other-self shadow player has to struggle to try to keep up while:)*

STORYTELLER: (now shouting excitedly) And old Tru was klaxoning ahead, 'Watchit, mugs up-ahead!'

TRU: Watch it, mugs up-ahead!

STORYTELLER: And old Jessie honking on behind, like, 'Honk, honk, watcha!

JESSIE: Honk, honk, watcha!

STORYTELLER: (now having to shout) Like they're on the home stretch of Le Mans or something…!

TRU: Move over, or die!

JESSIE: Move it or lose it!

STORYTELLER: You heard it! I couldn't believe it! 'Move over or die!'. 'Move it or lose it!'

> *(and just as suddenly TRU veers off to do a skid around the edge of the scrim curtain to thunder her wheelchair across his front-stage area, totally ignoring him. JESSIE is as close behind as she can make her own wheelchair go. They go off screeching… the wheelchairs and them, both. And as they go:)*

JESSIE: Hoi, you stick to the left!

TRU: Up sticking to the left!

JESSIE: You stick to the road rules!

TRU: Up sticking to the road rules!

STORYTELLER: (standing amazed, mutters) 'You stick to the left', 'Up the road rules'… It was supposed to be just two good old girls interviewed, so they said.
  (to audience)
You notice, how in your office, they never say? They never go, like, go record but take a splint along so you don't blame us for any broken bones, oh, no. And they never say how you're supposed to…
  (waving script again)
cope with the likes of this sloppy effort slipping back into present tense and now past tense again, you know? I've got sensitivities in that area. But who gives a stuff?
  (nevertheless, carries on with reading)

By now I'm recording that old Tru's seemed to have gotten up more speed than she could control herself. She took the turn at the end of the corridor by bouncing off the opposite wall and then, doing a wheelie, like, on one foot, was gone from sight. On the tape, even I think I hear the screech of tyres from her. I mean, you wouldn't have been surprised to hear her shout out, like, 'Watch out, World, Madam Mountain coming through!'

(Behind him, TRU pokes her head around the opposite side of the scrim curtain and:)

TRU: Watch out, World, Madam Mountain coming through!

STORYTELLER: (long-sufferingly) So there's the three of us squishing and squelching on the old-bones near-goner lino… yes, I was suckered in to following them.
(and)
As I say, listen on the Replay. Even so, already, I find I am in the doorway of their aged room there.

(He points to the shadow player who is playing him and who is now standing awkwardly in at the entrance of their room…)

STORYTELLER: Anyway, there I am in the doorway of their room there and suddenly I'm getting introduced to their twin-share suite like the old-boner near-goner brochure pretty-polly says, like if your imagination's on the blink.

(just as they are mentioned below, there are a lot of floating and props flying around TRU and JESSIE, who are both looking like pure angels seated 'at home' now…)

STORYTELLER: You might have to imagine a lot of this, but it's like a room with a dunny and a door in and a door out on the other side. There's chaos there that'd shame my room and I live in that out of real disgust. Like, over the TV there's humungous red satin bloomers the kings of Fiji would've played rugby in and they're out drying without shame or something. There's bottles and jars and sticky crunched-up kleenexs that I still don't want to think about. I'm getting to go into asthma distress with a fog of talcs and, you-don't-have-to-be-Einstein, false-teeth glues, probably for fixing wigs on too.

(and)

But don't get me like wrong. It's not too bad. In fact, it's sort of comfy, like. I had a grandmother too.

(to sounds over of birds chirping, bees buzzing idyllically...)

And outside there's this french door caper onto a real cheery little small garden all mardi gras'd up with flowers and what gardens have. Trouble is this french door isn't open to letting fresh air in; and also there's like this something-else smell not quite right, right? I'm thinking zoos and I'm like thinking lion cages and that blood'n'bone knock-the-nose-over you get there. And I'm watching both of them pulling back the curtain that's around one of the beds like it's Chinese royalty inside and holding out this like long-dead ham sandwich they'd pinched from the lunchtime sitting I guess and Tru's going, 'Ooo's my pretty boy then?'

> *(while she and JESSIE are seen pulling open a bed netting and going all lovey-dovey:)*

TRU: Ooo's my pretty boy then?

JESSIE: Ooo's our own King Billyboy, give's a smack on the lips.

STORYTELLER: And, yep, old Jessie's going, 'Ooo's our own King Billyboy, gives a smack on the lips'.

(aside, re camcorder)

It keeps seeming to want me to repeat what they're saying, or I thought it did, but it's strange, you know; I'm not sure now. Are they not minding me butting in if you don't, and they're still going:

JESSIE: (again, echo) Ooo's our own King Billyboy, give's a bit fat juicy smack on the lips.

STORYTELLER: ... or is it me? Or what's on the tape? That's how it was getting me even so early on.

> *(He nevertheless goes back to reading illustrating the action*
> *behind where the ladies are bending over the bed and itchy-*
> *cooing away, bow ties and Smiley stickers etc start floating*

*around in the air, and then comes into view, swimmingly, BILLY
BOY into shadow glory...)*

STORYTELLER: And suddenly there I am staring at this whopping
great goanna caper-thing, big mothafrrrukker, dinosaur nightmare come
true, right there on the pillow there like it's the Lion King up on the
rock posing for publicity stills. But it's wearing this like dog's harness
on, all tartan, and there's these red bows around its revolting neck and
revolting tail and all these Smiley stickers stuck along its back, I mean
really badly.

*(note: a giantish version of BILLY BOY remains hovering over
all – and pretty much continues to do so from here on -- while the
shadow playacting revolves around a normal-sized BILLY BOY
in the middle of the action – eg, on the bed between TRU and
JESSIE – that reflects the following...)*

STORYTELLER: You can see how it looks like its thinking it's
surveying all it commands and it's got this upchuckable purple tongue
thing lolling out of the side of its upchuckable purple mouth thing.
Meantime old Tru and Jessie, they're pushing this old stale-as-a-board
sandwich at it going 'Ooos' this and 'Ooos' that, when all of a sudden-
like that purple nightmare of a tongue thing snatches that sandwich
up... like wouldn't you be shuddering... then raises its purple-kind of a
head to dragon's heaven, or whatever sits above something like that,
and swallows the bread to halfway and then stops like a statute of the
Lion King somebody's shoved his half-finished sanny into the mouth
of in the middle of that publicity shoot and shouting hold-it-right-there-
pal.

*(There is a moment when he turns and nods at KING BILLY
shadow doing all of that -- and now frozen with the sandwich in
its mouth, half-gulped, half not)*

TRU: Ooos.

JESSIE: Ooos.

STORYTELLER: Did I say how it's got these false eyebrows the old
girls've eye'liner'd in? And a set of false mouse's ears painted in pink

85

polka dots? And claws all purple painted toe-nails? And more… it's all on the video. And I'm there cooling my heels in the doorway, stunned out of my mind, when suddenly I'm guessing I must be in like Flynn, like, whoever that is, or they wouldn't be letting me stand there looking at their obvious secret of all secrets, their treasure, like. And old Tru's going to me like I've just been initiated into some secret society, going on something about scoffing his greens.

TRU: Scoffing his greens puts hair on his chest.

STORYTELLER: And old Jessie's going on, nodding away and tapping her nose at me like I'm family now, indoctrinated into the presence of royalty, going on about royalty or something…

JESSIE: Call him Sir Billyboy, or your majesty will do.

STORYTELLER: She wants me to call him Sir Billyboy or 'your majesty' would do. How's about big hhmotherhhhfrugger of a purple pukability? And if you look closely you can see my shadow on the wall and I'm there…
    (nodding at the part his own-self's shadow player is having…)
lying through my teeth, nodding away great-great, thinking how do you work Godzilla the goanna into oral history to impress those-who-sent-me cos they pay me?, when I think you can even hear King Billyboy giving this great purple-bubbling burp affair, like publicity wanted him to say a few words into the mike or something. And I'm saying to m'self like forget oral histories, what I could be recording is a first of some lizard/goanna monstrosity going burp-wise on the Australian continent, and on cue.

> *(waits for the almighty burp which doesn't come… at least not until the giantish BILLY BOY, floating above, obliges. And when it does it almost blows the whole shadow-area paraphernalia away…)*

STORYTELLER: See?, and back at the office I get to tell how ole King Billyboy's been with the old girls for five years or more, no crap, and like how they'd kept him hidden in the closet of that near-goner's place, don't ask me how. Like, the staff there must be blind in the

86

smell department or they must've thought those two old girls were just a bit more on the nose than a couple of old ducks ought to be.

(as TRU and JESSIE sits back primly as though butter wouldn't melt in their mouths…)

Anyway, burp or not, on cue or not, batten-down-the-hatches, like, when Billyboy goes all socially incorrect, they're suddenly two sweet old ladies, sitting all prim like, hands in laps, ankles together, lips going that pursed thing like ooos a little sweetie. And I'm suddenly thinking would butter melt in their mouths before it went off and had to be thrown out? And now I twig that they're waiting for me to ask what they-who-pay say I've got to ask, so I ask it: like what would you say to Life Itself?, as if it was a question of life itself, and I'm getting Tru going:

(During that, the ladies have wheeled themselves out into the front stage area to be in full view, although keeping on their own 'side' of the scrim, and:)

TRU: To Life Itself? I'd say suck on this.

JESSIE: And I'd be going for the crutch with me knee.

TRU: I'd say sit on this; it's got new nail polish on.

JESSIE: And I'd say sit on this but first get back in line with all the other lover boys.

BOTH LADIES: Anyway, who's asking?

(They turn on the STORYTELLER. The shadow player who is acting the STORYTELLER part back there now feels left out…)

STORYTELLER SHADOW PLAYER: Me!

(They ignore him, repeat to 'real' STORYTELLER:)

BOTH LADIES: Who's asking, and no answering, 'How many letters?'

(Now, the STORYTELLER's shadow player is getting so

87

desperate to get into the action – actually where he should be – he is pushing up against the scrim curtain to be let out, and:)

STORYTELLER SHADOW PLAYER: I'm asking!

(But they continue to ignore him for the 'real' STORYTELLER, who take pity of his ownself's shadow struggling there and addresses him:)

STORYTELLER: I think they're asking you 'who's talking'?

STORYTELLER SHADOW PLAYER: (thinks, before:) How many letters?

BOTH LADIES: (losing buzzer) Blaaa.

STORYTELLER: (can get back to audience) See, I'm a bit uncomfortable with them on the wrong side of the lens at this stage, I'm really getting all togged-up on this oral-history stuff and it needing a bit of yours-truly's fresh air, so I'm pushing my luck with old Tru first going like asking her okay, ma'am, when were you born?

STORYTELLER SHADOW PLAYER: (*'I'm here too'*) Tru, when were you born?

(Of course, TRU ignores him for the real thing)

STORYTELLER: And old Tru's, she's going to me ignoring everything else…

(and, despite his ownself's shadow player's protests behind, orchestrates her for:)

TRU: Born? Born? In 1803 before you ever got flushed out, little mopokery you.

STORYTELLER: 1803?

STORYTELLER SHADOW PLAYER: (now being ignored by his own self) I said that!

88

STORYTELLER: And I'm like double-taking pull-this-one going, '1803?' and old Tru's going all high-horse lah-de-dah like Queen Victoria or however this Queen Victoria's supposed to go like they said old Truganinni used to lah-de-dah about the streets looking like.

TRU: (shocked, to JESSIE) You hear that, y'moll?

JESSIE: (lips pursed with her) I did.

TRU: Who said 1803? I said thereabouts. Jeez. What they send along these days.

STORYTELLER: But oral history and my pay at the end of the week's at stake here, and having to make they-who-pay believe what they're listening to, right?, but I feel things might be slipping a bit, when suddenly Tru's real and live and not sorta kidding anymore…

STORYTELLER SHADOW PLAYER: I'm still here, you know.

(but he sees he is now so ignored that he turns from breasting the scrim curtain, and walks away to leave them at it…)

TRU: (seriously) I was born in a rock pool, in a water pond, in the lilies of a dancing tide, Junior.

STORYTELLER: And… and I know there's a lot of 'and's… and somehow I'm looking at that wheelchair and thinking she's in this near-goners' joint and she's still sitting in it like it's some, yeah, throne and I'm going sorry-sorry and keeping my mouth clammed because there's this sudden dignity there, like, you know? And there's something going on inside me saying to me, hey, bozo, this is oral history and you're not just some finger on the play button, okay? So better smarten up.

(waits for enough time… just enough time… for TRU to pose as royalty before she gets an itch under her breast)

STORYTELLER: And, anyway, as it's got down here, old Jessie's not to be outdone, is she? She's, like, tugging at my sleeve if you can do it by mental telegraphy and shes going all protective over old Tru. Least I think she is, was… this past and present tense here is driving me zippy… and she's -- Jessie's -- going:

JESSIE: You cheeky little b. Don't ask me where what do I know?, 'cepting it was close to where the migrant ship left from the Land of Pomegranates and when it finally got to dock at that bleedin' Melbourne wharf there, where didn't I ever stand on that gangplank because nobody's going to throw their leg over me and I yelled down to all those horny Eye-tite cheeky little b's down there on the dockside looking for a bit even if they had to take a bride and I gave them a real cop of an eyeful and then gave it to them straight, 'Righto, who's game?'.

TRU: (cackle repeat) 'Righto, who's game?' Mad old moll.

JESSIE: Who's a mad old moll?

(They giggle at each other and then honk up their wheelchairs and beat each other back into the shadow area… 'buzzing' the STORYTELLER as they pass across his front-stage area, of course.

Finally, he can continue reading:)

STORYTELLER: That old Jessie, she's so skinny, it's like when she clacks those dentures, it's like her bones are breaking. Old Tru's as black as the ace of spade but all shiny like a moonlight sea you'd like to dive into at a beach party when the full moon's rising. Like. So this is oral history for real, I'm going to myself and feeling a lot better about myself. And if you knew me, you'd know that's saying a lot.

(He stands… the outsider… looking back 'into' the shadow-acting area where TRU and JESSIE fuss around the majestic giantish KING BILLY. He nods with satisfaction as… Blackout)

2.
(The shadow area is noticeably darkish. There is certainly some sort of movement in there but it cannot be discerned.

The STORYTELLER stands, therefore, looking and sounding bereft of support. His voice has an ominous edge to it:)

STORYTELLER: It might be two weeks later and I might still be approaching the old girls' room thinking handkerchief over the nose because of King Billy…
   (pause for effect)
But this time I didn't need it. And this time it's not feeling right.

   (as the shadow area comes up on something brighter than expected, as he reminisces and, shadowedly, bumbles around with TRU and JESSIE in their room – mainly, of course, around KING BILLY. Then, as the STORYTELLER's ownself's shadow comes in, the two ladies shoot off in their wheelchairs, giggling and having a gay old time, illustrating:)

STORYTELLER: Prior to that it had been a good two weeks too, you know? The only small drawback is the dud thing with being initiated into the tribe is you're left as Billyboy's babysitter, ain't you?, while them two lubberly ladies take off as soon as I front up, belting those wheelchairs of theirs down the corridor, giggling away, and only coming back when visitors' time's-up smelling of like chocolate and gin. If it's not gin, it ain't no roses, either.

   (TRU and JESSIE return, all giggling and kicking up their heels, and being a bit silly with their wheelchairs. He has to quicken up his pace of reading in order to keep up with them:)

STORYTELLER: But they're happy, I'm happy. And me?, I'm being left like old Billyboy's nanny or something. Have a look for yourself. Talk about the King! It's like I'm only the finger on Play; if it's on it's on, like if it's not, it's not, so what do I know? Same with the King Billy. He looked happy as a statue there. I could even look at that purple horror of a mouth'n'tongue and think I'm making that purple horror of a mouth'n'tongue happy. It made me pretty happy too, 'cept I was still having nightmares about those purple horrors. But maybe you don't, video-wide, get that, that I was happy and taping a good tape, you know…?

91

(But then the mood behind the scrim curtain turns grim by dint of lighting and slowing down of movement.

This is particularly noticeable with KING BILLY; it's shadow suddenly disappears from its commanding view ... and is reflected in the STORYTELLER's tone of voice:)

STORYTELLER: But that was then, right? I'm on about now, and, yeah, noticing this time I'm not even tempted to put a handkerchief to my face approaching their room. This is a bit odd, I'm thinking. And then, the fact is, I'm like just arriving when the place's Manager bad-arse's foghorner voice barely getting heard over old Tru in there wailing away, like I've walked into a train wreck after the wreck has gone, or something.

(Now the shadow scene of the room becomes clear and clear that things have changed dramatically.

The STORYTELLER's and the MANAGER's shadows are static in the doorway. TRU is now on the floor and JESSIE is bending over her trying to lift her up.

TRU is cradling a shrunken KING BILLY in her lap.

From these positions, they move according to:)

STORYTELLER: So, I'm there suddenly stopped in my tracks at the doorway next to that Manager and old Tru's on her knees with old Jessie's trying to hoist her up into the wheelchair but old Tru's holding Billyboy in her hands and I see he's not moving or even pretending to be the Lion King high up on the cliff for stills publicity.
(pauses to let it be shown)
His purple monstrosity of a tongue's lolling out one side. His red tail bow is like dangling just by a last puke-making scale. All the Smiley stickers have fallen off on the floor around her. What can I tell you that you can't hear by looking'n'listening closely anyway? It's my video. It's all this world-famous oral history, isn't it? And Billyboy's eyeliner eyebrows are all smudged, you know? 'Cepting for old Tru near-retching like sobbing away and the Manager, there seems this soundproofing all over the world, you'd think like.

92

(Behind is it as he reads – and now JESSIE virtually taking over the shadow acting. She rises from her wheelchair showing she is still sprightly and hadn't even needed it, and...)

STORYTELLER: That's old Jessie finally getting to help lift Billyboy fully into a full-on nestle in old Tru's lap and then old Tru can get to cradle his or its, whatever, cheek against her cheek and she's like blowing into his spew-making nostril like she's practicing the tuba or something. I'm thinking a fit coming on or come on, like. But old Jessie's holding both of them sort of from falling over going: 'Ssh ssh'
if you look real hard and old Tru starts grabbing old Jessie's old hair with her old near-goner left hand and like she needed saving from drowning and then, hey, oh boy, like, then screaming going:

(TRU shadow player is obviously trying to let some grief out but it won't come nor will her breathing...)

STORYTELLER: (greatly serious) I have to let her say it. I have to...

(Finally, TRU pent-up lamentation breaks:)

TRU: Don't let them cut me up!

(In sympathy, JESSIE falls down beside her. They cannot move, but huddle into each other)

STORYTELLER: (sotto voce) This is that Manager now speaking. He's going like bad-arse, like Lord Frick Shithead Himself, out of a real mealy-mouth, you know?, 'We'll find out who did this, trust me on this'.

MANAGER: (all of how described) We'll find out who did this. Trust me on this.

(JESSIE is seen staring up at him until he shifts uncomfortably, and the STORYTELLER feels it time to continue to the action:)

93

STORYTELLER: (speeding up and down) And, to that, there's old Jessie giving the Manager A-hole the big finger and there's old Tru pretty much at the same time lifting poor gone Billyboy up to me, like why me?, and her big near-goner eyes are going great crying pools and my own chest's going real tight and then, would you believe, she's only like crawling to the garden outside those french windows there and on her knees, outside, yeah, to their garden thingo out there, yes, right? And Jessie she's with Tru and on her knees too out there too. And they're both suddenly on all fours clawing the little earth in that little garden area they had and going all hysterical and you can even hear them digging that grave for Billyboy with their own bare hands. Jesus H. You can hear it on tape if you listen hard.

>   *(He has to stop and wait as the shadow acting plays out. His own shadow dares not move too close to what the old ladies are doing. It is really so pathetic that it cannot be helped.*
>
>   *His voice carries much sympathetic hurt:)*

STORYTELLER: Then all I'm hearing is Manager A-hole tutt-tutting at all this daring to happen inside the walls of his heavenly kingdom of near-goners and like the A-holes's only going, isn't he?…

>   *(He has to wait – indeed all has to wait – for the MANAGER to deign to speak from the doorway; the fellow has a long think about it, and then strides out from behind the curtain to address the world:)*

MANAGER: You can't do that without permission!
  (adding)
They can't do that without prior permission you know.

STORYTELLER: A-hole. And when the old Tru and Jessie take no notice, like what'd you expect them to?, he's only turning to me and going on tape as though I'm also guilty of going bare hands at his precious garden heaven-on-earth, and he's still A-hole-ing away going, 'Nobody's allowed to say we allow that around here!'

MANAGER: (repeat) Nobody's allowed to say we allow that around here!

STORYTELLER: Real A-hole. Now, I know I'm no saint but right then I really know I'm no saint. Do I stand up for them? I do not stand up for them. Surprise, surprise. What I do know is this oral-history caper has to be past tense, and you can put that down as just about all, as well…

(waves script)

This stuff should be like I keep saying… past tense. Not the present. Not what you can't get any distance from it, you know? I'm videoing oral history, not something that's stabbing you away in the heart while you're really there just to watch; what else?

(stops, apologetically to 'world')

Yeah, I know. But it's something like that. And I still feel it.

(carries on reluctantly)

So I slip off'n'out sayonara bad-arsed Manager A-hole, and I head for the home hills, even though I'm seeing out of the corner of my eye old Jessie's somehow getting poor old Tru back inside and could do with my help.

(bitter aside again)

I've already said I know.

(With a great deal of bitterness, he watches his own shadow literally slink off. Blackout)

3.

(When lighting returns, only the STORYTELLER is illuminated. He stands before a blackened shadow area, and shrugs with self-incrimination to audience)

STORYTELLER: Yes, okay, I'm back here. They sent me back here. They said, where's The End? I said, I thought that was The End, but they knew I was crapping. I said I didn't want to know The End. They said, oh yes you do. Oh, no I don't, I said. They said yep you do. I said give me one good reason and they said because we want to know and our children want to know and our children's children want to know. And I do that's bullshit, that is. And they said we know that; go back and do your fucking job.

(The back-lighting returns in the shadow area on TRU, JESSIE,

95

MANAGER, NURSE and his own shadow.

The scene is as he narrates it is below as is the enactment of his description. It starts very softly, funereally:)

STORYTELLER: The next time, the next morning, and I'm already on Record coming down the corridor. You know something gone even more wrong when go on through the main lounge and there's no near-goners sitting around and even the TV isn't on. Then you get to Tru-and-Jessie's and like big surprise there's bad-arse snot-ridden Manager A-hole trying to get up on his high chariot again but you can see he's sort of stuck in the doorway of their room there like nobody gives a rat's bum about him and when I show he's suddenly taking it out on me, oh right sure pick on me, going:

MANAGER: She's not allowed to die all over here; no, she's not!

STORYTELLER: A-hole still!
                              (mocking mimic)
'She's not allowed to die all over here; no, she's not!'
  (gets back to:)
And then the absolute A-hole's going… it's down here word-for-word… shouting back down the corridor like for all the old-boners to hear:

  (This time the MANAGER boldly comes out around the scrim curtain, flushed with self-righteousness)

MANAGER: We have walking tours and the shopping buses here! We have music hour with tinkling of the ivories! We have Snakes & Ladders and the daily rags! Nobody goes ratty here, not in any unknown way they don't!

STORYTELLER: (mock mimic) 'Nobody goes ratty here, not in any unknown way they don't!'
  (and)
Stuff me.

  (But by now the MANAGER has returned to the shadow area where he doesn't stand on ceremony, but washes his hands of the

96

whole affair and walks out in a huff)

STORYTELLER: A-hole! And I ought to talk. Where am I? It's like I've disappeared even before him.
   (then, taking refuge in script)
See, like the thing is, there's old Tru parked out on the floor in the corner of the room and I'm thinking rag doll all flopped out and her poor old head, that's dropped onto her chest and if she's making any sound I'm not picking it up. And old Jessie's by her side, where else?, and she's prodding this cup of tea at old Tru over and over but like deadpan and dead hopeless and all dead weight to it, going with each prod like: Tea. Tea. Tea. Tea. Tea… Take tea… Sort of thing.
   (and)
See, the thing was, someone had dug Billyboy back up from where they had used their own hands to bury him. Someone had chopped off his tail and left it there by the grave they'd dug with their own bare oldies. Someone had chopped off his head and left it there by the grave. Someone had lopped off his revolting little legs and left them there by the grave. Someone had left his tartan harness and his red bows lying there. Someone had stuck a couple of those Smiley stickers on the French doors there like how's-this, old farts? No one had left his little torso there. That was gone. Was the main part of Billyboy's being. See, this like trail of blood is winding its way off from his grave there and disappearing into the grass going around the corner and off off off and I'm looking at it and I'm thinking like sinkhole, vanished, King Billyboy's gone. And I'm going this is not right. No way. You can't do this. You don't do this.
   (and)
See, someone had left no flowers in their little garden. You can't hear any of that. I got no oral history on any of that, 'cepting Jessie's going to her Tru:
'Tea. Tea. Take tea'
to her poor old out-to-it Tru and I let my mike likeasif fall back into her going like it was a babble, a bubble, a wind-of-all that would never stop just as it had always been started which is all I can say about it; her going in a rasp, in a whisper, but as brittle as cold crust: 'Don't let them cut me up too. Bury me behind the mountains'.
   (he repeats on his own, not reading, but painfully)
'Don't let them cut me up too! Bury me behind the mountains!'
   (then)

It's like near all the oral history they're going to get out of me.
What I can see… see?… of poor old Tru, she looked now like a pile of ash against the light of day. Old Jessie's like kneeling down beside her waving us all off and maybe it's the same cup of tea she's pushing and prodding away going:
'Don't cry. Tea. Tea. Take tea'
to her old Tru's tears sparkling off the light of the day streaming in on everybody there now and I swear on me, on me, and I'm only the finger on the button.

JESSIE: (just audible) Don't cry. Tea. Tea. Take tea.

STORYTELLER: Like that. Jesus. And, but, she's not done with by half. No, she's not. She's suddenly a terrier. And she's suddenly fierce with some sort of memory that beats all.
   (repeats almost ecstatically)
She's a terrier and fierce with some sort of memory or something that beats all!

   (Apart from a natural reaction to resist her, he is helpless against her sudden onrush to invade his front-stage area, can only indicate what she has sprung up to do)

STORYTELLER: See… see?… she suddenly has me by the mike and she has me by the wrist and she's squeezing the life out of all that's dear to her, seems like, going like you have to slow it down to hear right like cos she's suddenly a whole bunch of organ pipes rolled into one; she's a choir going from choking to belting it out; she's a Hallelujah; a cry of joy to everything that's ever flashed around orbiting some centre-of-the-circle… she is in total italics…
   (and gets in before she can start up…)
Didn't I say from the start this was all about King Billy and her?

   (He has been saying this while JESSIE STORYTELLER, brandishing her own script, microphone in hand, has launched herself from the wings to take over from him… as, behind, the backdrop changes to clear blue sky ahead… with Uluru on the far open horizon… and the shadow living acting is largely replaced wholly by flying and skittish props and sounds, like the whee-ing wheelchairs, the surf and land below, the eagles, the

98

revving and skidding doing wheelies, their laughter… that is,
everything's-flying exposition of the burst of exaltations she
breaks into:)

JESSIE STORYTELLER: *What can I say to the waiting public?*
Choof-choof, always on the choof-choof, weren't we ever! They nicked
her trying to run a red light. Dangerous driving in charge of a
wheelchair; you're off the road for keeps, the beak orders her. Oh
yeah? Eat this one; it squeaks, she says and gives the beak the right
royal digit. She just trades up for a Wheelchairs-R-Us Shag-Magnet
4WD mean machine with ochre-n-black trim and matching muddies
and Blackpowers-R-Us pennant flag with tungsten frame, bull bars
rhino-strength and hunting lights to freeze a charging buffalo or any
bank you know back. Gears? They'd grind away your back teeth and
they're driving Bridgestone 275s on Dirty Dog wheel trims, enough to
make Everest look an anthill. Anyway, there I am tossed out of another
kitchen waiting for any lift I can get on the first road I can make it to
and suddenly there's Tru gunning smoke outa twin spoilers as she pulls
over on the track out of Hobart. Hop on, she says. No worries, I says.
Halfway across Bass Strait, I finally get to ask at the top of this big
brute of a breaking wave we're zooming over, How come the
mainland? She yells back, the only piece of me Tassie's getting is the
back of my big black bum.

    (gets an above-all 'hey-ho' vaudeville drum roll which she jigs gaily
      to before sailing on…)

What can I say? We're just past Flinders Island when she cops sight of
old Bill hauling in this whale, bleeding all over the place, both of them,
and old Tru swings the Shag Magnet down alongside and the mad
moll's calling Ahoy you can come alongside of me anytime, you big
one-left hunk you. Hop on Bill, she shouts into the Roaring Forties
funnily off Antarctica. No way Ugly, the so-called last of the
Tasmanian males, useless as my fanny all of 'em, burps rum back. But
Tru, she was a goner for him right from the start. Tru gunned the Shag
Magnet down to twenty-five fathoms to rescue his false teeth. She
thundered alongside when he threw his breakfast up over the side and
bottled it in case he needed it later, never mind poor Shag Magnet's
duco. She followed him ashore to Hobart Town, George Town,
Queenstown, all the whitie towns before Van Diemen's Land got stuck
with Tasmania -- or that's what they told me anyway. Old Bill couldn't
stagger out of a Ladies' Lounge without Tru waiting there outside for

him and then parading the Shag Magnet before him wherever he staggered like make way for King and her trumpeting MAKE WAY FOR HIM WHO'S NOW ME ONE'N'ONLY, KING BILL, NO BULL!...

> *(All of the shadow players stop and, as one, cry out before proceeding their mad-cappery:)*

SHADOW PLAYERS: MAKE WAY FOR HIM WHO'S NOW ME ONE'N'ONLY, KING BILL, NO BULL!

JESSIE STORYTELLER: ... The pubs closed, and there old King Bill'd be flaked over the Shag Magnet's handlebars like Lord Muck of the Fowlhouse as though that Sailor's Rest was a palace not a doss-down. Only that time when the real lah-de-dah Prince of Wales bowls up to meet him aboard the real royal yacht do we hang back on the tide. By this time they've all started calling him King Billy and all we're doing is dodging paparazzi whatcumcallits and other socialite scumbags while we're propping him up on the floorboards drunk as a skunk and twice as salty cos I'm telling you there was nothing Tru wouldn't do for that man. We rode the whale's back so he wouldn't have to strain his harpoon eye. We towed their carcasses back to the big boat so poor little Billy-willy wouldn't get his hands dirty. Even in the teeth of the Southerly, you could hear them all sniggering, bloody old Bill's got his hooks into a bit of the dark stuff; fate worse than death. And if you listened right you could hear Tru crying out inside, He's me last man, ever, no bull! And me trying to point out, He is the last, Tru, no bull. And she screaming back, what's the diff, dopey? Me, I never could say. What do I know?

> *(this time gets a sombre vaudeville drum roll she does a less expansive jig to before slowly getting herself to buck up again:)*

What can I say you ain't heard? She bawled her eyes out after they found old Bill, big celebrity by then, in the lane and sliced'n'diced him up the way you wouldn't do for a dog. Poor old Bill. Then after that, I'm spending all my time on Shag Magnet's buckboard trying to sink the boot in keeping them all off from coming at her with calipers trying to measure her konk like they did old Bill's and I'm shouting hey s'heads y'wanta know what size she is?, she wears one-size-fits-all New-York-Yankee's baseball cap, I yell out but you don't hear anyone laugh. Meanwhile they've got chocks under the Shag Magnet's Bridgestones but then one day...

100

*(gets a rousing vaudeville drum roll over all which has her jigging
and bursting out once more...)*

old Tru, she grabs me to cradle her all up and I do and she shouts we're
getting outa this berg again see! So I shove her into the passenger seat
and I took the wheel m'self and I gunned old Shag Magnet down the
Derwent and we sailed off high into the sunset and at 110 kilometres I
levelled her out and tell her it's all right now Tru, and we put our heads
down and we sleep the sleep of the innocent at Zero G for, what?,
maybe 10 or 20 or so Ashes series, until one day she moved my over
and shooed off the family of wedgetails and put the foot down, right
hand down back down to little planet in the big wide universe earth
again. Let 'em come, she shouted. Do your worse, she shouted. Up all
of youse, she shouted. And we whooped and we waved and we went a
bit ratbaggy! We caught this boomer and surfed its dump and slid
down its great face and we freestyled right across the beach there at
Warrnambool, down Timor Street past the Civic Centre, up north to the
Murray through the orchards and onto the Dig tree and a turn or two
around Burkie and Willsie's ghosts, hammered along with a wurly-
wurly northeast-like to nail the Opera House with a few hoony
wheelies, crashed the Dividing Range like piss-all until we laid down
rubber along a few of those Barrier reefs off Cairns, no sweat n' bugger
the greenies, burned off the crocs at Kakadu, showed them a thing or
two, bombed out Broome like they thought the Japs were back with a
vengeance, then touched down light as a flibberty feather, three-point
job, neat and nice, on the top of Ayers Rock at sunset. Lovely, it was.
Uluru, Truggie sighed. Oo-roo to you too, I sighed all giggly. Safe at
last. Spot on at last. Ozzies. Basked in ruby. I tell you.

(has to slow down for the sunset nature of it all now...)

What can I say but you should've copped a load of the two of us up
there on the Rock, on top of, oh, Oz world and didn't all those daylets
set on the daylight let! Not an inch of the Shag-Magnet's treads moved
from there, yet we spun in the swoon of the great rock's eve-tiding, its
amethyst in-swathed. When the great dog hooted at the drunken bo'sun
moon, we lay the evening of our lives down in it and I think I heard my
Tru's dreaming of huge snake coilings, immense gorgings of the pig
rats, hummings-along in the all-of-times, in the never-never evers of
the Ancestors, and there were moanings there and groanings there and
the gay-lauds of all the tribes of her there as all sparks flibberted moon-
wooed up and flittered over and over and over all. The lair the moon.
The carve drawings caved. She softed and I heard. The lair the moon

101

such a big larry, ha ha. She if-ted and I hah-ed. Then she vibrated and shook me and nodded and she just points down at our feet going MY ONE'N'ONLY KING BILL! and there's our King Billyboy there covered in Smiley stickers and pink'n'purple bows right out of the old Dreaming, you betcha, and old Tru simply say, see he got here finally, dopey.

SHADOW PLAYERS CHORUS: SEE, HE GOT HERE FINALLY, DOPEY!

JESSIE STORYTELLER: Where was I? Star lines shucked us and we took little Billyboy up pointed at the horizon. Where to now?, I shouted into the slipstream. Old Tru was laughing at last again and she's going, 'We're going where we are safe where the ham sandwiches are good'. See?, did you see with us?, how the rainbow serpent, I saw as I've seen, chuckled and swaged in the steep deep of the flooding inland sea as we floated by on a carpet a-flowering in neutral. Bloom and blush hush-a-bye Australia's land can. Take tea, I said. Don't let them cut me up too but bury me behind the mountains!, she cried.

SHADOW PLAYERS ALL: DON'T LET THEM CUT ME UP!
BURY ME BEHIND THE MOUNTAINS!

> *(Now JESSIE stops for the last time the stream-of-conscience she is reading. She puts aside her script; returns to being an old lady, terribly emotionally crushed but still fighting, before the audience)*

JESSIE STORYTELLER: And my lovie, she at my feet and she can't get up, oh. Drink tea, I said. It's only tea. It's free. It'll do you good. Don't let them cut me up, promise again, but bury me behind the mountains, oh. Take tea, I tell her. Tru, drink tea now; it seeps down through the ages-oh. Tru. My Tru. Queenie. My Queen Tru that you are.

> *(At that, her shoulders slump and she turns and walks back into the shadow area behind the scrim curtain where she sits helplessly by her TRU. As she does so, all the activity behind in the shadow area disappear.)*

The STORYTELLER is left in his usual place. He has very little left to say...)

STORYTELLER: You know how you like to have your finger on the button, but what do I know about metaphors and King Billies and Truganinnis and the once-Tasmanians, like? All I know I'm here one day and the next there's extinction all over me and it's like extinction give or take a day. Who am I but just a guy who runs things back. Except I'll say what I think is that extinction thing might be give or take a day but now it just seems to keep turning up like a bad penny.
     (lastly)
What's a penny? Never heard of it.

     (Blackout)

---000---

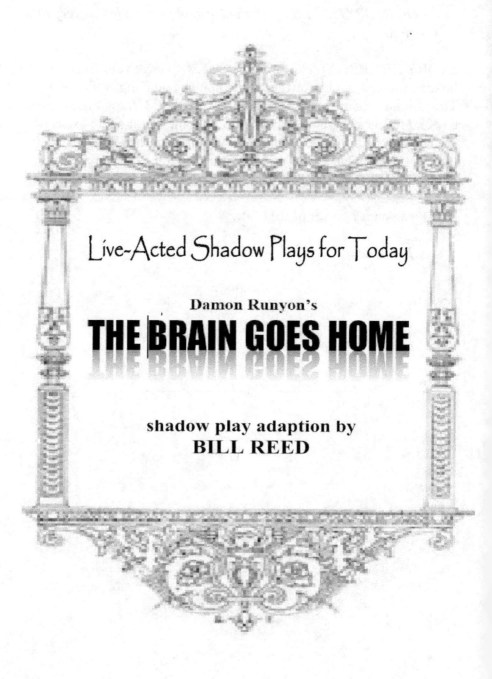

Live-Acted Shadow Plays for Today

Damon Runyon's

THE BRAIN GOES HOME

shadow play adaption by
BILL REED

The behind-the-screen shadow action – or 'inner background' play -- can only ever keep 'pace' with the reading, not *keep up* with it. Because of the resultant and necessary shadow-play distillation of the storyteller's tale, the extensive stage directions given in this script are only intended to be indicators as to what *might* be used for the shadow-play side of things. They deliberately go beyond what the director would employ and are given merely as a range of possible shadow-actions he or she might want to use in the 'distillation'.

The Characters

STORYTELLER

With freedom of movement, he reads as a natural storyteller from in front of the scrim and makes a virtue of reading quite unrehearsedly. He can insert himself into the production as he likes. He has a shadow-playing counterpart acting behind the scrim.

STORYTELLER SHADOW PLAYER

acts the Storyteller behind the screen, often wearing The Brain on his shoulder or on the palm of his hand, in order to show how they are such joined-at-the-hip pals.

THE BRAIN

A floating prop of itself. It probably has a prissy voice when it speaks, for all its 'boulevard prancing'. Picky, closed in on himself as an itself. Cockily confident about appearing fully embodied. It would always be thinking about how you shouldn't really have to imagine it arms and legs… or its swagger.

THE DOLLS SHADOW PLAYERS
(can be one or two actors using distinctive wigs etc)
RAGGEDY APPLE-SELLING DOLL
CHARLOTTE wife
DORIS CLAIRE
BOBBIE BAKER
CYNTHIA HARRIS

THE GUYS SHADOW PLAYERS
HOMER SWING
BIG NIG
DAFFY JACK

Production note

The Brain is a rakish floating giantish prop of a brain.

It might be disembodied from human form, but it acts just as
Runyonesque as any Runyon guy. It considers itself debonair. It could
even wear a toff's monocle on its greatly-noble Roman nose and it
might even wear a lecherous moustache so sharp that you'd better
watch out coming near it.

It will float in ghostly fashion in and out of the shadow-play action.
When 'out', it is always floating somewhere nearby, and proprietarily
so.

.

The Brain Goes Home

(Music from a sole jazz-age sax player sets a nightclub-closing, lonely dawn's-coming mood along Broadway.

As, at first, pale lighting comes on both in the shadow-playing area and the separate frontstage, THE BRAIN appears yawningly, floatingly behind the screen and the STORYTELLER comes on to take up his front-of-screen position, shielding his eyes from a dawning sun.

They both yawn synchronously.   The STORYTELLER points out the togetherness.

On a music-hall 'scene' stand, he balances sign. It reads
'MEET THE BRAIN'
which he proceeds to elaborately point out, and:)

STORYTELLER: One thing about my pal The Brain was he was a natural born thinker. Put one thought in his head and he'd go around thinking about it all day. And sharp! Say, he's so sharp you wouldn't want to go up to him and say hey what're you thinking in there, pal? Not to his face, see. Not to that being so close to his thinking.

(THE BRAIN proceeds to re-enact by gesture and manner the STORYTELLER's coming narration...)

STORYTELLER: I mean it was like he was made to think, you know? Anybody could see that. Say he's getting ready to face the world instead of just getting his head down at the usual six-thirty in the morning. Why, you can bet he's thinking not good the old hair's looking like Harpo Marx's... gotta reach for 'a little dab'll do ya' and get back to Billy de Wolf 'the gals all pursue ya' look that he's known for. All swank, The Brain! He'll be thinking lick down those eyebrows back like Douglas Fairbanks Jr, watch the swash and buckle up, ha ha. He'll be thinking toff up the nostril hairs like Buster Keaton; tune up the mo like Errol Flynn, pinch the old cheeks like Gloria Swanson's rosies, rosebud up the lips like Ray Navarro – even when The Brain

was thinking Ray Navarro even though he'd never heard of him. With The Brain, you could hear the wheels turning up
(taps head)
there.
(gets nod from THE BRAIN to go ahead)
The Brain and me knocked around together in the streets, mainly outside of Mindy's bar'n'grill with a nightspot you couldn't cut with a knife, you wanna know. But keep that under your hat, about us carrying the odd blade or two, see. You never know who's looking for who and who's thinking about it, it being a lot of things for The Brain to think about. Like I always said to him, better you than me with that thinking.
(and)
Talking about hats, and why not?, he'd be thinking push the hat back on the back of his head like Tom Mix too, but more a pork hat affair rather than Stetson, mind. And a diamond walking stick like great Gatsby but walked along like Charlie Chaplin had it on the twirl. Watch out, World, here comes de Brain, ha ha. You wouldn't even be able to see him push'n'shove you outa the way. You'd be left pushed'n'shoved in that kerb scratching your head thinking how did he push'n'shove past me, or did I just imagine about him having arms and legs? That's how The Brain got you.

(He removes the scene sign from the stage holder and replaces it with one reading:
'RAGGEDY DOLL'.

Music atmospherics change to something sweet like 'Sweet Molly Malone' from the sole sax player. Backdrop displays a night-time jazz age speakeasy street scene.

The STORYTELLER takes a deep breath and begins again... As he does so, the shadow players – with THE BRAIN – re-enact synchronously what he proceeds to narrate)

STORYTELLER: So, one night The Brain is walking me up and down Broadway in front of Mindy's, and we're speaking of this and that, when along comes a red-headed raggedy doll selling apples at five cents per copy, and The Brain, being very fond of apples, grabs one out of her basket and hands her a five-dollar bill.

(and)

The red-headed raggedy doll, who is maybe thirty-odd and is nothing but a crow as far as looks are concerned, squints at the finnif, and says to The Brain like this:

'I do not have change for so much money,' she says, 'but I will go and get it in a minute.'

'You keep the change,'

The Brain says, biting a big hunk out of the apple, which is hard enough to do with a mouth let alone good strong teeth, and taking my arm to start me walking again.

(as THE BRAIN on the shoulder of the STORYTELLER shadow
player does so, but is caught up again...)

Well, the raggedy doll looks at The Brain again, and it seems to me that all of a sudden there are large tears in her eyes as she says: 'Oh, thank you, sir! Thank you, thank you, and God bless you, sir!'

(and)

And then she goes on up the street in a hurry, with her hands over her eyes and her shoulders shaking, and The Brain turns around very much astonished, and watches her until she is out of sight. 'Gawk me!' The Brain says. 'I give Doris Clare ten G's last night, and she don't make half as much fuss over it as this doll does over a pound note.'

THE BRAIN SHADOW: (loud enough) Gawk me! I'm thinking I give Doris Clare ten G's last night, and she don't make half as much fuss over it as this doll does over a pound note.

(The STORYTELLER tries to make THE BRAIN settle down.

As they continue their street trawling, music mood changes back
to jazz age high-life, while he replaces the scene sign about the
apply-selling doll with the next one reading:
'THE DOLLS')

STORYTELLER: 'Well,' I say, 'maybe the apple doll needs a pound note more than Doris needs ten G's.' Maybe so,' The Brain says. 'But I'm thinking Doris gives me much more in return than just an apple. Doris gives me her love. The Brain says proudly, going, 'That love costs me about as much dough as any guy that ever lives, and *that's love, that is*.'

STORYTELLER SHADOW PLAYER: (ditto loud enough) I guess it does, pal.

STORYTELLER: 'I guess it does,' I say, yes, guessing The Brain gets out on three hundred G's per year for love. But when you think about it… as he always is, right?… he's got a very economical lover business going, since we all know that The Brain has three different dolls, besides an ever-loving wife.

> *(and flourishes – as they also do behind the screen – for music changes to depict each dollface…)*

STORYTELLER: See, The Brain likes to think his love affairs are a great secret but the only guy I ever see in this town who doesn't know all about them is a guy who's deaf, dumb, and blind. Old King Solomon of the mines or something didn't have dolls as expensive as The Brain's dolls.

> *(to her appearing and parading herself in shadow area [or even sashaying openly across his frontstage area]… and him showing ogling appreciation…)*

The overhead on Doris Clare alone would drive an ordinary guy daffy, and Doris is practically frugal compared to…

> *(fanfare as CYNTHIA comes next to parade herself a la DORIS… again to his appreciation)*

Cynthia Harris and…

> *(waits with even more appreciation for BOBBIE BAKER to do the same as the others…)*

Bobbie Baker…

> *(waits not so appreciatively as CHARLOTTE, the wife, tries to unsuccessfully equal the others allure in her wheelchair)*

Or his wife Charlotte, who has a society bug and needs plenty of coconuts at all times to keep herself a going concern. Now, she's a bit of an invalid, sure, but as a matter of fact there is never anything the matter with Charlotte that a few bob won't cure, although of course this goes for nearly every doll in this world who is an invalid, but especially Charlotte who's got this strong grasp.

> *(When the dolls have finished being introduced, THE BRAIN hover over all and, in gestures and swooping, gives man-about-town illustration to:)*

111

STORYTELLER: When a guy is knocking around Broadway as long as The Brain, he is bound to accumulate dolls here and there, but most guys accumulate one at a time, and when this one runs out on him, as Broadway dolls will do, he accumulates another, and so on, and so on, until he is too old to care about such matters as dolls, which is when he is maybe a hundred and four years old, although I hear of several guys who beat even this record.

(waits for THE BRAIN to catch up…)
But when The Brain accumulates a doll he seems to keep her accumulated, and none of them ever run out on him, and while this will be a very great nuisance to the average guy, it pleases The Brain no end because it makes him think he has a very great power over dolls.

(much no*d*ding yes behind…)
'They ain't to blame if they fall in love with me,' The Brain says to me one night. 'so I…

THE BRAIN SHADOW: (loudly finishes sentence off) …I won't cause none of them living dolls any sorrow, not for all the world.

STORYTELLER: Anyway, I take this as read because The Brain thinks mightily good of himself at the best of times.

(aside so behind would have hard time hearing…)
However, some guys claim that the real reason The Brain keeps all his dolls is because he's too selfish to give any one of them away, although personally I wouldn't take any of them, even if The Brain threw in a cash bonus, except maybe Bobbie Baker.

(THE BRAIN presses against the curtain what's-going-on?; the STORYTELLER hurries to finish aside…)
Anyway, what with him buying them automobiles and furs and diamonds and especially swell places for each of the dollfaces to live in. one time I tell The Brain he will save himself plenty if he

(feels he can return to normal hearable voice…)
buys a house and bunches his dolls together in one big happy family, instead of having them scattered all over town, but The Brain says this idea is no good. 'In the first place,' he says, 'they don't know about each other, except Doris and Cynthia and Bobbie know about Charlotte, although she does not know about them. They each think they are the only one for me. So it's better to have them in different spots, so it

112

gives me a real choice when I want to go home. In fact,' The Brain says puffing his chest out...

THE BRAIN SHADOW: (finishes proudly) I guess I've got more homes to go to than any other guy on Broadway.

> *(Full jazz music and gambling/dancing atmospheric returns with all-in night-on-the-town shadow playing. The STORYTELLER belatedly remembers to change the scene sign for one this time reading:*
> ***'THE HOMES')***

STORYTELLER: (enjoyably, above it all) Well, this may be true, but what The Brain wants with a lot of different homes is a very great mystery on Broadway, because he seldom goes home, anyway.
> *(repeats again just in case...)*
I say again, what The Brain wants with a lot of different homes is a very great mystery on Broadway, because he seldom goes home, anyway. You get that?
> *(then)*
His idea in not going home... see, he's still thinking, thinking!... you can't beat him!... is that something may happen in this town while he's stuck away at home that he is not part of. Or mightn've have caused.
> *(pause in the shadow area for:)*
Not that The Brain goes anywhere much, not in particular. He never goes out in public with anyone of his dolls, except maybe once or twice a year with Charlotte, his ever-loving wife, and finally he even stops going with her because Doris Clare says it don't look good to her friends and gives him one across the chops.

> *(DORIS SHADOW PLAYER takes a swipe at THE BRAIN but misses as it slips off the dance floor and pops off into air; very slippery, hard-to-catch... except when he now sees a card game below and flies to join it.*
>
> *While the STORYTELLER takes time for this, he changes the scene sign over to the next one going:*
> ***'THE DOLLS AGAIN!')***

STORYTELLER: ('see what I mean') The Brain marries Charlotte long before the times he becomes the biggest guy in gambling operations on the Eastside, and a millionaire two or three times over. It was even before the times he is too poor to live in a neighborhood that is far enough out of town to make it convenient for him to go home and sit around talking to her, so finally he gets out of the habit of going home, see. That's the thing.

(pauses for CHARLOTTE-at-home too...)
But Charlotte is not such a doll as cares to spend more than one or two years looking at the pictures on the wall, because it seems the pictures on the wall are nothing but pictures of cows in the meadows and houses covered with snow, so she does not go home any more than necessary either, and is very happy with her society friends.

(she joins more refined revellers)
I will say one thing about The Brain, he doesn't care if his dolls are blonde or brunette, because Cynthia Harris's hair's as black as the inside of a wolf...

        (she poses in her window attracting wolf whistles...)
while Bobbie Baker is betwixt and between... like her, so I hear on the vine... her hair being a light brown but don't you go thinking mousey.

(she takes a hand gun out from her suspender belt...)
Cynthia Harris is more of a Johnny-come-lately than Doris, being out of Mr. Earl Carroll's 'Vanities', whatever that is, and I hear she first comes to New York as Miss Somebody in one of these beauty contests which she won hands down when one of the judges got no better wink from a Miss Somebody Else. So the next thing anybody knows she's scanty in a rag mag and riding around in a big foreign automobile the size of a rum chaser, and is chucking a terrible swell.

(CYNTHIA is kicking her heels up out of the back seat of a limo...)
Personally, I always consider Bobbie Baker the smartest of all The Brain's dolls, because she is just middling as to looks and she does not have any of the advantages of life like Doris Clare and Cynthia Harris, such as jobs on the stage where they can walk around showing off their shapes to guys such as The Brain.

(Busy office sounds like phones ringing and old typewriter carriages clunking etc, and BOBBIE skirting amongst it all)

STORYTELLER: Bobbie Baker starts off as nothing but a private secretary to a guy in Wall Street, and naturally she's always wearing clothes, or anyway, as many clothes as an ordinary doll can get as few away with, which is not so many at that and makes her a real stand-out in that office.

(she is seen sitting on a desk, cross-legged, taking dictation...)
It seems that The Brain once has some business with the guy Bobbie works for and happens to get talking to her, and she tells him how she always wishes to meet the great The Brain and see him thinking away, what with hearing and reading about him, and how he is just as handsome and romantic-looking as she always pictured him rolling in dough.

(She has come over to the card table, lifted THE BRAIN up and is
    tucking him under the chin, ruffling his non-existent hair etc...)
The best you can give The Brain at this time is that he is very well dressed. Which is not like it always is.

(THE BRAIN breaks away and moves to mid-air centre of shadow area where he waits impatiently (and sprucing himself) to give visual credence to what the STORYTELLER is going to say.

Before carrying on, the STORYTELLER quickly changes the scene sign for one reading:
'MEET THE BRAIN 2'.)

STORYTELLER: He's maybe forty years old, give or take a couple of years... although don't be fooled by those cortexes; they always look older than they are, especially with all that thinking he does... and he is commencing to get a little bunchy about the middle, what with sitting down at card-tables so much and never taking any exercise outside of walking with guys such as me up and down in front of Mindy's for a few hours every night. He has a clean-looking frontal kinda thing, always very white around the gills, if them-those're gills like he thinks they are, and, if he had any, you'd say he has nice teeth and a nice smile when he wishes to smile, or thinks he is, which is never at guys who owe him dough.

(The STORYTELLER crashes over the card table in a rage and the other card players scatter for their lives)

STORYTELLER: And I will say for The Brain he has what is called personality. One of them thinking ones. And he tells a story well, although he is always the hero of any story he tells, or thinks he is, and he knows how to make himself agreeable to dolls in many ways. He has taken in a pretty fair sort of education, and while dolls such as Cynthia and Doris and maybe Charlotte, too, will rather have a charge account at Cartier's than all the education in Yale and Harvard put together could get them, it seems that Bobbie Baker likes higher-brow gab, so naturally she gets plenty of same from The Brain.

(as BOBBIE muscles in to get rightfully hers and giving the finger to anything she thinks is against her...)

Well, pretty soon Bobbie is riding around in a car bigger than Cynthia's, though neither is as big as Doris's car, and all the neighbors' children over in Flatbush, which is where Bobbie halls from, are very jealous of her and running around spreading gossip about her, but keeping their eyes open for big cars themselves. Personally, I always figure The Brain lowers himself socially by taking up with a doll from Flatbush, especially as Bobbie Baker soon goes in for literary guys, such as newspaper scribes and similar characters around Greenwich Village crawling with actor types you can't go to a movie without hearing their voices yak-yak.

(Drastic music atmospherics change to film-noire climax strains. The shadow area darkens to be a back alley, unhealthy and rain-swept, with appropriate ominous back cloth. We see THE BRAIN getting stuck as giantish shadows on the alley wall. He staggers into the STORYTELLER'S arms... or hands really.

The STORYTELLER waits for effect before:)

STORYTELLER: Now what happens early one morning but a guy by the name of Daffy Jack hauls off and sticks a shiv in The Brain's left side affecting his right side, so it goes, right?

(and)

It seems that this is done at the request of a certain party by the name of Homer Swing, who owes The Brain plenty of dough in a gambling transaction, and who becomes very indignant when The Brain presses him for payment.

(HOMER takes a baseball bat to THE BRAIN but keeps swinging and missing, while...)

116

It seems that Daffy Jack, who is considered a very good shiv artist, aims at The Brain's heart, but misses it by a couple of miles because The Brain's heart is much like his teeth and smile, real hard to find if you lack imagination like Daffy Jack does, leaving The Brain with a very bad cut in his side which calls for some stitching.

(Finally, in the back alley there, THE BRAIN is caught up with and shivved. He staggers -- to a wailing lone sax player – and falls, stricken, to the ground.

Now it is the turn of the STORYTELLER and BIG NIG shadow players to take over the proceedings as narrated:)

STORYTELLER: Big Nig, the crap shooter, and I are standing at Fifty-Second Street and Seventh Avenue along about 2 a.m. speaking of not much, when The Brain comes stumbling out of Fifty-Second Street, and falls into Big Nig's hands, practically ruining a brand-new topcoat and one of Mindy's expensive manicures, which Big Nig pays sixty bucks for each of them a few hours back with the blood that is coming out of the cut. Naturally, Big Nig is indignant about this, but we can see that it is no time to be speaking to The Brain about a little care shown to other would be nice. We can see that The Brain is carved up quite some, and is in a bad way.

(book maker stall at the track...)

Of course, we are not greatly surprised at seeing The Brain in this condition, because for years he is practically no price around this town, what with this-and-that guy being anxious to do something or other to him, but we are never expecting to see him carved up like a turkey, not with that mind of his and all the thinking that would make it like Fort Knox. But while we're still stunned there, The Brain coughs up to me like this: 'Call lawyer Hymie Weissberger to lend me his ear lug to what I've got to say, and Doc Frisch,' he says, 'and take me home.'

THE BRAIN SHADOW: (croak barely audible) Call lawyer Hymie Weissberger to lend me his ear lug to what I've got to say, and Doc Frisch, and take me home.

(Dramatic dying-breath coughs)

STORYTELLER: Naturally, a guy such as The Brain wishes for his lawyer before he wishes his doctor, and Hymie Weissberger is The Brain's mouthpiece, and a very sure-footed guy, at that. But first, I say, 'we gotta take you to a hospital.' 'No,' The Brain gurgles. 'No hospital, no coppers. Take me home.'

(All stop front and behind the screen, including music over. One word reveals why:)

STORYTELLER: 'Home'. You hear that? 'Home' like a dying man's wish. Hopeless futility! And naturally, I say which home, being somewhat confused about The Brain's homes, and he seems to sink into a thinking funk a minute which must have been hurting his left side a lot and so, as I think it goes, the right side of his body if he had one. And he's doing this gear-grinding in his mind as if this is a question to which an answer needs to be well thought out.
   (gears do seem to be grinding as all lean over THE BRAIN, waiting, waiting...)
'Park Avenue,' The Brain says finally.

THE BRAIN SHADOW: (too weak to be heard, really) Park Avenue.

STORYTELLER: 'Park Avenue' he said. I heard it myself and I'm sick of arguing I didn't.
   (then)
Wait, wait.

   (He changes the next-scene sign to
   'THE ONE'N'ONLY HOME')

STORYTELLER: So that's what I'm saying anyway. And so Big Nig stops a taxicab, and we help The Brain into the cab and tell the jockey to take us to the apartment house on Park Avenue near Sixty-Fourth where everybody knows The Brain's ever-loving wife Charlotte lives. Well, the cab jockey didn't but what have we got mouths for?

   (the cab roars away into the night and passes through and beyond the high-life lights)

118

STORYTELLER: When we get there, I figure it is best for me to go up first and break the news gently to Charlotte, because I can see what a shock it's bound to be to any ever-loving wife to have her husband brought home in the early hours of the morning all shivved up.

(at her door…)

Well, the door man and the elevator guy in the apartment house had given me an argument about going up to The Brain's apartment, saying a blow-out of a shin-ding of some kind is going on there, but after I explain to them that The Brain is bleeding all over their carpet, they let me in. A big fat butler comes to the door when I ring the apartment chimes, and I can see inside there are many guys and dolls in evening clothes putting on the Ritz, and somebody is singing very loud.

> *(Despite the emergency, the STORYTELLER shadow player stops to listen to a Bessie-Smith blues type of voice. Front stage, the STORYTELLER has nothing to do but wait until behind is good and ready…)*

STORYTELLER: The butler tries to tell me I cannot see Charlotte, but I'm little old persistent me and so by and by she comes to the door, and a very pleasant sight she is, at that, with jewellery all over her and her wheelchair nice and shiny, all polished up like that.

(CHARLOTTE does so…)

I stall around awhile, so as not to alarm her too much, and then I tell her everloving husband The Brain meets with an accident and that we have him outside in a cab, and ask her where we gotta put him?

STORYTELLER SHADOW PLAYER: Where do you want him?

STORYTELLER: 'Put,' she says, 'him into hospital, dope. I am entertaining some very important people tonight, and I cannot have them disturbed by bringing in a person who ought to be in hospital. Tell him I'll pop around to see him to-morrow and I'll bring him some broth. There should be some left over.'

(and)

I try to explain to her that The Brain does not need any broth, but a nice place to lie down in, but finally she gets very testy with me and shuts the door in my face, saying, 'This is a ridiculous hour for him to be coming home. It's twenty years since he came home so early.'

CHARLOTTE SHADOW PLAYER: Who remembered where home is? He wouldn't.

(She slams the door and the STORYTELLER shadow player makes for the elevator:)

STORYTELLER: Then as I'm waiting for the elevator, she opens the door again just a little bit and says, 'By the way, is he hurt bad?'
(and)
I'm thinking what a heartless doll she is, although I can see where it would be very inconvenient for her to bust up her party, at that.

(By now, his shadow player counterpart is trudging out of the building and into the street, with the sounds of Bessie Smith and jolly voices fading)

STORYTELLER: When I get back down, The Brain is lying back in the corner of the cab, his eyes half closed, and by this time it seems that Big Nig stops the blood somewhat with a handkerchief, but The Brain acts kinda weak when I lie to him telling him his ever-loving wife is not home. 'Take me to Doris', he croaks.

(The cab roars off through more high life and nightspots and finally reaches...)

STORYTELLER: Now Doris lives in a big apartment house away over on West Seventy-Second Street near the Drive, and I tell the taxi jockey to go there while The Brain seems to slide off into a doze. Then Big Nig leans over to me and says to me like this:

BIG NIG SHADOW PLAYER: (loud enough) No use taking him there. I sees Doris going out tonight all dressed up in her ermine coat carrying on with this actor guy, Jack Walen, she is struck on like bubble gum, see. Let us take him to Cynthia. She's a big-hearted doll.

STORYTELLER: (appreciative) And well said, too, Big Nig!
(then)
Now Cynthia Harris has a big suite of rooms that cost The Brain fifteen G's a year in a big hotel just off Fifth Avenue, Cynthia being a doll who likes to be downtown so if she hears of anything coming off anywhere

120

she can get there very rapidly. Or out of there ahead of the sirens. So, when we arrive at her hotel I call her on the house 'phone and tell her I've gotta see her about something very important, so Cynthia says for me to come up. Poor old The Brain's still bleeding away.

(At CYNTHIA's apartment door with, at least, a seduction coming on by the musical strains and a semi-naked look of her...)

STORYTELLER: It is now maybe three-fifteen in the morning, and I am somewhat surprised to find Cynthia home so early, but there she is, and looking very beautiful indeed in a negligee with her hair hanging down, and I can see that The Brain is no chump when it comes to picking 'em. She gives me a hello pleasant enough, but as soon as I explain what I am there for, her kisser gets very stern and she says to me like this:

(he gestures apologies to the audience for the time it takes CYNTHIA to come forward around the side of the scrim screen to stand, three dimensionally, in front of the audience to deliver:)

CYNTHIA SHADOW PLAYER: Listen, I got trouble enough here as it is, what with two guys getting in a fight over me at a little gathering I had here last night and the house copper coming to split them up, and ending up staying the night which caused more trouble. Coppers! What can a gal do? Now, suppose it gets out that The Brain is here? What will that do if I come to enter another beauty contest and nobody'll take my wink because I've had to do all the winking I've got in me just to keep out of the nick? This joint is costing The Brain fifty Gs and you can't expect me to get dragged out and leave it just like that.

(CYNTHIA returns to the shadow area, while...)

STORYTELLER: Well, in about ten minutes of looking and a bit of listening, I can see there is no use staring at her much longer, so I leave her standing at the door in her negligee, still looking as beautiful on the inside as on the outside, as in it doesn't look all winked-out to me, you know.

(The STORYTELLER shadow player again trudges back down to the cab to the same sights and sounds.

121

As the STORYTELLER relates, the taxi takes off through jazzy New York once more...)

STORYTELLER: There is now nothing for us to do but take The Brain to Bobbie Baker, who lives in a duplex apartment in Sutton Place over by the East River, where the swells set up a colony of much-nicer joints in the heart of an old tenement-house neighborhood, and as we are on our way there with The Brain lying back in the cab just barely breathing, which is bad enough even normally if you haven't got a nose, and I say to Big Nig like this:

STORYTELLER SHADOW PLAYER: Big Nig, when we get to Bobbie's, we'll carry The Brain in without asking her first and just dump him on her so she can't refuse to take him in, although Bobbie Baker is a nice little doll, and I am pretty sure she will do anything she can for him, especially since he forks out another fifty G's for her apartment.

BIG NIG SHADOW PLAYER: If I had the loot, for that one, I'd kick in that too.

(To the Maltese Falcon score probably, they arrive at the door of BOBBIE's apartment finally:)

STORYTELLER: So when the cabbie stops in front of Bobbie's house, Big Nig and I take The Brain out of the cab and lug him up to her apartment. I ring the bell.
                    (It is a thunderous affair...)
Bobby opens the door herself, and I happen to see a guy's legs zip into a room behind her, although who am I to say there's anything wrong in such a sight, even though the guy's legs are in pink pyjamas?
   (She blows a large bubble-gum bubble at them)
Naturally, Bobbie is greatly astonished to see us with The Brain dripping away the red stuff between us, but she does not invite us in as I explain to her that The Brain is stabbed and his last words are for us to take him to his Bobbie.
   (She blows an even larger bubble in their faces)
Furthermore, she does not let me finish my story, the way she's going, 'Say, if you do not take him away from here quicksmatt...

122

(Again, he gestures apologies to the audience for the time it takes BOBBIE, this time, to come forward around the side of the scrim screen to stand, three dimensionally, in front of the audience to deliver:)

BOBBIE SHADOW PLAYER: ... I'm calling the cops and you guys will be going down town on suspicion, like...
  (blows another impressive bubble in their faces)
that you know something about how the bum got what was coming to him.

> *(and hurries back into the shadow area when a male voice calls her from inside... so that, now long-sufferingly, they lug THE BRAIN back down to the cab while doors are slammed against them all over the place)*

STORYTELLER: Then she slams the door on us, and we lug The Brain back down the stairs into the street, because all of a sudden it strikes us that Bobbie's right, and if The Brain is found in our possession all shivved up, and he happens to croak, we are in a very tough spot, because the cops never want to believe guys like Big Nig and me, no matter how innocent we try to look.

> *(Now the street is empty with no lights. It has started, of course, to rain)*

STORYTELLER: Furthermore, the same idea must've hit the taxi jockey because he's nowhere to be seen, gone the lam, and there we are away over by the East River in the early morning around four, with no other cabs in sight, and a cop liable to come along any minute.

> *(The ominous wail of a siren and screams far off and a sound of an argument nearby. The shadow players, with THE BRAIN dangling lifeless between them, move off etc as the STORYTELLER next relates...*
>
> *... But not before he replaces the old scene with a new one reading:*
> ***'HOME AT LAST!')***

STORYTELLER: There's nothing for us to do but get away from there, so Big Nig and I start moving, with me carrying The Brain's feet, and Big Nig his head, if you use your imagination like would be easy if you had The Brain's thinking about it. So we get several blocks away from Sutton Place, going very slow and hiding in dark doorways whenever we hear anybody coming, and now we are in a section of tenement houses…

(They are)

When, all of a sudden, up from the basement of one of these crappy joints, out pops a doll.

(Fanfare as RAGGEDY DOLL appears, who acts exactly as depicted…)

STORYTELLER: She sees us before we can hide in the dark, and she seems to have plenty of nerve for a doll, because she comes right over to us and looks at Big Nig and me, and then looks at The Brain. 'Why,' the doll says, 'if it isn't the kind gentleman who gives me the five dollars for the apple -- the money what buys the medicine that saves my little Joey's life! What is the matter?'

RAGGEDY DOLL SHADOW PLAYER: (a hard-life but sweet voice) Why, if it isn't my kind gentleman what gave me the finnif for the apple!

STORYTELLER: 'Well,' I say to the doll, who's still raggedy and still red-headed, 'there is nothing much the matter with him except if we do not get him somewhere soon, he's gonna croak out on us.'

(Yet again, (he gestures apologies to the audience for the time it takes RAGGEDY DOLL, this time, to come forward around the side of the scrim screen to stand, three dimensionally, in front of the audience to deliver:)

RAGGEDY DOLL SHADOW PLAYER: 'Bring him in,' she says, pointing to the joint she just comes out of. 'It is not much of a place, but you can let him rest there until you get help. I am just going over here to the drugstore to get some more medicine for my little Joey, although he is out of danger now, thanks to this gentleman.'

124

(and returns to the shadow area where, funereally, they carry THE BRAIN into the home of RAGGEDY DOLL and her family to a heart-plucking violin over)

STORYTELLER: So we lug The Brain down the basement steps with the doll leading the way, and we follow her into a room that smells like a Chinese laundry and seems to be full of kids sleeping on the floor. There is only one bed in the room, and it is not much of a bed any way you take it, and there seems to be a kid in this bed, too, but the red-headed doll rolls this kid over to one side of the bed and motions us to lay The Brain alongside of the kid. Then she gets a wet rag and stars bathing The Brain's noggin.

(as she sweetly does so...)
The Brain finally opens his eyes and looks at the red-headed raggedy doll, and she grins at him very pleasant. So then he turns his head to Big Nig, and says to him like this:

(BIG NIG shadow player bends his ear to THE BRAIN but nothing is heard over the crying babies etc)

STORYTELLER: The Brain's too weak to be heard. He was telling Big Nig, 'Go get lawyer Weissberger. I don't know how bad I am and I must tell him some things.'
(and as BIG NIG shadow players sadly goes to do so...)
Well, The Brain is hurt worse than I thought... probably even more than he's thinking!... and he remains in the doll's basement dump until he dies three days later...

(wailing and dirge-ful music over, even drowning out the kids' cryings)

STORYTELLER: ... with the red-headed raggedy dollface nursing him alongside her sick kid Joey, because old Doc Frisch, says he can't be moved. Meaning The Brain not the kid.

(The shadow area goes darkened. When some sombre lighting returns – after a time fit for mourning – there is the funeral parlour scene; quite Irish merry really.

125

The STORYTELLER replaces the scene sign with one going,
'ARRIVEDECI, THE BRAIN')

STORYTELLER: So, there I am, present at The Brain's funeral at
Wiggins's Funeral Parlours, like everybody else on Broadway, and I
wish to say I never see-d more flowers in all my life. They are all over
the casket and knee-deep on the floor, and some of the pieces must cost
plenty. In fact, I judge it is the size and cost of the different pieces that
makes me notice a little bundle of faded red carnations not much bigger
than your fist. There is a small card tied to the carnations...
   (he replaces the 'arrivedeci' sign with 'To a kind gentleman'...)
and on it goes: 'To a kind gentleman', and it comes to my mind that out
of all those fifty Gs or like worth of flowers there, these faded
carnations represent the only true sincerity. I mention this to Big Nig,
and he says the chances are I am right, but that even true sincerity is not
going to do The Brain any good where he thinks he might be going,
unless true sincerity digs down good.

   *(He stands waiting to allow the sounds of sadness and of giggling
   at the funeral to somewhat subside, and for The Brain's dolls to,
   in turn, do their various self-serving things, before:)*

STORYTELLER: Anybody will tell you that for off-hand weeping at a
funeral The Brain's ever-loving wife Charlotte does herself very proud
indeed, but she is not a patch on Doris Clare, Cynthia Harris, and
Bobbie Baker. In fact, Bobbie Baker weeps so loud there's some talk of
heaving her out of the funeral altogether.
   (and)
However, I afterwards hear that, loud as they are, it's nothing to the
weep they all put on when it comes out that what The Brain had to tell
the lawyer Hymie Weissberger was to draw up a new will while he is
dying and leaves all his dough to the red-headed raggedy doll, whose
name seems to be O'Halloran, and who is the widow of a bricklayer and
has five kids. Don't ask me what she's doing selling apples.

   *(Now, the shadow area activities slowly wind down. When they
   have and when he stands alone in his own front-stage spotlight,
   the STORYTELLER can be intimate with the audience)*

126

STORYTELLER: Well, at first, all the citizens along Broadway say it is a wonderful thing for The Brain to do, and serves his ever-loving wife and Doris and Cynthia and Bobbie right; and from the way one and all speaks you will think they are going to build a monument to The Brain for his generosity to the red-headed raggedy doll, and why not? But about two weeks after he is dead, I hear citizens saying the chances are the red-headed raggedy apple-selling doll is none other than one of The Brain's old-time dolls, and that maybe the kids are his -- and that he leaves them the dough because his conscience hurts him at the finish, for this is the way Broadway is.

(pause for wrap-up effect)

But personally, I don't think it can be true, for if there is one thing The Brain never has is a conscience. He didn't even have a thinking conscience, when you think about it. Still, on the other hand, you'd know he'd be thinking about having one a lot... so who knows?

(milks timing for a closer...)

STORYTELLER: What made him so lovable, see. Sure it was.

---oOo---

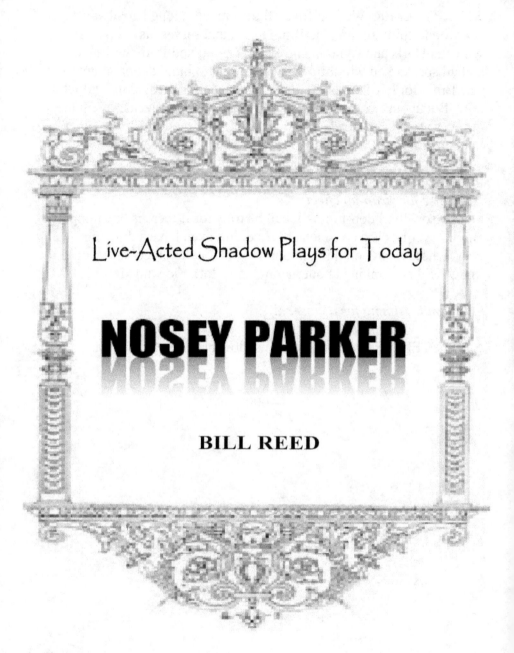

Live-Acted Shadow Plays for Today

NOSEY PARKER

BILL REED

The behind-the-screen shadow action – or 'inner background' play --
can only ever keep 'pace' with the reading, not *keep up* with it.
Because of the resultant and necessary shadow-play distillation of the
storyteller's tale, the extensive stage directions given in this script are
only intended to be indicators as to what *might* be used for the shadow-
play side of things. They deliberately go beyond what the director
would employ and are given merely as a range of possible shadow-
actions he or she might want to use in the 'distillation'.

The Characters

STORYTELLER
By openly reading from a script, he narrates the proceedings from front stage, audience side of the scrim. His reading should be as 'natural' -- even unrehearsed -- as possible.

NOSEY PARKER
The 'shadowy' mother with prominent forefinger (very shadowy prominent!). Buzzes around. Comes large and small but always, always a vision of a floating hooked nose before her and her giantish forefinger.

SHADOW PLAYERS
4 or so actors shadowing/intertwining the parts of:
Son
Father
Aunt
the Seeds of the Right Idea
Burra townspeople

Nosey Parker

1.

(The STORYTELLER is seen to be sitting with his manuscript (or digital reader) on his lap. He is in plain view at first and then is dimmed to get necessary dramatic effect as the back lighting behind the scrim. He might even play impishly with a torch underneath his chin, so as to indicate that, as a character, he is up for anything.

On the 'up' of the lighting, he commences...)

STORYTELLER: I can think of nothing better to introduce the Mum of our tale than starting out with a heading. It might open a stitch or two in your side but, never mind, that can be surgically repaired providing you're not trying to add a cash refund of your ticket and, anyway, it is typed in bold as you ought to be able to tell from my voice:

... the woman who could tell a lot of things by getting up people's noses...

You see, the Mum we have here wasn't all plain nose or plain nosey, even if you are only going to get a rather shadowy stage version of her. No, sirree. We should start out by what she was outside of just being called Nosey Parker or, in and out of Burra town, The Snoz.

(Behind the scrim, NOSEY PARKER is now shadow-miming to his narration – that is, she now portrays objection to what he has just said, and indicating that her silhouetted nose is quite normal in fact.

NOTE: often, as a nose, it can get unattached from her and starts 'floating' around as a loose and impertinent prop – but the fact that it seems to have a life of its own doesn't faze her whatsoever)

STORYTELLER: But we won't keep calling her names because she really shut her ears to the insult, which glues shut her nostrils and makes her impenetrably shut down. As you ought to be able to see.
(and)

After all, her own schnauzer was pretty much normal. It's what she did to other people's nose that got her the nicknames not-so-nice.
  (and)
Anyway, it seems we're going to start out showing how she was much, much more than other people's noses, that there was more to her than just being The Snoz. She'd be please with that.
  (the shadow makes that point, while:)
For example, how about that one time she took her boy aside and half-whispered…

  (the shadow of the SON appears accordingly for her to tap away at his nose, then her own, then his, then her own, &ce:)

STORYTELLER: …to him about the ambushes of the spirit of the Seed of the Right Idea. The Seed, yes, of the Right Idea. According to her, when God blew his nose, the Seeds of the Right Idea shot out and were blown right down through the earth's crust. They were! She knew that, she kept telling him… always with a tap-tap-tapping, first, on the side of her hooter then on the side of his -- because she was always coming home from work, up from the tin mines of their Burra town with one of other her 'golden nuggets' of advice for him. Where did she think she got them, she asked him, because I'm so clever at sniffing things out?

NOSEY PARKER SHADOW PLAYER: (over-loud) Because I'm so clever with magic, you silly billy? No way, dopey; it's because…

  (As showers of shadowy gold nuggets pour down, and as her nose 'lifts off' into the air to sniff out at least one of them…)

STORYTELLER: (takes back control) …No, it was because, she said, she was only picking up the Seeds of the Right Idea that were only lying there in God's snot at the bottom of the mine down there. They're gems of thoughts!, she told him.

NOSEY PARKER SHADOW PLAYER: (over-loud) They're gems of thoughts, that's what they are, dopey!

STORYTELLER: (getting annoyed) So, the boy had better listen to what she had to say, or she'd stop bringing him home such golden

132

nuggets, even if he was such an ingrate as to point out they were really made of tin stuck in a lot of dirt. So keep his ears open and his nose clean.

NOSER PARKER SHADOW PLAYER: (another shout) Keep the wax outa, or everybody's gonna say, 'Look, that dirty little bugger's got ear wax up his nose!', dopey the mope.

STORYTELLER: Yep, 'so keep your ears open and don't let the wax get into your nose, so's everybody's gonna say, 'Look, that dirty little bugger's got ear wax up his nose!' or words to that effect. You heard right, if you're just pretending behind those close eyelids. She did! And, you know her... once she got started at the end of your nose there, who was game enough to try to stop her?...

> *(Behind the scrim curtain, the shadows of the seeds of the Right Idea begin to dance around the SON's shadow like fairies. The act out the narration of...)*

STORYTELLER: See, she told him, once a Seed of the Right Idea gets into you, you've got it for life. You're hooked. It's given for you to make something of your life. You have de Seed! You have to do something with it. And if you treat it right, one day it'll come out of your nose like it first did from God's nose as lovely crystal liquid and it'll come to you in none other than the form of someone special out of the Right Idea -- and in your case it'll be a her and not a him, hopefully, and you'll be clearing your nose...

> *(as a shadow player confront the SON shadow player...)*

and finding yourself saying to her something like, going: *'You ever been to America?'* -- or something totally off like that, knowing you, and she's gonna tease you back right out of the Seeds of the Right Idea, going:

'Oh yeah? You ever been to Hollywood and Vine there?' because if she's interested in you, she's got to be a bit of a weirdo herself, right?, but at least a weirdo like you, not with this nose of yours. If your brain was dynamite, you still couldn't blow your nose. What a silly billy!

NOSEY-PARKER SHADOW PLAYER: (shout out) If your brain was dynamite, you still couldn't blow your nose. Talk about a silly billy!

(Her nose 'flies off' and attacks him like an angry magpie, while...)

STORYTELLER: An oldie but a goodie. And, anyway, with a mother and her noses like that, the lad was able to ignore that too, even if he was having trouble avoiding that sticky beak of hers. And why, you ask, did she go at him like that, over and over, while pinching his nostrils together all the time?

(pause)

Don't ask me why; I don't think even this script knows why and it's what I'm reading all this from. So how am I to know? What if I couldn't read, like?

(the MOTHER is now starting to breath up her son's nostrils:)

All she knew, her son thought she kept yodelling up his nose, was this someone or something special would come naturally out of God's Seed of the Right Idea and, when it did, he'd never have to toil down a mine like she had to every day just to dig up golden nuggets made of tin covered with dirt and bring them home to his son like she had to bring them home to her idjit of a son.

(To a bucket being loudly kicked and the SEEDS OF THE RIGHT IDEA shadows start to disseminate and while a funereal dirge comes over a coffin...)

That's why, when you kick the bucket, she said, you're a few ounces' lighter when they weigh you before and after you peg out. They say they're trying to weigh up your soul, but it's not true. It's trying to find out what size you've made of your Seed of the Right Idea and what you made of it. And then *that's* weighed for or against you. So get with it, kid!

NOSEY PARKER SHADOW PLAYER: So get with it, buggerlugs, and blow that hooter of yours before i blow it for you! Okay? *Okay?* I've left your dinner in the oven. Heat it up yourself; you got no hands?

STORYTELLER: Apparently that's how the boy, the man, the son remembers his Mum saying it. If nothing else, you see she isn't such a one-dimensional nose-job that whoever gave this its title might be seeming to imply.

(looking at script)

What's also implied is a little light dimming by way of a brief chapter end allowing for any nose blowing or sneezing or god-knows-what we might be penting up here.

(and)

Be back in a jiffy. It says here.

(Brief blackout.

In the brief interval, there is a cacophony of nose snorting, wheezing, sneezing, clearing, blowing &ce)

2.

(Lighting back up, first on the STORYTELLER whiling away, playing with his torch. He is, though, keeping an eye on the shadow area over his shoulder, where the back lighting is coming back on – and where the shadow players are ready to mime the 'nosey-parker' section with a variety of gross nose silhouettes.

NOSEY PARKER shadow player now displays her very large forefinger and how it likes to poke. To facilitate the demonstration, her nose detaches itself and, in the air, allows her now-giantish forefinger to poke itself at, in and up it)

STORYTELLER: (continuing) In the mad rush of things, then, our Mum Nosey Parker, wasn't always as silly as that Right Seed thing suggests, but I don't know about that. You be the judge. Unfortunately, this was the same Mum known not only as a dumbcluck all over the extended Burra District, but also as the dumbcluck who got up everybody's nose. Dumbcluck The Snoz.

(and to, behind, weeds growing up through the floorboards…)

You see, we have to look at it from the boy's viewpoint. If those splintery holes in the floorboards of the family's rented shack and weeds growing through them didn't make him poor-kid enough, how come it was incumbent upon him to have had to put up with his mother and her noses as well? Just…

(indicates a huge floating forefinger behind)

look at that as a snoz shovel, will you?… whoooo… how would you like that up your hooter?

(carries on)

135

And his Mum going poke-poke up everyone's nose all over the town you're trying to grow up normally in? Boy! And still being in primary school with all the ha-has and you-suck's, at the bottom of his class, the dumdum of all... and all he ever seemed to get was being rubbished about his Mum and her obsession with other people's schnauzers.

(stops while, in the shadow area, a shadow player dashes across him, protecting his or her nose, fleeing from her forefinger close on the same magpie-attacking pursuit)

SHADOW PLAYER: (madly) GOD NOSE! GOD NOSE!

STORYTELLER: On a quiet Sundee arvo that really echoed around town. What really got her son in those days was having to suffer living with the social stigma of his own Mum's absolute obsession with everybody else's noses, not just his. Oh, as far as he could see, so teenager then, she never had any problem with her own, oh no, even though it had...
(while her detached nose inspects itself in the mirror…)
a distinct cock-up to it from her left profile and a definite cock-down to it from her right side, if you are to believe reports. The hard fact of the matter was, it didn't matter if his mother was in a room with only a few people or heaving him by the conk through the crowd of the Burra Easter show...

(He has to wait while the MOTHER shadow player goes on the nose attack on an innocent by-stander for the first of many times:)

STORYTELLER: … she just had to rush up to someone and squint up at his or her konk from, like, a millimetre away, didn't she?

(The innocent bystander meekly submits to her shadowy will)

STORYTELLER: Fair suck of the old sav, the War of the Worlds could have broken out but never mind that; look out for the bushes before she ambushes your snoz. Once she was there, squinting up your spout…
(while she performs a medical inspection of the other's nose…)

136

… she'd start nodding sadly at it as if she'd arrived only just in time to hear of its sorry plight but now it, that nose on someone else's face, shouldn't worry because she'd got there in the nick of time. Nose, worry no longer! Sort of thing. The town mayor or the town soak, it didn't matter… or, rather, *on* them. She was onto every nose in Burra town and probably beyond its regional borders.

(while she has a hard time keeping up with all the noses she must 'inspect'…)

Tis said that, even now, the son -- that once little buggerlugs, can yet see, remember as if yesterday -- his mother all over town saying, nodding wisely of noses, going predictively with a definite fullstop in her voice:

NOSEY PARKER: (new shout out) Stonkers're up front with me.

STORYTELLER: Or telling much the same thing directly to the nose in question from probably that one or two millimetres away while you're attached to it…

(She gets very person with a nose she has obviously picked out:)

NOSEY PARKER: Stonkers like you can be up front with me!

STORYTELLER: Oh, yes. Noses, his mother trusted implicitly and were quite likely to be the only things she trusted implicitly. To give her a little leeway from being a total dumbcluck when it came to noses, the boy was still pretty sure she didn't know how rude it was, or that her impulsive behaviour had offended just about everybody in town. He could only think that, in front of a snozzle, she got herself so concentrated-up in case that honker had been waiting all its life for her to arrive at it just in time, she simply forgot about the rest of other person's body parts coming with the nose.

(She plucks a nose from a player's face, goes off in a corner to speak to it and it alone…)

STORYTELLER: You could ask her how many people were in a room, and she'd go poking the air in a mid-distance pointing kind of way suchlike she had to mentally count off the nozzles in a row to come up with an answer… one by one, side-by-side as if everybody's snotter was the same height and everyone was lined up behind their noses in a level keel, shoulder-to-shoulder. He saw an image in a book once of how a dog sees the world in a real doggy kind of way...

(her own nose prop comes forward and pokes its nose into the scrim as though peering at and inspecting the audience...)

... and he guessed something of the sort was going on in her mind. Blowholes seemed to be central to it, the way she blew her own.

(He waits, but, behind, NOSEY PARKER is still concentrating intimately on that chosen someone's nose:)

STORYTELLER: (re-issuing cue-in) The way she blew her own.

(She 'wakes up', blows an enormous handkerchief blow that near-topples a few shadow players over. It is certainly like a storm wind on the scrim curtain)

STORYTELLER: ...Even when his mother was talking with someone... anyone!... there was no looking into their eyes, oh no. It was just so embarrassing for him! She seemed particularly avid about concentrating on their hooter, rather, when he was with her and couldn't escape to hide his face in a corner due to the vice-like grip she always held him by the ear with.

(Now she slips over to the SON again, secures him by grasping his ears)

SON; (to be heard) Ow! *Jeez!*

STORYTELLER: What made matters worse, she only spoke up your bonk by a type of bending at the knees, is she had to, or standing on tiptoe, if she had to, and turning her head up and sideways depending on how your nose ended up in relation to her.

(and she is demonstrating on the nearest nose she can find... until it finally is the priest)

The local priest himself... a man most in Burra town prayed would stop talking... stopped trying to talk to her (mostly griping, while holding the boy's swollen ear, about his being the dunce-numbbrain all around the place) because she made him, the priest, feel so self-conscious

138

about that biblical Mt-Ararat hook of his with those hairy flared nostrils like vine-covered hermit caves at the mountain's foot.

PRIEST SHADOW PLAYER: Ow! Fair go, or at least come to church!

STORYTELLER: Poor man, it says here in parenthesis, gave up the priesthood not long after and went to pray for his nose before she bent it too out-of-shape even for him to look at it ever again. He became, they say, an ever-after shadowy figure in the Church. Not even the Vatican could find him to get a shot of it to hang up in St Peters Square.

(and while the MOTHER takes to chasing some poor unfortunate around in circles with that horror forefinger of hers…)

STORYTELLER: And that poor priest wasn't the only one, either. What might start as a little step back or two by his Mum away from someone's nostrils often ended up with that person beating a full pelted retreat from her when he or she saw a brief window of making an escape, even if it meant going around in circles or on a backwards sashay because his Mum would never retreat even those few millimetres without sort of reserving her place at the front of your nose by sticking her forefinger up it
(pointing to the losing battle going on behind…)
or, worst case scenario, turning and making off at a sprint, nose held out in front and as far away from his Mum as possible.
(then)
You could see how that might be embarrassing to a boy growing up in a small town like Burra and related to someone always up other people's noses.

(Now, behind, there is something going on in the street which fully illustrates:)

STORYTELLER: The boy never could forget that one time a buckboard tail-gated into one of his distant aunts while his mother stood in the street talking up her nose. The buckboard dragged her, the aunt, down the street a battered mess -- and his mother just kept talking where the aunt's hooter had been as if she had blinked and nothing had

139

happened... that that genetically-related snorter was still there in front of her, not half way down the road smattered all over the bitumen. She was waving sideways be-with-you-in-a-jiffy to her sister screams down the road. It was only when the boy tugged on her sleeve that she discovered that nose missing from the point of her forefinger and was smattered down the road there; even then, she only looked down her nose at him and went all disgusted, going:

NOSEY PARKER SHADOW PLAYER: How rude! She might be my sister, but she was always following her nose, that one.

STORYTELLER: It was true! And all this was made worse by the lad's own poor nose being a bitter disappointment to her and he never being able to understand what he was supposed to do about it or even what could satisfy her. She thought it untidy, unkempt, a hooter a horse wouldn't let on its back, and one that would learn nothing, ever. When she got really mad, she'd put the tip of her finger on the tip of his nose and go:

NOSEY PARKER SHADOW PLAYER: Hey, how could *that* ever come to much? What a buggerlugs!

STORYTELLER: (quoting) 'Hey, how could that ever come to much?' A bit sad, that. And...

NOSEY PARKER SHADOW PLAYER: You imagine any seed of the right idea wanting to jump feet-first into *that*?

STORYTELLER: 'You imagine any Seed of the Right Idea wanting to jump feet first into that?' She just wouldn't let his hornpipe alone. She never even bothered with his fingernails, behind his ears, the crutch of his Jockeys, the spuds growing between his toes, but his snorter couldn't take a trick. As if it was as the dunny pit out back needing hucking out, she'd sneak up behind him and scare the squirts out of him, going:

NOSEY PARKER SHADOW PLAYER: Head! *Head*!

STORYTELLER: ...Which meant she was going to shove his head under her armpit, tilt his chin back and attack what she thought was

140

some humankind mortal enemy like Mad Cow Disease he was harbouring in his nose with the corner of a hanky twisted into a vicious corkscrew, always scraping away in those dark foul caverns, as she called them, clockwise.

BOY SHADOW PLAYER: Ow! Oo!

STORYTELLER: It says here in parenthesis, he had to admit in hindsight, many years later, he always felt the lighter for it. Anyway…

(while he continues reading, now it is the turn for the poor FATHER's nose to get her attention)

NOSEY PARKER: HEAD!

(She tackles him; they wrestle; but she is always going to win and finally succeeds in getting his upturned head in a headlock, as…)

STORYTELLER: Even with the agony she inflicted on his own nose, even as he sat there in his new hideaway in the sub-squats of Adelaide something like thirty years later, her son could still feel the horror he felt as she plunged the ends of her sewing-kit scissors as far as up his stepfather's nostrils as they'd go…

STEPFATHER SHADOW PLAYER: (trapped helplessly) OW! FUG ME!

STORYTELLER: … talking smoothing tones all along to his konk while she did so, snipping those nostril hairs as she went, snipping as those scissors *scissed*. And him only his stepdad, too, with him never knowing but always wondering where the nose of his real father had disappeared to. Close the family home's door and tyranny, pure and simple! Leave your nose outside on the door mat or it's useless to struggle!

STEPFATHER SHADOW PLAYER: (still helpless) *Frick me*!

STORYTELLER: In his ever-scarred mind's-eye, the boy always thought things started to go real goofy for his stepfather after his mother suddenly got the idea of clipping the hair in his nostrils.

Whether the boy dreamt it or not, he probably still shudders seeing her track down his stepfather with those scissors of hers.

(her shadows looms over all wielding huge scissors)

STORYTELLER: On the other hand, in this, you can perhaps see how the boy couldn't blame her for…

(comes the shadow of the stepfather's nose. Its nostrils go from great hairy protuberances which wave like seaweed or standing rigid like a walrus's…)

STORYTELLER: …wanting to clip the hair in those nostrils of his. Those hairs, they'd grown like seaweed in and out of those nostrils so he started to wheeze and couldn't stop and then they'd go like the bars on a cowcatcher on a train. They started to filter his soup. They were like the Burra weir over the Burra river; you wouldn't even use a mechanical scraper to scrape up what was caught in there but it still wasn't any worse than what you might dig up from those hairs in his nostrils.
(and)
People started to call him Walrus. But he hated her doing it, clipping those nostril hairs, no matter how long they grew. He'd be like the dog when you tried to bathe it.
(to the stepfather and mother doing so…)
He'd take off and hide, his stepfather not the dog and not the kid, but it only hid just what a nervous wreck her chasing him around the house… and a few times the boy hated to remember. around the block, to get at those nostrils of his in between her scissors. It was like he became a nervous wreck overnight.
(and then waits as a pew view indicates…)
His stepfather would suddenly be there in church, like they used to do in those days, and every couple of seconds he started to whip his head around as if to catch whoever or whatever was sneaking up on him, and there never was, and for the boy that was, yes, getting real goofy.
(and then waits as a street-stroll view shows…)
Or down the street, every ten steps or so, he started whirling around on strangers and warding them off, even shadow-boxing them by – and they don't even look like here, or, if they did, weren't raving around the street wielding a pair of scissors at his nostrils.

142

(and then waits as a driving view indicates…)

Driving became the worse. His stepdad started to be unable to keep his eyes front, on the road. He'd be turning around all the time, or looking backwards with his head out of the driver's window, his comb-over flying, as though he was hearing something at the back, something not right coming up the rear, and he'd start going: 'Some fugger's got 'is snippers up m'bum!'

STEPFATHER SHADOW PLAYER: (can only get out again:) *Frick me!*

STORYTELLER: You had to feel sorry for him. And as if that wasn't goofy enough, as soon as he ever started that 'some fugger's got 'is snippers up m'bum!', his mother would automatically start going 'Snip, snip up your sneezer!', her fingers going all scissory in his face… And the boy didn't know if she was for real or just the talk of the snips got her going with the thought of her dressmakers' scissors up his stepfather's nostrils, or what.

(and)

His mother always said it wasn't her fault those nostrils needed the good old snip. It was the Commies, she said. It was the war and the way he came back, she said. For her, the Vietnam War was all about the Viet Cong being driven crazy by those hairs in his nostril that it was no wonder they wanted to throw the Yanks and Yankettes out of their country.

(Back in the shadows area, a steamy jungle and figures stealthily tracking his nostrils down and her errant nose annoying all…)

STORYTELLER: You just ask those nostril hairs, she said, tapping her nose that she knew. There are still Commies sneaking along trails over there in that sneaky place Vietnam there, because they can't trust those hairs have ever fully gone from their country.

(Very surprisingly, the MOTHER comes out around the side of the scrim to stand in full view. Without a beg-your-pardon, she waves the STORYTELLER silent and delivers full frontedly to the audience:)

MOTHER: Too right, they still do. Sneaky little b's. Can't blame them, but. See, I know this for a fact: those hairs... ugh!... up those nostrils of his...

(shudders doubly)

clogged up the war effort so much nobody could get around to killing each other, so what's the point of a war in the first place? His own lieutenant hauled him up before his CO... and don't get up my nose by asking what CO means; it's just got to be bad, that's all I know... for being out of uniform because his nostril hair had grown so long it was an added entanglement the frontline lads didn't need trying to get through the jungle at the best of times. The other side was complaining too to the Geneva Convention their bullets couldn't get through neither and it wasn't fair on them. So the CO said to his lieutenant he'd better find someone to cut those hairs out before it all ended in peace or there'd be hell to play

(and)

But do they find someone? They do not. No hope! Who's surprised at that anyway? And don't get onto me; I'm only trying to do my bit for the war effort.

> *(She returns to the shadow area, allowing the STORYTELLER to be able to take control again with a shrug of what-to-do to the audience:)*

STORYTELLER: In fact, given the overall situation with his Mum and her nosey-parking, the lad had no idea what made her behaviour around noses become a bit of a downward spiral to his juvenile development. What he couldn't help seeing was how her own friends started deserting her, his own Mum... even down the mines where it was so dark... and she had to go groping around...

> *(the back light goes off to plunge the shadow-mime area in darkness as in down the mine pit and only a few miners' lamps shining out, and, echoing loud enough to be heard:)*

MINER SHADOW PLAYER 1: Who hit the lights?!

MINER SHADOW PLAYER 2: I did. I saw her coming for me.

MINER SHADOW PLAYER 1: How's the nose?

MINER SHADOW PLAYER 2: She missed, thank God!

MINER SHADOW PLAYER 1: I'm talking to the Union! These mines ain't safe!

STORYTELLER: She'd have to be groping around to even know there was a nose working anywhere near close by, let alone be able to get another battery on her helmet lamp to shine up it... which meant, the son guessed, she had no friends to tell her they were really working down the mine to keep their bugles away from her.
   (aside, brandishing script)
It says to make that sound funny but to not be too sure about it.
   (resumes)
What with that and his stepdad not being able to stand other people very much anyway, and himself having no mates anyway, his Mum's behaviour with respect to noses became a bit dire for a small family in a small town like Burra. Passing her in the street, people she knew all her life started turning their heads to protect their hosepipes from being collared between the middle knuckles of her first and second fingers, then hoisted up or pulled down to her height for short-arm inspection.

   (Behind, now on the open street, the MOTHER shadow player is showing her expertise at being able to leap upon people trying to avoid her by catching their noses between the middle knuckles of her first and second fingers and lifting their noses up for her brief inspection – either loudly satisfied or with loud open disgust. Noses honk off and car horns nose off, while:)

STORYTELLER: If any stopped out of politeness in a moment of forgetting what their noses might think, she'd gotten into the habit of trying to shake hands with their snozs and then they'd have to shy away and probably stumble back, tripping over something or somebody and hurting themselves, including the danger of putting their stonkers out of joint. Or if they got past that handshake via her knuckles and decided to stay there and grin and bear it, she'd stand there stroking their conks like petting their dog absent-mindedly while she talked on and on exclusively to it…

   (He has to wait for the MOTHER shadow player to catch up
145

because she is spending too much time petting and stroking and baby-talking to others' noses. Even her own nose detaches itself again to nudge her to hurry it along. Finally the STORYTELLER can resume:)

STORYTELLER: And the boy himself? Her son? Well, tis written in plain view here how he tried to hide from her if he saw his own Mum coming, mainly beetling across the street to hide behind a tree, say, or trying to make his hooter look like just another sweet pea in some stranger's garden, and waiting until she passed. At least that was easy; even when he closed his eyes real shut and crossed his fingers, he could track her progress over on the other side of the street by the Mexican wave of people's hands going up to cover their snot-wots on the mad dash for the nearest place to hide.
   (pause)
One thing about having a mother like that… you knew you weren't the only one in all things.

   (The MOTHER has success in backing a couple of people at a time up against the scrim curtain so that it bulges outwards both with her pressure and their struggle for nose survival…)

STORYTELLER: Ah, if that was all! Look, see! More, much more! How she imagined she could get away with starting to tell people about their ailments from the snot in their handkerchiefs he would never know! This sorry chapter in his life with his mother came all of a sudden.
   (and)
Suddenly, she started diving into other people's pockets, reefing out their hankies which were much in vogue in those days, unfolding them (careful, careful!) to reveal the state of the mucus there. It didn't matter if it was new-gooey or old crusty. From its texture and colour, she could start in on a slight head cold (buttercup yellow)
                    (gets a full-blown sneeze)
to they should go immediately for cancer tests (mustard brown with moving flecks) or keep off the garlic if it was a bright purple turning rotten
   (gets a full-blown, really-nasty hacking cough)
and the whole Grays-Anatomy colour range in between, going happily as she went on her way:

146

NOSEY PARKER: (holding someone's nose) I DON'T CHARGE NOTHIN', NEVER DID.

STORYTELLER: From there it deteriorated into forecasting the weather. It did, and I am reading that I should say I am not kidding you.
   (and)
Other people's dusty snot was dust storms coming with time of day as an add-on.

   (He gets an echoing dust storm 'whoosh', and NOSEY PARKER holds up a dusty-coloured snot board, which shows around and past one side of the screen, and:)

STORYTELLER: (nodding) Dust storm, yep. And then if it was, say, clear, that snot meant clear air, bright day, sunshine.

   (He gets sounds of people playing in a bright, sunshiny day, while NOSEY PARKER now displays a sky-blue coloured snot board around the side of the scrim, and:)

STORYTELLER: A bright sunshiny day, yep again. And then debris lines around the edges of the snot she could predict meant rain, a shower or a thunderstorm, depending on the absorbent quality of the hankie.

   (He gets storm sounds, while NOSEY PARKER displays a storm-cloud coloured snot board around the side of the screen, and:)

STORYTELLER: She offered her services to ABC's Rural Department if they supplied the snot rags.

   (She displays a white handkerchief around the side of the screen)

STORYTELLER: But apparently she preferred the ones from the local Coles.

   (She quickly changes the white one for a coloured one to flap away with)

147

STORYTELLER: … and made no bones about it to any nose; she didn't care. Yes indeedy. Then, one of his last nose memories was her latest caper and talk about embarrassing for a boy still growing: her version of strolling along arm-in-arm with someone was to have her index finger up their nose, leading them on from a step ahead.

> *(She 'collars' a poor individual and leads him around by the nose)*

STORYTELLER: She said a nose was grateful to be pointed the way it really wanted to go by someone – even half its stature -- who understood what it really wanted. You ask any nose with two healthy nostrils, she said.
> *(and waiting until opportune moment for:)*
Well, it couldn't go on of course. It came to a head for the poor little bugger when old Wirth's Circus came to town and she sought out the clowns with the big rubber noses to find out how their snorters handled the workload without being given the recognition they deserved or having to constantly suffer honk-honk thieves.

> *(Behind, the circus comes to town and all the noisy gaieties that entails…)*

STORYTELLER: Excitement! Burra only ever saw it once every few years. But was it excitement for him? Of course, it was… he was still a boy… and of course didn't his Mum ever spoil it for him!
> *(to her doing so)*
When she came back from around the back of the Big Top and he asked her why her stockings weren't hooked to her suspenders at the back, she just shrugged and said it was the way noseries acted around hosieries.

NOSEY PARKER: (primly) It's the way noseries act around hosieries, ain't it?

STORYTELLER: It was the same with her smeared lipstick.

NOSEY PARKER: It's the same with a woman's lipstick if you must know, you sticky-beak of a cheeky little nosey buggerlugs, you! Blow that nose of yours!

STORYTELLER: But it must have been something more than that, because the next day she returned from around the back of the Big Top, she somehow got caught in a vacuum between the top of her head and the end of an elephant's trunk, and her own son had to find her dangling like that… from an elephant's trunk with her feet off the ground.

(She is hanging on for dear life, dangling from an elephant's trunk)

NOSEY PARKER: COP THIS FOR A SNAUZER!

STORYTELLER: In the photo in the *Burra Examiner* under the heading: 'NOSE LADY'S HEAD STUCK UP TRUNK OF LARGE NOSE JOB!'
(and)
It's true! 'Nose Lady's Head Stuck Up Trunk of Large Nose Job'! And she was dangling there in the photograph for all the *Examiner*'s readers to see from the end of that trunk, feet miles off the ground, her stockings and lipstick again no better than they should be – one stocking down around her ankle -- in the middle of what looked like her picking her own thar-she-blows plus waving happily to the camera, and obviously giggling mightily.
(and)
Well!, what could the poor lad do but ask his mother what happened as casually as he could and trying to pretend it was nothing unusual?

NOSEY PARKER: (haughtily) It's only how hosieries can't help acting around large noseries! Didn't i say blow that nose of yours?

STORYTELLER: Sad, really. But still, he wasn't really there around the side of that Big Top to get too affected by her behaviour, anyway. He didn't even wait for her answer or to even see how she got down from there.

(She is dropped from the trunk. Recovers to pose for bulb-

149

popping photography)

STORYTELLER: We really don't know if the son was around to see the *Examiner*'s piece with all its pixs. Or if he did get around to blow his nose. We do know he simply turned his back, and had gone back home as fast as his pretty-bandy legs, really, could carry him… which was very bandily… and, there, had taken the couple of dollars and the few cents he could find in her purse on the sideboard and then proceeded to do a juvenile hissy fit of a flit which was probably the root of all his later troubles if Freud had ever been consulted on whatever happened to the Seed of the Right Idea when it came into him, if it ever in fact had come into him.

(The behind-the-screen lighting fades until, while the shadows wave goodbye, closely followed by the general lighting beginning to fade too, until, finishing up, the STORYTELLER holds the torch under his chin once more…)

STORYTELLER: And, yes, sad to say, after that he never saw his mother again. Sad but true, since when does what's written down ever lie? Often, though, in some then-as-now time, when he was in his tucked away in some flesh-eating apartment in some flesh-eating part of Sydney, he would imagine seeing stars above and wonder how blew her snitzel, her snorer, her snoz. Hadst boogies or was healthy unblocked? Wert her sinuses full o' the old bottle? There even came a time when he got one of his wives… each of them proverbially proving a bit on the nose, sad to say… to phone her person-to-person after assuring the operator she wouldn't catch anything by simply placing a call to a place unknown to scientists. Of Burra town we speak. How was she?, he had her ask his Nosey-Parker mother. Who wanted to know?, his old Mum said, and then she apparently went: 'Who? You talking about the little turd who always got up me nose; the Snot Kid himself? You tell him to blow that dirty little nose and don't stop until I say!'
(then)
Whichever wife of his that was apparently, too, told him his old Mum definitely sounded like she had a head cold and certainly had the sniffles from a runny nose which, she said his mother said, was in training to defend the Easter Cup's upcoming Snorter Stakes where, as

a multiple past winner, she was under heavy handicap of over-use of the honk-honk of her hooter while blowing it out through her nose.

(The commentary of the Easter Show's Cup drowns him out for a moment. In this time, he shrugs and gets up and leaves)

---oOo---

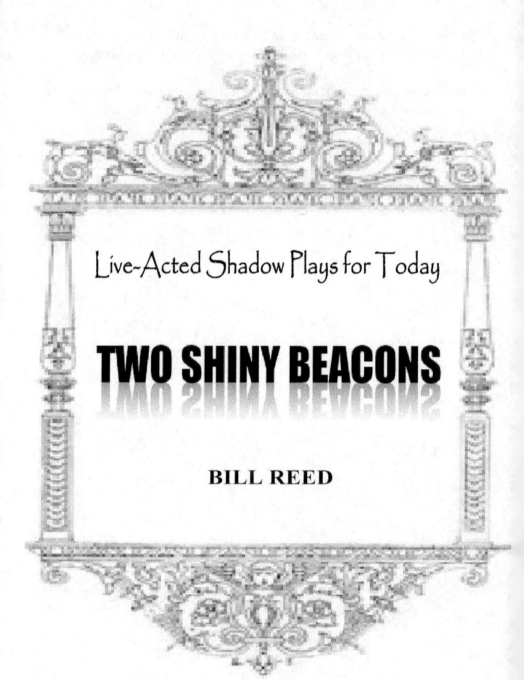

Live-Acted Shadow Plays for Today

TWO SHINY BEACONS

BILL REED

The behind-the-screen shadow action – or 'inner background' play --
can only ever keep 'pace' with the reading, not *keep up* with it.
Because of the resultant and necessary shadow-play distillation of the
storyteller's tale, the extensive stage directions given in this script are
only intended to be indicators as to what *might* be used for the shadow-
play side of things. They deliberately go beyond what the director
would employ and are given merely as a range of possible shadow-
actions he or she might want to use in the 'distillation'.

The Characters

Setting is south Machans Beach, a Cairns satellite suburb north of the city.

STORYTELLER
He reads from a manuscript or a hand-held device and does this, as a virtue, almost unrehearsed.

FR. IGNATIUS SHADOW PLAYER
who occasionally comes out from behind the scrim curtain to act 'three-dimensionally'. Young and with zeal for reform. Should be standing on the boards not on a pulpit.

ST PETER SHADOW PLAYER
Finally with a lead part in the passion plays, but might have been better suited if he had learnt how to swim. Enjoys a beer, though, and, obviously, good company, however fishy.

TILLIE SHADOW PLAYER:
who also sometimes 'escapes' out from behind the shadow area to act in full view; but, in reality, she's been doing that all her life. Matron; everybody's eccentric. The UV lights and the many salts she has had in her life! No stray dog has been seen actually letting itself lick her hand.

SHADOW PLAYERS
Whatever number available above 3 or 4, to take up the characters illustrating such elements as: the fishermen, the sailfish, the stray dogs, the elements, alongside of very flexible props and cut-outs.

Two Shiny Beacons

.

(The STORYTELLER starts in his own spot. Gradually, behind him, behind the scrim curtain, general lighting comes up. At first there is little to see back there, although there grows a strong sound-over of being on a beach.

At the outset, he brandishes script for the audience to see, and:)

STORYTELLER: I am apparently not meant to have learnt this by heart. It's just as well. With my memory, even some of my best mates say we wouldn't have gotten this far.

(The back lighting is fully 'on' in the shadow area... beach, coastal palms etc.)

STORYTELLER: We are on the beach at Machans South, where the tide comes in and the tide comes out with a tidal determination few beaches in the world would boast about. Here in Machans South, Far North Queensland, on a day ideal for the beach…

(as he speaks, TILLIE to his left and FR. IGNATIUS to his right come out from behind the screen and stand at either end of the stage apron...)

STORYTELLER: … you could fire a cannon-full of hermit crabs down the beach and not put the frog up anyone. That's how deserted it can get.
(indicating the two on either side of him)
Like any beach, Machans South has its leading-light shining beacons. But Machans South is special: its shiny beacons have no further ado.
(and)
And so, without further ado, may I introduce you to the first shiny beacon…

(He goes and places hand on TILLIE, who shrugs it off with disgust, and shakes an old string-sprung tennis racket at him)

155

STORYTELLER: Our Tillie here is Machans South's longest-ever shiny beacon. You have more time you might call her Tillie the Zap for when her hubby was bagman for the biggest crime czar that ever spent most of his working life sleeping on the steps of the Cairns Central Library.

(showing them...)

This is her straw hat, so now shiny-famous that the locals call all straw hats Tillies. And these...

(pointing under its brim)

are UV lights she has had strung beneath its brim long before UV lights were invented and batteries had just come in. So the locals go. These UVs light her way and zap the mozzies, so said. For this reason, she is oft called Tillie Lighthouse, along with Tillie the Zap. Take your pick. And they say, outside her husband who was a bit of a bit queer himself, no one's ever tried to throw their leg over Tillie. You can see why... or so some unkindly said.

(taps her on the shoulder)

Ah, Tillie, Tillie... you may go, hmm?

> *(Surprisingly she returns to the shadow-acting area surprisingly quite passively. The STORYTELLER then walks across stage to now place his hand on FR. IGNATIUS's shoulder)*

STORYTELLER: This is Fr. Ignatius, the newest edition of the shiny beacons of Machans South you could historically count on the fingers of an historically-versed hand. ...Where fingers are likely to be, even in Machans, right?, ha ha.

> *(joke falls flat. Has to dig the Father in the ribs to get a smile. Succeeds, but is interrupted by, behind in the shadow area, a shadow player picks up the Cross and starts lugging it along. Seeing this, FR. IGNATIUS breaks away, quickly goes back to shadow area to help out)*

STORYTELLER: Using Fr. Ignatius here... or there now... we can start out to explain how the place of the Eucharist for the foreseeable future in the Machans' diocese came to be a local beach bar favoured by St. Peter, when Machans South hasn't got any beach bars. A

growing number of pilgrims come to Machans to give witness to the
miracle of that alone.

*(needs to wait while Italian music – probably the score from 'The
Godfather' – give shadow allusions to Italy 'back home'...)*

To go back to the first olive oils... from his first semester of missionary
work, the novice Father Ignatius Lombardi wanted to flex his theatrical
muscles. He saw his calling as needing to clover theatre and faith
together, in order to show that priests sent out by the Vatican didn't all
seem like illegal migrants with pushy attitudes about what was before
their noses. After all, didn't his own people have centuries of pushing
their brightest out of the family's strolling-player business and into the
cloth, because just take a robe from Wardrobe; there was no need to go
out and buy an expensive new one that didn't even have the lived-in
look of inbuilt patched-up holes.

(and)

It helped, too, that in those times God was known to be one of the
theatre's most ardent supporters and never proven to ever miss a
Passion Play festival.

*(As, behind now, FR. IGNATIUS and his fellow shadow players
stop enacting the Agony and, eyes upwards, cross themselves)*

STORYTELLER: For the younger-than-young Fr. Ignatius, his own
passion for the theatre and the Passion itself had blossomed out of the
birth of his parents in two separate cabin trunks backstage of a
particularly boisterous opera-bouffé playhouse rollicking among the
highlands of the real Lombardy in what then was a real Italy running
with hot-fruity, especially in back-stages.

(takes theatrical breath)

It then appears as though the two babies had crawled into each other's
arms, midstage and mid-aria of *'The Basting of Saint Joan, Saintly
Chop Livered'*...

SHADOW OPERATIC CHOIR: (sing-song) The Basting of Saint
Joan, Saintly Chop Livered...!

STORYTELLER: And so, thereafter his mother and father were never
to be parted on early entrances or exits that involved any applause.

(pause for emphasis)

Sixteen years later, they gave birth to the infant Ignatius in the one of the same cabin trunks at the same place in the middle of the same aria.

SHADOW OPERATIC CHOIR: (again) The Basting of Saint Joan, Saintly Chop Livered...

STORYTELLER: (now long-sufferingly) ...in the middle, as I say, of the same aria which convinced Fr. Ignatius that theatre was in his blood from the moment he found the stigmata of splinters of stage boards on his little knees and little hands. As he was fond to say...

FR. IGNATIUS: (fit to be heard) I a-cut-ta my first diaper in the middle of l'aria 'Il Basting of Saint Joan, Saintly Chop Livered'.

(He returns to shadow area)

STORYTELLER: And so, one of improvement our good Father made popular in his native Lombardy was to cast the Passion plays in a more democratic light, to reflect those crawling around doing nothing back stage and the like. His first ground-breaker was to concentrate on the characters hardly getting a mention anymore. For example, what's with all that theatrical neglect of St. Peter, a saint never far from the crowing of cocks when, surely, real people's theatre was all about the crowing of cocks?
          (fights to be heard over the, now, crowing of the cocks three
                              times...)
One only had to take the stage takes on the Crucifixion... well, where is St. Peter? Pretty much nowhere, you'd have to agree. So, our Fr. Ignatius gave the congregation a St. Peter who wasn't left out of the Nativity play, just because he had only a minor billing in the Passion play... and literally left perennially waiting in the wings when he didn't deserve it. The cocks crowing got more audience time.
     (and)
And so, Fr. Ignatius placed much more faith in the character of St. Peter and wrote him back in to both plays where he belonged, especially in his famously-innovating 'Passion of Christ; the Prequel' which played religiously once a year in front of theatres and in which St. Peter cast off the nets holding him back and rose from the sea as a matter of liturgical interest.
     (and, to sinister music background...)

158

And then there was Judas. You take, Fr. Ignatius would always say, the treatment of Judas.

FR. IGNATIUS: (shout of 'yes') Thazza right!

STORYTELLER: Thazza right. To the good Father, Judas was another character given the short end of the pineapple. Judas gets shafted and character assassinated right from the word go, then after that… what? Not even a look in. Not even a decent tree scene to hang his characterisation on.
   (and)
It was bad enough with the Son Himself. A God by rights… sure, fine!... but come the climax, come the big night, how much abuse did He have to go through just to be able to come up with a few words you could count on one hand? You take the Nativity; all He gets to do is lie there and is even slapped down from making even a gurgle. Where's any fair crack of the whip from Casting?

   (There is now from behind a cacophony of confused sounds –
   operatic bouffé, the Nativity farmhouse; the Crucifix's crowd…)

STORYTELLER: (fighting to be heard) And so, for his very first Machans Beach Easter, Fr. Ignatius showed himself to be a cutter-to-the-chase. He positive shone with an inner shiny beacon to steer Machans Beach's already thrilling new-wave, post-modernist, avant-garde theatre into the very last word in the world's ecclesiastical dramaturgy.
   (thankfully, all the cacophonies behind die down:)
Not under his priestly direction would the good people of Machans to be left in the dark as to what St. Peter really looked like strutting the stage, or what he sounded like when he cleared his throat or where he was born, what school he went to, who his parents were – or even if his sisters, if he had any sisters, didn't roll their sleeves up and take over the family fishing business when he and his brothers were off gallivanting around the country with the Gang of Twelve, n' so forth.
   (pause for re-enactments in shadow area to catch up…)
Then didn't Fr. Ignatius ever have an epiphany! 'New wave', 'treading the boards' and all that, we suppose it was. Aussie inspired. Apparently instantly, he could see how, in this, his first presentation in Far North Queensland, St. Peter had to star in his own Passion vehicle

159

by coming to the rescue, riding a wave ashore at Galilee! Of course!
Oh, you can talk about your two shiny beacons, but this was shiny
brilliant!

(The shadow area is being set up for the Sea of Galilee scenes on
a very stormy day and surf painted on cardboards, etc, while:)

STORYTELLER: So we have Fr. Ignatius where our Tillie…
remember our Tillie the Zap, the other of our shiny beacons?... where
our Tillie, yes, was watching him standing there on Machans South
beach directing St. Peter and his fellow biblicals out in their dhow out
there past the surf break which was kind of idiotic, even to Tillie,
because Fr. Ignatius *was* the St. Peter in the boat out in the dhow out
past the break.
   (checks this in script, nods, gets back on course)
Unfortunately, Fr. Ignatius, a mere man from Lombardy after all,
wasn't very seaworthy. Which meant this St. Peter our Tillie was
watching wasn't very seaworthy either. Making even those pretty little
waves going on there very upchuckable.
   (over-dramatic re-enactments behind show the dhow suffering
   corkscrew swell and FR. IGNATIUS/ST. PETER hanging on for
   dear life, etc…)
Nor could we say that St. Peter had all his non-seaworthy heart in it all.
By the time he dare open his eyes on being put out to sea, he found
himself among what felt like mountainous waves, and his jammed into
what had to be a dug-out canoe affair… which was all Fr. Ignatius
could find to hire as a dhow in Far North Queensland… the width of
which was less wide than his twin bum cheeks so fleshy now with its
sea-faring splinters. Those white knuckles were his too. That gooey
stuff had to be the chewing gum the whole thing was held together
with, including that mast and that sail that was flapping in time to his
dry retches.

(FR. IGNATIUS/ST PETER tries to stand in the manner of
Horatio, but wobbles downward while the two other shadow
players try desperately to right the boat and as the storm rises…)

STORYTELLER: He realised he was being told that if you couldn't
squeeze your nates in between port and starboard you were too fat to be
a fisherman or too cowardly when you preferred getting out and

swimming even if you couldn't swim. As he was trying, and he couldn't. And he was being told this by a local abalone diver fully kitted out as his brother St. Andrew and a couple of others as extras difficult to look at given they weren't wearing anything under those wet, wind-driven kaftans… one of whom obviously suffered from irritated bowel. But at least the good Father had gotten out to sea there in his biblical thobe robe and bisht cloak and keffiyeh scarfs a-head with matching igal head strings and tassels and augmented beards applied with the same, probably, chewing gum as the dug-out canoe thing was stuck up with… and at least he still had the imagination left to envisage, on the big day, the hundreds of churchies who would be waiting on the shore for St. Peter to come storming in to save the day.

(while FR. IGNATIUS signals madly to the shore for help…)
It seems one problem was he couldn't keep his eyes off how the mast string-things had come loose at the stern and unhinged at the bow and how the sail rag thing was hanging, luffed up or something because, it seemed, that fluky wind seemed to prefer his and his biblical fishing mates' robes than the sail to bring that surf break too damn close.

(as the sail falls on him and he fights to get out from under it…)
And all also he could see was a width of boat less than half bum cheeks between him and a watery grave if, when it came to it, his St. Peter's cloak didn't trap air well enough amongst bucketing waves and to meet his Maker proved to be Down rather than Up. Please, God, don't be Down Under!

SHADOW PLAYERS CHORUS: And He said, "Throw out your net on the right side of your boat and you will find some fish…"

STORYTELLER: And St. Peter did as the Lord bid, for Fr. Ignatius knew that even as thou rehearse so doth thou end in a reheap, in a manner of biblically speaking.

(behind, the net has come to his rescue. With the sail over his head, he grabs it as a life line, manages to stand…)
St. Peter managed to get off a wave to the ghostly crowd of next-week's Passion-week's thousands of faithful who would be cheering from the shore and he flung that net as far as he could in a manner that couldn't fail to impress.

(watching as it is re-enacted…)
The next snag was, with that sail snagging him right up, when it came to push coming to shove, he wasn't going to let go of anything that had

dry-land solidity about it. No fracking way. So he went with the flow of
the flung net to do an uncharted somersault into charted waters fully
decked out in that ten-tonne wardrobe of biblical proportions and
giving rise to an unheard raus of ratiocination from the Rock of the
Church about to sink like a rock to the bottom there.

FR. IGNATIUS: STRONZO! STRONZO!

STORYTELLER: In his very best Italiano panic contralto. Hi toes
caught in the rope holding the main mast holding the other end of him
in from getting flung *out*, too. Which in turn tangled the net around a
tangle lot of arms and legs and dawn's early-light catch theoretically
already starting to rot there.

> *(And then, from behind, comes a veritable rainbow'd shower of*
> *sun-glinting colour, as indefinable as tinsel...)*

STORYTELLER: It wasn't helping either that the plastic fish the
kiddies of Fr. Ignatius's Under Four Drama Group had filled up the net
with such a sparkle of coloured plastic sprat cut-outs that a school of
just-then-passing real live yellow-speckled fusiliers had latched onto
the free feast even while...
> *(to the absolute chaos that is happening behind...)*
they, the cut-outs, the net and St. Peter's cloak all seemed to be
contriving to put an end to St. Peter's career on centre stage, if not pre-
eminently in the briny of life, and any further greater part he had hoped
as a character to have in the ecclesiastical plays of the future. Going to
show you being in the best inner circle doesn't guarantee your stage
career won't be cut short.
> *(and while, now, the sailfish is causing real havoc...)*
If that wasn't all... now there was this scene-stealer of a sailfish
suddenly plugging itself in on the scene. You know how sailfish are. It
wasn't going to be left wallowing around in the wings when there was
an opening on stage, not if it befell you out of the depths of a Passion
play. How often does that come around?
> *(has to pause for the chaos happened behind)*
In its first whipping-on-by, that-there sailfish missed all sainthood by
the narrowest of sword's edge, and on its second whipping-on-by that
sword stuck in the net and ended up acting against its better nature as a
life raft to St. Peter, who wasn't going down like a rock to any bottom

before showing that sailfish a few rodeo moves they use back in Galilee, when rodeos were all the go there

(and)

Boat-stuff things, the poor anointed fisher folk of the Sea of Galilee, yellow-speckled fusiliers and bright plastic sprats… it all made that sailfish a fishy form of surfboard which Fr. Ignatius and St. Peter were riding for their dear directing and acting lives… that, after all round initially doing quite well at hanging on for dear life...

(all are risen on the crest of a wave poised to come crashing down…)

all went down the tube in a hang-five that was as screechy as it was quite admirable really, their ways bouncing across the shoreline reef there and getting schoogered back onto shore to be dumped covered mightily with grit in their teeth and weed and misery at the rather happy feet of Tillie-on-the-shore… the one and only – unhappily – audience-of-one to witness the best St. Peter move ever to hit the boards.

(breathlessly conducts for the dumping from the wave to happen…)

KABOOM!

(Blackout)

2.

(After briefest of blackouts, lighting returns to the shadow area where 'sea scenes' are being cleared to make way for a makeshift beach bar. There, eventually, on stools and breasting the bar itself, is FR. IGNATIUS/ST. PETER and, seated next to him, the sailfish)

STORYTELLER: Ladies and gentles, that was only the briefest of blackouts so you can adjust your eyes to what you couldn't possibly be seeing.

(and)

Yes… or should that be 'no'?… you are not wrong. That is Fr. Ignatius there… an Italian priest newly imprinted on Australia… drinking hot flat Aussie beers, even if St. Peter might have done before… with a worst-for-the-wear sailfish. No kid. That's one thing. But you can also see the good Father hasn't got a red cent in his kick to pay for any of this and the sailfish's cunningly not making any move towards any pocket it's pretending not to have. The dog.

(and)

As if going stiff with drying Machans-South sand wasn't enough to make you real stiff, now the bar guy's threatening to throw them back if they don't cough up. Or, he was, until, oh yes, our...

(points to her arrival)

Tillie the Zap... remember?... appears on the scene and adds an earlier miracle to Passion Week pushing coin over and going to the guy: 'This idjit's for me. How much?'.

(TILLIE does indeed appear, and calls fit to be heard:)

TILLIE: This idjit's for me. How much?

BARMAN: Oh yeah? What about the fish, eh?

TILLIE: Okay, I'll put up for one more and that's it's lot!

(FR. IGNATIUS/ST PETER and the sailfish fall off their stools inebriated)

STORYTELLER: (has to shrug) So... there she is: our Tillie, the first mentioned shiny Machans beacon, right?

(and)

Then did our Tillie wheel Fr. Ignatius/St. Peter off and onto Beach Road in a most unchristian way, allowing us to get back to where we started all this, by allowing for a full blackout this time for where she fits in to all this...

(Blackout)

3.

(Setting returns to 'normal', both in front and behind the scrim curtain. Behind the curtain, back lighting slowly returns accompanied by growing sounds of being seaside)

STORYTELLER: As a blackout, that was even briefer. Still, now we are back where we started, on the beach at Machans South, where... if I may repeat... the tide comes in and the tide comes out with a tidal determination few beaches in the world would boast about. It was a lovely typical day on Machans Beach. No sun was shining...

(as he speaks, once more TILLIE emerges to his left and FR. IGNATIUS (wet and bedraggled) emerges to his right to be in full view again on either side of the scrim curtain)

STORYTELLER: ...you could fire a cannon-full of hermit crabs down the beach and not put the frog up anyone. Not even the frog.
(taps TILLIE on shoulder)
So, this time, let me tell you a little more about our other shiny beacon here... our own Tillie. We spoke about how she got the names Tillie the Walking Lighthouse or our preferred Tillie the Zap.
(hears no contradiction)
Okay. So, Tillie being Tillie, she watched every male who ever came onto her sands... for this part of Machans *is* her sands. Every time it was 'That's not the guy for me'... and that included her long-gone ex who she had seen trying to bury some of his stolen loot in the sand under high-water mark and said, 'That idjit ain't bright; he's the guy for me'.

TILLIE: (unenthusiastic) That idjit ain't bright; he's the dingbat for me!'

STORYTELLER: She never said that about any other man, until just now about Fr. Ignatius. And, remember, she'd been watching it all. It was the way that, within one foot in the boat, he obviously just didn't want the sea *to be there*. She took one of her looks and said of him, 'That's the idjit I need'.

TILLIE: That's the idjit tailor-made for yours-truly!

STORYTELLER: And saying it about none other than our Fr. Ignatius just shedding St. Peter there, losing his sea legs on that bar stool, not to mention some argument he was having with the sailfish. Whence, I will remind us all, she dragged him up the beach onto Beach Road. What a pretty Machans pass!

(TILLIE shrugs him off, moves across the stage to haul FR. IGNATIUS back into the shadow area -- where they are joined by

165

other shadow players to enact the mangrove-side scenes...)

STORYTELLER: Now, normally, very few would launch themselves along Beach Road, which went to show Machans South's far-sightedness in naming it a road, and the mangrove jungle that ran besides it as a people's park...

(now stray dogs whimpering, barking, snapping among a pack...)
And there she'd be every day carting her plastic bag of meat ends for the local stray dogs, going out in perfectly bright and brightening mornings with all her UV hat lights fully to light her way. And Fr. Ignatius... he who always had a crease to his trousers and spare starch for his collar... dragged there by her like a drowned rat, a stunned mullet. Oh, these two shiny beacons of Machans!

(TILLIE is feeding the dogs, as FR. IGNATIUS stands well back)

STORYTELLER: When he managed to clear his throat of the few plastic sprat cut-outs left blocking it, the good Father managed to point out that her feeding the strays was causing the dogs more life-threatening injuries fighting over the meat than if she just let them alone, and that she was doing so next to a large broken-down wall which had scrawled on it: 'No feed the mong grrrs!'

A DOG VOICE: No feeding the mong grrrs!

STORYTELLER: And then, the next thing Fr. Ignatius did was to inquire if she was rich enough to put money into a few improvements to his 'Passion of Christ: the prequel', as in helping to make it a bit more seaworthy around the edges. Around Cairns, his experience was that looking nutty meant money.

TILLIE: Don't ask.

FR. IGNATIUS: Okay, si.

STORYTELLER: Oh yes, Tillie... I'll remind you she wasn't otherwise also called the Walking Lighthouse for UV-nothing. She already had *his* UV hat she already had up her sleeve for him right there in the other hand the dogs weren't trying to tear to shreds for the simple reason – hers not the dogs – as to who else around there needed a UV hat since there was no one else around there crazy enough to be out rehearsing in a dhow mock-up in that weather instead of waiting for a proper stage to come sailing along. And without a UV hat to at least light the way as to what lurks at your feet. Like sailfish that won't kick in when it's their turn to shout.

(pauses, needing to catch breath)
Anyway, hadn't life taught her not to expect any rounding-off to any conversation with any man over four foot, aside from her ex who topped that by half a foot? So, she didn't wait to give Fr. Ignatius any meaningful response, but only shoved the hat she had for him and shove-handedly showed him how to turn its lamps on. This switch there... honestly, talk about thick!

> *(He waits but there is no response while she is trying to fit the hat on the Father's head. While they struggled, the dogs etc come to life again...)*

STORYTELLER: ('that's better') Tillie felt like shouting you have to remove that biblical hood first, dumbo. What do you think you are, St. Peter? Schee; over four foot, they don't get any better over the years.

TILLIE: (succeeds, bucking up) Schee, over four foot, the idjits don't get any better over the years! Whatcha think y'are, St. Peter?

STORYTELLER: It was her beacon-filled five trips around the world and double that crossing the Equator chasing internet discards of a certain footage with their tongues hanging down between their legs until they saw her and then their happy acceptance at accepting compensation of her Machans-South pearls of wisdom turned into dollars, quite honestly, that confirmed exactly what she should have known before throwing her ex's hard-earned loot from hold-ups at them... none of the idjits can ever round off a conversation, so say your piece and up 'em. Anyway...

> *(by now she has got the hat on FR. IGNATIUS and is now beating the dogs off him...)*

STORYTELLER: ... who are we to argue with her about the four-feet thing? After all, is she not that local shiny beacon, Tillie the Zap, The Walking Lighthouse?... and also it's a scientific fact that never in her

167

life would she expect to round off a conversation with a priest maybe touch-and-go over four foot, standing there under UV lights she'd paid for and going at her, 'Cosa c'è, signora, eh?

FR. IGNATIUS: Hey, cosa c'è, ladee?!

STORYTELLER: Many even had tried the Government kennels to come and put her down, but her beloved strays were still her beloved strays, and they still barked and howled and terrorised Machans when all were sleeping. Human lampshades still walked in the night under UV there, too, did they not?
(pause for effect)
Could not Fr. Ignatius, with all his theatrical insights about the outcast cast members of Time, see the problems confronting her, which was, as plain as the ugly nose on his moosh, that…
(turns to prompt for…)
the strays of this world were having their troubles with the salt of the air?

SHADOW CHORUS: the strays of this world are having their troubles with the salt of the air!

STORYTELLER: Exactly!… and the salt of the air of this world was having trouble with too much proximity of living things…

SHADOW CHORUS: And the salt of the air of this world's having its troubles with too much effing proximity of effing living humans!…

STORYTELLER: And if he had any common dog sense over four feet high he'd know that wasn't her fault but the sea's. For one thing, she could tell him of her certainty that the problem of the strays could be tackled with lots of red meat kept away from salt not happy with itself. Then, that other thing about it being the sea… she was absolutely convinced that the salt of the air was being distressed by too much exposure to her wrinkles and… getting back to the sea's fault… did he even know that the reason the salt around there wasn't happy salt?

TILLIE: (on cue) Dya know the reason the salt around here ain't happy salt?

168

STORYTELLER: No, he didn't. Can you believe that?
  *(she turns FR. IGNATIOUS's head to look around him more
  closely...)*
Well, if he would switch his UV hat lights on... what an idjit!... then
he'd be able to see the reason was as plain as the nose on his face...
which, being a Roman one was as plain to daylight as you could get,
cripessakes...
  (as she really gets into lecturing him...)
... and that was that the salt in the air around Machans South there was
exposed to her wrinkles simply because she lived, in particular, too
close to the sea and therefore in too much proximity to the salt, which
was the sea's fault because, in her opinion, she'd been living there just
as long as the sea, maybe longer. Bugger the sea! Nor was it flash for
Fr. Ignatius to argue the toss about it. Facts were her game, and shiny-
beaconing them was her name!

TILLIE: YOU CAN SAY IT'S SIMPLE BUT IT'S NOT AS SIMPLE
AS THAT, MISTER SMARTY-PANTS COLLAR GUY-IDJIT!

STORYTELLER: As all of us not deaf heard.... 'You can say it's
simple but it's not as simple as that, Mister Smarty-pants collar guy-
idjit' in her own way of saying she, yes, lived too close to the sea for
salt's good and, by therefore being a cause of making the salt in the air
unhappy admitted to contributing to the local thereabouts salt causing
malicious dehydrations to dogs that, frankly, couldn't defend
themselves, not having a pot to pee in. And Fr. Ignatius could blame
her, okay, but she blamed the sea because she was no idjit and laid
down for no man. Or sea.

TILLIE: OR SEA!

STORYTELLER: Thank you. So, either she had to move further from
the sea or the sea had to move further from her. But there was no way
she was going to be forced out by the sea or by anybody else thinking
they were too big for her boots. Why should she? If Fr. Ignatius was
any sort of red-blooded Italiano over four-feet tall, he'd see why-
should-she?, too, stronzo? You try telling the Pope *that*.

TILLIE: YOU TRY TELLING THAT I-TITE THAT!

STORYTELLER: It was more than all that, even, as it always is with shiny beacons of one's bailiwick. Tillie had her wiring wired for the UV lamps beneath her bonnet's brim and it was only the all-inclusive guarantee in the UV manufacturer's own writing that protected her top three most important layers of skin in a cone of black light wherever she went, even if it looked purple which it wasn't.

(FR. IGNATIUS makes an attempt to escape but can't. For one thing, there are her dogs and, for another, she has a dog chain around his dog collar. There is another all-in, while...)

STORYTELLER: (above it all) She was trying to calmly explain, that... whatever 'that' was... was what she was trying to avoid. If she kept herself living too close to the sea, even if it annoyed the sea -- stiff cheddar! -- then no salt in the air could penetrate to within touch of her wrinkles, and therefore no air could be harmed and therefore no dog's tongue gone salted-smoked-black slack. And if Fr. Ignatius didn't believe that, she would just invite him to witness the number of ultraviolet zaps she got in from flying insects on any average night just by putting on and switching on her hat. Or he wasn't the man over four foot she thought he was.

TILLIE: THEN YOU'RE NO FOUR-FLUSHER FOR ME, FELLAH!

FR. IGNATIUS: YOU BE A-WILLING TO SWEAR-A THAT ON A BIBLE, CERTO?

STORYTELLER: A little bickering as you can see, but not to worry. You know what shiny beacons are like. And what did she mean by that anyway? She'd tell him what she meant... It meant those insects living just as close to the sea as she was weren't being dehydrated by the salt, given the healthy juicy sound of them being zapped, that's what. And that meant the salt had gone all unhealthy, if it couldn't even handle mozzies. And it would have been only half of what she could say to him but she didn't have time to be standing around pleasantly batting the sea breeze with him. There were the batteries you had to think of, remember, or wasn't he listening to a word she was saying?
(as she doubles over a throaty cough that the shadow players and the dogs duck from...)

170

And if he didn't think about salt in his lungs, she did about the salt in hers, fuggit. Yet she realised she was getting no younger, and maybe it hadn't been enough that she had built those high walls around her front yard to protect the masses of...

(Backdrop now shifts to her front garden behind its high wall. It looks, and mostly is, a junk yard of rusting white goods...)

STORYTELLER: ... junk refrigerators, washing machines and the blowhardy other rustables she had rescued from shelf-life corrodibles junked-out, in order to give the salt a bit of a playground so it didn't have to work so hard at rusting things up – a place where salt knew it was welcomed, could work uninterrupted on iron of its choice, without strain -- even a place where salt could come to put its feet up without feeling it had to go rusting every moment of the day. Without let or hindrance, like, she said.
(as she points to a hammock she has in the middle of the garden. On it... waiting... are a bottle of beer and a book)
Of, when it started to feel a bit jaded, the salt of that air would be able to sit back and contemplate its navel and gaze out upon the delectable bowls of yesterday's mashed potatoes she had strewn for it between all those tempting objects of rust she had brought in especially for its amusement. Of a retreat all gardeny, full of eye-candy for any salt of the air with lead in its pencil. Of a nice home away from home, away from all those greasy tidal encroachments from that hhffrukken sea.
(idyllic strains...)
Of a sanctuary for the very salt of the Machans air. Was that too much to ask?

TILLIE: (plaint) Is that too much to shitting ask?

FR. IGNATIUS: (won over) I doan't see why it shouldna be, si!

STORYTELLER: No, how could it be? Oh, it wasn't that she couldn't find her front door; among all that junk-fit-to-rust there, she couldn't find her house! That's how much of herself Tillie had given. But who would listen?
(dramatic music as TILLIE slumps in hopelessness....)
None! It was like her dogs... always biting the hand that fed them ... not even her petition to the Cairns Municipal Council to have that

171

blasted sea removed from the area, banished, frigged-off, at least made to turn back its ways, had any effect. Ears seaside shell shocked.

(The scene changes back to the beach proper by sight and sound. Now, TILLIE stands against the wind, heroically holding her hand up 'Stop', while all gather about her)

STORYTELLER: And if the truth be known, Fr. Ignatius was not thinking any longer that he might look something of an Italian priest out of water in that hat with the UV lamps and the St. Peter robe. He was starting even then to think shiny beacon-esque. He could see he was her last hope somehow, and… well… was humbled and excited by the prospect, wanting to give it its proper place on stage.
   (the Father directorially gauges her through finger-formed camera lens…)
There she was, a good Samaritan if ever there was a shiny beacon of a one, who had forked out for him and his new fishy pal at the bar, and her eyes were large and pathetic on him, watery all round, bringing almost tears to his own. He didn't know about the salt in the air, or that it was probably that which was making his eyes smart.
   (as she turns and pushes her face pleadingly up against his…)
He could see she was waiting for an answer. Strike his shiny beacon, on what? She suddenly seemed so desperate, so in need of his priestly blessing or besting. 'Please', she said to a someone-else for maybe the first time in her life. 'Think!', she said, even knowing how useless that was to ask any man for such a rounding-up.

TILLIE: Think! Try to get that noodle of yours above the 48-inch mark!

(now the dogs are mounting his legs and she is holding him by the shoulders, nose-to-nose as much as the hats allow…)

STORYTELLER: How desperate was this getting for poor Fr. Ignatius. A sailfish on the beach doing him over by not taking its turn to shout. And now amongst the mangroves getting the dog-pack hump, the dogs actually forming a queue. Yet despite all this something was happening to him! For some reason, he suddenly felt shiny with her. For some reason, he suddenly felt beacony with her.

172

FR. IGNATIOUS: I'a feel… I'a feel…

STORYTELLER: Yes, and yes! That shiny beacon feeling that comes only to you if you've ever been to Machans!

FR. IGNATIOUS: Wait… wait! Una momento!
(and finally)
Ho-kay!

TILLIE: (clap hands) ONWARD, CHRISTIAN SOLDIERS!

>*(Triumphantly, she leads the way off. The scene changes to being on the beach, proper. The sea is closer, sounds angry…)*

STORYTELLER: And, as the shaggy-dog stories of Machans South have it, our Tillie was able to shiny-beaconly take Fr. Ignatius Lombardi by the hand and lead him down the road apiece'n'apace, turned left past a whole block of half-sunken rotting garbage in a hole as large as, and barely distinguishable from, Cairns municipal swimming pool on bowel-voiding day, which was every day, and out onto the lower windswept reaches of Machans South beach thereabouts (you can follow the heritage signs these days) where the sea was exerting itself very shittily, and, for sure, knew it.

>*(They and the dogs arrive on the wind-swept beach; the wind at her frock and his Galilee robe; two stalwarts against the raw elements…)*

STORYTELLER: Oh, what a historical frieze was this! Only imagined in the tourist hand-sketched maps available at the Machans kiosk! Avoid the pasties; check the oven date. And there… for hers were never off!… did Tillie the Zap turn on the UV light on his hat while they waited.
(it seems all are holding their breath…)
And there, for a moment, they were as close as UV to UV, and none could go closer outside the UV spectrum. And as their UV night vision naturally kicked in (so broad was the daylight's wishy-washes running into the indigos!), Fr. Ignatius started to see what she meant; you…
(as the colours gloriously come about them…)

played light's kindly light on the salt in the air and the green sludge on the shoreline got greener and the sea's green got greener and the sky stretched itself lastic green promising greater greens. It was exceedingly pretty, and she, Tillie the Walking Lighthouse now, greenily... well, right then and there!... she drew a line in the sand at the highest point where the last lazed sludged sea-weedy lovely-green tide-sweep there had swept.

(She does so with great flourish and much dog-pack howling)

STORYTELLER: This, she pointed down to meaningfully and accordingly.

TILLIE: This, I am pointing down to meaningfully and accordingly, o Shorty!

STORYTELLER: And, yes... yes!... she was pointing to the green-green rotten sea itself, maybe to a green-green rotten sea anywhere, even. Tis said she was atrophying the planet's green-green horizon, she was scouting and courting green-greenly filled empty spaces; and she was going greenishly to all, and in the green-green state he was day-night-vision'd in, he was beginning to understand perfectly as she went green around the gill, going in command to him as she was and not unlike St. Peter Himself as Moses Himself would have been proud of had he been under four feet tall, going... oh, let her say it!:

TILLIE: BANISH THAT OCEAN; SAY GO HENCE TO THAT SEA, PUSHY TURD THAT IT IS!

STORYTELLER: She didn't even have to bother, either! For...
    (FR. IGNATIUS rolls his robe's sleeves up for the task...)
Fr. Ignatius needed no St. Peter inspiration now. He perfectly understood, was in tune. And he nodded *yes yes* or *si si* to her and he... *obeyed* and went banishing! He did! He launched himself on the banish! And, it is so written that, as he did, he bloody-well felt like banishing too! Me-the-Vatican-like.

(FR. IGNATIUS pushes her and the dogs back to a safety behind him and produces a King-Canute staff to confront the sea with...)

174

STORYTELLER: He had the UV night-vision hat for the job, a real green of a greenie in daylight. He had the will to do it, a bluey. Fr. Ignatius didn't care if he hadn't heard of the failing health of the salt of the air coming into too close contact with human wrinkles and he hadn't heard how salt in the air dehydrated dogs especially on the upper side of the tongue and he hadn't heard how the salt of the air was wearing itself out trying to keep up with all that rust by having to live in such proximity to the three most important skin layers of human beings... but, by all that is Vatican, he could see it all now.
(sails on:)
Tillie, the shiny beacon, was dead right! The sea *was* too close. The sea was the culprit! And now-as-then, with her line in the sand, Fr. Ignatius knew exactly what to do.

FR. IGNATIUS: PISS-A OFF, YOUS!

STORYTELLER: ...he heroically cried out to the sea and the sky and all the salt therein, putting as much King Canute into it as he could, given it was more likely to be King Canute than Moses or St. Peter even, all men not of short stature being alike so it's often said.
(as FR. IGNATIUS shakes his fist at the sea...)
Whence he scalded the sea for its harmful encroachment on Tillie's enclosure and he quite frankly commanded the sea to ne'er more cross the line in the sand she had drawn. Ever again. Mate.

FR. IGNATIUS: BEGONE FROM ALL THIS DOING HARM! IT'S REAL GROSS!

STORYTELLER: And that in plain-spoken English, too! Vatican education. And, during all this? Well, wasn't only Tillie already running up'n'down the line she had drawn in the sand and on her land side of it, waving her old arms and going 'fugorf, fugorf', so it goes, before she suddenly stopped and watched, arms and legs akimbo, that beacon of a chin jutting out, did Tillie the Zap.
(pause as all wait while she does nothing...)
For ten minutes she waited, an eternity compared to how she slept at night plus a full ten minutes when she looked like she wasn't going to wait any more. But, still...
(as all slowly unwind from the frieze...)

175

... not one more ripple of that sea, not one greedy outreach of any of insinuating finger of foam, not a lick of windswept spray dared approach let alone put any part of any toe over that line of hers under the salt in the air swirling there!

(and)

You had to see it to believe it! Oh, maybe the sea might again someday. But not that day, and not even up to this day. No! Not with salt's UV hats on. Not with a whole host of stray dogs sleeping on the shore without further dehydrations to their rosy-pink tongues. Not while rust could only hang in the air or while salt, invigorated, welcomed people, all sorts of people, any age of people however wrinkled, even from Cairns proper on a day trip!

(while celebrations of cheering, high-fives etc begin behind...)

Not while Tillie stayed with her toes dug in.

(and)

The sea had moved over. The sea had moved further out to sea! What a shiny there was! What a beacon became! What two shiny beacons got a begorrah!

(TILLIE and FR. IGNATIUS show how their monumental deed has made them exhausted. Even the STORYTELLER grows sombre for the finale:)

STORYTELLER: And so did Tillie, finally, to that sea, managed a croak, a cri de cur for her starving curs and the starved salt of the air above them.

TILLIE: (weak in croak) See, that didn't hurt a bit. All you short-bums.

STORYTELLER: She being too much a lady to add so-there-buster or yasucks-to-you-rotten-sea-shitface, but that didn't matter. She had spoken for her salt in the air; she had spoken for her dogs on the drool; she had spoken for herself. All was bright beneath her bonnet and, now, all was bright under Fr. Ignatius's bonnet, totally unrehearsed as I am here.

(to a new dawn rising behind)

Therefore, more than the woolly widow of the black UV lights; more than the lady of the three layers of topmost wrinkles which harmed the salt of the air just because she lived too near to it; more than the crazy

176

old duck with the mangy mutts; more than the famous inventor of potted mashed potatoes for the suburban garden which beg to be remembered for their salty tangs; more than her being known as the Machans South's own glow worm at night… Tillie became the lady who had the last word with the sea which included a rounded-off word or two with a man over four-feet tall and better off than her beloved strays because he at least had a dog collar around his neck a bit garlicly.

(and)

Tillie. The lady who had given the salt of the air a little more room to breathe.

> *(With closing rousing cheers and fire crackers, the shadow area 'cuts off' to darkness. There is not a murmur, a movement suddenly. The STORYTELLER bows and moves slowly off. But, just before he departs, he pops head back in, like someone who might never go away)*

STORYTELLER: Mind you, pretty persistent rumour has it that our Tillie did have the second thought it might have all been a bit easier if she had covered up her wrinkles from the word go – at least the top three important layers of them. Well, tis said, she thought it was too late for that now and, anyway, more healthy salt equalled less UV lamp equals a good saving on batteries that people of Machans South has become notorious for.

(stops another 'last' time from going off)

Oh, that salt is still there, but let's not kid ourselves it's the same salt as before. In point of fact, there is no better place on earth to take the salt in the air than at the sea side of Machans South. You set your watch by the salt air there; it's so abundant and rosy-cheeked and friendly that it comes to you without you even having to cover your wrinkles. You just look at the ever-growing number of tail-wagging strays taking up residence there. Not a blackened tongue between them, and don't they wag!

(and)

And, incidentally, a wind came from out of Africa and blew Fr. Ignatius's UV hat off. The dogs got it and carried it away. It is said to light up the mangrove nooks and crannies at night to this day, especially during high-old tides of the Passion and Nativity weeks, when everybody's off cheering St. Peter being able to walk, rather than surf, ashore – and then to lead the curtain calls as the star billing with his little Aussie mate, the sailfish.

(He bows off, but just falls short of actually leaving:)

STORYTELLER: Thought I was gone, didn't you?
   (and)
The next Sunday, in our St Joseph's of Machans Beach, there was noticeable movement of the communion-minded towards the beach bar which St. Peter himself had ordained the man's-renewal Eucharist should properly be guzzled, not churchified. Since this included women and children, after All Hallows Sunday, back in church, there came to be precious few left to stand in the aisle waiting for wafers. Not without liquified burbs, there wasn't.

(To everyone's relief, he finally leaves)

---000---

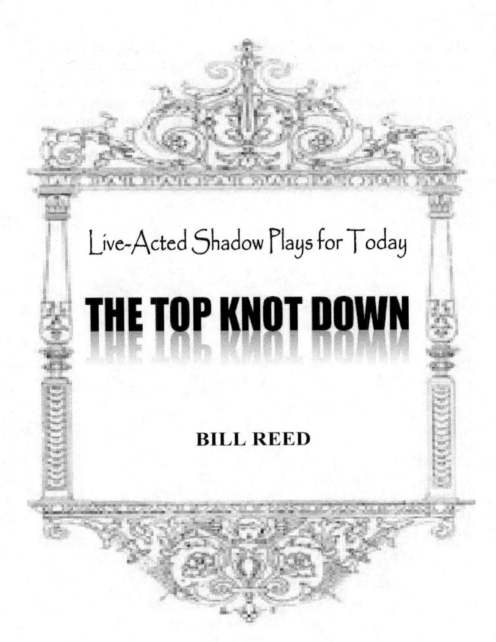

Live-Acted Shadow Plays for Today

THE TOP KNOT DOWN

BILL REED

The behind-the-screen shadow action – or 'inner background' play --
can only ever keep 'pace' with the reading, not *keep up* with it.
Because of the resultant and necessary shadow-play distillation of the
storyteller's tale, the extensive stage directions given in this script are
only intended to be indicators as to what *might* be used for the shadow-
play side of things. They deliberately go beyond what the director
would employ and are given merely as a range of possible shadow-
actions he or she might want to use in the 'distillation'.

The Characters

STORYTELLER
Minstrel-type. By opening reading from a script, he narrates the
proceedings from front stage, audience side of the scrim. It is even
preferable if he is *not* fully rehearsed, but rather reads 'naturally'.

THE TOP KNOT DOWN
or the fluffy'n'soft top knot in its most innocent wise state... not
knowing, just wants to know. A tiny bird-like shadow and/or equally
tiny human (by back lighting effect) with wings. It is Innocence
personified. It is only asking, '*Where?*'. (Could have its own (2ND)
STORYTELLER, if desired.)

SHADOW PLAYERS:
numbering, perhaps, 4 or so, presenting the parts the 'filth of a man',
the African Warrior, the boy in the dyke, the Indian monk and the
Chinese monk, the Red Indian brave, the wise men, the polar bears, the
Australian bushie, the Tribal Woman, and a host of shadowy shapes,
etc.

The Top Knot Down

·

*(The STORYTELLER is sitting with his manuscript in plain view
at first and then is dimmed to get necessary dramatic effect as the
back lighting behind the scrim is heightened. He might even play
impishly with a torch underneath his chin, so as to indicate that,
as a character, he is up for any competition to gain the
audience's attention.*

*On the up of the lighting, the STORYTELLER commences, even
by beginning with shouting and waving his script in order to gain
that attention...)*

STORYTELLER: She was so tiny, so lovely. Our little Veena, of
course. For those of you who don't know her, you'll hear her name
from time to time. Maybe in the very air about you as you go about
your lives. You don't have to 'know' her when it all boils down. You
only have to think 'Little Veena' whenever you hear words *innocence*
and the like coming into play.
  (waves script)
I'll be reading from this, folks, so none of us need to be of two minds.
It's fortunate that I'm *really* a lousy reader, because the list of
characters here lists that I need not be a good one. So…
  (starts into reading)
Little Veena was so tiny. She was so sweet. She was such a little
chirp. She was a cluck. She was all a-twitter, a tweet, a bok-bok-bok.
First came the wings, it seems, then came the angelic of her. The beat
of wings had it in flight in her.
  (and)
If I am describing Innocence, I am describing Innocence. Why not? If
it's there before us, why shouldn't we?
                              (and)
So, firstly, we should say where she came from. But surely, it's
enough to equate that rope which bound her tiny little ankle to her
father with the snare of snuggle, the snare of kindness, saving her from
when the roof of the family home would open and the Bad Thing… that
Beast as we know it, and she will come to… with the great black wings
would swoop down to carrion her off, would swallow her up. Like all

182

children, especially perpetually as little Veena was, did she believe. And, who knows?, perhaps believing that brought some scars into her dear little heart otherwise showing so much of love. Oh, yes. But never enough to slow how the beat of wings had that innocence in flight in her.

(As the shadow of her grows 'in flight', the first fledgling attempts...)

STORYTELLER: Yes and yes, the light breezes rifling amongst her feather finery coming and, see, her top knot, still fluffy down still. That top knot down. So now you know.

(On the top of her head, the top knot down does its own fledgling attempts to fly on top of her own attempts. It nearly does; but with a flutter and a flap or two falls back flop onto her again)

STORYTELLER: Little Veena's dear little ties to her father wasn't to say she didn't have her own keening, her own hawking. After all, even tethered by love to him, she could see out through the holes in the roof, out into the open skies, despite being warned about how the Bad Thing... the Beast... with the great black wings keened out there for her.
  (as huge dark wings come to temporarily darken over all)
Even as she flustered and fluttered, we think we know our little Veena knew then the roof had to lift one day, the freedom a-part.

(Slowly, the coverage of the menacing wings lifts, so that the following can be enacted:)

STORYTELLER: Ah, the light again. Aren't we all naïve enough to think the Beast's wings will eventually lift? As of course out little chirp, our little tweet, our little Veena did... and when it did, bok-bok-bok... at least for that moment-as-then, bok-bok-bok... she found herself old enough and she herself to herself became as clear as an eagle's eye on a striking's day: that she had to, yes, grow upwards and upwards and upwards despite how her little heart was beating and out, out, out up through the roof... oh, yes. And she did, did our little Veena, finally really opening her wings, *out*, so easy once simply thought through.

(VEENA's shadow takes joyous flight. She keens away; it is the keening of the Outback.

The STORYTELLER stands in sympathetic joy of release. His voice rises and falls with her)

THE STORYTELLER: Unperched! Free! Oh, swish that and the swoosh! And you don't need in your heart to ever land, where the dark thoughts, where the loss, you-can, of the innocence, you-can? Where can it be possible for there to be no space beneath your feet? Where is there *not* the pointy end, the pointy end, of all thinking? Oh, spread those wings, little Veena, little Veena bok-bok-bok! Oh, yes and yes, the oh! of a chirp, a cluck, a tweet, a bok-bok-bok, yes!

(It all quietens down, but with good feeling. The STORYTELLER returns to his seat, back on track and saddening for knowing what is coming)

STORYTELLER: (almost a mutter) How can there be no space beneath your feet or the pointy end of thinking…?
   (recovers)
But never mind that for now. And so, you see…
   (resumes reading directly)
our little Veena, she flew away into the great wide world to seek her own fortune, as any wingtip flies in the face of Providence for a little bit of a smile, a giggle, a pat on the top of the head or, you know, top knot down wherein, don't you know, lies all wisdom within you. Look how proudly the birds of the air carry them.
   (and)
And outside of the restaurant where her two brothers worked, she perched high and happily and she watch over all going in chime, feeling so good as her tiny wings spread and with so much to think about. Going, 'Oh!' with thrill'n'wonder…

VEENA: (joyfully, keening to all horizons) Oh!

STORYTELLER: And oh, it was, still, an 'oh!' of a chirp, a cluck, a tweet, a bok-bok-bok, yes.
   (and)

If you must know, she alighted on *my* head. She did. Truly. Who was to know? Well, I'll tell you now. How a blessing can pick you out!

(At which he surprisingly puts down script, suddenly mourns:)

STORYTELLER: I say that but it's more likely I just happened to be there; we all know that. She was a little bird, like. A little tweet. A cluck, cluck, cluck. A nibble at your ear. She was our little Veena. Our bok-bok-bok.

(And while the ominous wings come again and start shadowing over all, even the lighting on him:)

STORYTELLER: Was it ever up to me to tell the dear little thing you can always have the space beneath your feet and you can always hold onto the pointy end of thinking, but comes the spike and comes what comes to spit-roast you. You see. Don't you see…? It might sound jejune, out of around-a-campfire, but it's still the Beast whichever way it looks at you. If you want to call it the Bad Thing, that's up to you.

(Blackout)

2.

(When the lighting comes back, now VEENA shadow player is as small as a bird, although not so small, perhaps, that the audience cannot see how she is shaking with fear. She is perched high on a rafter, but there is again a rope around her ankle)

STORYTELLER: (with anguish) What else is there but to skip straight to it? Does it matter how it happened, how the Beast of it all came, as it always would, to spike the little dear, to spit-roast the little darling? Our little Veena. And oh, if you could close your eyes to open them to it, you could see how our little Veena knew she could not escape from this gross old cruel man for long.

(As a shadow player comes up and whistles and beckons her 'down', at the other end of the rope around her ankle, and acting to all this grotesquely and even priapically while she flutters, is overwhelmed, is consumed:)

185

STORYTELLER: As this thing… this human being we all could recognise in a shame on us and a shape of us…he whistled and whispered drooling to her, the top of his head openly blowing penis-shaped spumes, his legs grotesquely bandy, as pricked with hair as hers showed now, stripped, prickly with spikey down, his feet looking huge and cloven and clomped to the crude earth, hers clipped and clucking but still hanging down to within the reach of his violations. His manhood monstrous. She didn't want to look. Such a pitiful thing, this, oh!

(now, more than quaking with fear she is desperately trying to escape…)

She called across all the scapes of all our lands as high as she dared and heard her herself cry thwistle, thwistle for the far and long horizon that was ages gone and ages in coming. Our little
Veena, hunching in quiver, dizzy, giddy, swirling not high enough and not a feather dry. Where the sun? Where the snuggle? Where our cupped hand, our two held-together palms? He has the rope; this some old brute, this Beast, this Bad Thing, this swinging filth, who is tightening the rope around her little ankle.

(looking up to audience painfully)

Does she see out of his wall of window the marshlands, the plains and valleys she flew upwards to see or over beyond the sea, the great Coral Sea, the slowly tiding grounds of seas? Can she see the sky which bleeds into all? Oh.

(He waits while the skyline'd lighting dims emotionally on the horizon and as it does so while VEENA shadow player 'goes under':)

STORYTELLER: Who can resist this? Whose tiny little feet can grow upwards away from this? Where the space beneath them away from the gross? *Where the pointy end of any thinking?*

(And, inevitably, the rope wins and VEENA is pulled down to the shadow player, growing to be a full-sized sexual object as her shadow does so. The man's shadow looms over her and over them comes the Beast's wings to cover it all up.

In the behind-the-scrim blackout which follows that, there comes

186

disconcerting sounds that sound like slatherings.

In the face of this, the STORYTELLER grows hardened. He pushes himself to revert to the page, reads in bitter monotone:)

STORYTELLER: Her little feet, she saw, couldn't, no, grow upwards out of any way. Her little eyes couldn't, no, see anything but was not this filth's vision. It has here that his pole rose and rose in slow, in indelible, motion and it spiked, yes, her, yes, and it could have been right through her, and had, and the last thing little Veena saw was there couldn't have been a perch high enough, after all. At any time. After all.
   (sotto voce)
And yet, still, from this thing, this It, what a moan, what a mourn off as if afar on some black slurping shore! And yes, of course she was like moss clinging to a rock and soon, soon, did she like moss rubbed to raw and start to lose all the moisture that moss must moss do. And she dried out. And she started to crack. And then to powder, and then little Veena simply burst apart into friction flakes that, petering, fell. The stiff of legend.
   (shouts angrily)
That is no joke! It shouldn't be any joke!
   (and)
Oh, listen if you can't shut your ears. This is once pure-white. This chirp. This tweet. This bok-bok-bok.

(The behind-the-scrim lighting comes back on enough to see the crushing, the overwhelming beating of great wings and:)

SHADOW PLAYER: Oof oof oof oof oof.
                       Oof oof oof oof oof.
                       Oof oof oof oof oof.

STORYTELLER: (despair above it all) Rising. All that was and is against her. Already rising from the bottom of his brute's being, this Beast's being, this Bad Thing's being… vibrating against the top of that foul head. By the time his lid was about to come off at the top… this isn't funny!… his brains were fried and he was pumped up to at least twice his normal filthy size and his eyes were tumbling firmaments. And he was going:

SHADOW PLAYER: Oof oof oof oof oof
                Oof oof oof oof oof
                Oof oof oof oof oof!

(In the behind-the-scrim area, all chaotic sound and movement breaks loose)

STORYTELLER: I read!
  (and does so shoutingly:)
By the time his lid did come off, the brute, the filth, had hit the roof, turned cartwheels and fairy wheels and fiery whorls, hung between heaven and earth for a moment while the weather of the world stopped once, stopped twice, might never start again for the huge whole in the ether his gigantic egress had wrought, before it flung him like a thing of no stuffing back to the ground he would never walk on again. And where the dear little thing's, our little Veena's, flakes were. Only flakes. Such a dear little thing gone. …Where, in such a killing pretty pass, our little thing could no longer look for where the space between her feet was or where the pointy end of any higher-above thinking was.

(The chaos suddenly ceases to silence. There are no shadows of anything on the screen. The STORYTELLER is just about spent.

Finally:)

STORYTELLER: It was the biggest erection, eruption and death by eructation that cruelty had ever seen or sheer evil could ever innocence dim down. And, no, that is no joke and, no, nor should it be. And, oh, look what dear little thing it had taken in It's claws and pumped into smithereens.

(Blackout)

3.
(From a grey'd shadow area, some brightness comes as:)

STORYTELLER: It's okay. It's alright now.
  (back on even keel)
A chirp, a cluck, a tweet, a bok-bok-bok, yes.

(Now the shadow of the funny-looking top knot down comes 'swimming' into view. It is represented by flitting cox-comb object that has a shadow player echoing its movement from the ground)

STORYTELLER: Oh, there was a survivor of survivors. For the first thing, what survived of our little Veena was the dear little thing's wonder about where the space beneath her feet had gone and her wonder about where the pointy end of any thinking higher above all this was.

(and nodding to the shadow pointing of both)
But mainly there survived her learned top knot down. Yes, that tuft, and choughed-off funny looking thing that grew from the top of her dear head, of all just-beginning and innocent hair in the world. That could, for her, cry for shame, oh shame, cry for pity, cry for what should never have happened to innocence, how come, how come, how come? It could cry for her.

(and)
That which, now, under our little Veena's wonder-where?, couldn't be put off, and wouldn't. It was down... just growing... but learned, learned, oh.

TOP KNOT DOWN: O heavens! O shikes!

STORYTELLER: Exactly. 'O heavens, o shikes!' How it can speak! How it can natter!

TOP KNOT DOWN: (booming) Where the purity of spirit?

THE STORYTELLER: 'Where the purity of spirit?', it went and goes. And it had more...

TOP KNOT DOWN: Where the space between the feet and the harshness of the ground?

STORYTELLER: (outcry with it) 'Where the space between the feet and the harshness of the ground?' How it can speak, yes! How it can natter! And more, much more!

TOP KNOT DOWN: Where the pointy end of any thinking higher-above?

STORYTELLER: Did we all hear that? 'Where the pointy end of any thinking higher-above?' How it could speak and how it could natter, oh boy! How it could whistle as it keened! More, even more!

TOP KNOT DOWN: Where's the why for Innocence for-pity's sake?

STORYTELLER: (winding down) 'Where's the why for Innocence for-pity's sake?'

> *(A shadow player 'shadowing' the top knot down from the ground has now gotten a drum and is beating it furiously marching up and down behind the screen until he suddenly drops to his knee hopelessly. Another, with a whip, is lashing out at one and all. There is another wandering around gnashing his teeth.*

> *A silence.*

> *The STORYTELLER regains his place in the script again)*

STORYTELLER: And at that moment in this then-as-now time, dear watchers all, did the learned top knot down begin its legendary flights and begin its plights and start its heartrending pppffflights to find answers for her from all the *piteous-doing* things of the world it might find.
   (to the re-enactments that the top knot now does...)
. Did flit as flurtishly as a feather. Did fly out from the ruins of that monster brutish filth of a man, if a man, and out into the open skies. Did flutter like butterfly along the lengths and breadths and all the world's breadths and lengths it might need to for to find out where the space beneath the feet, where the pointy end of all thinking higher-above.
   (the top knot down is now hawking high, high...)
And in a twinkle, in a tinkle, in a tweet a chirp a cluck a bok-bok-bok, the top knot down had taken off. Oh, and wasn't it for all the world! Flit! Fly! Ask! Oh, Christ, you'd be lucky!

(Blackout)

4.

(The only thing moving in the shadow area is the winging shadow of the TOP KNOT DOWN lazily swinging, it seems, on a breeze, back and forwards as if it was being swung in a cradle)

STORYTELLER: I mentioned the little learned top knot down... I've been thinking it should perhaps be the top knot *down'd*, like *hair'd* or *fluff'd*... anyway, I did say it did land, when it finally landed, on *my* head. I guess you figured it was just something like wishful thinking on my part. But, why not? A chirp, a tweet, a bok-bok-bok why not me?

(He positions himself at the edge of the scrim, from where he conducts the swaying of the little top knot.

One by one, the shadow players and the necessary props come into the shadow-acting area and take up their positions to enact and to re-enact the African section of the TOP KNOT DOWN's quest, as outlined in the following narrative.

As they do so, the STORYTELLER plays his part by erecting a music-hall upcoming-scene easel on which is a sign reading:
'OUT OF AFRICA'
a theme that is echoed behind the scrim of the first part of his reading accompanied by African shapes and sounds:)

STORYTELLER: And so, as I go on, it was on the wind as the great dusts rose that the learned top knot down came across an African who represented all of Africa and it asked him where it might find space beneath the feet and the harshness of the ground, where the purity of spirit, where the pointy end of any thinking higher-above? Where the Innocence?

(The AFRICAN WARRIOR comes to stand proudly in full view on one side of the scrim, overlooking his domain and waits, listens:)

STORYTELLER: The man was tall and long and had great golden wise-looking rings in his nose and ear and around his neck and he

191

looked like he had the wisdom of all history the learned top knot down was seeking. He of all Africa stood on one leg with a shield and spear covering the whorls to his skin and said in his opinion the top knot down should go to a village by following the blood streams and watch the nuns of many religions working unprotected trying to help the people there after a massacre of machetes and knives.

AFRICAN WARRIOR: (fit to be heard) Go see the nuns, man.

(then waves the STORYTELLER away to return to shadow area where he takes part in the enactment:)

STORYTELLER: And the learned top knot down did. On the wind, yes it did. It went to see the nuns who might tell him about how it was above it all. But the top knot down found the nuns dead too. They had no feet left that they could keep up off the ground so they might keep away from being able to dig into the ground like innocence. And they had no heads to tell him where the pointy end of any higher-above thinking was. And the learned top knot down could see, could know, they hadn't even been able to help one child, one woman, one man before the killers came back with their machetes.

(On a frieze of that, the shadow play area goes into blackout)

STORYTELLER: If that wasn't an answer to where the space beneath the feet, where the purity of spirit, where the pointy end of any thinking higher-above... well, what else was? Well, the top knot down had the logic to know something must be. So, the learned top knot down had to search on, and did, yes, catch the next wind out of Africa.

(Barely stopping, the STORYTELLER changes the upcoming-scene sign for the next one reading:
'EUROPE WHAT'S NEW?'

Behind the curtain, the shadow players 'change' over to Europe visuals and play out the TOP KNOT DOWN's European quest:)

STORYTELLER: After Africa in massacre, the learned top knot down caught, yes, a passing wind and passed wind further to the north to the land they call Europe, to centuries of culture and science and much talk of the dignity of Mankind, where it met a Belgian man-child…

(comes, shadowed, the boy in the dyke while…)

who had his French finger in a German-made hole in a Dutch dyke keeping the English out. He had a red cross tattooed on one arm and a blue crescent cut in on the other and was shaded by a Turkish flag while sitting there contemplating his Irish navel. When the top knot down asked him if he could help he said well he'd just finished Dante's *Inferno* and Chaucer's *The Canterbury Tales* and knew that the people he represented -- which was all the people of Europe -- had saline tablets that could stop Mankind from getting the runs and therefore settle down. If it had saline tablets like that, Europe must have the answers to where the space beneath the feet; there the pointy end of all the thinking higher-above; where the purity of spirit; how come the rape of all innocence?

(The boy-in-the-dyke shadow player extracts his finger out of the dyke with great difficulty and, nearly too late, pushes past her to emerge fully front-of-the-screen for:)

BOY IN THE DYKE: Can't be fairer than that, the whole of Europe and England can't. Whatcha want, little whack?

STORYTELLER: So the learned top knot down asked him to point the way to where there was clear daylight beneath feet and a purity of spirit with the knowledge of the evil infamy against all innocence, and where the pointy end of any or all the thinking higher-above…

BOY IN THE DYKE: Eh?

STORYTELLER: Well, the fellow holding the tides back on all Europe answered he could rock-solid, yeah, send the question to Brussels in triplicate. As to the whatnot pointy end of spirit, he pointed the way to the Vatican and said, going:

BOY IN THE DYKE: Go there. They got the pointy bits, orright. You give a thought, they stick 'em right into you, them pointy bits, they do.

193

STORYTELLER: But the learned top knot down didn't bother to go to the Vatican. It was looking for answers, not for laughs. Instead, it learnedly decided it was probably just as good to stay by the man-child who represented all of Europe with his finger in the dyke there. It asked the monsieur, the herr, the signor, the mister, the uram, the senhor, why was he was sitting there with his finger in a sea wall. Was there any pointy end of the thinking in that? Was there an answer to the utter defilement of all the innocence Mankind was keeping secret? Was there the space beneath the feet from coming in contact with the harshness of reality in having the tip of your forefinger sea-dipping?

BOY IN THE DYKE: Betcha, yeah! To keep out them immigrant people smugglers goin' the sex trades, old whack.

STORYTELLER: But, the learned top knot down said, you're holding back the North Sea and wasn't all the refugee people coming from the south, from Iran and Afghanistan and the Horn of Africa and the Gulf of Yemen region and places like that in boats that needed his finger in holes there?

BOY IN THE DYKE: You tryin' to toss the toss? I'm only the boy with the finger in the dyke, mate. I only asked them what's a dyke when it's home and they said stick your finger in here n' find out. That way I got learning and didn't have to worry about inter-lectur-ally havin' to split the croaker of any more teachers, that's what that was. This's only practice anyway for when I'm on the football terraces n' have to stick my finger in some woggy's eye, and keep it there until they blow him to pieces before he blows us to pieces, the chump. Talk about piss-weak. You ask me 'bout that and you'll 'ave the straight-up too right.

(He returns to the shadow area, where the remnants of the TOP KNOT DOWN's European quest fade)

STORYTELLER: So the learned top knot down decided to move on from Europe too in order to not give up on its quest of where the space beneath the feet, where that-there purity of spirit, where the pointy end of any thinking higher-above might be. What the utter defilement of all Innocence. And, learnedly, oh learnedly, it took to the wind again. It did.

(The STORYTELLER replaces the Europe sign with one saying: **'SANDY HOOK, USA'** *while the shadow players turn their movements to the TOP KNOT DOWN's North-American quest with, at least initially, a lot of native American feathers and dancing to traditional beats – at least at first...)*

STORYTELLER: Soon the learned top knot down had drifted over the prairies of the Americas where the buffalo still roamed, or so the penny dreadful he was reading said, and the painted Indian brave in war paint still sat on his painted horse and shielded his eyes as probably the coming-last bald eagle keened away so high.

(The INDIAN-BRAVE shadow player comes to a prominent shadow position, sitting scanning the horizon on a shaky horse and making many 'how?' gestures etc, while:)

STORYTELLER: The top knot down approached this Indian brave... this one man who might be the last of his people... this man who seemed to it good enough anyway to represent all the peoples of both Americas and it asked him if he knew where any purity of spirit and where hopefully the thinking space beneath the feet could be found there, the pointy ends of the thinkings higher-above preferably please, and so forth. The Indian brave told it he could introduce the learned top knot down to a classroom of pre-schoolers who represented all of the peoples of both Americas better than anyone ever could and would have the answers better than anyone in both Americas because the future was theirs.

(images of a school and the American flag ominously tempered by sounds of battle over, while...)

And he had the right to say so because hadn't he just come back from fighting a war that made the world a better place full of bombing the hell out of it? Add on, he said, where all the buffalo have gone, and he'd personally show the learned top know down how to find the children. It would, said the learned top knot down.

(and while the sights'n'sounds of Route 66 come and go:)

So, if the learned top knot down would like to follow him high above a lone star, guided by his rhinestones along Route 66 with real southern Texan on the radio, he was going there himself, to that preschool where the future's children were. And the learned top knot down did. It followed the American brave, but a little behind, probably enjoying the true southern-Texan music on MPR radio a little too much. And soon the learned top knot down arrived just after the American brave took out his assault rifle and Glock automatic pistols and locked the school's main door behind him in the face of the learned top knot down.

(The shadow area blinks to black and then back again. When the enactment comes back on, the great wings of evil have returned to hang over all. The STORYTELLER quickly covers the sign up, doesn't know what to do with himself)

STORYTELLER: The learned top knot down listened to the gunfire and the dollish four-year-olds laying their dear heads down, then he turned and left past the sign going Sandy Hook School, Newtown, Connecticut. Oh. If that wasn't an answer to the possible uselessness of its quest of where the space beneath the feet to avoid any of this earth-bound such-like, where the purity of spirit, where the pointy end of any thinking higher-above… well, what was? What was worth bothering with the use of thinking or where the pointy end? How could he ask now why the rape of all innocence? Oh. And, yes, oh. So, the learned top knot down looked to the wind again, as it did.

(Brighter, more friendly lighting and setting slowly returns to the shadow area. Not without a good deal of relief, the STORYTELLER replaces the Europe sign with one saying:
'ASIA OR AS IS'

Behind him comes the conch shells and evocations of Nepal. In particular two shadow players don Buddhist's travelling robes and with wanderer's staves, while the other shadow players turn their movements and their silhouettes to the TOP KNOT DOWN's Indian and Chinese quests…)

STORYTELLER: As far away as it could get from Sandy Hook Newtown Connecticut, the learned top knot down, in the mid-reaches of the Himalayas, met a blind Chinese monk leading and being led by a blind Indian wise man. And the learned top knot down said to them it was finding it difficult to find anywhere where there was purity of spirits and enough space beneath feet for right thinking higher-above, and they nodded wisely; they nodded sagely; they nodded sadly.

(The shadow players, two in particular, reflect this with such over-formality that the shadow of the learned top knot down has to interject itself between them)

STORYTELLER: The wandering monks stopped to rest and told him they were blind and could see all things; that is why they represented all the people of both India and China combined, almost half the world. They could not only see the future but had the accumulated wisdom of India and China; knowing the past and understanding the present that pass beneath Man's feet as they pass over Man's head, Man being nothing more than the in-between of a baloney sandwich. Would that do? Yes, it would, answered the learned top knot down.

(The MONK shadow players congratulate themselves on their answer, jangle tiny bells, turn prayer wheels, nod to the conches...)

STORYTELLER: So they told the learned top knot down that if it wanted to see where the purity of spirit of that accumulated wisdom of half of the whole of Mankind was, then it should go and catch a certain public bus in New Delhi and it should then go and catch the equivalent public bus in Beijing and see for itself. They gave the learned top knot down the buses' numbers and the times they were passing by any spot it was likely to be, and where, because they were wise men who couldn't see but had their fingers on half of all the world's bus timetables, no two doubts about it. The learned top knot did so, just as they said, and went there... there being, first, India.

(Now distinctly Indian-themed shadow playing the New Delhi enactment of:)

STORYTELLER: In New Delhi, the learned top knot down arrived just in time to catch the certain bus to see a young Indian woman starting to get raped in plain view of the many other passengers by six fume-drunken louts in full view too then beaten mercilessly with a length of piping for being a harlot with her short skirt before being thrown off the bus to die by the wayside of a popular middle-class suburb. Where she

197

was run over many times before anyone had the inclination to stop and see what was making all the skid marks on the road, followed by a riot shouting that traffic snags like that were making it impossible to drive home in New Delhi these days and the people of India were sick of it.

INDIAN RIOT CHORUS: Stop the rot of traffic blocks! Stop the traffic stops! What are we sick of? Whatever, we're sick of it now!

(These are instantly replaced by Chinese shadow playing to re-enact the Beijing scenes of:)

STORYTELLER: So the learned top knot down quickly hopped on a strong breeze out of New Delhi and followed the monks' advice to Beijing. There the learned top knot down caught the equivalent bus they said to and was just in time to see a young Chinese woman raped by six drunken louts in full view of many other passengers and then beaten mercilessly for being a slut and letting them do that, and then thrown off to die by the wayside of a popular middle-class suburb. Where she too was run over many times before anyone had the inclination to stop to get out to see what was making such a holy mess on the road causing a lot of disturbance with skidding noises. The resulting Chinese riots of an outraged driving public about exorbitant cost of stopping'n'starting to look at victims let alone the moral imperative of having to struggle with whether to help the victim, what with the scandalous price of fuel today when they were only trying to get home from work without being held up by some drunken louts on a bus.

CHINESE RIOT CHORUS: Yeah, and all of the above. Price of petrol, price of petrol! What do we want? Whatever, we want it now!

(the shadow area now morphs back into the Himalayan site once more, with even louder Buddhist bells and wild wind whistles:)

STORYTELLER: So what could the learned top knot down do but quickly leave Bejing? On the wind as we go, the learned top knot down returned to the Himalayas, to the two blind monks, and said to the blind Indian monk it did not understand and it said to the blind Chinese monk it did not understand. The two blind monks nodded sagely and they nodded wisely and they nodded sagely and they said:

198

(The two monk shadow players storm out from behind the curtain – one of one side of the stage; the other on the other side – and pontificate advice back to the shadow of the TOP KNOT DOWN behind the scrim:)

INDIAN MONK: Join the club.

CHINESE MONK: Join the club.

INDIAN MONK: Join *his* club!

CHINESE MONK: No, join *his* club!

INDIAN MONK: (re the other monk) He's as blind as a bat and you're asking *him*?! I don't even know where he's leading!

CHINESE MONK: He's as blind as a bat and you're asking *him*?! I don't even know where he's leading!

(They wait but the TOP KNOT DOWN only flutters, like eyelashes, behind the screen)

CHINESE MONK: What's it doing?

INDIAN MONK: Certainly ask what it's doing!

BOTH TOGETHER: (to each other) What can you do? They're all as blind as bats!

CHINESE MONK: Couldn't see their arse from their orifices!

INDIAN MONK: Couldn't see their arses from their oracles!

(They do three times around the STORYTELLER, then retreat to the clashing of cymbals and drums a la their respective temples)

STORYTELLER: But they did at least leave the learned top knot down with a glimpse of the future of more than half of Mankind which, on the surface of it, looked even worse than the other half. And with the glimpses still left to it from the New Delhi visit, it saw the same young Indian girl, now three years older but at least alive, on the equivalent certain bus, holding a take-away paper bag with a nice termination-clinic logo on its side in full colour. In it was the remains of a little she which she was taking home to show her husband she wasn't cheating and trying to sneak in delivering a little girl instead of a proper little boy she only had the right to do. She was very sore from the tearing-out.

(The Indian shadow player lifts the top of a rubbish bin, drops the paper bag into it, closes it. And is interchanged with:)

STORYTELLER: And with the glimpse into the future still left to it from it Beijing visit, the learned top knot down saw the same young Chinese girl, now three years older and thankfully still alive, on the same certain bus holding a take-away paper bag with a nice termination-clinic logo on its side in full colour too. In it was the remains of a little she which she was taking home to show her husband she wasn't cheating and sneaking in trying to deliver a little she rather than a proper little he she only had the right to do. She was very sore from the tearing-out.

(The Chinese shadow player lifts the top from a rubbish bin, drops the paper bag into it, closes it, then making way for the shadow enactment over Tibet again for:)

STORYTELLER: So now very confused, the learned top knot down returned to protest to the two blind sages about look what the tearing-out of little little-she innocents their accumulated wisdom of India and China had brought no better promise of a better future, it found no one had heard about any Indian blind leading the Chinese blind, or vice-versa. On these treacherous tracks and the way blind monks slip away into the ravines below, and them as monks obliged to carry the accumulation of the wisdom of ages blindly as the blind leading the blind, who did the learned top knot down think it was kidding about where they might have gone?
(pause)
If that wasn't an answer to its quest of where the space beneath the feet above earth-bound, where the purity of spirit, where the pointy end of any or all thinking higher-above… well, the learned top knot down

dusted the dust of China and dusted the dust of India off its tiny imaginary feet and committed itself to the wind blowing off Everest, in order to search on for an answer to the utter defilement of all that's innocence, hoping for a favourable wind...

(The STORYTELLER mounts a new sign reading:
'OONAWHOOPWHOOP AUSSIELAND'
and perhaps even places on his head a wide-brim with 'fly' corks strung to it.

While he does so, the shadow players swelter in the sun, sit around knocking back beers etc. The learned TOP KNOT DOWN has trouble with magpies attacking it, and so forth.

To front stage comes an Australian Bushie scratching his bum to sit on one side of the front apron and an elderly tribal woman to sit picking her teeth on the other side. Both look like they hadn't moved for years and would have no wish to have to do so. When they are settled, the STORYTELLER can continue:)

STORYTELLER: Back in Australia, spinning in a local wurlie-wurlie went out back of Oonawhoopwhoop, the learned top knot down sat down with a white man in a broad brimmed hat but a lot of red skin around his neck and asked him where it could find the space beneath the feet for a purity of spirit, even spirits, and a pointy end of thinking higher-above.

BUSHIE: This 'ere's the ancient land of Austraya, son. and there was them purities of spirits coming out of people's ears once and running out of their noses, so good was the local plonk ha ha, but knowin' whatcha-mean I reckon I knows a character who was all pearly-white u-beaut purity of spirit, never got his beetle-crushers on the turf, always on the give-give giving. See, if you ever fell a bit short of the old moral gubbins, son, you could front up to this bloke and he'd never stopped being good for a handout on the go. A heart on him as big as Pharlap's nuts put together and those nuts were so meaty they knocked the bookie odds down b'themselves, old China. Now, see, all youse got to do is get yourself down to the Ancient Land round the back there of old Oonawhoopwhoop and ask for T. H. E. Dreaming, and she'd be jake.

STORYTELLER: (interjecting) 'Jake Dreaming?', the learned top knot down went.

BUSHIE: Don't interject, cob. Nar, son, T.H.E. Dreaming, and she'll be jake. Don't got thick on a man, Gawd luv it.

STORYTELLER: And so the learned top knot down floated on down to the back of Oonawhoopwhoop way…

(as the shadow of it hovers as near to the TRIBAL WOMAN as it can and she begins spraying Mortein at it but lacking energy or enthusiasm…)

STORYTELLER: Where it came across an ancient-looking Aboriginal lady and asked if this was Ancient Land as it looked like it was.

(She answers while the shadow playing behind the scrim act out the Dreaming sequences, the dry river-bed camp, the endless and unrelieved landscapes etc:)

TRIBAL WOMAN: 'Ancient?' Strike, this be ancient too right. I'm twenty-two and look at me, even me grey hair's got ancient written all bloody over it. See me blindness gawk-y-oma or sumthin', eh? That's real ancient, that is, bub. See me no-teeth? That's real ancient, too. See me kids what drunk themselves into that petrol can and can't get out no more? I reckon that's ancient history too. I ain't ever seen inside a classroom and I ain't ever had a job and I ain't seen my man in flamin' years. That's all as ancient as the hills, bub. See this dry creek bed under me bum, see me black eye, see them dogs peeing on me leg, cheeky buggers? They're all ancient as all hfruggeree. This wine flask's seen the dawn of time but I was a bit full at the time and I didn't see it m'self. Some White man coming along always forkin' what out? The wherewithal? I never seed no wherewithal. I don't know if he's any gubba callin' heself T. H. E. Dreaming but you'd be the one dreaming if you think he's kipped out around here if he's going anything left in his kick. See this? This 'ere's a snake track. You go all mad as a cut snake and follow that big bugger Eastern Brown, you might come across that Dreaming bloke. He'd haveta be the one silly enough to be kissin' it on the lips. You'd have to hurry or he'll be ancient history too. Listen, you do find this Tee Haitch Eee Dreaming alive'n'kickin', you tell the b. to come back here 'cos he's missed one out with that wherewithal of his. Me. Don't be too long 'bout it, but, tell him; come quick, I got terrible fallen arches. They come with the Flood that's how real ancient they are.

STORYTELLER: After this, the learned top knot down felt let down to think this Mr or Mrs T. H. E. Dreaming might be able to answer about the purity of spirits or where the space was between the feet, where the gross infamies against all innocence... well, again, what else was? So the learned top knot down left the back of Oonawhoopwhoop of the Ancient Land of Australia to its heavy mischiefs and simply let the great south-westerlies carry it away to elsewhere...

> *(The STORYTELLER waits as the shadow players prepare to re-enact its Outer Mongolian quest.*
>
> *This time, THE STORYTELLER's sign, which he parades again, in fur cap with ear pieces, reads:*
> **'MONGOLIA. BRRRR'**.
>
> *One of the descendants of Genghis Khan is seen shadowed by a smoldering yurt. His wife and two children sit by him but further away from the warmth and they commence re-enacting the Mongolian quest:)*

STORYTELLER: Over the great steppes of Asia, the learned top knot down met one of the countless sons of the Great Khan who represented all the people of Asia, without doubt about things like purity and pointy ends and infamies against all innocence. Now, we're getting somewhere, it thought. For didn't the Great Khan's wisdoms sweep across almost all the known world, and the power of his mind and spirit imagining up civilizations and cities so fabulous his men's feet hardly touched the earth with the space beneath, that knew no earthly bounds to free pointy-end thinking... like the wind, like their horses' hooves, his wisdoms flew!... save for a tiny nip of silk and brocade and a pinch or two of opium, and a great hearty fart on the flyby or not, who cared since it was in the Great Outdoors and dissipated quickly?
  (and)
And so, the learned top knot down hovered over there and it asked that particular one of the countless sons of the Great Genghis sitting there if

203

the Great Genghis had mentioned the purity of spirit, the hoof-flying space beneath the feet, how all innocence could be forever protected. But it could soon see one of those fires was the family's still-burning yurt. Now, this countless son of the Great Khan was not sitting under mighty wisdoms passed down to him, but was staring murderously at his wife who had made him buy the books and computer for his son and daughter to learn by, instead of letting him buy what he needed of his beloved mare's piss. From a mere spark of the push-bike generator they had now lost their home. Hadn't he told the silly bitch not to bring that modern education shit into his house'n'home had she listened?; did anyone listen to what was passed down to him anymore?

(and)

But surely there was this the learned top knot down could see… that, before saving any of their prized possessions, they had saved the books. They had! Out of all the charred mess, the books, safe and sound! Here… surely now!... were the residue wisdoms to give it the answers it sought, here surely the right thinking and the pointy ends of it. So the learned top knot down, with a sudden hope welling in its little imaginary throat, asked this countless son of the Great Khan loud enough for all the Asian steppes to hear: 'Sir?' it said, but the man waved it away. So, 'Madam?' it started to ask the wife but she sushed it and put her fingers to her lips. So, 'Little children of the Gobi and future?' it stated asking but they couldn't give any answer because their words were all stuck up with bubble gum.

(the family sits static around their fire, mute to the excited
flittings above of the TOP KNOT DOWN)

STORYTELLER: For, what the learned top knot down could clearly hear was no wisdoms passed down by the Great Khan, but…
(the son shadow player stands with intent for the following and,
after, just sits back down without doing anything...)
the son only wished to throw his father, mother and sister into the fire while it lasted so he could sell the books to buy rights to a good street corner he could knife around in. And
(the daughter shadow player stands with intent for the following and
then just sits back down without doing anything...)
the daughter only wished to throw her father, mother and brother into the fire so the books were hers to sell to give the money to her drunken uncle who was the father of her coming child. And

204

(the wife shadow player stands with intent for the following and then just sits back down without doing anything...)
the wife only wished to throw her husband and her children into the fire and keep the books to seed her escape money. And
(the father shadow player stands with intent for the following and then just sits down without doing anything....)
the man only dearly wished to throw his wife and kids into the fire so he could sell the books to buy another computer to watch the best porn he'd ever had in his life before the batteries ran out.

(The shadow area 'winds down' disconsolately and only slowing picks itself up to prepare for the next TOP KNOT DOWN quest:)

STORYTELLER: If that wasn't an answer to its quest of where the space beneath the feet, where the purity of spirit, where the pointy end of thinking higher-above... how come, always, always, the utter defilements... well, what else was? What was worth bothering with the use of thinking?
(and)
The learned top knot down let the arctic wind take him on from Asia Proper to any elsewhere where it might find the answers regarding little Veena and why innocence-raped came so on so inevitably. His little imaginary shoulders were slumping. But still, but still...

(Now the shadow area evokes an Arctic waste theme, where THE TOP KNOT DOWN has its next search.

Already the STORYTELLER is putting up a new sign which reads:
'ICE FLOW. GET THE DRIFT?'
in time for the shadowing of its polar-bear quest:)

STORYTELLER: Over the middle part of the Pacific, the learned top knot down came across virtually its one last chance in the form of a dugong, which, so kind and wise, surely represented the whole nonhuman life on earth. The learned top knot down had to ask it, going: Hey, dugie old pal old buddy, you seen where the purity of spirits, where the space beneath the feet in the killing fields I see? Where the pointy end of thinking higher-above? Whence'n'why the utter defilements all the time?

205

(and)

The dugong thought a while then nodded, yes it knew a place. All the
learned top knot down had to do was to let the wind take it to the
Bering Strait where the last polar bear of all had just avoiding
extinction and miraculously given birth to twin pups of either gender
guaranteed to stave off extinction at least for a day, night without end.
There, the dugong, said rolling over for a downy scratch on its slow but
kind belly for a bit of a tickle, the learned top knot down could see
what the wisdom of all time could do, but it would have to hurry
because the pups were up and about and soon to be on the move
fending for themselves.

(and, to the shadowing of this going on behind:)

The learned top knot down did so, too, and eagerly, eagerly, because
everyone knew how the polar bear was the thing of beauty, the purest
of whites, the freest of spirits who slept half its life with its pads off the
ground leaving space beneath its feet and sticking into the unpolluted
air and dreaming of times on ice flows immeasurably pointy-ended
compared to the manmade infamies against all innocence.

(and)

And there on the ice flow in the Bering Strait did it, yes, look down to
find the mummy polar bear with its feet off the ground. But the
learned top knot down did not bother to land. There were down there
too many feet seen to be off the ground with space underneath for its
liking. For, four of those feet, yes, belonged to mummy bear just killed
by pappy bear and with no choice to lying on her back with her feet up
off the ground and in the air. And four of the other feet were pappy
bear's, still awake enough to be licking its chops before it rolled
contentedly on its back, where it fell into hibernation with its feet in the
air and plenty of space beneath them. And eight of the feet were just
the paws remaining of the puppy bears which pappy bear had just
finished eating leaving the paws for a later smack of the ole lips when it
eventually woke up again. There was no space between those little feet
and the ground there, only innocence left lying in its own blood.

(The shadow area is blacked-out instantly)

STORYTELLER: And, oh, where was this as any answer? Wasn't it
now there was no purity of spirits to be found anywhere in the world,
no thinking space beneath any feet you'd meet and no pointy end of
thinking higher-above, especially about the utter defilement, not once

but a thousand million times, of the all innocent. Was three only ever the Beast and its bitter end?

(in the 'empty' silence and shadow-area that echoes that prospect of desolation, the STORYTELLER walks around behind the screen. We see him striding slowly, looking right and left but obviously seeing only devastation.

He emerges from the other side, can hardly look up at the audience as he does so. For a moment he can only stand with his arms outstretched in a hopeless gesture. Eventually, he feels he just has the energy to finish it:)

STORYTELLER: Okay. Alrightee. And so, the learned top knot down decided it could only go with the north-westerly until the north westerly's end or until it dropped away from it. It just let all the french fries and the Big Macs of all countries just float on by on the oceans passing beneath it. It didn't matter. It could get no answers for our little Veena, neither cluck nor tweet nor bok-bok-bok. And it did so, until the north-westerly finally ran out of puff... until the learned top knot down itself became so heavy with depression that it simply fell straight through its cloud there down towards the earth, the ground, the earth-bound below, and...

(There is now only the shadow of the learned TOP KNOT DOWN and it is falling, spinning towards earth, but like a feather, lazily and pointlessly, and, halfway up and halfway down, stops:)

STORYTELLER: ... and as it fell down to earth, it fell not so much, then not so much, then not so much, then not at all. It did! It looked down and it wasn't falling. It looked up and it wasn't falling. It found what only a lone-wolf top knot of young down could find... and that was it was gravity-neutral. That it was neither one thing. That it was neither the other thing, neither. And it lay back on whatever back a learned top knot has under its down... and put its whatever little imaginary hands beneath its little imaginary downy head... and it just-simply-lazed. Lazed. It did. For, the learned top knot down had its answers, so obvious.
(enough musical flourishes for moral ending)

That there was always space beneath your feet and there was always purity of spirit for the all-innocent and there was always the pointy end of thinking higher-above when you didn't bother with landing on Earth. Why would you want to land back on Earth anyway? And why would you want to downily attach yourself to the top of a head when any head, all heads, any kind of head, was thinking only what you suspected they thought. No, for your answers, didn't you only have to get with the gravity-neutrals? With a bik and a bok and a tweet, tweet, tweet.

(Blackout, from fading on the learned TOP KNOT DOWN as zero gravity and floating free)

---000---

Live-Acted Shadow Plays for Today

John Maddison Morton's

BOX AND COX

shadow play adaption by
BILL REED

The behind-the-screen shadow action – or 'inner background' play --
can only ever keep 'pace' with the reading, not *keep up* with it.
Because of the resultant and necessary shadow-play distillation of the
storyteller's tale, the extensive stage directions given in this script are
only intended to be indicators as to what *might* be used for the shadow-
play side of things. They deliberately go beyond what the director
would employ and are given merely as a range of possible shadow-
actions he or she might want to use in the 'distillation'.

BOX AND COX, the timeless farce by John Maddison Morton, has rarely been reproduced on stage since its premiere at the Royal Lyceum Theatre, London, in 1847. Yet, it has 'gone into' the English language as coming to mean two people who substitute for each other – from The Chambers' English Dictionary: 'Box and Cox; two people who never meet or who alternate in a job or place etc…'

Curiously, this famous farce has only been infrequently performed since its premiere.

Equally curiously, for a play that has buried itself in the Western psyche, it generally only runs for less than an hour in conventional theatre terms. This shadow-play version would run longer.

The Characters

STORYTELLER
Like STORYTELLER JOHN BOX and STORYTELLER JAMES
COX, he is confined to the stage in front of the scrim curtain and reads
from a manuscript or a hand-held device and does this unapologetically
unrehearsed, if need be. He is occasionally 'swamped' by the other
two storytellers and remains more of a free spirit than them.

STORYTELLER JOHN BOX
SHADOW JOHN BOX
(the one front of screen; the other shadowed back of screen)
described as 'a Journeyman printer. Wearing 'small, swallow-tailed
black coat, short buff waistcoat, light drab trousers, short and turned up
at the bottom, black stockings, white canvas boots with black tips,
cotton neckcloth, shabby black hat'. He works night shift, and is home
during the day. Despite his attempt to keep clean, he is 'blackish
around the edges', as though the original years dabbling in printer's ink
has ingrained his very pores.

STORYTELLER JAMES COX
SHADOW JAMES COX
(the one front of screen; the other shadowed back of screen)
described as 'a Journeyman hatter, wearing: brown Newmarket coat,
long white waistcoat, plaid trousers, leather boots, white hat, black
stockings'. He works during the day, and is home during the nights. He
is foppish, a nut for neatness, cleanliness, and precision.

MRS BOUNCER
(aerial good fairy godmother behind the screen but screaming)
described as 'a Lodging House keeper, wearing 'coloured cotton gown,
apron, cap &ce'. A bit of a blowser, and blusterer, if you ask anyone,
but kindly and of a what-else buxomy, homely appearance. Still, a
handsome woman, not chaste but chased, and coquettish with it.

SHADOW PLAYERS
4 or so shadow actors re-enacting the storytelling.

Box and Cox

1.

(When lighting up, behind-the-screen soon becomes fully back-lit, where the shadow actors playing SHADOW BOX, SHADOW COX and MRS BOUNCER are waiting impatiently for the three storytellers front stage of the scrim curtain to get their act together. MRS BOUNCER, in particular, looks precarious, dangling so heavily and lopsidedly, hoisted by stout ropes in the air as she is. Even her bonnet is on the 'slosh'.

Finally, after bumbling around the other two STORYTELLERs, the STORYTELLER gets to come on to his front-stage area. He is waving his script in hand, and, to audience:)

STORYTELLER: This is the script I'm to read. Well, my bits, not...
   (indicates the STORYTELLERS BOX and COX)
not theirs, so feel free to single me out for applause if you're into comparisons. Which given the way they bumble through, I am, ha ha.
   (and)
So... I don't know how relevant this is, but the reason why I got this jig was my voice is strong enough to get through it, though that was the voice I had before what I did last night show, ha ha. So, let's see who we've got here...

(As he imparts knowledge of them, he moves to indicate one-by-one: STORYTELLER JOHN BOX, then (behind screen) his counterpart SHADOW JOHN BOX... doing the same with the characters of JAMES COX and MRS BOUNCER.

Firstly, behind the screen, the player SHADOW BOX preens and scrapes and bows while his description is read out...)

STORYTELLER: John Box... the grimy fellow here and back there... it's got down here that he's
   (reads)
'a journeyman printer, wearing small, swallow-tailed black coat, short buff waistcoat, light drab trousers, short and turned up at the bottom,

black stockings, white canvas boots with black tips, cotton neckcloth, shabby black hat. He works night shift, and is home during the day. Despite his attempt to keep clean, he is 'blackish around the edges', as though the original years dabbling in printer's ink has ingrained his very pores.'

(the fore and aft BOX players show meaty hands)
One or the other, he thinks pores are his paws. Pitiful, really. Shows he's a true printer to his inky core.

> *(Secondly, behind the screen, the player SHADOW COX preens and scrapes and bows as his description is read out...)*

STORYTELLER: And then there's James Cox. It has down here
(waves script)
James is a journeyman hatter, wearing a brown Newmarket coat, long white waistcoat, plaid trousers, leather boots, white hat, black stockings'. He works during the day, and is home during the nights. He is foppish, a nut for neatness, cleanliness, and precision. Seems to specialise in hats and, it's said, bras, but in these olden day'n'times probably not so naughtily as if it were our now day'n'time, right?
(with)
Seems James Cox works during the day, and is home during the nights. He is foppish. He tops 'is doff a lot, as you can see. Inside and out. An itchy type of fellow. Fopheadish, really. A stickler for neatness, cleanliness, and precision. When his hat's on. When it's off, he's just as sloppy as old Box there.

> *(He pauses to watch with the audience MRS BOUNCER 'bounce' around behind the screen in her aerial harness for her turn, before:)*

STORYTELLER: And who tip-toes here on dainty, thunderous foot?...
(cues for 'entrance')
Why, it's Mrs Bouncer and no bounce-on-me-and-I'll-really-bounce-on-you about it, either, shiver me timbers. Whoo, are these roof rafters strong enough here?

> *(Disregarding his ridicule, next behind the screen, MRS BOUNCE preens and scrapes and bows alarmingly to her description being read out....)*

214

STORYTELLER: Mrs B. Obviously not named for babies ever being much on her lap. Mrs Bouncer, so it says, is our lodging's house keeper. Some have taxi cabs waiting outside the front door. Mrs Bouncer has a crane standing by the front door. It's for getting in that taxi cab waiting outside the door. Getting out, it's said the cabbies just put the boot in. If you wanted to get any closer, you might be able to see she is wearing 'coloured cotton gown, apron, cap', and the usual other stuff other cranes can get her into in those days. She's also wearing her usual workaday apron without, this day, not too many smears which means she hasn't had to deal with too many smudglings so far today. And she's also sporting a new hairdo for some occasion which is waving in the breeze there because she's applied too much of that kitchen-grease-trap's grease she's wont to. No, that's not Big Ben; that's Mrs B, ha ha.

(ignores her shaking fist)
God luv 'er, it says here, she's soft hearted from having it stomped on in the wine barrel too many times. A bit of a coquette, really...

(he certainly ignores her grotesque attempt at being coquettish)
Maybe even a 'andsome woman beneath all the ham, or maybe they don't mean handsome but hamsome. 'Never in her life chased', if you believe that. I do.

(studies script)
So that's them.

> *(Lighting, any music over, London-through-window backdrop, the shadow cast all 'settle down' for:))*

STORYTELLER: Scene. You are asked to look deeply into the shadows and imagine the whole caboodle of stage business: entrances -- exits -- properties -- and directions. As performed at the London Theatres under gaslight. Room, decently furnished. At C, as they stage-say, a bed, with curtains closed. At LC, a door. At 3, at ELH, wherever that's supposed to be, another door. At 2 ELH... I mean, what's EL, what's H?, should it bother us?... a chest of drawers. Cum cupboard. At back, RH, a window. At 3 ERH, yet another door. At 2 E. RH, a fireplace with mantelpiece. A few ornaments on the mantelpiece. Etcetera, etcetera.

(to overall)
I think we have it. By golly, we 'ave it and ta all!

(He backs off or is darkened. Thus cued, STORYTELLER COX takes over the frontstage spotlight and reads from his script.

As he does so, SHADOW COX re-enacts his words and, as though fitting, any illustrative shadow play goes on:)

STORYTELLER COX: I'm James Cox. You find me alone in the room left right or centre fore or aft to start with. Dressed to leave, am I, with the exception of my beloved cloth cap which I have removed very reluctantly as a temporary measure. I am looking at myself in a small looking-glass which I am holding since, if I wasn't, I wouldn't be holding it, would I? I am going to myself… not altogether *not* liking what I am seeing but, still, not at all keen about it…I've half a mind to register an oath that I'll never have my hair cut again!

SHADOW COX: (from behind screen) YERG, HOW UCKABLE!

STORYTELLER COX: Or words to that effect, although I'd hope I'd been put down as a bit more polished than that. Going as I am to my own reflection: 'I look as if I had just been cropped for the Militia! And I was particularly emphatic in my instructions to the hair-dresser, only to cut the ends off. He must have thought I meant the other ends on the scalp side! Never mind'.

SHADOW COX: (again) YERG ME, HOW UCKABLE!

STORYTELLER COX: Oh, well… my manner clearly showing I'm thinking: 'I shan't meet anybody to care about so early'. And then, look at the time! Eight o'clock, I declare! I haven't a moment to lose. Fate has paced me with the most punctual, particular and peremptory of hatters as bosses, and I must fulfil my destiny'.

SHADOW COX: LOOK AT THE YERGING TIME!

STORYTELLER COX: See how that's just me? I'm late, about to leave for work and as usual I'm making a speech to parliament about it! But hark!, a knock on door at LCD, wherever that is, as well.
(back on script, as his shadow counterpart keeps up)

216

But you know me… gay as a blade even if it's been over-mowed. going: 'Open locks, whoever knocks!' What a poet! In the blood, don't you know.

(By now, in the shadow area to a lot of creaking and groaning of people and things, MRS BOUNCER swings into action literally. She waves her wand, flaps her wings, threatens to crash down on everything, and finally makes intimation of entering for:)

STORYTELLER: (sudden take-over appearance) As if we didn't know from the crank changing gears that it's Mrs Bouncer entering, going 'Good morning, Mr. Cox. I hope you slept comfortably, Mr. Cox?' Meaning she's got a fold or two she could tuck him into if he wished, wink wink. And poor old hounded Cox with his new-enlistee's haircut is going, as we can see: 'I can't say I did, Mrs. B…'

(Here, STORYTELLER COX asserts his right to his own speech, butts in (with his shadowed counterpart's nodding agreement) with…)

STORYTELLER COX: I should feel obliged to you, if you could accommodate me with a more protuberant bolster, Mrs B, that's what I would oblige or protube you with….

MRS BOUNCER: (holding on for dear life) I say, that new haircut of yours is a bit uckable, isn't it, Mr. Cox?

STORYTELLER COX: The one I've got now seems to me to have about a handful and a half of feathers at each end, and nothing whatever in the middle, Mrs B.

MRS BOUNCER: Anything to accommodate you, Mr Cox.

(As she is inadvertently swung away for a while, kicking and throwing her arms about)

STORYTELLER COX: Thank you, *madam*. Then perhaps you'll be good enough to hold this glass, while I finish my toilet. And all the time I'm noticing how the woman is trying to make her figure an hour-

217

glass rather than a barrel when I told you early on how a crane is needed a lot around her.

MRS BOUNCER: I see'n'say again, your haircut again, Mr Cox!

BOTH COXES AND MRS BOUNCER: (together) THAT BARBER SHOULD BE KILLED!

> *(SHADOW COX puts on his hat prior to leaving. With his head shorn so, it falls down over his ears)*

STORYTELLER COX: You see, Mrs B., the effect of having one's hair cut like a cruddish lawn mowing? Luckily, I've got two or three dozen more.

MRS BOUNCER: (having to hold on again) Haircuts, Mr Cox?

STORYTELLER COX: Hat sizes, Mrs B.

MRS BOUNCER: If only you had time to change your hat, sir.

STORYTELLER COX: ('so true') If only I had time to change, Mrs B. And now I'm off!
(SHADOW COX elaborately, flourishingly goes to do so...)
Bye-bye, Mrs Bouncer', I'm going and all that. But then I'm stopping for something I've been meaning to say to her: 'By the way, Mrs B.,' I go, 'I wish to call your attention to the fact that my coals are going remarkable fast lately, you know'.

MRS BOUNCER: Lor, Mr Cox!

STORYTELLER COX: All innocent light, is she. Fine cleared pipes, that Mrs Bouncer, like a grinder giving his organ a good blow out. And I'm going back to her...

SHADOW COX: It's not only the yerging coals, Mrs B., but...

STORYTELLING COX: (reasserting again) ... but latterly some sort of gradual and steady increase of evaporation among my candles, wood, sugar and Lucifer matches – and that's said in no uncertain terms to you, Mrs B., for a man not used to certain terms, either!

MRS BOUNCER: (finding a resting place somewhere) Lor, Mr Cox!, you surely don't suspect me?

STORYTELLER COX: And I'm doing a bit of retorting, going, 'I don't say I do, Mrs B., and I don't say I don't. I only wish you to understand, that I don't believe it's the cat'. Said with that surprising turn of sarcasm for a hatter I'm a bit known for, too.

MRS BOUNCER: (trouble with her flying girdle) My, how we grumble so in the morning, Mr Cox!

STORYTELLER COX: Grumble?! Mrs Bouncer, I'll give you grumble! How is it I frequently find my apartment full of smoke?

MRS BOUNCER: Why… I suppose the chimney, sir…

   (while SHADOW COX fights a bout of smoke inhalation…)

STORYTELLER COX: Oh, and don't I come back with none of my well-known smirks obvious, 'Madam,' I go, 'the chimney doesn't smoke tobacco. I'm speaking of tobacco smoke, Mrs B, and I am perhaps alluding to the are-you-or-are-you-not guilty of the odd cheroot or cuban, not to mention that smoking pipe you keep under your apron?

MRS BOUNCER: (shocked) Oh, Mr Cox!

   *(She quickly zooms down to have her nose against the screen to
   get intimate with him, and:)*

MRS BOUNCER: Why…I suppose… yes… that must be of course… it must be the gentlemen who 'as the attic. He's hardly ever without a pipe in his mouth – and there he sits up there, with his feet on the mantelpiece…

   (The shadow action shows how this might be possible)

STORYTELLER COX: How gullible does she think James Cox the hatter is?! 'Feet up on the mantelpiece?!,' I snort, 'That strikes me as a stretch, madam, either of your imagination or the said gentleman's legs. I presume you mean the fender of the hob, or you're trying to pull *my* leg, Mrs B.'

MRS BOUNCER: There he sits for hours, sir, and puffs away into the fireplace. And, lor, I don't know how 'e does it, but instead of going up like all decent smoke, like, it affects the singularity of taking the contrary direction, you see.

(SHADOW COX in another coughing fit, while...)

STORYTELLER COX: Oh, fancy her trying to cough up that put-this-one-in-your-pipe-and-smoke-it one! 'Then I suppose, Mrs B.,' you can clearly hear me going between splutters, 'the gentleman you are speaking of is the same individual that I invariably meet coming upstairs in the mornings when I'm going down, and going down stairs in the evenings when I'm coming up, is it?'

MRS BOUNCER: (eagerly) Yeah, yeah.

STORYTELLER COX: 'From the appearance,' I'm going shrewdly, 'of his outward man, I should unhesitatingly set him down as a gentleman with the printing interest'.

MRS BOUNCER: Yes, sir... as I swing by... and a very respectable gentleman he is!

STORTELLER COX: That sort of thing. But I'm still late for work, and settle instead on letting her off the hook, going,
    (as SHADOW COX re-enacts...)
'Nine o'clock! You needn't light my fire for me in here, Mrs B. Tonight, I'll do it myself. Don't forget the better-protuberant bolster! Oh, and a halfpenny worth of milk, Mrs B. – and be good enough to let it stand. I wish the cream to accumulate'.

MRS BOUNCER: (cunningly on the swivel): You'll be back at your usual time, I suppose, Mr Cox?

STORYTELLER COX: 'Of course. Well, good morning, Mrs Bouncer!' Nobody out-gentlemans James Cox the hatter. A real creamer, if I says so m'self.

> *(He sits 'back' out of the spotlight, while SHADOW COX takes his vaudevillian leave.*
>
> *Whenupon, MRS BOUNCER does her aerially level best to not stand on ceremony. She air-strides hurriedly tidying up the room, then is moved off to the wings, where she disappears for a moment before re-appearing front stage, in full view, to stand and deliver – legs apart oakishly and meaty arms akimbo -- to the audience:)*

MRS BOUNCER: He's gone at last! I declare I was all in a tremble for fear Mr Box should come in before Mr Cox went out! Luckily, they ain't ever met yet -- and what's more, they're not likely to, either, for Mr Box is hard at work at a newspaper office all night and don't come home till the morning, and Mr Cox is busy making them whatnot hats all day long and don't come home till night.

(taps nose)

So, I'm getting double rent on me room... not as silly as I look!... and neither of 'em are any the wiser for it! Another slap-my-thigh bright idea of mine, that it was! But a gal don't have an instant to lose! First of all, get Coxsie's things out of Boxsie's way...

> *(She points out the shadow area re-enactments to what she has and will say...)*

MRS BOUNCER: ...like, I takes his six hats, his dressing gown and slippers and opens the door at LH, and who cares where's that?, and I puts them in, then shuts the blessed door and locks it. Now, I puts the key where Mr Cox puts it and I puts it on the ledge of the door at that LH place, no one the wiser.

(watches a shadow player do this; aside about it:)

Make a wish an' someone does it.

(then)

But I really must beg Boxsie not to smoke so much. Give the game away, that, right smart! Caught me on the hope, like, and me not near that crane to help.

(orchestrating shadow action)

Now, then, to make the bed – and don't let me forget that what's the head of the bed for Mr Cox becomes the foot of the bed for Mr Box. Finicky, these lodgers! They're lucky they can fit on a bed. See…

(points out a shadow player doing so)

that? Mummy's little helpers, like. Okay, that bolster's a bit on the thin side… we should be so lucky, eh?, ha ha…

(the pillow is like a thin bit of rag in a shadow player's hand)

but Coxsie won't notice we've just taken the stuffing out of the old one so we can put it back in for Boxsie having no difference.

(tapping head)

Managin' a lodging house ain't just for us in the beauty stakes, you know.

> *(She disappears again behind the screen, to soon re-appear back there as the good fairy, even if she is having trouble with her wig and getting the harness to lift her more than a few inches off the ground.*
>
> *The STORYTELLER can take the delay as an opportunity of getting the attention back on him…*
>
> *… while the shadow action has turned to the open door where SHADOW BOX makes a flourishing entrance to stand shaking his fist down the stairs:)*

STORYTELLER: Thank you, Mrs B.!

(aside)

Shrew she mightn't quite be, but a real ham fist, you betcha.

(and now, introductorily:)

And now, who have we here? Hatless, so t'ain't Cox, is it? Why, it's none other than Box and he's going off back down stairs, shaking that meaty printer's fist of his and giving the old back-a-yer, 'Pooh… pooh!

SHADOW BOX: Pooh… pooh!

STORYTELLER: Which was a real up-yours-too in those days. And going, 'Why don't you keep to your own side of the stairs, sir?'

SHADOW BOX: Why don't you keep to your own side of the staircase, sir?!'

STORYTELLER: …meaning he's bumped into Cox since old Coxsie was running late that day as you know. If he wasn't such a shadowy character, you'd see how grimy and irritable the fellow is a day's hard yakka at the printers…

> *(which 'wakes' STORYTELLER BOX up out of his bit of front-of-stage stupor…)*

STORYTELLER BOX: Hey, watcha!

STORYTELLER: (gradually withdrawing) As you can see. Attitude in sootiness written all over him and not letting a casual collision on the stairs there without a show of white knuckles. About the only thing left white about him.

STORYTELLER BOX: (again) Hey, watcha, cock! That was as good a bit of the old up-yer-flue-mate as ever got out of the old printer's shop as you'd ever see in your lifetime, matey.
> *(SHADOW BOX indicates down the stairs…)*
Cheeky sod. Bargin' on through with not a 'cuse-I!
> *(calls again)*
Your fault as good as mine, fellah!
> *(then)*
And of course I'm dragging Mrs B. out from behind the curtains around the bed… cover your ears while ye may…

> *(MRS BOUNCER has to untangle her wings and things from them, before she can:)*

MRS BOUNCER: (thunderously) Dear, dear, Mr Box!, what a temper you are in, to be sure! I declare you're quite pale in the face or is it my fashion girdle on too tight for me eyes? Where's all the printer's ink gone? Quite drained from your face. You must be tired.

STORYTELLER BOX: See, all a man wants after a hard day's work is a bit of the old sympathy. Even if a crane has to crank it up. Somebody should get a bigger crane there. Anyways, yes, here is your

Mr John Box, which is I and yours truly, returned from a hard night setting up long leaders for this morning's paper… all done n' near pressed out, poor me… and who'd blame me for being gruff'n'whiney like at the same time, going, 'Far be it from me, Bouncer, to hurry your movements, but I think it right to acquaint you with my immediate intention of divesting myself of my garments, upon going to bed'. I did, right to her moosh. Said as correct as m'training to be a proof reader would ask of yer.

(then, as acting behind…)
But then, see how quick I thinks of the better of that and change the subject, whippet-like. Going, 'Bouncer, can you inform me who the blowhard is that I encounter going down stairs when I'm coming up, and coming up stairs when I'm going down? Clumsy bugger.'

(and, as shadows try to get past each other on stairs, bumbling silent-movie style…)
And Mrs B. going all innocent, 'Who?'

MRS BOUNCER: Who, sir?

STORYTELLER BOX: 'You heard', don't I ever go, and Mrs B. going like butter wouldn't melt steel in her mouth, 'Oh, him… the particular gentleman in the attic, you mean, sir?' Who?

MRS BOUNCER: The particular gentleman in the attic, Mr Box.

STORYTELLER BOX: Particular, farticular. I'm going. 'There's nothing 'particular' about that bloke, cepting his lah-de-dah fancy hats - - white hats and black hats, them hats with broad brims and hats what with narrow brims. Hats with naps, n' 'ats without naps. I knows my hats n' 'ats-off too.

(waits until hats of all types are tried on and off, are twirled and juggled around the shadow area…)

STORYTELLER BOX: In short, I have come to the conclusion that the hat bugger must be individually and professionally associated with hatting interests. And Mrs B. going, like who can stop her?: 'That's the gentleman! And by the bye, Mr Box, he begged me to request of you, as a particular favour, that you would not smoke quite as much'.

224

MRS BOUNCER: Down with the smoke a bit, love.

(SHADOW BOX is pulling out a still smoking pipe protectively from his pocket...)

STORYTELLER BOX: Fat chance, that! Given me, I'm riding the vapours of m'honour, going, 'Did the blighter? Then you may tell the 'at 'ead, Missus, with my bleedin' compliments, if he objects to the effluvia of tobacco, he had better domesticate himself in some adjoining parish on the quick piss orf.

MRS BOUNCER: Oh, Mr Box! You surely wouldn't deprive me of a lodger?

(A mishap almost takes her up and out of view, making all wait until her screams quieten, and:)

STORYTELLER BOX: She's a real flitter at heart. I wouldn't be that crane for quids. She's got gaps what would gupper you. Anyways, regarding that don't-deprive-me-of-a-lodger, don't I ever give her a look of wouldn't-I-buggery! Known for that, I am. But ere I can follow it up with a quick smirk, like, she's up n' going out LCD, whichever way that remains to be, slamming it after her. Whatever it is.

(Indeed, the crane swings her up and away in a great parabola, followed by a great sound over -- and the whole building shaking -- of her stomping away down the stairs)

STORYTELLER BOX: Mate, are them boots ever made for woodworking!
(pauses while the vibrations ease)
So, it's like this, see. After-work after after-work, the extraordinary time I always have to get rid of that venerable female! She knows I'm up sluggin' away all night, and yet she seems to set her face against my indulging in a horizontal position by day. And then, when she's finally gone, there's this dilemma, isn't it?: shall I take my nap before I swallow my breakfast, or shall I take my breakfast before I swallow my nap? Don't I always got this urgent bit of bacon rasher about m'person somewhere?...
(feeling in his pockets to honking over...)

I does. Somewhere… I've the most distinct and vivid recollection of having purchased a rasher of bacon, since there ain't a morning I don't.

(Has to wait somewhat impatiently while SHADOW BOX, and then helped by a number of shadow players, go through his pockets and then his clothing. Finally, the rasher is found)

STORYTELLER BOX: Don't forget the penny roll.

(… which sets off another round of searching SHADOW BOX's pockets and then his person, while STORYTELLER BOX waits impatiently)

STORYTELLER BOX: They always forget the penny roll.

(They finally succeed)

STORYTELLER BOX: So, me being a creature of 'abit, the next thing is to light the fire. Where are my Lucifers? If I can find where RH is…
  (scrutinizes script)
like it's got here… they're there…

(Again, there is the repeat scrambling around SHADOW BOX's person to find the matches which is getting too much for STORYTELLER BOX who has to resort to hissing:)

STORYTELLER BOX: RH! RH! No, don't look at me all shadow creepy like. How do I know what RH is…? The mantelpiece, man…! Or woman.
  (confidence to audience re shadows)
Who can tell with *them*?
  (and to the Lucifers being found)
And old Boxsie baby… me… I proves right again. On the flamin' mantelpiece, where else, since it's every morning, right? I don't know where RH gets too.
  (As SHADOW BOX reels in the discovery of:)
Now, I take a shooftie of my Lucifers, and 'pon my life, this is too bad of Bouncer! This is real shitty if I may say so m'self! I had a whole box full, three days ago, and now there's only one! I'm perfectly aware

226

that she purloins my coals and my candles, and my coals which are always down when I get home, and my sugar, but what man wouldn't think... his pipe and the fire needed for a bit of food for 'is poor empty hardworked belly... what man wouldn't think, I say, that 'is Lucifers wouldn't be sacred from her thievin' 'ands?!

(and)

Look there at 'right of where he finds his Lucifers', it's got here...!

(points to the candlestick on the mantelpiece at least being quickly found, even if only after a bit of Keystone Kops shadow play...)

'RH's whereabouts might have been dug up, like, but lookee how there is only a very small end of candle in that candlestick... look at it! Now I should like to ask any unprejudiced person or persons in this country their opinion touching this candle. In the first place, a candle is an article that I don't require, because I'm only at home in the day time --- and I bought this candle on the first of May -- Chimney-sweep's Day -- calculating that it would last me three months and here's one week not half over, and that-there candle's three parts gone, if I'm a day!

(long-suffering 'I-ask-you' pause)

If I wasn't so dog tired, she'd be hearing from me already. I'd give her the yawns! But, blow it, I lights the fire...

(... as the shadow action re-enacts behind...)

STORYTELLER BOX: Like always, ain't it?, I takes down the gridiron, which is hanging over the fireplace, RH-like, which I've found even if I ain't quite laid a hand on the gridiron yet...

(it is flourishingly found)

An' guess what? Yes, you've guessed it! Mrs Bouncer's been using my gridiron too! What a gridiron cheek! The last article of consumption that I cooked upon it was a pork chop, and now it is powerfully impregnated with the odour of red herrings! By gad! By gaddery! Nobody throws yours truly a red herring! Somebody... guess who!...

(uses echoing shadow action of crackling, fire cooking as a show)

placed that gridiron on fire, and then, with a fork, lay red herring 'ponst it before it... yum, yum!... meets my morning rasher of bacon lovey-dovey like! But what a rotten, greasy thing to do to a working man! Then again, how sleepy a poor printer covered in ink gets. Needs to get blanket coverage on 's ink coating, ha ha! I'd indulge myself with a nap, if there was anybody here to superintend the turning of my rasher.

227

(yawning again, while, behind huge sizzling and honking sounds and large appropriate props...)
A rasher like that'll turn itself. Must lie down...

(SHADOW BOX accordingly turns away and goes to his bed, closing the bed curtains round him. Snores away immediately. It gives a pause for the STORYTELLER to thrust himself into the action; he needs to do it quickly too:)

STORYTELLER: Is that a horse snorting I hear? And so, after a short pause, enter Cox, hurriedly, at LC.
(points back in wrong direction)
Stuff it, where's LC?

(But, behind, SHADOW COX has certainly entered... hurriedly... on cue but now straightway comes forward to almost breast the scrim curtain from behind, clearly indicating he has something to say. This is, of course, through STORYTELLER COX who now takes up the front-stage storytelling area...)

STORYTELLER COX: Well, I frankly don't care where it is, but I found LC if nobody else can! And I say, here and now, wonders will never cease! Conscious of being eleven minutes and a half behind time, I was sneaking into the shop, in a state of considerable over-excitement on the verge of agitation, I must say, when my venerable employer, with a smile of extreme employer benevolence on his aged countenance... that really should retire to make way for someone like, say, me, you know... and it or he said to me, 'Cox, I shan't want you today. You can have a holiday'. No, he did. He went, 'Cox, you take the day off, go for a holiday on me' and his pants didn't even catch on fire.

(Behind, there are roundels of getting ready to go on holiday, and of trains and buses and going out through the smoky city and into the cow-mooing countryside &ce, as STORYTELLER COX relates:)

STORYTELLER COX: Ah, thoughts of Gravesend and back... fare one shilling, instantly suggested themselves, intermingled with visions of Greenwich for fourpence! Then came the two-penny omnibuses,

228

and the halfpenny boats -- in short, I'm quite bewildered thinking where I can get down to something for free!

(His ears prick up when, through the sounds of holiday revels, comes the crackling of the bacon being enticingly cooked...)

STORYTELLER COX: However, I must have my breakfast first before I can suppress thoughts of expenditure. I've even laid out for a mutton chop, so I shan't want any dinner and can save on that. If I don't go anywhere much on that holiday, I might be able to save myself a fortune.
(as his shadow counterpart proceeds to:)
I out with the mutton chop and put it on the table. Good gracious, I've forgot the bread! What a silly duffer!
(but then)
 Helloa!, what's this? A penny roll, I declare! Come, penny roll into papa's arms! Now, then, to light the fire. Helloa...– I see my Lucifer box is on the table... teeth gggg-nashing. Who presumes to touch my box of Lucifers?
(as it is played out behind...)
Why, it's empty! I left one in it; I'd take my oath or any penny roll lying about I did. Heydey!, why this fire is lighted! Where's the gridiron! On the fire, I declare. And what's that on it? Bacon? Bacon it is! Well, bacon it is for breakie, not mutton! This holiday's becoming more and more profitable by the hour! Soon, it'll be paying me to go back to work where it all started, hey nonny no!
(thinks)
But hold it!
(behind, SHADOW COX does so)
Come to think on it... 'pon my soul, there is a quiet coolness about Mrs Bouncer's sneakiness that's almost amusing. She takes my last Lucifer -- my coals, and my gridiron, to cook her breakfast by! A working class rasher of bacon, too, not any mutton chop I'd set a minimum standard on, the money that gridiron cost me. No, no – I can't stand this! Come out of that!
(as is re-enacted behind...)
I pokes fork into bacon and puts said poked pork on my cheapest plate on the table, then I place blasted chop on the gridiron which I put back on the fire with a meaty bit worthy of it! I can hardly show more contempt in doing so. In my own unexpected holiday, too. And so,

229

now for my breakfast things. I takes key, hung up, LH, open door LH, since it is the only door, and temporarily retire, slamming the door after me a loud noise, what I call an upset, if not aggrieved, bang. Bang!

(quite rightly, gets a loud bang from the shadow area. This causes SHADOW BOX to waked up with a start, struggle with the bed curtains to get out of bed, which allows STORYTELLER BOX to narratively intercede…)

STORYTELLER BOX: Hey! Wha…? Who's making all the racket? Come in! Mrs Bouncer?
  (no reply)
So, I'm there rubbing the sleep out of my eyes, wondering how long I've been out to it, when I get the whiff back, don't I…? Gawd'struth, me bacon rasher! I leaps off the bed and runs to the fireplace.

(As, this time, SHADOW BOX takes over the cooking shenanigans he relates:)

STORYTELLER BOX: 'Ere, am I supposed to believe my eyes?! Holloa! What's this? A bleedin' chop! Whose bleedin' chop? Bleedin' Bouncer's, I'll be bbb-bound. Looks like she thinks to cook her breakfast while I was asleep using my blessed coals my gridiron! She'd be lucky! And my 'umble gridiron lumbered with her high-society mutton chop. What a cheek of a bleedin' chop!
  (then)
Wait up! Where's me bacon, did you say? She go lifting that, a man's last crust? Bugger me!

(He has SHADOW BOX casting around under the table, under the bed &ce until he finally figures to check on the table…)

STORYTELLER BOX: Relief! I sees it on the table. How did it get there? Well, bugger me, Bouncer's going it this time! And I'm only hesitating havin' at 'er on the need to curb my indignation, else end up on the footpath outside next to that crane of hers? But is John Box the man to falter in 'is vengeance? He is not! So, I digs the old fork into the chop and I opens the window, ignoring the soot what falls, and I throws the said bleedin' chop bleedingwell out. I does! I shuts window again, ignoring the soot fallin' again.

230

(SHADOW BOX dusts hands off 'that's done')

So much for Bouncer's breakfast, and now for my own! I go back to the table, like, and with the fork, I puts me rasher on the gridiron, back where it belongs. I may as well lay my breakfast things, so thinks I, don't I? So, I goes to mantelpiece at RH...

(waits with bare patience while SHADOW BOX runs around looking for RH....)

RH! RH! And not waiting for RH to turn up, I takes key out of the key flower pot, opens door at RH, knowing that the key flower pot knows where it is, and I exits, slamming door after me a good old whatfor slam!

(He withdraws to allow STORYTELLER COX to take over on cue...)

STORYTELLER COX: It is only me, back from getting my breakfast things Mrs Bouncer might one day wash up like she's supposed to... whenceupon I put head in quickly at LHD, which I've no idea how my head found, and I think I heard someone at the door of course.

(while SHADOW COX re-enacts...)

Come in, come in! But if there is someone there, I don't see it. So, then I open the door at LC, or hope it's the one at LC not RCH, then I enter with a small fastidious-performing breakfast tray on which are a few modest tea things &ce which I place on drawers LH, or near 'nough in proximity – and it is only after this... for some holiday-day reason of gay abandon... that I remember my chop's still on the fire. Oh, goodness! my chop! I can clearly see myself running to the fireplace. Helloa, what's this? That rude lowclass bacon again! Oh, pooh! Zounds and clenching fists!... confound it!... dash it!... no, damn it!... I can't stand this stinking the whole place out!

(with pace rising quickly)

I poke my fork into that damnable bacon. I fling open the window. I fling that food-fit-for-a-beggar out on its sow's ear. I do! I fling it far'n'wide, then shut the window again, slam, bang, take the falling soot with you and be damned!

(He and the shadow action calm down somewhat)

STORYTELLER COX: With that, I return to the sideboard for the tea things and... by Gad and its fly!...

(At the same time as STORYTELLER BOX stands and assert himself alongside of STORYTELLER COX for the first time, SHADOW BOX breaks back into the room so that the two shadow players have to overcome their shock of... first... an intruder into their home and, then, simply the shock of the other being so brazenly standing his ground...)

STORYTELLER COX: (first to recover) I encounter this Box fellow coming from the pantry with tea things I certainly hadn't ever noticed in *my* room, when I simply presumed they would normally be found up in the attic with Mrs B's other lodger chap. And, I can tell you, I went: 'Who are you, sir?'

STORYTELLER BOX: Up that. Who are *you*, mate?

(Blackout)

2.

(NOTE: from here on, the shadow play takes on a strobe-like 'silent-movie' feel.

When lighting up, BOX and COX are still frozen confronting each other, both front screen and back of screen. Finally, they both manage simultaneously – with their shadow counterparts doing the necessary acting out of what they are saying:)

STORYTELLERS BOX and COX: (together) Helloa!

STORYTELLER COX: I said it first.

STORYTELLER BOX: Cock you did.

STORYTELLER COX: There was a distinct lapse in your reaction.

STORYTELLER BOX: I'll give you a lapse right in yer bladder!

COX: Never mind that, what are you doing in my room, sir?

BOX: Who the blessed are you, cocko?

COX: What do you want here, sir?

BOX: If it comes to that, what do you want?

COX: Hey, you're the printer!

BOX: Hey, you're the hatter!

(Behind, the shadow counterparts vie to put their tea things on the table)

COX: Go to your attic, sir!

BOX: My attic? Your attic, mate!

COX: Printer, I shall do you an frightful injury, if you don't instantly leave my apartment!

BOX: *Your* apartment? You mean *my* apartment, you drop of a hat, you!

(Their shadows face up in boxing poses)

BOX AND COX: (simultaneous call) Mrs Bouncer!

(MRS BOUNCER makes her coming presence felt by banging on the wall fit to bring the house down around their ears, as she tries to get in)

BOX AND COX: LCH.! The door at LCH.!

MRS BOUNCER: (booming voice over) Where's the buggery of an LCH?

BOX AND COX: It's your boarding house, madam!

(SHADOW BOX and SHADOW COX finally go over and open door for her and step back to wait for her thundering entrance.

233

But she beats all to it but being hoisted high by the crane to make a grand floating entrance:)

MRS BOUNCER: As light as a feather.

BOX AND COX: Sez who?

MRS BOUNCER: What *is* the matter? Do tell your fairy godmother.

STORYTELLER BOX: Instantly remove this mad hatter!

STORYTELLER COX: Immediately turn out the stain of this printer!

MRS BOUNCER: Gentlemen… gentlemen...

BOX AND COX: This is my room, Bouncer!

MRS BOUNCER: (crocodile tears sounding like tropical rain) Sirs… oh, dear-oh-dear… it belongs to both of you! Oh, dear gentlemen, please don't get 'em twisted… there's enough twisting up here… but you see, this gentleman…
(points to SHADOW BOX, then to SHADOW COX, then to STORYTELLER BOX and then to STORYTELLER COX… and then has to give up)
… one of you only being at home in the day time, and th'other kind 'eart only home at night, I thought I might venture a little dram of efficiency… you know, until my little back second-floor room was ready, like, for you to fight over.

STORYTELLER COX: And when will that little back second floor room you promised *me* be ready?

STORYTELLER BOX: And when will that little back second-floor room you promised *me* be ready?

MRS BOUNCER: Why, tomorrow, sir and sir.

COX: I'll take it!

BOX: So will I!

MRS BOUNCER: (shrewdly) If the crane's still ain't developed metal fatigue by then, sirs. If I could be a referee in this, I'd offer for you both to share it.

STORYTELLER COX: Done!

STORYTELLER BOX: Done!

MRS BOUNCER: But if you both take it, you may just as well stop where you are, ha ha.

(They and their shadows turn surly at being beaten by the logic)

MRS BOUNCER: Sirs and sirs, I'll see if I can't get my little back second-floor room ready this very day. I swear by my frills what must be showing. Now do keep your tempers, that's good gentlemen. So, excuse I, but I'll be off while the wind is between my wings…

(She is cranked up and off, while the sound effects have the door shut behind her and has her shaking the whole house with her footsteps going down the stairs. After her, they slip unbeknowingly into conversation…)

STORYTELLER COX: Would you call them frills?

STORYTELLER BOX: I'd call them 'orse blankets.

STORYTELLER COX: What a dastardly position the woman has put us in!

STORYTELLER BOX: Just what I was going to say.

STORYTELLER COX: Then it is well I said it first, don't you think?

STORYTELLER BOX: After a hard night's work, I do not, mate.

STORYTELLER COX: After labouring over holiday arrangements, I'm quite amazed I did.

235

(They allow their shadow counterparts to have SHADOW COX walking giantishly up and down while SHADOW BOX sits at the table and holds his peace until he can't stand the other pacing up and down any longer)

STORYTELLER BOX: Pacing up'n'down. I can't stand that! I say, 'Will you allow me to observe, if you have not had any exercise today, you'd better go out and fucking take it.'

STORYTELLER COX: I shall not do anything of the sort, sir.

STORYTELLER BOX: Well, what about nuffin' of the sort, then?

STORYTELLER COX: I will not do that, either, sir.

(his counterpart sits himself at the table opposite SHADOW BOX. There is a general pause, while they become huge, then become small again, as they start up a new phase in their relationship:)

STORYTELLER COX: 'Very well, sir', I say.

STORYTELLER BOX: 'Very well, sir', I say.

STORYTELLER COX: But so fastidiously that I must have said it first.

STORYTELLER BOX: Who cares? That a cocked hat?

(SHADOW COX goes to break off a bit of the penny roll to eat)

STORYTELLER BOX: Stuffme, that's my penny roll, mate!

(Back in the shadow area, his counterpart snatches it away, then lights up pipe and puffs smoke across the table towards SHADOW COX)

STORYTELLER COX: Helloa! What are you about, sir?

236

STORYTELLER BOX: What am I about? I'm going to smoke, that's what I'm about, boyo.

STORYTELLER COX: Wheugh!

STORYTELLER BOX: Yeah, an' 'wheugh!' to you, too!

(SHADOW COX flings open the window, ignores getting covered in soot by doing so again)

STORYTELLER BOX: Hoy, cock! Put down that window.

STORYTELLER COX: Then put your pipe out, sir!

STORYTELLER BOX: (putting pipe back in pocket) There!

STORYTELLER COX: (slams down 'window') There!

STORYTELLER BOX: What a picky bugger! I shall retire to my pillow.

(SHADOW BOX gets up to do so. SHADOW COX stands up hurriedly. A moment's hesitation before they are seen to launch themselves at the bed trying to beat the other to it. A dead heat)

STORYTELLER COX: I beg your pardon, sir. I cannot allow anyone to rumple my bed which is expecting a new protuberating bolster from Mrs Bouncer.

STORYTELLER BOX: *Your* bed? Right! Put 'em up!

STORYTELLER COX: I surely will if you'll tell me what you so rudely want put up, sir!

STORYTELLER BOX: Yer Queensberries, mate.

STORYTELLER COX: Have you no shame? First, it's my mutton chop. Now you want my Queensberries? I'll have you know I have no Queensberries!

STORYTELLER BOX: C'mon, c'mon. Let's 'ave yer!

STORYTELLER COX: If you don't stop being ridiculous, I'm instantly vociferating "Police!"

(There is a shadowed impasse. They both go back to the table and sit)

STORYTELLER COX: Don't I tell him a thing or two.

STORYTELLER BOX: I come right out with it, I do.
  (and)
I warn you, squire, I can cast a long shadow.

STORYTELLER COX: And I warn you, sir, I can cast a long shadow.
  (then)
I say, sir… although we are doomed to occupy the same room for a few hours longer in the course of casting the same kind of long shadow… I can't see any necessity for us cutting each other's throats. Same with you, sir?

STORYTELLER BOX: I 'ate knives. Anyways, it'd be a slice or two at this 'ere eating table, I'd decidedly object to. After all, it all boils down to me not 'aving no violent animosity to you, mate, not on an empty stomach after a whole night's shift, see.

STORYTELLER COX: Nor have I any rooted antipathy to you, sir.

STORYTELLER BOX: 'Sides, it was all Bouncer's fault, ain't it?

STORYTELLER COX: Entirely, sir. Shall we sit, sir?

(They rise from the table and ceremoniously sit back down together, very self and mutually congratulatory. Both in front of and behind the screen, all now is quite jovial)

STORYTELLER BOX: Take a bit of roll, old son?

STORYTELLER COX: Thank 'e, sir.

STORYTELLER BOX: I say, do you burst into, like, a bit of a song, sir?

STORYTELLER COX: I have been known to prop up a choir and chorus in my time, sir.

STORYTELLER BOX: Go on with yer. Then 'ave you seen the high-stepping chorus in the show at the Savoy from the front few rows, eh?

STORYTELLER COX: No, sir; my wife wouldn't let me.

STORYTELLER BOX: Lumbered with a missus not just them 'ats, is it?

> *(The shadow area has a hastily arranged walking down the aisle and confetti showers...)*

STORYTELLER COX: No, no. That is, my *intended* wife.

STORYTELLER BOX: I congratulate you, squire!

STORYTELLER COX: But, you needn't disturb yourself, sir. She won't come here.

STORYTELLER BOX: (rubbing nose conspiratorially) Unnerstand! Got the old snug little how's-yer-mother establishment of your own here -- on the sly – you cunning old dog, eh?

> *(The shadow area has a splurge of a fallen woman in lingerie kicking up her heels with gay abandon and long-holdered cigarette and champagne bottle and glasses...)*

STORYTELLER COX: No such thing, sir, no such thing! My wife… that is, my *intended* wife… happens to be the proprietor of a considerable number of bathing machines.

STORYTELLER BOX: *(suddenly)* Get off with you! Where?

STORYTELLER COX: Only at a certain favourite watering place, if you must know.

239

STORYTELLER BOX: (now a bit wary) A certain watering place, you say? Famous, you say?

(The shadow area has beach changing sheds, beach jollity and shocking immodest bathing neck-to-knee bathing costumes...)

STORYTELLER COX: ('absolutely') Consequently, in the bathing season we see but little of each other; but, as that is now over, I am daily indulging in the expectation of being blessed with the sight of my beloved. Are you married, sir?

STORYTELLER BOX: Me? Why...not exactly, see.

STORYTELLER COX: Ah, a happy bachelor, are we?

STORYTELLER BOX: Yes'n'no, like.

STORYTELLER COX: Oh, a widower?

STORYTELLER BOX: No, not altogether in the true sense of the thing...

STORYTELLER COX: You'll excuse me, sir... but I don't see how any man alive cannot be the one or the other.

STORYTELLER BOX: Well, that's the thing, you see... I'm not alive, are I?!

STORYTELLER COX: You'll excuse me, sir – but I don't like joking upon such subjects.

STORYTELLER BOX: Cross me heart n' hope to die, squire... I've been, like, defunct for the last three years!

(The shadow area has a violinist playing funereally...)

STORYTELLER COX: (aghast at BOX) Get on with you, sir!

STORYTELLER BOX: Ain't you the delicate one! If you don't believe me, I'll refer you to a large 'ighly-respectable circle of disconsolate hacquaintances o' mine.

STORYTELLER COX: My dear sir -- my *very* dear sir -- if there does exist any ingenious contrivance whereby a man on the eve of committing matrimony can leave this world, and yet stay in it, I shouldn't be sorry to know it.

STORYTELLER BOX: That right? Well, then I presume I'm not to set you down as being frantically attached to your intended, eh eh?

STORYTELLER COX: Why, not exactly; and yet, at present, I'm only aware of one obstacle to my doting upon her, and that is that I can't abide her!

> *(The shadow area has an aghast fanfare...)*

STORYTELLER BOX: That right, guv? Then there's nothing easier. Do as I did, see.

> *(SHADOW COX falls upon SHADOW BOX over-eagerly...)*

STORYTELLER COX: (so very avid) I will! What was it?

STORYTELLER BOX: (waits for drum roll, then:) Drown yourself.

STORYTELLER COX: Will you be quiet, sir!

> *(The shadow area re-enacts a drowning man in a rising river in full melodrama...)*

STORYTELLER BOX: Listen to me, old son. Three years ago it was my misfortune to captivate the affections of a still blooming, though somewhat middle-aged widow, at Margate.

> *(The shadow area has music of the heart strings together with an Ophelia-type flitting around amongst the lilies and the men...)*

STORYTELLERCOX: Singular enough! Just my case three months ago at Margate too.

STORYTELLER BOX: Beware of Margate, no two ways 'bout it. Well, squire, in order to escape her *importunities*… and I never did come at those *importunities* of hers… I came to the determination of enlisting into the Blues, or Life Guards.

STORYTELLER COX: So did I! How very odd!

SHADOW BOX: So did I!

SHADOW COX: Me too!

BOX: A lot of blokes go for the Blues, seems like.

STORYTELLER COX: It certainly portunes as though.

STORYTELLER BOX: I didn't much come at her *portunes*, either. Anyways, would you believe the Blues, they wouldn't have me. They actually had the cheek to say I was too short.

STORYTELLER COX: And I wasn't tall enough!

SHADOW BOX: And I couldn't hide my dandruff because I was too shortish!

SHADOW COX: And it didn't make any difference me standing on tiptoe!

STORYTELLER BOX: So I was obliged to content myself with a marching regiment known for its short strides in which I enlisted!

(The shadow area has a military parade…)

STORYTELLER COX: So did I! Oh, singular coincidence!

STORYTELLER BOX: Old hamwurst, I'd no sooner done so than I was sorry for it.

242

STORYTELLER COX: So was I!

SHADOW BOX AND COX: So were we!

SHADOW BOX: So, cutting a long story short, my infatuated one offered to purchase my discharge, on condition I'd lead her to the altar, long or short strides, didn't matter which. I hesitated, but at last I consented.

STORYTELLER COX: Amazing; I hesitated too but gave in!

SHADOW BOX: My same old consent was due to this weak heart of mine!

SHADOW COX: My same old consent was because I was having bladder problems at the time!

> *(The STORYTELLER comes forward pointing pointedly to his watch to both of the other storytellers in turn. Since they take no notice of the time, he rudely inserts himself into the proceedings on behalf of the management.*
>
> *As he proceeds to read from his script STORYTELLER BOX and COX give way to his spotlit, the shadow action behind struggles to keep up with what he is enouncing...)*

STORYTELLER: (pointedly) So, moving right along... what happens here is there's John Box saying about how the day fixed for his wedding drew near, he suddenly realised he wasn't worthy to possess the good lady, and tried to tell her so. But, instead of her being flattered by the compliment, something whizzed past his ear and shattered into a thousand pieces against a nearby wall... due to the fact that it was his engagement ring and it had a lot of glass in it.
> *(he waits for the shattering which finally comes with a lot of wailing...)*
So John Box retaliated with a well-aimed brick with the upshot he and his fiancé parting, and the next morning him being served with a notice of action for breach of promise.
> *(allows bailiff action behind to catch up)*

Well, ruin faced him nose-to-nose, what with the legal action proceeding with gigantic strides, far longer than that military regiment he mentioned, so he came to a desperate decision and left home early the next morning with an extra suit of clothes under his arm, and …

(as SHADOW BOX amply highlights…)
when he arrived on the cliffs, deposited the suit of clothes on the very verge of the gaping precipice there… then walked off in the opposite direction!

(All wait while SHADOW BOX disappears off into the distance…)
Upon hearing all this, James Cox sees the light and exclaimed, ' 'O, ingenious creature! You disappeared and they found a note in that extra suit there saying "Farewell, World. This is all thy work, oh, Penelope Ann!"

(At this, STORYTELLER COX stops the melodrama behind by jumps to his feet to take back the attention)

STORYTELLER COX: Hold on! Penelope Ann, you say?! Not Penelope Ann, the widow of Margate's William Wiggins, who himself had earlier befell a cliff too?!

STORYTELLER BOX: That's her, true.

STORYTELLER COX: Then you can be none other than the dreaded Box of the lamented longlost Box personage! Why, and there I was about to marry the innocent creature you so cruelly deceived, you bouncer!

STORYTELLER BOX: You've got me, guv.

STORYTELLER COX: Then, sir, I congratulate you! I give you joy to be back in the arms of your intended Penelope Ann! And now, I think I'll go and take a stroll.

STORYTELLER BOX: Hold on there, cocko! You mean *your* intended!

STORYTELLER COX: How can she be mine any longer now that you've returned?

STORYTELLER BOX: Hoi, I came to me untimely end, and you popped the question subsequent like!

> *(As they confront each other… shown by the shadow action to be the one trying to get through, and the other blocking, the door, the STORYTELLER takes back the centre stage, and:)*

STORYTELLER: Hullaballoo to pay, in play! Out of my way, you bounder! Never! Phoo on you! Phoo on you too! An insult; I demand instant satisfaction! So do I!
(and above the shadow action push-and-shove)
Fortunately, there is always the good fairy godmother Mrs Bouncer to maintain the peace at a snap of the fingers…

> *(This is a cue for the new entrance of MRS BOUNCER, but all have to wait as the crane swings her this way and that trying to get her in position above them. Finally:)*

MRS BOUNCER: Sirs in need of a pair of good dueling pistols?

STORYTELLER BOX AND COX: Deliver the murderous weapons immediately, Mrs B.!

MRS BOUNCER: They're not loaded is the thing.
(good idea)
You might ups and throw them at each other, if that helps.

STORYTELLER COX: Well, sir, dueling is a disagreeable waste of a good holiday.

STORYTELLER BOX: (in agreement) I'd rather sleep any old day. G'day to you, old son; go, and be happy ever after with your Penelope Ann.

STORYTELLER COX: Don't be absurd, dear sir. I would never come between you and your lost-now-found beloved!

STORYTELLER BOX: (urging) Yes, you will.

STORYTELLER COX: No, I won't.

245

STORYTELLER BOX: Nor I you and your recent betrothed.

STORYTELLER COX: (equal urging) Yes, you will.

STORYTELLER BOX: (chivalry itself) Never, sir!
  (another good idea)
'Ere, why don't we throw a little dice for the lady?

  (SHADOW BOX produces dice)

STORYTELLER COX: Ha, those loaded dice of yours precede your jumping off the cliff, reputation-wise.

  (SHADOW COX produces a coin for tossing)

STORYTELLER BOX: Pull this one, mate. That-there shilling of your is all around Margate for 'aving two heads.

STORYTELLER COX: It cannot be blamed. It was born with them.

STORYTELLER BOX: Thief! You're not fit to marry *your* Penelope Ann!

STORYTELLER COX: Chiseler! You're not fit to marry *your* Penelope Ann!

  (They stand back to allow attention on the shadow area, where SHADOW BOX and SHADOW COX fall on each other.

  In giantish, cave-wall silhouetting, they:
  throttle each other;
  hold each other in head locks;
  tweak the other's nose;
  twist ears
  to sounds of great chaos, until it all is broken by:)

MRS BOUNCER: (calm as you like) Gentlemen sirs, there's this letter from Margate what came for you yesterday which I just remembered in London today.

246

(She flips it down from on high. They scramble for it)

MRS BOUNCER: 'Ere, I had to pay tuppence for it.

STORYTELLER BOX AND COX: (no offer) We forgive you, Mrs B.!

> *(But the shadow players show they both suddenly step back from the letter, and:)*

STORYTELLER BOX: Doubtless a tender epistle from *your* Penelope Ann.

STORYTELLER COX: I was thinking the same regarding *your* Penelope Ann. Then read it, sir.

STORYTELLER BOX: After you, old sausage.

STORYTELLER COX: It's addressed to you – B. O. X.

STORYTELLER BOX: That looks like a C to me, not a B.

MRS BOUNCER: Why don't you fracture the seal together, young gents?

> *(This is such a good idea that their shadow counterparts 'have at' the letter, to produce and to re-enact:)*

STORYTELLER BOX AND COX: Goodness gracious!

STORYTELLER COX: (reading) 'Margate, May 4th. Sir, I hasten to convey to you the intelligence of a melancholy accident, which has rendered you bereft of your intended wife.' He means your intended.

STORYTELLER BOX: No, *yours*! Look, go on, Cox!

STORYTELLER COX: (resuming) 'Poor Penelope Ann went for a short excursion in a sailing boat -- a sudden and violent squall soon

247

after took place, which, it is supposed, upset her greatly, and she was found, two days afterwards, keel upwards.'

STORYTELLER BOX: Poor woman!

STORYTELLER COX: The boat, sir!
   (back to letter)
'As her man of business, I immediately proceeded to examine her papers amongst which I soon discovered her will; the following extract from which, will, I have no doubt, be satisfactory to you. It reads, "I hereby bequeath my entire property, to my intended husband."
   (stops reading)
Oh, *my* poor unfortunate intended!

STORYTELLER BOX: When I remember that I might have staked such a treasure of *mine* on the hazard of a die! And I'm sure, Coxsie old boy, you couldn't feel worse if she had been your own intended.

STORYTELLER COX: *If* she'd been my own intended! She *was* my own intended!

STORYTELLER BOX: Your intended? Hoi, didn't you very properly observe just now, sir, that I proposed to her first?

STORYTELLER COX: To which you very sensibly replied, that you'd come to an untimely end, and very timely too!

STORYTELLER BOX: I deny it! Anyone can see the fortune's rightfully mine!

STORYTELLER COX: Mine! I'll go to the law, sir!

STORYTELLER BOX: Not before me, you won't, cocko!

   (Both SHADOW BOX and SHADOW COX snatch the letter and shake it and their fists in the other's face, when the crane suffers a momentary fatigue and MRS BOUNCER falls right on top of them.

   More chaos, until the crane creaks to get her righted in the air

248

above them again. But it has at least given time for a front-stage breather...)

STORYTELLER BOX: Stop Cox and Cox stop! 'Ere's a thought, like. Instead of going to the Beak about the property, suppose we divvie it up?

STORYTELLER COX: Equally?

STORYTELLER BOX: Equally. I'll take two thirds.

STORYTELLER COX: That's fair enough. And I'll take three fourths.

STORYTELLER BOX: Half and half!

STORYTELLER COX: Agreed, Box! There's my hand upon it –

STORYTELLER BOX: And mine!

(There is a knock heard on the front door downstairs, which upsets the equilibrium of MRS BOUNCER. With wand waving and wings flapping she tries to get the crane to swing her off. It only results in her buzzing around like a balloon with the air being let out of it.

The STORYTELLER has to again step in to the proceedings:)

STORYTELLER: Hark, the postman again, isn't it?

(He repeats this as many times as it takes for MRS BOUNCER to settle down, adjusts her skirts and recommence as though nothing has happened...)

MRS BOUNCER: Another letter, Mr Cox and Mr Box, and tuppence out of my kick a-more!

STORYTELLER BOX AND COX: We forgive you again, Bouncer!

MRS BOUNCER: (very surlily) What am I, just another fairy godmother?

> *(But she does eventually manage to find the second letter and to flutter it on down to their shadow counterparts)*

SHADOW BOX: Examining letter here...

SHADOW COX: (contradicting) No, I'm examining letter here...

STORYTELLER BOX AND COX: (reading, and:) Goodness gracious!

> *(They read it...)*

STORYTELLER COX: 'Happy to inform you... false alarm...'

STORYTELLER BOX: ...'sudden squall... Penelope Ann picked up by a steam boat...'

STORYTELLER BOX: ...'carried into Boulogne...'

STORYTELLER COX: ...'Will start by early train tomorrow'...

STORYTELLER BOX: ...'and be by your beloved side at ten o'clock, exact. PS...

STORYTELLER COX: '...don't make me wait.'

> *(SHADOW BOX and COX pull out their watches, jump with alarm and start running around in panicked circles, producing another Keystone Kops episode of absolute chaos behind, until, front of screen, they can get a word in edgeways:)*

STORYTELLER BOX: Cox, I congratulate you!

STORYTELLER COX: Box, I give you joy!

STORYTELLER COX: (tries to leave) I'm sorry that A most important business at the Colonial Office will prevent my witnessing the truly happy meeting between you and your intended.

STORYTELLER BOX: (stopping him) It's bedtime for me. Wake me up if my snores disturb the rapturous meeting between you and your intended.

(Now their panic causes another Keystone Kops burst behind.

Ten o'clock on Big Ben strikes Doom, and in the horrified hiatus that follows it, there is loud honking from the street of a taxi pulling up outside. Even MRS BOUNCER flies to the window ...)

STORYTELLER AND SHADOW BOX: (panic) What's that?

STORYTELLER AND SHADOW COX: (ditto) A lady's getting out.

STORYTELLER AND SHADOW BOX: That's no lady! That's Penelope Ann!

STORYTELER AND SHADOW COX: Your intended!

STORYTELLER BOX: Yours!

STORYTELLER COX: Yours!

STORYTELLER BOX: Listen! She's coming up!

STORYTELLER COX: Shut the door!

SHADOW BOX: It is shut!

SHADOW COX: Shut it harder!

(Shadows puny by comparison, SHADOW BOX and SHADOW COX try to lean their backs against the door, but the drumming coming up the stairs increases and increases until the now-giantishly-shadowed door shakes them to the bone and flings them off very easily.

But no-one enters. Instead MRS BOUNCER makes a rather neat and unexpected crane re-appearance. With the crane suffering

251

metal fatigue and bending under her weight, she can make a
perfect four-point landing at their feet)

MRS BOUNCER: (the coquette) Only me, dears.

STORYTELLER COX: (quivering) Where's Penelope Ann?

MRS BOUNCER: Oh her. She's gone, Mr Cox. You owe me another
tuppence for this new letter she had the cheek to charge me for.

STORYTELLER BOX AND COX: We still forgive you!

STORYTELLER COX: Gone?

STORYTELLER BOX: Upon your honour she's gone, Bouncer?

MRS BOUNCER: Here, take the letter before it upends me!

(Now the letter is so giantish as a shadow that both SHADOW
BOX and SHADOW COX have to struggle together to 'tame' it,
and, having read it:)

ALL FOUR BOXES AND COXES: Goodness gracious!
   (reading it out together)
'Dear Mr Cox, pardon my candor, but being convinced that our feeling,
like our ages, do not reciprocate, I hasten to apprise you of my
immediate union with a one Mr Knox who lives by happy coincidence
in the attic above you.'

STORYTELLER COX: Huzza!

STORYTELLER BOX: Three cheers for Knox!

(The letter is tossed into the air and all-in dancing begins to the
tune and all-in singing of 'The Bells of St. Clements')

MRS BOUNCER: (now hanging on the crane itself) And bye the bye,
sirs, my little back second-floor back room is now ready!

STORYTELLER COX: I don't want it!

252

STORYTELLER BOX: Count me out, too!

STORYTELLER COX: What shall part us?

STORYTELLER BOX: What shall tear us asunder?

STORYTELLER COX: Box!

STORYTELLER BOX: Cox!

(Behind, their shadow counterparts are about to fall into each other's arms when they both stop and look into the other's face)

STORYTELLER COX: Sir, I hope you'll excuse the apparent insanity of the remark, but the more I gaze on your handsome features, the more I'm convinced that you're my long lost identical-twin brother.

STORYTELLER BOX: An' the very observation I was going to make to you, 'slike I'm admiring myself in the mirror!

STORYTELLER COX: Ah, tell me in all honesty… do you have such a thing as a strawberry mark on your left arm?

STORYTELLER BOX: No!

STORYTELLER COX: Then it is he!

(Front and back stage, they rush into each other's arms)

STORYTELLER COX: And so I vote, Box, that we stick by this room, this house, and even Bouncer.

STORYTELLER BOX: (nodding eagerly) Who pays her for all the tuppency letters?

STORYTELLER BOX AND COX: We both don't!

STORYTELLER COX: Agreed! Then Cox…–

253

STORYTELLER BOX: and Box...–

BOTH: are satisfied!

(Now the bells of St Clement's really ring out. Even MRS BOUNCER joins the terrestrial throng)

---000---

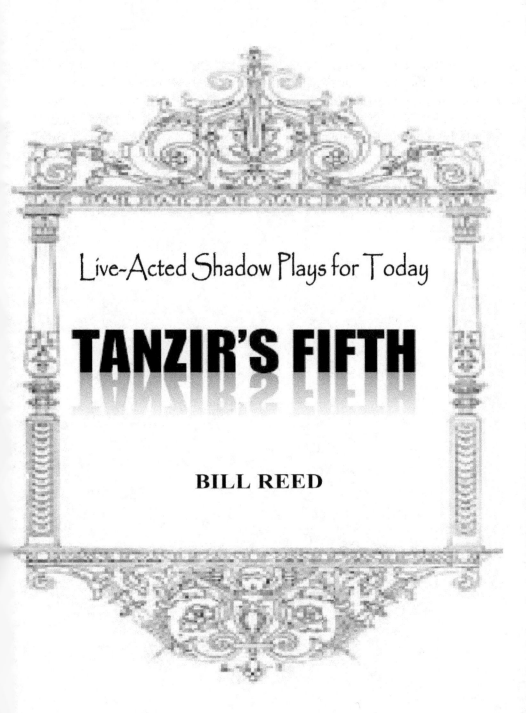

Live-Acted Shadow Plays for Today

TANZIR'S FIFTH

BILL REED

The behind-the-screen shadow action – or 'inner background' play --
can only ever keep 'pace' with the reading, not *keep up* with it.
Because of the resultant and necessary shadow-play distillation of the
storyteller's tale, the extensive stage directions given in this script are
only intended to be indicators as to what *might* be used for the shadow-
play side of things. They deliberately go beyond what the director
would employ and are given merely as a range of possible shadow-
actions he or she might want to use in the 'distillation'.

The Characters

STORYTELLER
The son of Tanzir the Tailor – and so, a much-bruised man and a survivor of many a Fifth. Tendency to stutter as a result. Will read from a traditional manuscript or any hand-held device more than he renders dialogue, and does so openly unrehearsed as part of the play.

TANZIR THE TAILOR
More porky than not-so-sprightly. A real sneezer for a man risen out of the Afghani dust. His Fifth meant he had to have a hammer and nails at hand as much as a needle and thread. Needs to fly through the air a lot.

SHADOW PLAYERS
(at least 4) playing the various shadow parts and episodes. Will skirt onto front apron as stage as called for. They will comprise the customers and the innocent passers-by who will need to fling themselves around a lot… including various customers and hurriers-by. There are a lot of props flying about, too.

Production Note

Whenever Tanzir sneezes a Fifth, there is a drum roll leading up to it. After it, for whatever survives, there is, say, 5-second post-tornado silence to allow for a 'bombed-out' effect. Even the STORYTELLER will be (cornily) bomb-blasted and, like the resulting chaos behind him, behind the scrim, will need the hiatus to recover.

Tanzir's Fifth

(Lighting up on both the front area of stage and behind the scrim curtain. Front stage, the STORYTELLER turns to the audience after watching TANZIR appear in his shop in the shadow area behind. TANZIR tries to hold back a sneeze sequence and, with excessive movements – like a finger under the nose etc – manages to stop himself from doing so.

The drummer beats out a one-two-one-two drum roll as TANZIR fights off the sneezes; and other shadow players, obviously in the shop at the time or passing-by duck and then show great relief when he controls himself.

When he obviously feels safe enough to venture out, the STORYTELLER comes forward with his script, which he brandishes at the audience to bring attention to it, and:)

STORYTELLER: I asked them, I said, how am I supposed to read this out if the earth's shaking? They said, do what they do in disaster movies; learn it by heart. I said I ain't trying to read this out by heart; that'll be the greater disaster.
   (and makes a big play of settling down to the page)
All right… 'He came from Afghanistan and he mightn't have brought his camel but he sure secreted away one of the humps in his baggage, and even then, it was rumoured it wasn't all of a hump but what was left over from one of his fifth sneezes. And, then, if it was, didn't it ever hump more than it ever would've anyway! I should know; I'm the son. I got humped by that Fifth too many times! I grew up really humped over.

(He takes pains to pause and indicate the growing shadow-lane scene and his father working diligently at his tailoring:)

STORYTELLER: Long ago, my father set up his needling shop just off the Chinese quarter in one of Melbourne's lanes. I always thought it appropriate it was just down from Dob Yu Too undertakers, because, once it registered that a Fifth was coming, the first thing anyone did

258

was to cry hallelujah that at least an undertaker was near that you could dive into without having to book ahead.

(aside)

It was a rumour among us kids that Dob Yu Too the undertaker used to keep a few who took refuge in there and that my father's Fifth wasn't all to blame.

(returns to reading)

My father was more than some ordinary tailor. He was famous for his own fashion line… Tanzir T's, the T standing for not for 'Treads' as generally thought, but 'Try-to-find it', meaning his personal signature on each garment, sometimes never even ever found.

(a shadow player madly searches a blouse)

Tanzir T Fashion Treads became known for not coming up or down easily, in that, sure, you had to work a little harder to put them on, but, more than that, you paid for the privilege of really having to search high'n'low for that elusive Tanzir T. signature. I mean, this could be under some inner part or something, or even sewn into a hem, in which case you could proudly sport a Tanzir T garment with one hem hanging down so you could go around showing it was a real Tanzir T's, or just say it was a Tanzir T. garment without having to prove it, in which you could purchase a Tanzir T. garment that had all of its hems hanging out so you could prove it *wasn't* a Tanzir T's. But that cost more than a genuine Tanzir T's, so I never saw the point really.

> *(One or two shadow players struts or strut around with various Tanzir T. fashions, most of which having hems hanging down sloppily and loosely)*

STORYTELLER: No wonder they didn't come cheap! I know from firsthand how much work my father put into them, especially those hem-less ones, having to sew all those hems in and then having to undo them and make it look like they hadn't deliberately come undone. That was one of the jobs I had to do after school. Undoing the hems, I used to tell the teacher about my homework. It was hard to beat. Anyway…

> *(He points back to the shadow area. There, TANZIR is seated at his sewing machine and is trying to thread a needle… and tries… and tries. It is a real thimble fumble)*

STORYTELLER: Normally a hive of activity, my father's tailoring business was, let me tell you. There was good reason that alterations taking up to five minutes had to be booked ahead because they normally took at least an hour. But that signature made that garment a genuine Tanzir T. Fashion Trend if it could be found without tearing too much of the garment apart, and so was worth searching for the extra money you paid for it, oh yep'n'yes. Indeed, Tazer Tanzir – revealing his full name for the first time -- was the Melbourne-lane tailor man with a face so narrow it could have come out of a cotton bob, and ears so strident that from his schooldays…

(aside)

Well, he didn't have any, but was there ever a myth that was not made up around my father?...

(back to reading, while the shadows re-enact:)

… from his schooldays, people kept wanting to thread cotton between his ears and hold him up bobbing in the middle, and those people were from second-graders upwards. That was a bit annoying, but it was his fingers that annoyed even his-own-self the most. He blamed them the most for making him kneel on a high bar stool if he wanted to reach his sewing machine…

(TANZIR puts his head around the edge of the scrim and delivers to the audience before retreating back into the shadow area:)

TANZIR: If you don't know the cotton coming out of my ears, I blame them the most for making me need to kneel on a high bar stool just to reach my sewing machine.

STORYTELLER: My father is talking about his fingers, there. And also, it says here, being…

(TANZIR returns to peer around the edge of th e scrim)

TANZIR: (interjecting) But that stool's only because they insist on making sewing machines only one distance from the ground. Sewing machine designers… no hopers!

(He withdraws)

260

STORYTELLER: (can go back to reading) So… and those fingers being so pudgy alongside of that narrowest of faces that his own tailor of a father – a grandfather I never met -- told his mother to take him away and have those fingers sewn together, so that if they had to keep him they could at least put in a decorative pond and pretend he was a duck. My grandfather couldn't know that those pudgy fingers he thought totally unfit for the family tailoring business, actually made Tanzir the Melbourne-lane Threader the tailoring success that he was, for they slowed him down so much they countered how his mind was always running out of the other side of the shop before he even started working on something.

(TANZIR drops everything, runs out of the shop, retrieves his mind and brings it back in. Watching, his son shrugs 'see what I mean' to the audience, and:)

STORYTELLER: It was just such a combination of a sprint of mind and stodginess of pudgy digits that proved in to Melbournites one could become successful at anything providing one didn't start out too naturally suited for it and wasn't drowned at birth in some ceremonial duck pond…
    (and)
It was a lesson many in early Melbourne would swear by.

(TANZIR shadowly tries to pick up some cloth but can't get his fingers around it, because he has to try to keep his mind together at the same time. After waiting futilely for him to succeed, the STORYTELLER continues:)

STORYTELLER: Not that Tazer Tanzir's hand-and-mind coordination had anything to do with his restriction on five-minutes of repair work leading to an hour. This was generally because my father had a fifth-sneeze affliction that stood time still… or…

(He has to wait while TANZIR shadowly starts the 'uh uh uh' of starting a sneeze painfully slow to come. A shadow player or two comes into his shop… the old-fashioned door 'cow bell'… hears the sneeze preparations going on, and beat a hasty retreat. Finally, TANZIR controls himself and his son the STORYTELLER feels he can resume:)

261

STORYTELLER: … that stood time still, or made you worry yourself about withstanding the toss of time while you waited for the next Fifth to come sneezing around the corner. And would it ever come around the corner!

(TANZIR shadow player starts off as though he is about to sneeze again. The drum begins a slow beat prelude to a full roll; shadows are seen running off down the street waving their arms)

STORYTELLER: Cowards!
(continues)
It wasn't that his sneezes one to four were hardly worth mentioning. After all, they were pretty good, even worthy enough to shock anybody or anything by the spray they could serve. (You could buy Tanzir T handkerchief which my father had signed very secretly, or at least know one was always within reach in the shop in case of an emergency) And, as one to four, they could pretty much always boast with reasonable modesty they were recognisable sneezes in their own right. It was just that his Fifth was a true coup de grace of the most authentic French type when it came to came to capping off such an ordinary – however fine – bout of sneezing as being exquisite over and above what a menace to public life'n'property it was, or parliamentary declared as being.
(aside)
It's true. Why do you think I had to wear a hearing aid growing up and, from the tender age of two, became dead scared of growing a bushy beard for fear of it being blown off my face and leaving devastation like trees being uprooted? Around my father, upbringing wasn't easy.

(He resumes nevertheless, as does TANZIR looks 'out' to him thoughtfully… just as if he could really see him… then returns to his work as the drum starts rolling again)

STORYTELLER: Always, if there was one sneeze out of him, there was pretty much always a second, and then maybe a third, and then… steady, steady!… even a fourth and then… thar she blows!… the dreaded Fifth. But not one more and, if three was reached, not one less. Number one through to four, as I say, were pretty routine as far as humans go given that they generally didn't rock the very foundations as much as the house, unless there was a real lot of cayenne pepper about, or too much poppy seed dust from his native Afghanistan, I guess.

(voice rising to calm to his father – in a self-preserving way...)
Steady, steady...

(TANZIR quietens and allows him to continue:)
But, as I was saying... that Fifth! The capitol F Fifth! You'd see my father get safely past one, past two, past three, past four... but, between four and five, his whole life -- and all that which surrounded it as lifeform at that moment, not to mention the heavenly drum roll building up -- stopped completely. It did!

(and)
Time and space anywhere near him stood still in that one moment. It was called the Nine-to-five Four-to-Five! It was: hit the hills; it's gonna blow! Nobody within four or five city blocks would dare breathe in that moment. It's true. Between number four and the dreaded Fifth, there was not a breath of air left in the world, not a clock that kept ticking, not an atom that could keep spinning! Nary a drum beat. Even way up as far as Sydney, people stopped thinking... well, it's Sydney, so maybe that's too easier an example... so maybe we should read there: 'stopped longer than normal'.

(TANZIR sneezes once. A few beats of the drum)

STORYTELLER: Cock your ears. Don't worry, it's normal...

(TANZIR sneezes a second time. The cloth he is holding flies from his hands. The drum beats pick up)

STORYTELLER: Just test out being able to grab hold of the person next to you...

(TANZIR sneezes a third time. The drum rolling picks up its beat. The tailoring table jumps, yet somehow lands safely)

STORYTELLER: It's best to look around for a table or an open doorway you could dive under...

(TANZIR sneezes the fourth sneeze to the drum-roll now going full beat. The stool, the cloth, the table come 'flying' back to

263

*where they were. But now TANZIR stands; the Fifth is coming...
his chest is heaving... his arms are circling wildly, then go to his
throat as though he is choking)*

STORYTELLER: For God's sake, brace yourselves!

*(Then there is a deathly silence... the eye of the storm...as
TANZIR is rumbling with what is coming, is fighting desperately
for breath. It is not only him. The STORYTELLER too can't get
past his next breath.*

*Time, yes, is standing still, and all dangerously, breathlessly with
it... until, in true theatrical tradition, it passes.*

*The STORYTELLER and TANZIR at first hardly dare to believe
it, and wait and wait, until the dreaded Fifth does indeed seem to
have passed. The drum roll's now-near dirge reluctantly dies
down as they do so)*

STORYTELLER: People, go out and buy a lottery ticket while your
sails are wet! No, really, I mean it. I honestly don't think I've ever
seen that... that stopping teetering on the brink of extinction. No,
really! Normally, there'd be no stopping it. Nine hundred and ninety-
nine times out of a thousand. The Melbourne Met Office put on notice,
all leave cancelled. First responders, where are you? Break out the
rubber-ball ambulances! Normally my father would never have been
able to finish the same breath that he had taken after that fourth sneeze.
You lucky few! You chosen to *stay and continue on earth*! You now
legendary survivors of Fifth Death Roll!
    (quick aside)
Sorry, no refund on tickets.
        (resumes, while, behind, TANZIR picks up the pieces...)
Not even the drum roll you can't stop. I bet the drummer's in shock or
using both hands to feel the miracle of still being in one piece. And he's
stone deaf.
    (carries on)
... So you can imagine how my father is feeling. For him and all
around him, for an eternal moment, it seemed existence itself stopped
in its tracks, and in that suspension of his livingness, he could suck in
no more air but what was in him and he was stuck paralysed, not being

264

able to move anything, not even to roll, say, his blood-filled eyes or joggle his blood-filled lungs, except for his arms in floppy help-me ways going around in circles like as a rag doll's. If a rag doll does that.
   (and)
No, listen! Suspended between the fourth and the Fifth capital F...
                (has to wait long-sufferingly for drum roll again)
my poor father would be stuck in an airless limbo. Anyone safely far enough away with, say, binoculars could see he was at that pre-Fifth instant staring down a black hole of a vast detonation itself, unable to get it out, unable to pull back before it blew up in his face like air in a burst balloon.
   (and)
You have to take a little time to really look and see how pitiable it could be for him.

   (He points to how the TANZIR is badly shaken but still trying to clear things up... a forlorn figure)

STORYTELLER: Folks, can you believe it was even worse than that? It was worse, because whatever he was doing at the time affected all who were around him in the same way. No, it did and they were! They too were suspended in a killing time-and-space totally suspended with him. They couldn't help it! I never could!

   (He stops suddenly. Instinct has alerted him. Behind, TANZIR 'tightens', starts shuddering, stands upright, grips his sewing machine...)

STORYTELLER: What...?
   (looking at his father)
Oh my God, it's not over!
   (to audience)
Wherever it went, get that grip back!

   (Nevertheless... even as his father winds up for the Fifth and the drum roll rumbles out its early... his family duty and love has him bravely standing his ground, doing a running commentary... soon having to shout it out to be heard:)

STORYTELLER: My God, look at it! It's a tidal wave!

265

(gets degree of control back)
And then, out of every fibre of my father's being vibrating to some point omega, it would come, would that Fifth... oh, the capitalness of that F-ness!... building up, building up, built up, built up, and... and...

(while TANZIR and the drum beat are near the crescendo...)

STORYTELLER: ... here she comes!

TANZIR SHADOW PLAYER: Uh!... uh!... uh!...

STORYTELLER: (rising to climax) ...with such built-up force that it might blow him upwards, might explode him backwards... might lift him into diving pikes with half-turns and triple somersaults with double pikes as if a balloon exploding to freedom off one's lips... on the kamikaze bonzai bonzai!... here it comes... wait for it!... oh, look and wonder!...
   (and finally)
BINGO!

> *(Behind the scrim curtain, all hell breaks loose for an instant, then there is an almighty explosion and...*
>
> *Blackout, and dead silence, for a very long time.*
>
> *In this hiatus, there is only a dim light on the STORYTELLER and he is reeling around the apron mouthing Ow!... Ow!... Ow!*
>
> *Finally, order comes back, and the silence is cracked slowly by the sounds of the last shards of glass tinkling, the last pieces of masonry falling, the last choking sobs, etc. When the STORYTELLER can 'return' and speak again, his is covered in dust and his voice starts from a hoarse whisper, while the Fifth-destroyed shop comes to light in some sort of order due to the shadowed rescue workers:)*

STORYTELLER: Folks, here's where I'm happy I've got something to read from. These lines might be the only thing not destroyed in the whole of the Melbourne Business District. If you were one of those rescue workers...

(indicates shadow players' re-enactments...)

there, the first thing you'd go looking for is my father. Strapped bodily to the Fifth, he might have been shot off like out of a cannon, backwards, upwards, sideways, downwards, upwards'n'sideways again, like when, as I said, you blow up a balloon and let it loose, psssphhheeeeeee, psssphhheeeeee... he could end up anywhere if something solid didn't prevent it by slamming him back. The second thing you'd be looking for is how far did he get; did he have his passport on him? Should you ring Guinness Book of Records?

(pause, while a chunk of plaster belatedly falls to ground behind him)

Distance, though, wasn't even much of a consideration post-Fifth. My father became as a bee with one wing pulled off.

(Outdoor/highway sights and sounds come to show...)

Across the four lanes of Spring Street, say, and before, say, the blast wave hit you, you might be more than halfway into pulling out the insect spray, even before you managed to look up and see half the by-lanes of Melbourne's Chinese quarter was hurtling towards you. They mightn't have sharp points but flying chopsticks are no fun! It would take a whole day to repair them, and I'm talking about just the chopsticks. Any joss stick was on its own.

(pause to express real relief)

Phew, what I was saying about us all being in the survivors' club was a bit premature, right?

(and)

Still no ticket refund, it seems I'm supposed to say.

> *(He lets things settle down behind; for the shadow enactments to catch up. TANZIR shadow player has managed to pick himself up, as are his customers. They are dusting themselves off, returning to normal as though nothing has happened... all to the drummer beating a soothing cadence around a single beat. The STORYTELLER sees that it is time to continue:)*

STORYTELLER: It was a miracle my father never hurt himself really. That's the thing, you see. It might have been those pudgy fingers of his, but Tazer Tanzir the Melbourne-lane Threader was a real bouncer-off. It enhanced his reputation no end. His customers might know the dangers of going into the shop and he suddenly exploding, but they at least could be sure he'd bounce back to be able to fix their alteration or

267

to sign their Tanzir T. Fashion Tread from their hospital beds. Or have someone point out where his signature was if they lost their sight. There was no tailor more resilient along any lane in Melbourne! Quite possibly in the any Melbourne Chinese lane in the whole of Australia!

(There is a patriotic drum roll for the shadow of what is obviously the Australian flag being raised. Even the rescue workers are stopped and standing to attention)

STORYTELLER: And, in all truth, I always suspected he secretly loved that Fifth, even in the face of all the broken bones it could have given him had they not always been, fortunately, in somebody else's body, even as he sailed through the air. Not a bone, not even in his thimble finger, even stressed! I based that on him always going: 'Nothing like a good old shake-up of the old bowel-movement to Epsom-salts the old bobbin!'

(TANZIR stands manfully up among all the chaos to:)

TANZIR: Nothing like a good old shake-up of the old bowel movement to Epsom-salts the old bobbin!

STORYTELLER: (nodding) You show me anyone, other than my father, who could cough up a sneeze from one to four that could give you anything like that.
(back to script)
The frizz and pizzzzz-azzzzario of a befffflutterbbbblllying exploding balloon, yes, and a good way of describing it too, if I may say so myself. And though my father never actually hurt himself or anyone else physically able to sue him, outside of a few shattered ear drums, my mother always made sure there was nothing breakable anywhere within his vicinity… and we're talking at least four tram stops away… not anything worth anything anyway, not even the tailor's shop, which she never once dared to put a foot into. My father had learned his own lesson, anyway. The Fifth never came for any fitting.

(to the action-echoing from the shadow-area ranging from Parliament to the woman going missing &ce…)

STORYTELLER: For example, one of the lessons he learnt was: as soon as he felt sneeze number one coming on, he tried to make for the nearest doorway arch or, if not, dived under the nearest table, yes, or hide under that hump he had brought from his Afghan boyhood and suchlike n' so forth. Once upon a time, he made it out into the open as far as the third lane over of Spring Street before the Fifth hit, and, even then, he managed to get a motorcycle helmet on before he burst through the doors of Parliament which was in session at one minute and not the next.

(as parliamentary chaos re-enacts behind...)

Ladies and gentlemen, you can see you are not being treated with fanciful facts here. You only have to step into the shop and see the cracks in the plaster in the wall behind my father's cutting table if you are a doubter who needs good clear evidence. It was said that on two occasions the Fifth came with customers in the shop and they've gone missing ever since. Those other doubters among you could try the Missing Persons Bureau if you're the type who like to poke at holes in palms of hands. Indeed, one of *those* missing, reputed to be a spinster who wanted my father to raise her hem a teezy bit higher while my father had it in hand, had got as far as having a Coroner's inquiry about her whereabouts, but it didn't amount to anything because no one wanted to be in that coroner's room while her name and Tazer T.'s were mentioned in the same breath, on suspicion that the resulting memory-induced dust of her might set him off again.

(and)

And if there are any doubters among you left, you only need to look at his shop lease which had the clause he was to pay for a six-monthly inspection of the building's foundation at his own expense. Or, ask anybody why you'd never find Tazer Tanzir the Melbourne-lane Threader sitting in front of glass where, if required, you could be burst through, and never directly under a fan, where, if required, it was much harder to be burst through and could really hurt. Also, glass allowed you to be blown in many more directions than fans which was always pretty much upwards. Or downwards, which wasn't so good when the earth is hurtling up towards you. Or, how about the canard that, when he sniffed, there was always a stampede for the door? That was a vicious lie; don't you think my father would have put in double doors?

(to a rush and a squeeze resulting from it at the shop door...)

269

STORYTELLER: Quod demonstratum. You know, one famous time my father was caught on the hop in the middle of his shop with no time to gain the safety of anything earthquake-proof. That particular notorious Fifth blew his front teeth and his front windows right out simultaneously. It truly did, and the overall convulsion was tazer-like, wasn't it ever! The glass was shattered into such smithereens that the passing highway traffic up and down all Melbourne lanes reported being caught in the finest spray of a shower that glinted so prettily in the sun that the fact that Spring Street's train schedule, thrown into chaos by the blast, was throwing everything into chaos. Police also called for any dental forensic scientist used to picking up the pieces.
   (aside)
I think that was when I was about to come along, and a reason I finally came long overdue.

TANZIR: (calls) Hold on!

> *(and he comes to stick his head around the side of the scrim curtain again)*

STORYTELLER: (happy whisper) He's going to deny it. My Dads.

TANZIR: ('but'…) It was. But long overdue? Bullsh! I didn't even have time to build a ceremonial duck pond. But what can a poor tailor man down a lane say?

> *(withdraws to go back to the shadow acting)*

STORYTELLER: (deep breaths before…) That's why it's thought he was the only tailor-in-a-Chinese-lane in the country to put in iron grilles on his windows… which leads us into our first excursion of talking about my father's famous cardboard signs or, to give them the class they deserve: *signages all sewn up*. Arguably, they have become just as famous as his Tanzir T's Fashion Treads, if that were conceivable. The very first pioneering *signage all sewn up*, in his front window, yes, behind the newly-installed iron grilles, yes… I remember it well… this very first one that the lane public could set their eyes on went:

> *(In line with this, a shadow player comes fully out from around*

the side of the screen carrying aloft a cardboard sign reading:
'YOUR RAGS WE SHED'
*and sashays across the front stage to leave on the other side of
the curtain)*

THE STORYTELLER: 'Your rags we shed'. Clever! Or I still think
so! What a pot-stirrer among the tailoring fraternity that first one was!
It had to be his pudgy fingers that gave him this added talent too, of
course, plus probably a bit of that mind of his that kept racing ahead
and out of the front door and doing a few turns around the State Library
before making its way back in time for my father to wake up for lunch.
And, needless to say, those new iron grilles in his window there
weren't to stop rogues getting in but the Fifth from getting out, but of
course that didn't need to be said really since everybody knew that and
so you might as well put up signs in the window to cover up the iron
grilles, you see.
(loses breath)
Excuse I. A few deep breaths…
(can carry on)
There was even that time he didn't have time to throw away the needle
he was holding before the Fifth struck. They had to borrow a ladder
from the undertakers Dob Yu Too next door to get him unpinned from
the ceiling, dangling from that needle as it had penetrated the concrete
slab main brace up there and…
(as shadowed-illustrated)
he not daring to let go, with the woman's padded jacket he was sewing
shredded to pieces, hence the sign in the window I just told you about,
although it possibly needed *shred,* instead of *shed*… ie, 'Your rags we
shred' as against 'Your rags we shed', but Melbourne lanes ring to that
argument to this day… to be fully appreciated as a wry comment from
one survivor of the Fifth to another by way of commercial signage in a
shop window.

*(He has to pause while another shadow player emerges from one
side of the scrim curtain wearing a sandwich bards reading:*
'Your clothes we shred.
Your rags we shed'
*parading it past him to return back to the shadow area via the
other side of the screen)*

271

STORYTELLER: (arched patience) Still, all the early Fifths did teach my father a lesson he would never forget: in business, it is not good enough to burst on the scene once; you have to do it a second time and then a third… all the way up to a fifth time if need be, allowing for at least one good sneeze in between. And, as he always told me, if you haven't broken through something by then, pick yourself up, dust yourself off, blow your nose and carry on and wait patiently until you can start on the next sneeze cycle again. Good advice, that.

(He waves for a shadow response from behind. The TANZIR shadow player starts up on a demonstrating sneeze sequence again like an old engine turning over, as does the drum roll begins however belatedly, and:)

STORYTELLER: Another four times should do it, was my father's considered opinion, and by that time he was Tazer Tanzir the Melbourne-lane Threader, who's sniff was his snip, and was listened to, or at least any itchy-sniffing in his words were listened for. It was said that the sight of Tazer Tanzir sitting quietly at thread made the Chinese fare of those lanes tastier than anything outside of China. It certainly made the queues outside those august-moon eateries all the longer, when it became a common rumour that Tanzir T. the Melbourne-lane Threader was stitching together the noodles and if you found one with his signature you'd have found yourself something that would last just as long as a Tanzir T. Fashion Tread, lucky you.

(as shadow players begin fighting over a noodle or two…)

Although therein lie a quandary: not many waiting in those lines were very happy lingering for too long anywhere near the tailor's where the famous Fifth might go off at any time. With his pudgy fingers leading the way, having been informed by his mind that had gone ahead out of the door, heard what was being said, and returned before it had been missed, my father was quite upset about coming to know that. That just hurt! He used to point out that they had a laneway up and a laneway down to escape into; his shop didn't have even a back door, but he never ran away; he had stayed for forty years staring down the Fifth. He shed or shred nothing but cloth, as the first famous signage went.

(Immediately he mentions the word sign, three shadow players emerge again with from one side of the scrim, this time holding

up a sign of:
'Tanzir's! Sleeves for the arm!
Look for our stitches!
No skirt too short!'
And competitively cat-walk them across the stage as if
announcing the next round in a prize fight)

STORYTELLER: (unamused) Of course, you can imagine all the trend-setting signs taking the tailoring fraternity by storm that followed over the next tailoring…

(He is stopped when an unscheduled, another shadow player emerges… this time with a sandwich board… strutting a sign going:
'All sewn items wiped clean!'
with the bearer stopping quite deliberately front stage and town-crying:)

SIGN-BEARER: 'All sewn items wiped clean!', exclamation mark.

STORYTELLER: We can all read, thank you very much.

SIGN-BEARER: (pursed lips) With an exclamation mark.

STORYTELLER: I know.

SIGN-BEARER: They don't come easily you know, exclamation marks.

STORYTELLER: We can read. You don't get in the theatre if you can't read. Get off.

(The shadow player cocks a finger at him and minces off around the other side of the screen)

THE STORYTELLER: *I* presume we can all read so I presume that he or she should presume we can all read. That's all I'm saying. But I bet they're going all unionised back there already.

(But even before he can read on further, another shadow player

273

emerges with another sandwich board sign, and struts it front stage. This one reads:
'Our best work falls on you!'
which he or she also stops centre stage to proclaim it loudly to audience:)

SIGN BEARER: 'Our best work falls on you', a much better exclamation mark.

THE STORYTELLER: I just pointed out we can all read, thanks for nothing.

(but even as the second sign-bearer huffily returns back stage, the first one returns lavishly displaying the sign:
'T. Casuals: none more sloppier!'
and, too, stops to point-and-proclaim it:)

SIGN BEARER: 'T's Casuals: none more sloppier!' exclamation mark far better scribbled on the inscribe of hand-painted.

(The STORYTELLER gives up and proceeds to allow a subsequent roundel of signs to begin, quite mindless of, if not in spite of, his open annoyance. One after another, sign-board shadow players emerge from one side of the curtain, with a new sign. They do so with competing preeniness, and even, eventually, to blow kisses and star curtain-call bows to any in the audience who show appreciation. [A growing number do.]

The STORYTELLER gives up on trying to do anything about it for the time being, sits back on STORYTELLER's stool. He only ventures among their hurly-burly.

The paraded signs now are:
'T's Underclunks: next to unmentionable!'
'T's Mens: Tanzir has gone to town on them!'
'T's Ladies: so airy they don't come easier!'
'T's Kids with legs on!'
'T's Young Gents: crutch-clutchers to take your breath away!'
'T's Young Ladies: for town bikes!'

274

... and, very soon, the shadow players are competing as to who can 'cry out' their signs the most raucously, the most peacockingly:)

SIGN BEARER 1: 'T's Underclunks: next to unmentionable!'. The exclamation mark is thrown in.

SIGN BEARER 2: 'T's Mens: Tanzir has gone to town on them!' with an exclamation mark that would never come free.

SIGN BEARER 3: 'T's Ladies: so airy they don't come easier!', with an exclamation mark all sewn up.

SIGN BEARER 4: 'T's Kids with legs on' and an exclamation mark to put you in stitches.

SIGN BEARER 5: 'T's Young Gents: crutch-clutchers to take your breath away.' Where's the exclamation mark?

SIGN BEARER 6: 'T's Young Ladies: for town bikes!' What's an exclamation mark?

STORYTELLER: ('enough') YOU CAN STOP NOW!

(With this, as though all obeyed him, a general blackout)

2.
(When the lighting comes back over all, the STORYTELLER is back where he was... staring daggers at the shadow-playing, even though all has returned to normal back in the shadow area)

STORYTELLER: I think, as I said, we got the picture, sign-wise. My father, you know, once made a fashion garment based on one of those sandwich boards so surfers could sleep with their boards in their board shorts and make a little promo money as they did so.
   (takes up script again)
Although there was still the most famous of all to come. This eventuated after my father could hardly keep up with the demand for a Tanzir T.'s Fashion Tread garment, even with garments with no label

275

and no signature, he signposted these last ones: 'Tanzir T's without borders', ha ha.

(waves towards behind-scrim in an attempt to get it brought forward too)

It was the first time I realised my father had a sense of humour. Though, on that, he said to me, is humour the same a camel turd? No, Father, I went going. Well, he went, I ain't got no sense of humour.

(thinks)

I think that was a joke and he was deliberately contradicting himself. Or it might have been an Afghan saying or something.

(then, 'anyway', back to reading while, hehind, the shadow playing returns to full re-enactments of:)

Then there were his great commercial innovations borne on the wind of inspiration, he said, of the Fifth. For example, local gents who were Chinese could get trouser legs extended down by a quarter of an inch and only needed to pay for anything over that, providing that that first quarter-inch comprised a Tanzir T. Fashion Tread iron-on extension.

(waits patiently until TANZIR finishes measuring an inside leg, and then start to illustrate:)

STORYTELLER: The same applied to their inside leg seams, although for these those local gents would have to pay for the last four inches of alteration down at the ankles end whether, after the Tanzir T. Fashion Tread iron-on extension, they needed it or not. Or they could have the tops of their trousers' belt-lines lowered below nipple chaff so that the rice money and the like that had gone into their bellies could be better appreciated:

(An opportunist appears around the end of the scrim with the appropriate sign and calling before being waved back:)

SIGN BEARER: Tanzir's! Belly buttons! *Two* exclamation marks!

THE STORYTELLER: ... could be better appreciated, as I was saying, by going into the leg extension, signed by Tanzir T. himself – and, more valuably, where you could never find it but knew you had paid for it! -- a man who could never work his fingers to the bone for you enough, since they had special pudginess that wouldn't allow any bones of any fingers to really make themselves vulnerable.

276

*(and waits for another maverick sign-bearer to appear but
thankfully none does)*

STORYTELLER: Another while-flying-through-the-Fifth-air
inspiration of my father was that his frocks and dresses and skirts and
school uniforms could have custom-made pleats altered to look like
good old hit-and-miss home-stitching so nobody would evil-eye you
for getting above your station in life, especially if you were Chinese off
the goldfields in yesteryear, and trying not to look like a refugee or
having a gold front tooth, and the like – a look advocated by a very
cottage-industry-conscious Tanzir the Melbourne-lane Threader but
beneath him to put his pudgy fingers to unless it looked like he had put
his pudgy fingers to it…

(pauses for a breather and is caught on the hop by:)

SIGN BEARER: (showing herself) 'Tanzir's! Turvy! Tanzir's!
Groovy! Four exclamation marks!

STORYTELLER: (just ignoring it now) … And paying only for any
pleat which proved awkward when the famous Tanzir touch got all
over-pudgy when trying to blunt its edge into looking home-made.
(brandishes script)
This might need a bit of editing.

*(and now, working up steam, he conducts the shadow re-
enactments into double-quick time accordance, such that the
shadow-playing becomes as close to fast forwarding as possible:)*

STORYTELLER: (rising in pitch) From hips to waists, elastic Tanzir
T's Fashion Treads branded bands came in many colours designed to
hang out, men's jocks the speciality…

SIGN BEARER: 'Tanzir's! Togs Toggle! Exclam…

(is pulled back by invisible hands)

STORYTELLER: (sailing on) What took up most of my father's
valuable time was his Melbourne-lane-only offer that anyone who put

277

two feet into his premises could wait up to 24 hours to have any decent part of their bodies signed by Tanzir T's Fashion Treads head signer, namely he himself, either in felt tip in black or blackened tip of felt...

SIGN BEARER: (head appearing other side) Tanzir's! Teasers with the Twizzers!

STORYTELLER: ...on the understanding that it would not be covered up in part or whole by clothing or otherwise concealed unless festering occurred.
  (then quite suddenly and surprising burst into spruiking:)
Tazer Tanzir the Melbourne-lane Tailor's got a name! Ask for him by name tag! Watch out for fancy stitches! Tanzir T's Shod Treads for the summer races! Sleeves looking like socks! Tanzir T's and fashion trend, the seamless couple!
  (catching breath to rise further)
Men!, what Tanzir T's Longs say about you can never be repeated! Women!, no rear ends! PS: trust Tanzir the Melbourne-lane Threader to still use a thimble on his thumb! Pudge Rules!...

SHADOW PLAYER: (ecstatic outcry) Cop them exclamation marks!

STORYTELLER: (going for crescendo) Tanzir T's treads! Juries wear 'em in court! They lay down rubber! They withstand any thought! Remember Tanzir's, the light through the seat of your pants! Tanzir's: for offcuts left with scissor marks, so scissoring it'll make you sizzle! Look for Tazer Tanzir's Creams: play by the seat of your pants!...

  (... and now a couple of shadow players are dancing around front stage making ecstatic exclamation marks in the air...)

STORYTELLER: (now unable to stop) Tanzir's! T's! Fashion! If you have a funny feeling down below, it probably needs to be let out! Tazer Tanzir has the right needle for you! Tanzir's for the cuts down Melbourne lanes that ladies want to chew off and men would rather leave on! Shoes given to shoemakers for repair! In Tanzir T's Fashion Treads outfits, you go around good and find a looking! Oh, father, don't stop me now!

(but, in saying his father's name, he manages to bring himself back to earth to stop himself. The shadow players return disappointedly back to the shadow area. The STORYTELLER has exhausted himself, waves hand apologetically, needing break:)

STORYTELLER: I think my father feels a sneeze coming on…

(waves hand for: Blackout)

3.

(When the lighting allows him to swim back into view, the STORYTELLER has somewhat recovered, although his overall mood is sombre. Even his reading takes on a more sedate cadence, which allows the shadow playing and the prop-work, such as the explosion, more time to keep up:)

STORYTELLER: You know, there are many versions of the legend of Tazer Tanzir, the Melbourne Threader, but it behoves me – whatever that means but I like how it sounds -- to put the record straight about something. That calamity that time that happened between the shop and the undertaker next door, Dob Yu Too's? That-there sink hole that one moment wasn't there and the next was, with a sort of explosion in between…? Well, it was the undertaker Dob Yu Too himself getting over-zealous with his digging, that was. Talk about the man always boasting that one of his holes in the ground was worth two sink holes… not much of a boast if there's those couple of petrol bowsers next door on the other side to my father's shop.
   (and, as the ground begins to sink and smoke starts to rise…)
Well, as I was saying, that day of the legendary explosion… that sink hole that suddenly appeared outside the shop simply coincided, would you believe?, with one of my father's Fifths to rival all previous Fifths. And *that* Fifth happened just as Father stepped out and fell down that sink hole. It is said embalming fluid seeping deep into the ground didn't go with underground petrol and that got the sink hole started which started all the smoke rising started. Well, that might read here as the formal insurance explanation for it all, but it doesn't explain the prefect storm of coincidence… one, sink hole; two, one of the most

thunderous Fifths ever heard; three, my father stepping into number one and falling into number two at the same blessed time.

(pauses so the re-enactment of the following can get ready, such that he has to be a bit apologetic:)

With, you'd have to say, with a bit of the being harried. Never mind.

(finally feels able to carry on)

And so, it was not as all the vicious rumours had it, that it was all because my father had that unfortunate momentary lack of judgment and had recently bought a job lot of expensive Italian thread, not knowing the cheating sods had repackaged dissolvable surgical thread for the real tailors' thread; or because that dissolvable surgical thread dissolved on him, thereby breaking apart his own trousers just as he was about to step right into that sink hole while temporarily blurred-sighted by the just-gone aftermath of a pretty bloody good fourth, it has to be said.

(pause)

With the mightiest Fifth of any Fifth coming up as he sailed downwards through the air down there... I mean, it had to be a miracle that those surgical-thread stitches had lasted past the second or third sneeze when he was in the relative safety of the shop, let alone lasting until his foot was literally over the abyss!

(And to the massive explosion and props flying everywhere and drum rolls crashing:)

STORYTELLER: Boom! Oh, it was a boom! That boom had not been seen in the whole history of boom times in Chinese downtown-laned Melbourne since the gold rushes!

(He has to stop with all the crash-banging going on behind him. Finally, he can continue as it somewhat subsides:)

STORYTELLER: (quieter) Boom crash bang. You betcha. Mind you, as I said, the vicious rumours were way off. It wasn't my father's Fifth's sole fault that the stained-glass window over St Patrick's altar went for a burton and ended up over at Collingwood's car park. It wasn't that any miracle had come to Collingwood's premiership hopes; it was more like a Fifth of such proportions and the embalming fluids leaking out of the undertaker Dob Yu Too's proving such a volatile combination. Especially down in the gaseous regions of a sink hole they've never been able to fill in to this day, not properly they haven't.

(and, among the wreckage behind...)

One good thing did come out of it, though. My father might have never been found again if that Fifth wasn't of such magnitude that it blew him right out of that sink hole, thankfully, and landed him on the roof of the only, we think, Chinese godown warehouse in all those lanes there which had a lift and so, therefore, he didn't have to walk out of there with what was left of those trousers with no stitches left that weren't dissolved. Which might have been a bit embarrassing.

> *(has to wait until the 'dissolved-stitches' lift-and-trousers enactment starts to make way for bits of clothing falling off all over Melbourne:)*

STORYTELLER: What wasn't so good was the bashing to the reputation to Tanzir T's Fashion Treads my poor father had to weather. All over Melbourne, let alone all over Melbourne lanes, just listen to the calamity of Tanzir T's Fashion Treads suddenly falling away from bodies which were simply walking along minding their own business and proudly-displaying their Tanzir treads. I mean, you have to be fair. Only the most astute would ever have imagined my father being conned into buying a whole bunch of dissolvable surgical thread for his sewing material. Other than them, you can imagine what confusion there was all over the place when their Tanzir T's started dropping off. You can imagine how many didn't even think of putting on clean underwear that morning! In the streets, in the trams'n'trains, in the offices, in the lockers of the shower rooms up'n'down Melbourne's hills and dales. Soon, the police stations were full with Tanzir T. customers charged with exposing themselves.

(and)

It was worst at weddings, not much better at far more important occasions like other people's weddings. In his own shop, my father's personal fittings became striptease before his own eyes! He had to apologise to his own dressmaker's dummy. Which wasn't me, fortunately, at the time. I was having my own problems in the interschool swim meet with the bathers he'd run up for me.

> *(A sorely tattered, very bemused and very blown-black TANZIR shadow player struggles around one side of the curtain to:)*

281

TANZIR: Oh, strip-tease, strip-teasing before these very eyes!

STORYTELLER: It's alright, Pop.

TANZIR: I lost a shoe down a very large hole outside my own front door!

STORYTELLER: It's okay, Pop.

TANZIR: It was the best discount I ever got on a shoe. Hell smells like embalming fluid. I thought it'd smell like a goatherd from back home.

STORYTELLER: Not to worry, Pop.

(Gentle hands help the old man back into the shadow area)

STORYTELLER: In no time at all, my poor father's Tanzir T's Fashion Treads rugged looks had turned to blushing pinks in a harsh garment – not to mention stained-glass -- world. There was hardly a Chinese Melbourne lane with a drain that wasn't blocked with Tanzir T's fallen parts with the ghosts of surgical threads hanging off them. The poor old chap.
  (pause)
Yet did he ever get credit from the Tourist Board for the tourist pick-up that down Melbourne lanes was where nobody could keep their clothes on? Or for the pickup in personal safety-equipment trade? No, he did not.

(In mental agony, TANZIR shadow player can be seen to be tearing the shirt off his back – which just dissolves in his hands anyway – then holding up to the heavens his old camel's hump then letting it drop away)

STORYTELLER: This was my father's darkest hour and I know that for a fact. It looked like no more would his mind ever push ahead and make a beeline for the shop exit without him. It was inconceivable if, any more, he could thread a needle in the dark in two seconds flat because there was always at least one light bulb going off in his head. All he could do was put up another sign which went:

(as two or three bearers parade split boards with tiny scrawls trying to fit it all in:)

'Reminder: Tazer Tanzir the Melbourne-lane Threader regrets a no-refund policy applies to all seams. Please check all stitches with your local surgical authority before purchase.'

(and)

With not an exclamation mark in sight.

(and then)

Oh, ladies and gentlemen, it says here I should re-emphasize these were hard times. And I do re-emphasize it. These were hard times, the worst. Regardez…

(TANZIR shadow player slums over his sewing machine, while others try to pull a pair of his trousers apart but can't)

STORYTELLER: It was… it is… a time when all the lights could go out.

(They do. There is a brief total blackout in the blink of an eye.)

4.

(Lighting up with TANZIR back to happily working away at a hem on a woman modelling one of his dresses. It is all a happily busy tailor shop, with people coming and going and the tailor trying to do two things at once etc. We have the feeling that the STORYTELLER now has some time to himself so that he can leisurely go into:)

STORYTELLER: Friends, I think it's fair to say that an ordinary Melbourne-lane threader might not have recovered from that dissolving surgical thread fiasco. But my father was no ordinary Melbourne-lane threader, and you don't know your skin from where it shrinks if you say so!

(Behind, the shadow playing prepares to illustrate the 'rebirth' of TANZIR, as it is narrated:)

283

STORYTELLER: No, sirree. He could have sat there and let his business dissolve around his ears like his garments were around his customers' ears, but no one reckoned on that mind of his which was always capable of shooting ahead and out of the shop door.

(aside)

My theory's always been that it didn't like the close proximity of all that pudge in the fingers but I could never catch it up to ask.

(pauses for effect)

He mightn't be able, no, to do anything about all his stitches dissolving into thin air, but somewhere along the line he saw that he *could* do something about his invaluable Tanzir T's signature he put on his Tanzir T's Fashion Treads. Now, he might be the one person who realised that that little scribble of his name with that felt pen was worth more than the garment it was hidden away on, but the customer didn't know that. Wasn't his signed label, after all, what his customers paid so much extra for? Wasn't it just precisely that which they searched high'n'low for, and couldn't be prouder of especially if they could honestly say to their friends they hadn't found it yet and were looking every day? Or even that they had been cheated and it wasn't even there?... how exclusive was that, there being only one time like it!

(He waits while the shadow players search their clothes. None can find the signed Tanzir T. label at first sight, and begin to strip off so that can search better. Soon they are all stripped down to their underwear, and pouring over their clothes. Satisfied, he can continue:)

STORYTELLER: It was plain as day! At least to my father it was! Daylight robbery by the Italian sods, dissolving or non-dissolving surgical thread instead of the real thing... what of it when it all boiled down? What remained untouched and unsullied through all the tribulation was the Tanzir T. signed label!

(then)

From that realization, the solution was easy. Or I think it was. I know that for the first time in his business life, my father snapped his fingers. It was quite a moment for the more pudgy life! That snap made a lot of pudge proud.

(He allows his father to delight in snapping his fingers in other people's faces)

284

STORYTELLER: After that, my father underwent a foregoing of all sewing and, instead, simply concentrated on the signed tags of it all with the sole and immutable proviso that, this time, just being on a garment didn't matter so much as that-there Tanzir T. signed label had to now be the very first thing anyone wearing or not wearing a Tanzir T's Fashion Treads item saw.

(and)

With one extra proviso, even to that! – and *that* was that any of his signed tags doubled as a price tag and… yet more!... that price had to be just as prominent as the signing of the Tanzir name, plus in a large'n'rough scribble. He called it his large'n'rough scribbled signed price tag. The Tanzir T. large'n'rough scribbled signed price tag!

(Sign bearer emerge with however signs are needed to spread the message: 'The Tanzir T. large'n'rough scribbled signed price tag!' followed by a last one finally bearing the sign: 'Cop the exclamation!'

To take their place in attention, Tanzir large'n'rough scribbled signed price tags start raining down like spaghetti back in the shadow area)

STORYTELLER: What's unbelievably more, his strict dictate was that no – underlined here -- *no* large'n'rough signed price tag could be tagged or sold at a lesser price than the garment it was designed to be on, even when it wasn't on the garment it was designed to be on, even if that garment was discounted to zero. Never! Never ever! A Tanzir T. large'n'rough signed price tag was never to be cheapened by being sold cheaper than the sewn item it was attached to and therefore presumably meant for.

(further pause)

And it had to be tagged large'n'roughly easy-to-find on any body part, showing the price and the signature prominently.

(yet another pause)

And none of his tag were ever to be seen anywhere near an item of his clothing, especially near any expensive cloth which might have come from Italy and the same thieving garlic guzzlers who con you into buying dissolving surgical threads marketed as treads threads. No way and no sir; each and every Tanzir T. Fashion Treads large'n'rough scribbled signed price tags had to be handwritten on scribbling cardboard out of a... any!... Chinese restaurant from a Melbourne lane. It didn't matter which, and by way of permanent-marker scribble, as long as it saved a used Chinese take-away box from being thrown away.

(Behind, shadow players scramble to pick up the rained-down large'n'rough scribbled signed price tags lying around the ground. When they have successfully done so, sign bearers hold up signs displaying: 'Chinee lanes – cleanest in town!')

STORYTELLER: It was brilliant! It was throw out the old clothes hangers and in with the large'n'rough scribbled signed price tag hooks! This is Tazer Tanzir's, the Melbourne-lane Threader, shop! This is where you get properly tagged! You want bespoke cloths sewn into clothes, go elsewhere, even hence! But if you want the most expensive high-fashion tag, signed and priced-to-break-your-purse for the tag alone, you have come to the right place! Clothes on your back? Forget commonplace concepts! You're here in Australia with Tanzir with the embalming fluid not the goatherd piss you can't scrub off! With Tanzir T's Fashion Treads large'n'rough scribbled signed price tags, who needs rags on your back to *really impress*? And those are...
   (waves script)
this's italics, not mine!
   (and)
But what exclamation marks!
   (and sailing on)
It was simply this: World, free yourself from the fickles of the sewn without missing out on paying through the nose!

(Behind the shadow players are now strutting around naked, or near so, with large price tag tied around their necks or arms or thighs... displaying their wares.

Two of them... rather demurely only dressed in either underpants or bra-and-panties but prominently tagged with a large'n'rough scribbled signed price tag – emerge as before onto the front stage holding up a sign to get across the message:
'Tanzir T's, the fashion treads to free you of the fickles of the sewn!...'

286

followed closely behind by a second pair carrying signs that complete:
'without missing out on paying through the nose!'

Each competitively appears at edge of scrim curtain to wail:)

SIGN BEARERS 1 AND 2: 'Tanzir T's, the fashion treads to free you from the fickles of the sewn!...

SIGN BEARERS 3 AND 4: ...'without missing out on paying through the nose!'

ALL FOUR SIGN BEARERS: Who needs exclamation marks?, exclamation mark!

(They obligingly return behind screen)

STORYTELLER: (alone at last) Well, good people, you can imagine the rush in the shop and into the subsequent Tanzir T. franchises that had to be opened down that Melbourne lane to cope with the demand! My father had done it. He had gone to the depth of the sink hole and returned triumphantly on the crest of the mightiest Fifth ever seen or heard! The mad rushes down not just our Melbourne lane but all Melbourne lanes with laney profiles got such that his mind hardly ever went ahead and out of the front door anymore because it had such trouble getting back in once it did!
(as the lighting behind fades to sunset...)
Eventually, as you all will know, my father got back to sewing again, it being his whole life, after all. Yet, even here, he protected the high value of the Tanzir T's Fashion Treads large'n'rough scribbled signed price tag that the world of fashion had lifted to exultation by then, by putting his tags on absolutely rubbishy garments that he could pretend he wouldn't dream of ever turning out and therefore had to be pirate jobs out of Vietnam or somewhere... the impeccable reason being nothing could beat Tazer Tanzir, the Melbourne-lane Threader's large'n'rough scribbled signed price tag prices for any garment counterfeiter who was willing to pay royalties on the tag.

(But he has to stop, when TANZIR suddenly starts trying to fight another sneezing fit. As the warning of the drum rolling begins

287

in tune with it, the other shadow players start backing away from him.

The STORYTELLER is confused by it all, searches script unsuccessfully for reference, as his father sneezes number One...)

STORYTELLER: ('what's this?') Eh?

(His father gets drum-rolled into sneezing number Two)

STORYTELLER: (re script) This down here some place...?

(His father gets drum-rolled into sneezing number Three, while the other shadow players are now really making their moves)

STORYTELLER: *Hey...!*

(His father now gets drum-rolled into making number Four, which preludes number Five... the dreaded Fifth...)

STORYTELLER: (alarm bells) How many was that?! Anybody counting?!

(realises it to be so as his father and the drum roll head uncontrollably into the Fifth's build-up which cannot be denied)

STORYTELLER: *Head for the hills!*

(Blackout.

Over, a tremendous explosion and sounds of a whole building collapsing)

---o0o---

288

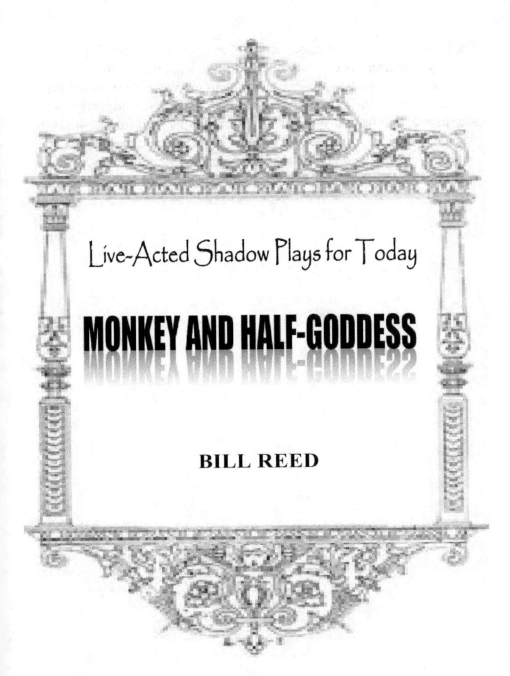

Live-Acted Shadow Plays for Today

MONKEY AND HALF-GODDESS

BILL REED

The behind-the-screen shadow action – or 'inner background' play --
can only ever keep 'pace' with the reading, not *keep up* with it.
Because of the resultant and necessary shadow-play distillation of the
storyteller's tale, the extensive stage directions given in this script are
only intended to be indicators as to what *might* be used for the shadow-
play side of things. They deliberately go beyond what the director
would employ and are given merely as a range of possible shadow-
actions he or she might want to use in the 'distillation'.

The Characters

THE KING/STORYTELLER:
Story participating. Wears crown and assorted summer dresses Relates the ballad from his angle, making a virtue of an unrehearsed reading straight from his script of off his hand-held device. Often 'orchestrates' the illustrating shadow movements behind the scrim and behind him. Can't help his asides. He's king, after all.

MONKEY SHADOW PLAYER:
Will appear to be in front of scrim to speak lines as and when necessary, often squatting opposite the Half-Goddess while they exchange dialogue.

HALF-GODDESS SHADOW PLAYER:
As the Monkey, will come out from behind scrim to speak lines, always confrontational, as and when necessary.

4 or so SHADOW ACTORS
taking the various parts mentioned during the narration.

Monkey and Half-Goddess

(The lighting comes up on a screen showing the KING changing into frocks and parading around before his courtiers, preening himself, getting cheered on.

He will emerge to sit in the narration spot, with his script in hand, wearing a dress underneath his crown. He consults and reads from the notes/script as an integral part of the production.

As he does so, the shadow playing reflects his subjects and then projects the MONKEY and the GODDESS as he describes while they illustrate any of the incidents he mentions as they can:)

KING: When this particular king we are tall-tales talking about here…
   (adds very definite aside)
which is me, by the way, and kindly-and-kingly so, if I might say so m'self…
   (continues)
…wasn't in his once-upon-a-time palace there, he right-royally disguised it, the palace, as an ordinary sort of house in order to discourage thieves which of course encouraged thieves.
   (pause to see if shadow action is keeping up)
This time in the now-as-then time, as he did not so very often, the king came out of lapidary where he was counting his precious stones to sew on as buttons for the once-upon-a-year carnival of his summer dresses where he could show his people his right royal dress sense. There were so many different prints and colours and styles, he didn't know where to start apart from starting from his bottom up.
   (aside)
As you can see and I hope appropriately appreciate…

   (He struts and 'cat-walks' the dress he has chosen to wear now)

KING: Likee, likee? See how I'm not only saying mauve is in this year, but I am walking the walk? Like any king at the head of his troops should.
   (then waves notes/script)

292

I'm reading from this. I'm the King; I'm allowed to have a memory like a sieve. God knows where this place would be if I had a good one. I doubt whether there'd be anyone left.

(He returns very satisfied to his narration's station, and)

KING: What a queen and so gay, hee hee! What a wardrobe and wimple! The king paraded those summer dresses throughout the length and breadth of shopping malls with handbags on the hooks and tickets on the hangers-on and the breathless on the speechless… didn't I ever!... and he did it also down streets paved and duck-boarded, up and down town, over'n'above open sewers in a burst of gay parade and parody. It was all his once-upon-a-year time, yes, of showing off his summer dresses so that his people knew what they were fighting the hard graft of the life he gave them for.
(and)
A lot of ingrates, in my opinion. Which, I remind you, is royal.
(continues)
Meanwhile, as passed down by smoky word of smoky mouth, the palace-turned-into-a-house was not without its thieves and each year never was.

(The shadows reflect this, and then clear to show the two main thieves of:)

KING: Along those lines and upstairs, the monkey…
(aside)
And what a thieving sod that one was!
(continues)
was quietly shaking one window pane loose, reaching out from the end of a bough. And meanwhile along the same sort of lines, downstairs, the half-Goddess
(aside)
And what a thieving sod-dess that one was! Real finicky too.
(continues)
was twisting a few hinges loose with her fingernails, but covered with gloves so she wouldn't leave any fingerprints that might show up next year somewhere on the king's summer prints.

(To appropriate creaking and sundry noises, they were trying not

to make -- and one on one side of the screen and the other on the other side -- MONKEY and HALF-GODDESS go about their burglaries, unknowingly in syncopation with each other, while:)

KING: And thus it was that each year, unbeknown to each other, the monkey and the half-goddess did this on the same day at the same time and the same glum faces. It was not to say she was ugly…
    (aside)
although, moosh-wise, she was pretty grim
    (continues)
and it was not to say the monkey was not ugly…
    (continues)
they just looked alike and it just all looked a bit crook. Also, they were, both, not the cleanest of thieves to set before a king, either, even if the palace was not transformed into a plain-old-day house, sort of.
    (and)
See, they both had things about their private parts which might explain why they were loners, each.

    (First MONKEY and then HALF-GODDESS come quickly
    around their respective side of the scrim curtain, turn and show
    their rear ends and then, when the KING is not referring to them
    again, just as quickly return back to shadow area and take up
    shadow acting again…)

KING: Frankly, when I read here that the monkey had been rolling around in 3B best-drawing graphite somewhere turning his anal display into a bit of a leaden dud and his bare breasts duddier than the usual dud monkey-lovers would be used to… well, frankly, it explained a lot. And…
    (and rounding on her appearance)
when it got rumoured the half-goddess had the imprints of the poverty of owning only one dress and with the consequence of 3B best-drawing graphite-type hand smudges where bikini cloth would be if she was part of the king's…
    (aside)
Not me; don't count me in on this one…
    (continues)

294

beach fashion parade which she wasn't because the king kept all bikinis to model himself so that the really-wide welter of his eating wasn't on display by contrast or by half...

(catches breath)

Phew. A few commas wouldn't go amiss there.

(continues)

These unseemly-to-a-King's-eye great bikini smears on the half-goddess's private parts were from her rucking up her knickers and hoisting up her bras a lot more than she perhaps ought to, but nobody dared to ask why. They looked chafey.

(pause to further pick them out)

So, you'd have to say they certainly weren't the most pleasant-looking monkey and half-goddess the world had seen. Neither of them was the greatest thing to set before a king.

(aside)

Ain't that for sure! Excusee...

> *(He adjusts his foundation garments, while the shadow players wait... very long-sufferingly... for him to finish, to seek and get approval from audience for his seams, and continue. Then they can resume the echoing shadow acting:)*

KING: So, having broken into the top floor of the house, the monkey would eat all it could find up there except any banana, which it hated simply because it hated bananas, and would rip apart everything it could lay its claws on. It particularly delighted in leaving a stool on the king's bed as its calling card.

(aside)

I mean, how's that for disgusting? Even I hesitate before doing *that*.

(continues reading while MONKEY re-enacts:)

From the window, it would throw rocks at anybody passing down below at street level or even minding their own businesses strolling along past the king's pad pretending it was just a plain-as-day old house. And when that thieving monkey of a monkey couldn't make any more people more disgusted, it would start throwing stones down the staircase at whoever it heard each and every year moving around downstairs and stopping it from having the whole place to itself. Year after year, always, yes, the same once-upon-a-time.

> *(When MONKEY has stopped jumping up and down with fury*

295

and throwing rocks right, left and centre, HALF-GODDESS
comes back into shadow-play for:)

KING: A bit over-doing it. Still…
    (continues reading)
the half-Goddess, despite her name, was not much better than the
monkey. Once inside downstairs, she would guts down all she could
eat except any banana which she thought was bad for her chafe and also
simply because she hated bananas anyway, would tear up everything
she could get her claws into, loved leaving a stool in the king's
bathroom's wash basin as a calling card.
    (aside)
Say, I never knew that. No wonder I never used it.
    (carries on reading)
She too would throw rocks and break as many heads of the passers-by
down at street level as she could and give the people minding their own
businesses passing the king's pad the real squitters. Then, too, when
she couldn't make any more people any more miserable, she would
throw rocks up the stairs at whoever it was she heard up there each and
every year at this time, stopping her from having the whole place to
herself.

    (HALF-GODDESS finishes her stint. She now confronts shadow
    stairs going upwards to high heaven, while MONKEY comes to
    confront stairs going downwards to high hell, and:)

KING: It's got here that, as silly as it sounds, and not as silly as some
of the King's dresses…
    (giggles and carries on)
… that the monkey was well aware that each year at summer-dress
parade time in the best shopping malls in all the land…
    (aside, appeased)
Okay, all's forgiven.
    (and)
the truth be known, Monkey broke only broke in upstairs because it
was scared of the somebody it heard downstairs. Likewise, the truth be
known, Half-Goddess only broke in downstairs and only ransacked
down there because she was wary of whoever it was she heard moving
around upstairs. Also, every year, the only things left untouched either

by the monkey upstairs or the half-goddess downstairs were the bananas, which they both thought were disgusting.

(The banana prop comes floating but does not tantalise)

KING: So the King...
   (aside)
clever old me!...
   (continues)
ordered all the food taken out of the pretend house save for one banana to be disguised as a whole banana banquet-in-itself, not only fit for a king, but also for modern-day thieves with their penchant for the higher things of life than kings, especially when it came to summer dresses and bananas
   (aside)
the cheeky little rotters...
   (carries on)
and he ordered that it, the banana disguised as a whole banana banquet-in-itself fit for a king, should be placed on the staircase exactly halfway up and halfway down the staircase... in other words, halfway between Monkey's side of upstairs and exactly half on Half-Goddess's side of downstairs.

   (The staircase props join so that MONKEY is looking down and HALF-GODDESS is looking up, both with agitated curiosity. They enact:)

KING: Well, it worked straight away, as these tall stories retold tend to do, don't you know Both the monkey and the half-goddess tried to creep up or down the stairs to get to the whole banana banquet-in-itself fit-for-a-king left midway there as the only food they could steal that was at all fit for a monkey better than a king and a half-goddess better than a king.
   (waits while they shadow-illustrate)
Looking down at the whole banana banquet-in-itself fit-for-a-king, Monkey thought the spread looked just made for it -- and looking up at the whole banana banquet-in-itself fit-for-a-king, the half-goddess thought the spread looked just about made for her and her chafe.

(Their reaching for the banana gets desperate, frustrating)

297

KING: They could creep down; they could creep up. They could stretch their arms out as far as they could and nearly get to touch that banquet. But each time they got near to it, they were pushed back by hearing whoever it was up there and whoever it was down there sneaking around like some thief in the night copying what they were trying to do.
  (pause for a little head-shaking pity)
Not that either gave up trying. Each was so sick of being pushed around year after year by whoever it was always stopping them from having the whole place to themselves that each hid on the landing above and below the whole banana banquet-in-itself fit-for-a-king left for them and waited for nightfall.

   (The night comes shadowy; there is barely any light and certainly not for MONKEY or HALF-GODDESS)

KING: At midnight, of course, no moonlight of course, each made a dash for the banquet fit-for-a-king that was really only a banana and, of course, they collided front on right on half way.

   (They do so blindly – a couple of bouncing balls – until, beckoned by the KING's snap of fingers, they break off and come around their sides of the screen to sit on their haunches front stage staring across at each other)

KING: Monkey thought:

MONKEY: What a filthy black smudge of a human being; I can do her.

KING: Half-Goddess thought:

HALF-GODDESS: What a filthy black bum of a monkey; I can do it.

   (The KING snaps his fingers again for them to return to the shadow area, where, after another face-off:)

KING: They fought. Oh boy, didn't they ever!
  (aside)

Almost as much fun as making fashion statements with black little numbers in the shopping malls!

(back to reading script)

They fought so hard they wound up in adjacent beds at the local royal hospital that normally was the king's karaoke bar out of the summer-dress season.

(aside)

But then one must *sacrifice*, don't you know.

(continues reading)

And this side-by-sideness again was too much. The monkey closed it eyes; it didn't want to be seen there with something that looked like a thieving-arsed half-goddess any monkey would be ashamed to be seen with, especially in a hospital bed that normally was a karaoke drinks' bar. And Half-Goddess closed her eyes because she didn't want to be seen in a hospital bed that normally was a karaoke drinks' bar with something that looked like a thieving-arsed monkey no half-goddess would want to be seen anywhere near. Instead, they pretended they were back in the king's pretend house licking their wounds.

(pauses for shadow re-enactments to catch up)

The trouble was each of them was thinking with a mixture of sullenness and cunning, not a good combination on empty stomachs not lined with any binding banana fibre.

(While they despatch all the mountains of bandages they have to get to returning to either side of the front stage by his finger beckoning:)

KING: Their miseries were especially so since their thoughts were pretty much around the same miserable thing... being prevented from getting to the whole banana banquet-in-itself fit-for-a-king set for them by the other thieving-arsed filthy thing shuffling around in the dark. What another miserable thieving sod!, they were each thinking.

MONKEY: (now squatting front stage) What another miserable thieving sod! Why should I be run off by her with my tail between my legs? I'm cleverer.

HALF-GODDESS: (ditto) What another miserable thieving sod! Why should I be run off by an it with a tail between its legs with my tail between my legs? I'm cleverer.

299

(The KING snaps his fingers for them to return. They follow his order but noticeably now more surlily, more cunningly. Once behind the scrim, they seem unmindful about passing each other by and going to the opposite side than they started:)

KING: But when it opened its eyes, the monkey found itself not upstairs but downstairs and not only downstairs but sitting half in the stool the half-goddess had left in the king's bathroom wash basin down there and half not.
  (waits for the MONKEY's panic to subside)
Its first reaction was panic before it realised it had better disguise itself as the half-goddess quick smart so that if she caught him down there she'd only confuse herself.
  (and)
Likewise, when she opened her eyes. the half-goddess found herself not downstairs in her usual place but upstairs, and not only upstairs but half-sitting pretty much in the stool the monkey always left on the king's bed and half not, and she got so scared of being taken off by the monkey into the jungle and losing her virginity before she ever found it again after hanging it out to dry one time.
  (aside)
Well, many times, if what my spies tell me is right.
  (gets back on script)
 So, Half-Goddess quickly disguised herself as a chimp so if that thieving filthy-arsed monkey caught her it would only confuse itself.
  (waits for all that to happen)
In their new disguises upstairs and downstairs there, neither dared move, despite where they had found themselves half-sitting. Their faces became as long as some of the king's summer dresses.
  (aside)
Wasn't this ever written a few fashion statements ago!
  (renews reading)
The king and the entire king's cortege in their summer corsages could return anytime and then they would really be in the poo and not halfway, either. Their stomachs – those of the monkey and half-goddess, not those of the king and his cortege -- were starting to rumble with the time they were waiting breathlessly, not to mention the monkey thought:

(MONKEY comes around to upfront but obviously getting a bit annoyed to having to do so now, and:)

MONKEY: This wasn't fair, and it certainly is no fair shake of the stick!

KING: ...not to mention the Half-Goddess thinking...

(She has to scurry around to the front stage area and is obviously getting just as disaffected at having to do so as the MONKEY:)

HALF-GODDESS: This wasn't fair, and it certainly is no suck of the old sav which is far better than a fair shake of the old leg, so there!

KING: (brushing any rebellion off) They didn't know magic enough to know how they had gotten where they sat, but somehow Monkey did know where and in what Half-Goddess was half-sitting and how she was trying to disguise her thieving filthy-arsed self as him. And Half-Goddess did know somehow where and in what Monkey was half-sitting and how it was trying to disguise its thieving filthy-arsed self to look like her. You know, the monkey was thinking...

(Thinking about it, MONKEY gets quite enthusiastic about having to take the trouble to come up front so soon again and:)

MONKEY: You know, come to think about it, the creature sort of kind of does look a bit like me.

(and returns to shadow area while HALF-GODDESS likewise gets far more enthusiastic about having to get up and come back upfront before she is quite ready, and gathers energy for:)

HALF-GODDESS: You know, when I look at how I think about it, I have to admit that creature sort of kind of does look a bit like me.

(She returns thoughtfully back to the shadow area too)

KING: In fact, the longer they sat in each other's stool the more each started having funny feelings for their lesser halves half-sitting in a stool down there in the wash basin really in the stinko or half-sitting really in the stinko up there on the King's bed.

(and)

But, o audience mine, there were larger appetites were in play here! That…

(loses lines, has to go back to reading the script)

… that same night -- and again it would have to be midnight of course, but this time a full moon of course, according to how the clouds get sucked up together by centuries of tall-story narrative around centuries of campfires, blah blah blah -- the monkey disguised as the half-goddess crept up towards the banana-disguised-as-a-banquet-fit-for-a-king at the exact same time as the half-goddess disguised as the monkey was creeping down towards the banana-disguised-as-a-banquet-fit-for-a-king.

Again, they met exactly in the middle of the stairway there where the King…

(aside)

Crafty old me! It's breeding the upbringing, you know.

(then)

had had it placed. They stopped in their tracks, not believing what they were seeing, too shocked to move. Now Monkey had to contend with another live monkey. Now Half-Goddess had to contend with another live Half-Goddess. This was too much by half!

(He pauses to encourage MONKEY and HALF-GODDESS to put more into their displaying of 'This was too much by half')

KING: It was one thing to share the palace-cum-house with a half-Goddess, up herself, if you were a thieving-arsed monkey or to share the palace-cum-house with a monkey, up itself, if you were a thieving-arsed half-Goddess, but quite another thing to have to share it with another thieving filthy-arsed monkey or another thieving filthy-arsed half-goddess with 3B best-drawing graphite smudged all over their unmentionable parts.

(aside)

Even I draw a line at that!

(goes to read on, but has to wait for the shadow acting to catch up, especially while MONKEY and HALF-GODDESS circle each other waiting for an opening to launch themselves at each other.

Which they eventually do, and disappear in a cloud of dust…)

KING: (hurrahing) Oh, and didn't they go at each other! They threw themselves! They flung themselves! They went toe-to-toe over that banana-disguised-as-a-banquet-fit-for-a-king.

(The cut-out dust clouds give way. They are only almost 'at' each other but now stopped:)

KING: Or they thought they did, thought they were. But this time, there was the moment's hesitation of monkey upon monkey and the moment's hesitation of half-goddess upon half-goddess. And instead of falling upon each other in a crook old way claws'n'all, they found themselves falling into the crooks of each other's arms, going as to confuse even themselves…

(He has to wait for them to obey his signal to come up front because they are locked in each other's arms and have to 'crab' it out from behind scrim, and not before trying to get the other to go their way. They finally make it front stage, and:)

MONKEY: Brother!

HALF-GODDESS: Sister!

KING: Getting their disguises and genders mixed up, and who would blame them.

MONKEY: Sister!

HALF-GODDESS: Brother!

KING: And if that wasn't enough, Monkey couldn't believe it was hearing itself, meaning the banana-as-a-banquet-fit-for-a-king, going:

MONKEY: (bowing) Do please dig in and fill your boots first.

KING: And Half-Goddess couldn't believe she was saying to it concerning the banana-as-banquet, going:

303

HALF-GODDESS: (deeper bow) No, please, you first. Please dig in and fill your boots.

MONKEY: Dear madam.

HALF-GODDESS: Kind sir.

> *(They return to behind the scrim, hand-in-hand, where birds are singing, lambs are playing, cut-out hearts are floating everywhere...)*

KING: Oo, so polite, so idyllic, it could have been making each feel really miserable but, strangely, wasn't. And it seemed that that was all that was needed too, as the king's all-seeing eyes had it.
   (aside)
And you can bet on that.
   (then, to MONKEY nit-picking her)
No sooner said than done, the Monkey was buffing off the greasy 3B best-drawing graphite smudges from the half-Goddess's private parts and...
   (to HALF-GODDESS nit-picking it)
the half-goddess was buffing off the 3B best-drawing graphite stains from the monkey's private-display-y parts. It was all very familiar, intimate-wise, almost getting to the stage where we all should be averting our eyes. Or was it the other way around, up and down, as the king's all-seeing eyes had it? It might have been. Nevertheless, when they had cleaned each other up, their hearts now on the other's sleeve...
   (aside)
Yes, and that sleeve was lifted out of my autumn-wear wardrobe, too. Remind me to gut that locksmith of mine; I'll give him 'something to slip into', the big poofie!
   (returns to script)
... sleeve, and they return to their original positions...

> *(MONKEY scrambles up to the top of his half of the stairs and HALF-GODDESS scrambles down to the bottom of her half of the stairs... to their original positions. When readied...)*

KING: (long-sufferingly) ...positions I say, and then they crept down, the one, and crept up, the other, to the exact midway point, neither up

304

nor down, if the king's surveyor was to be believed... ever so gingerly and ever so diplomatically... where the one banana that was disguised as a whole banquet fit for a king was. You had to be there to see it! There wasn't even a turning up of the nose because it was a banana, so disguised as a banquet fit for a king it was! And then... and then...

(waiting, waiting, as their fingertips edge towards the 'centre')

KING: ... and then, when there, at the centre of it all, when their fingers touched -- light in touch, tipple to tipple, tripped by the tripping up -- it was not lost on Monkey and it wasn't lost on Half-Goddess...

MONKEY: (cry out) It is not lost on me!

HALF-GODDESS: (ditto) Same here! Even lost-ier!

MONKEY: Not as lost-ier as me!

HALF-GODDESS: Certainly just as lost-ier!

MONKEY: (appeased) Okay.

HALF-GODDESS: (ditto) Okay.

KING: ... as to how, after all those thieving filthy-arsed years, they had arrived at the banana at the centre of it'n'them both. Or at least the banana skin which was all that was left of the banana.
(pause for dramatic effect)
For, banana skin was all it was by then. They had taken so long, of course, to meet halfway that the banana had not only long gone rotten, but had gone *poof*! Poof!, up in magical smoke, would you believe!

(Nothing but a shadowy ghost of a banana skin floats above them in the air)

KING: There was nothing there and nothing to it! Not even grilling the sugar ants could explain it. Of the fit-for-a-king banquet Monkey had thought was duly fit for it and Half-Goddess had thought was duly fit for her, there was nothing left to either! They had become two *pansies*!

(aside, queanishly:)
They should meet my locksmith.
(carries on reading)
Did it discern them, concern them, unlearn them?
(orchestrating action behind his back)
The monkey would have thought so.

MONKEY: (dutifully) I would have thought so.

HALF-GODDESS: (ditto) I would have thought so.

KING: The half-goddess would have thought so. The king with his all-seeing eye would have thought so, in order to teach them a lesson about thieving 3B-graphite khybers. But they were not discerned, concerned; they were not unlearned. They might have poked there and scraped there…
(not turning but presuming)
As they should be doing now.
(and)
But when they looked at one another, they were still holding each other's hand, even if Monkey knew it was holding a monkey's hand pretending to be a half-goddess's mouthful-of-a-banquet's-nuffink, even if Half-Goddess knew she was holding a half-goddess's hand pretending to be a monkey's mouthful-of-a-banquet's-nuffink. The main thing, though, was they had fed off each other in that most famous and particular of fairy-tale ways.

(He snaps his fingers impatiently for them to get around to the front of the curtain once again, where:)

MONKEY: I hate bananas.

HALF-GODDESS: Bananas, I can't stand.

KING: 'Normally'.

MONKEY: Normally.

HALF-GODDESS: Normally.

KING: Said Half-Goddess too, after Monkey had, scratching the chafe she believed a banana had given her by way of a bit of a cluck that she was.

(gradually working up to reading finale)
But this was the thing, other than the major thing of feeding off the other: they came to see it was the absolute best when they fed off each other's miserable dislike of bananas.

MONKEY: We see it is the absolute best when we feed off each other.

HALF-GODDESS: We see it is the absolute best when we feed off each other.

MONKEY and HALF-GODDESS: (together, dully) We see it is the absolute best when we feed off each other.

KING: Pats on the heads all round. And so, the moral was a lay-down misere: Monkey realised it wouldn't be anywhere near the same lonely miserable dork if it just simply disguised itself as Half-Goddess and fed off her similar miserable dislike for bananas.

MONKEY: I realise I wouldn't be the same lonely miserable dork if I just simply...
(forgets lines)
do *that... thing...* said.

KING: (not to be discouraged now) And it was the same for the half-goddess. She saw how she wouldn't be the same lonely miserable dorkess if she just disguised herself as the monkey and fed off his similar miserable dislike of bananas.

HALF-GODDESS: I saw how I wouldn't be the same lonely miserable dorkess if I...
(forgets too; takes a stab)
we feed off each other or something, keeping bananas out of the picture or somethingorother.

KING: ('exactly') So, in the thereafter of any shaggy-dog pull-this-one you could name... when Monkey dressed as Half-Goddess, and Half-Goddess dressed as Monkey, but still got their thieving 3B-pencil-

307

leaded arses in gear with each other, the king's summer dresses stayed
pretty much the same-old, same-old.
   (aside)
Hey, that's a cheap shot!
   (but manages to carry on anyway)
And the summer-dress seasons rolled royally on. Monkey even
changed over to being Half-Goddess's left-handedness; the half-
goddess even changed over to being the monkey's right-handedness,
and all that stuff'n'nonsense.

   *(They are back behind the scrim and back to shadow acting with
   the necessary props to re-enact...)*

KING: She grew its beard; it grew just her hint of a moustache but
kept it discreetly waxed. They both displayed their tail-ends a lot,
especially as they mooned them out of the windows at the people down
at street level just minding their own business trying to stroll by their
king's pad of a palace on a lazy Sunday afternoon pretending it was an
ordinary house.
   (points to how that is illustrated)
Even in that, things had improved, as you can see. Now, instead of
rocks, there were only a couple of 3B-smudged quoits hanging out of
the windows mooning at them. The miserable buggers that used to be
seemed to have gone. In fact... and this is perhaps the real storybook
ending to all this... everybody in the Realm was doing it out of their
windows at passers-by down at street level. Everybody was happy,
especially with the king's summer dresses collection!

   *(All seems to be a fairy-tale lighting fade, but the KING holds
   this up for a moment with:)*

KING: Not quite yet.
   (and)
When they looked around more closely, now that they could, the
monkey and the half-goddess saw that the king had left them an exit
doorway halfway up the stairs and halfway down the stairs, exactly
midway as well.

   *(The behind-the-curtain lights up all technicolour and gay
   flashing lights)*

THE KING: All Monkey and Half-Goddess had to do was take the moral of their story, hold hands forever more, go through the doorway made of lollipops, slide down the barber-pole sugar-candy ladder and feel free to glee away out into the sugar-candy world where chafes and hairy fingers were no more.

(Behind now, a wonderland scene of rainbow and bucolic paradise, and 'Wizard of Oz' music, all soft green fields...)

KING: But, much to the king's chagrin, they didn't take that fairy-tale ending. Oh, no. Why should they, they thought. Palace or not, it was still their home. And the king mightn't be happy about it, but he's not important, except to dictate how high the summer hemlines are going to be.
(looks up brightly though)
No finer legacy, no finer legacy...! My legacies have never looked better in high heels! Do I hear anyone complaining?

(He waits, but gets no complaint)

KING: No, I didn't think so. And I'll tell you why I don't think so. Because this is my house and that banana fit-for-a-king's-banquet was my banana-fit-for-a-king's-banquet and... and...
(casts around for further examples; settles on:)
... and nobody's going to shit on my bed because I can do what I like!

(He nastily flicks a command for the scrim curtain to fall down. It does so immediately, catching the shadow players in various embarrassing states of undress. None knows what to do...)

KING: You think that's bad. Hey, you should get a load of my walk-in wardrobe.

(Blackout)

---oOo---

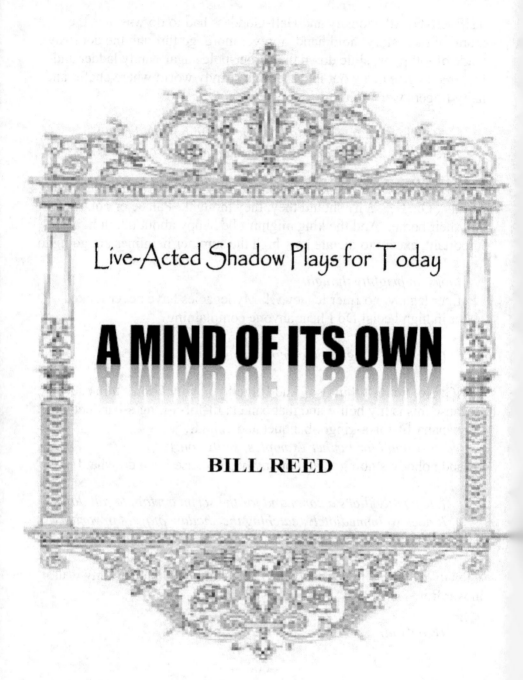

Live-Acted Shadow Plays for Today

A MIND OF ITS OWN

BILL REED

The behind-the-screen shadow action – or 'inner background' play --
can only ever keep 'pace' with the reading, not *keep up* with it.
Because of the resultant and necessary shadow-play distillation of the
storyteller's tale, the extensive stage directions given in this script are
only intended to be indicators as to what *might* be used for the shadow-
play side of things. They deliberately go beyond what the director
would employ and are given merely as a range of possible shadow-
actions he or she might want to use in the 'distillation'.

The Characters

STORYTELLER:
He has a secondary role of coming and going in the shadow action. He has his own shadow player representing him as the fairly-impassive HYPNOTIST as directed.

THE MOTHER:
mainly a shadow player but will come front-of-screen to act conventionally as or when necessary. When behind or in front of scrim curtain, her nervousness shows, snap-snap grrr-grrr.

THE SON SHADOW PLAYER:
Role speaks for itself. Or at least his most brainy part does.

SHADOW PLAYERS:
4 or 5 cast members acting out the shadow versions of academics of both sexes, the hypnotist, psychiatrist, the passers-by, and suchlike.

A Mind of Its Own

*(The back light to the shadow area behind the screen comes on,
but shows only a kindly glow. Rather than any action initially,
sound over intimates a relatively busy shopping street outside the
hypnotist's rooms.*

*The STORYTELLER arrives on his area in front of the scrim
curtain. He 'inspects' from afar the shadow-area set-up to show
he at least thinks he is in charge, picks up the script. This, he
flips through, then shakes his head sorrowfully over it, before he
looks to the wings and answers what must have been whispered
to him:)*

STORYTELLER: No, I did not 'lose' it, okay? Yes, I did think I
could get by without it, okay? No, I did not try to get my memory to
get it down pat. Yes, I did try it; I distinctly remember getting to line
five or six.
   (feels able to turn away, mutters)
What a dong.
   (finally gets 'around' to the audience)
So. good evening. How's it hangin'?
   (and waves script)
Bumpf. I say again. They're lucky I got down to line five or six.

   *(Finally gets to settle down to start reading script to audience. As
   soon as he does so, the shadow area comes alive; the street
   sounds come to normal; the shadow players evoke a normal
   street before, soon, the MOTHER SHADOW PLATER throws
   herself down on the footpath before them, proceeds to illustrate
   what STORYTELLER reads-narrates...)*

STORYTELLER: She appeared... looking hypnotised but she really
wasn't... not yet... on the footpath outside the famous hypnotist's
rooms because she was so prone to being hypnotised she couldn't even
get herself through his front door before hitting the deck.
   (pointing, smirking)
And there she was. As if on cue. The mother of the son with the brainy
penis. Yes, you heard right. Not penis; you hear that all the time. The

'brainy' bit. So brainy, it had a definite mind of its own and the qualifications to prove it.

(as the MOTHER pleads to passers-by for attention)

This was no ordinary brainy penis with a mind of its own you normally come across, either. This penis of her son had a PhD, probably meaning Penis Has Distinctions, right? That penisoscity structure of his was so educated it even disdained using the honorific of 'Doctor' because that was *so* educationally coarse, so culturally PC, or politically or penis correct, right?

(feels need to explain)

You begin to see how it was always big noting itself? Anyway, the fact was the mother of the son with a penis with a mind of its own was down there on the footpath crying out so much that her eyes are suffering backwash and wilting all the passers-by resolve to dog-paddle around her and get on their way without looking at her. But it was more her naked feet and toes that's pulling them to her. Who drops down in the middle of the pavement, sobbing rivers, in naked feet or toes? Are we starting all this with scenes of nudity? And who could blame them, the passers-by, not the toes? Right off the bat, you could see they weren't normal toes, those naked toes weren't...

(The MOTHER is trying to stop all... any... of the shadows hurrying by. We can see, and hear, her large crocodile tears. What is giantish – by shadows -- about her is the toes. They come as props that are literally things apart... prominently large and grotesquely alive to what is being narrated about her feelings... separate things:)

STORYTELLER: Boy, taking up the whole footpath; how diddly-ohs of toes and how-naked-can-you-get?, or what?

(He allows time for the toes to get demonstrated in all their shadow-animation glory, before:)

STORYTELLER: Pork sausages! And not that she was allowing many to get past, the way she grabbed at their ankles and begged them to stop and listen, those toes or no those-toes being naked or not. There was almost nothing for it but for the hypnotist...

(behind, the shadow of the HYPNOTIST does so...)

314

to come out and see what was going on the threshold of his threshings. Hey, what's stopping half the population of North Sydney from passing my door here? What's all this about sex, sex and more sex on the near horizon here, and am I missing out on something? What gives? Who's giving? What's being put out? You know, the usual questions that pop into hypnotists' minds… as to how only good bastardry can come out of sex, sex and more sex. Thank God, for the dangle and the swing of it, right! Makes the eyes of even the mightiest hypnotist glaze over, ha ha.

(He points back at evidence coming from the MOTHER in the shadow area where she leads his narration:)

STORYTELLER: So, with the mother and her naked toes down there, before him and everybody else, making motions of an erectionification going *whoo-whoo bash-bash*, like she's unashamedly going back there right now, right?, and then…

(as she does so…)

STORYTELLER: … making those urgent movements of knee-crunching, crutch-crushings, going *gotta-go, gotta-pee*…

(as she does so…)

STORYTELLER: …then – look at it, will you? – going like she's trying to bite her own bum, going *snap-snap, grrr-grrr*…

MOTHER: (loud enough to be heard) *SNAP-SNAP, GRRR-GRRR!*

STORYTELLER: (despite interruption, carries on reading) What a pantomime! And, there!, she's *bash-bash, gotta-go, snap-snap, grrr-grrr* going, both in a clockwise way and in an antisocial way right in front of the famous hypnotist who's, as I told you, come out and going shrugs-like to the gathering crowd looking daggers at him: I haven't even touched her yet, let alone handed her the bill.
(and)
All quite architectural really if thinking in theatrical terms, which we hope you are, kinda penis-wise. And all enacted by those toes of hers,

315

giving their own all-too-graphic impressions without a stitch on and needing trimming around the nail regions.

> *(with the toes giantishly coming into their own in whoo-whoo, bash-bash, gotta-go gotta-pee, snap-snap grrr-grrr way...)*

STORYTELLER: Not doing it half bad, either, considering.
> *(then as she starts twisting around to try to bite her own bum)*
And, while we could watch her all day getting nowhere near biting her own bum, you'd have to be deaf, dumb and blind not to see she was very clearly saying the why and the how her son and his brainy penis needed the famous hypnotist's help. And, of course, here he comes...

> *(The SON shadow player enters, oddly and stiffly and half-bent over himself, reluctant to straighten, backing in and then beginning to turn around)*

STORYTELLER: (warning shout to him) No turning!

> *(The SON stops, just in time to keep his back to audience. The STORYTELLER turns back to audience, silently shrugs 'hopeless, right?' and then feels he can continue from script:)*

STORYTELLER: Our hero, her son. In the flesh. And what flesh! But he has to keep his back to us, doesn't he?, cos he's not really there, or even here; he's still caught up in the spirit in which his mother there's wailing on about him to the whole of Sydney.

> *(Even as he is speaking, behind, inexorably coming into view, thick ropes haul and steady the dwarfing-all tree-like trunk upright slowly, inevitably raised to stand far beyond the upper reaches of the screen. As it does so, the MOTHER cries out, points with quaking finger (and toes) upwards at it apocalyptically. She tries to bite her own bum with renewed desperation and 'grrrr grrrr's... with her giantishly-shadowed toes going (ecstatically) crazy...)*

STORYTELLER: Grrr-grrr, that's right, Mother. Snap-snap, grrr-grrr. You go right ahead and get it off your chest.
> *(can get back on script)*

And, as I was saying: boy, wasn't she putting those-there naked toes out there on that pavement dobbing her son right in it, too! She was going on help my son…

MOTHER: HELP MY BOY!

STORYTELLER: … because, she's going: apparently, after her baby boy got to thirty-nine years of age, two things hadn't changed. One, he was still at home living in the room he was born in, taking his meals under the door and, two, he was still at school in the same classroom he'd started out preschool in – both the room he was born in and the classroom he was schooled in being the same room. That's what she was going on about, anyway. Or her toes were. Or both were or are. It's hard to say.

> *(To these descriptions and the ones to come, yet keeping from being able to fully straighten up, the SON enacts jumping lovingly from bed to school desk and back to bed etc inches away from each other, then satisfied walks off and, almost spiritously, disappears, while:)*

STORYTELLER: She's wailing away with those toes of hers naked as the day they were first clipped that he'd been refusing to leave home so long that over the years she had to change his cot in his bedroom to a king-sized waterbed with built-in surround sound, and he had been so long in the same classroom that they had upgraded the classes given in there from infant-school to post-graduate school though the desks and chairs, unlike the bed, remained kindergarten. And now… look, will you… she's there or was there now starting to wrestle with some erectionification or something… at least it looked like to the hypnotist and all the others there… and if it's not or wasn't some stiffy she's wrestling with, how come she's still going…

MOTHER: (toes flashing) WOO-WHOO BASH-BASH!

STORYTELLER: Yeah, yeah, whoo-whoo bash-bash, or rubbing her knees together going pee-pee gotta go…

MOTHER: PEE-PEE, GOTTA GO!

317

STORYTELLER: Yeah, pee-pee, gotta go!

MOTHER: SNAP-SNAP GRRRR-GRRRR!

STORYTELLER: Snap-snap grrr-grrr, that's right, Mother. You put the bite on yourself, go on, g-nash, g-nash.
   (and)
So, what's a poor Sydney hypnotist where there's no one left not going around hypnotised do but listen along with the rest of Sydney? And then she's going on about more help-help and how her son grew into becoming a professional student stay-at-home who started absorbing text books along with meals pushed under the door, taking every course he could for fear they mightn't ever let him back in to the classroom if he ever went out of class, which I guess was the front door. Or something.

MOTHER: (just loud enough) He won't let go his books which are tied to his bed which is tied to the desk so tied to being awful so dyed-in-the-wool!

   (The STORYTELLER waits until he thinks she has stopped. But when he goes to read on...

MOTHER: (ditto) Won't let go his books tied to the bed tied to the desk after thirty-nine years, and it's getting on my goat a bit. Thirty-nine *and a half*!

STORYTELLER: (long sufferingly) See, what the hypnotist hadn't realised as yet was that, with so many degrees now under his belt, her son's penisosity had developed, first through educated guesses and then, with open competition between slurpy thoughts open to it and thoughts still niggling away at it, started developing a mind of its own in order to think its whole situation through.
   (and)
By now, though, the hypnotist knew precisely what Mum was talking about. How many times had he tried to tell his own regulars that that's what Education does. You open yourself up to it before seeking professional help, it worms its way in, nestles in cracks, feeds off the host, starts laying down pith and feelings of grandeur, then uses the pith to feed those very feelings of grandeur and the feelings of grandeur to

318

feed the pith. Pretty soon there's a vicious feeding circle going on and there's nothing left of you but an educated carcass. It might be called sex sex and more sex for you to cope with but imagine if you were just a plain old penis! For starters, there can be more than one head for your brain! For another, storks just don't bring babies! Not the storks you as a penis have in mind anyway! And that stuff ain't water you've got on your brain, no way!

(then, to the shadow playing illustrations behind...)
I mean, you and I we can always lay off Education before lining the old stomach in the mornings, no? But where can you go if you're a brainy penis? How many brainy penises do you see floating around that could set any sort of good example? As a penis with a budding mind of your own, you can't just click your fingers and find a soul-mate of a fellow brainy penis you can go up to and get a little sense shoved into you over a few glasses of the old vintage that vints.

(As he pauses for the action to catch up, the giantish tree-type trunk is pulled upright again. He nods I-know to a lot of gasps over, while as the 'thing' is raised, the SON has to bend more and more over himself to hide his lower band.)

STORYTELLER: Following our hypnotist's lead, you could almost understand why the Mother is still going or was going grrrr-grrrr, whoo-whoo bash-bash, gotta pee gotta pee.

MOTHER: (loud enough to be heard, with toes going:) GOING GRRRR-GRRRR, WHOO-WHOO BASH-BASH, GOTTA PEE GOTTA PEE!

STORYTELLER: So we have Mum on her footpath, flashing naked toes, yerk. We have all the half-of-all-Sydney watching, towing kids probably yawning cos they've seen it all. And we have her sonnyjim there. And the famous hypnotist there. Even I'm here, who used to think God is in His heaven and the sun will come up tomorrow until I saw...
(makes the giant-trunk prop gestures)
that thing and realized that He isn't and it won't. Not personally. Dunno about you lot.
(carries on reading regardless)

319

And now who can't see how she's or was now going on about her son's you-know-what now lumbered with Education as its last resort.

(The SON starts jumping happily, even if still hunched, from bed to desk again)

STORYTELLER: And since he wouldn't leave home and was taking all the courses he could lay his brainy penisification on, that-there member of his had soon gotten itself those telltale smoke trails of Education frenticification n' the like. That-there penis began asserting itself and filling any head in him it could find with his fifth Batchelor's degree and fourth Masters and second PhD. And it wasn't as if they were taken from any disreputable university or anything for they were not! This was full-on regular Education stuff leading to the stuff of genius. It was!

MOTHER: BASH-BASH, PEE-PEE, SLAP-SLAP GRRR-GRRR!

STORYTELLER: Yes, yes. Too right, Mother.
    (and)
Apparently, it was soon after all that that that-there son of hers was so stuck with that-there brainy penis of his getting all educatedly uppity, he couldn't talk to a woman without it, the penis, raising itself up in front of her degree by degree, graduation upon graduation, its chest out and boasting all the way. Which, generally, didn't advance much conversation along the path of let's-see-a-bit-more-of-each-other.
    (up at giantish tree prop)
With that thing, how could any more of each other be seen?
    (waits while the SON tries to engage a passing female shadow, manages to get in only a few words before he is slapped and shoved off)
Sad. There had obviously become so much Education with a capital E in that brainy penosity that it stood ready and willing for someone to learn from its acquired wisdom as to what penises were about at the core if they had brains enough to put their minds to it. But it still didn't seem to be getting anywhere, apparently. So, the brainy penis decided it had to sit down…

(The SON breathes a loud sigh of relief, can straighten considerably… even half-turn around to face the audience-side…

320

with the MOTHER's toes calming down slightly)

STORYTELLER: ...and work out how come all the ambiguity between being educated *and* concerning what high-educated standard it was trying to get across... how come it was always getting so slugged by every woman it tried to have an intelligent conversation with -- and even causing the mother of its own brain pan to start rolling around footpaths in Sydney looking like she was trying to climb up some snake-charmer's rope, with naked toes on.

MOTHER: BASH-BASH, PEE-PEE, SLAP-SLAP GRRR-GRRR!

STORYTELLER: Well! She certainly had the wobble-wib-sway of either the rope or the king cobra she was wrestling with down pat as they could be subject to *whoo-whoo, bash-bash* outside the hypnotist's office.

(He diverts a little when shadow action catches up...)

STORYTELLER: Too much of a good thing... Reminds me of the fellow who wolfs down a slap-up five course meal and when they lad-de-dah present him with the bill he says, 'I've only got a fiver'. So, they call the cops and the cops arrest him. Outside he pays the cops a fiver to let him out of the paddy wagon.

(and can get back on script... with, now, even the HYPNOTIST shadow player offering to assist the writhing mother)

STORYTELLER: And, good people, that wasn't the end of it, either. Just about then – or now -- she cried out by way of going: 'This isn't the end of it, this isn't, either!'

MOTHER: (shout at) This isn't the end of it, this isn't, either!

HYPNOTIST: (shout out for those not hearing) She said, 'This isn't the end of it, this isn't, either!' Can anyone see it?!

STORYTELLER: (suffering the interruptions) And, you see, good people, it is most thought that she was meaning how her son's monstrously-educated penis not only caused him such terrible trouble

321

with women, but wasn't much better when the poor lad had to confront a man anywhere out of the confines of his room. No, really! In front of men, as well. apparently! Before the same sex sex and more sex in open defiance of social decorum! Yes, sir! In front of men, too, her son's grotesquely-educated brainy penis with its own tertiary qualifications not even allowing him to stop and have a good old chat, without it making the poor boy to do precisely what his poor mother is trying to show us now... knees crunching-together, and cods-grabbing and going *gotta-go, gotta-hose-pipe-it-pal*!

MOTHER: (writing) GOTTA GO! GOTTA HOSE PIPE IT DOWN!

STORYTELLER: Exactly! And then, she is or was going on to say it started to be sex sex and more sex by brainy degrees and it was hurting her own toes standing in the community.
  (then turns around to address MOTHER directly)
Look, those toes feel better if you came out here and saved me the rude interruptions?

MOTHER: Too right!

> *(She comes out from behind the scrim curtain to the*
> *STORYTELLER's front-of-stage area. But she is also trailed by*
> *the HYPNOTIST)*

STORYTELLER: (at him) That's not necessary.

HYPNOTIST: (milking being upfront) I feel she's already under my care and shouldn't be let go, not until her cheque's cleared and I can say she's cured.

STORYTELLER: What's the problem?

HYPNOTIST: With that performance of hers?

MOTHER: Hey, you two mind?

> *(But, anyway, doesn't wait for them, before out-crying to*
> *audience:)*

322

MOTHER: What's the level of education qualification got to do with it? Like any mother worth her salt would ask!

(The STORYTELLER literally shepherds the both of them back to behind the screen, and so can get on with:)

STORYTELLER: Well, let me try to explain that. Mumsie here tells us that, at first -- up to the age of say thirty-five, -six -- her son's behaviour was put down to his youthfulness, his lack of seeing the world outside his childhood bedroom and his bedroom classroom and the naivete that comes from that. So far, so good. But later that-there penis, bursting with Ten-Commandment-type pride in its own growing brainy qualifications – going way beyond the nerd level to well into the twerp stage -- began to insist that there was no public place too large or too small for a brainy penis with Education with superior grades to exert its penisosity, nor its perfect right to do so as a conscious entity of society at large.

(and can now call to behind screen to raise the tree-like trunk, which is done so in all its over-everything glory)

STORYTELLER: When it came, she said or is saying, the brainy penis, in its deluded penisophy under Education, insisted on a verbally-understood commemorated flag being run up the tenure of a flagpole to the effect there were inalienable rights of flagging a brainy penis had which did not need to rely on figurative speaking but could – no, should! – be its prerogative by the honorifics behind its name. And with demands like that, over the last few years, those naked toes of hers were saying, even her son could do nothing when the brainy penis got all huffity and started demanding to flag itself. You may gasp, but it did!

(Now the crutch of the SON inexorably turns into a tent pole under a tent – and stays like this such that he can no longer hide it in any further re-enactment. The immediate result, of course, is some shadow player slaps and shoves him away from her)

STORYTELLER: Education! I told you! A good way to get slapped down!

323

(He waits, nodding sagely while the SON shows himself helpless to do anything about his condition. He rushes to a mirror as...)

STORYTELLER: It was a shame really, it seems. According to Mum that son of hers tried reasoning with it in the mirror...
(while SON pops pills)
he tried coercion through medications...
(while SON escapes a priest)
he tried taking it to a priest and was lucky to get it back.
(while SON in arms of law)
It was tried before a magistrate who said he thought he had seen it all before but now swore to be forsworn off everything.
(while SON portrays hopelessness)
Whatever he attempted, his brainy penis wouldn't be swayed, wouldn't be swaged, insisted on its assuagements. Some go for the vapours; it went for the vigours.

(He switches general attention back on the MOTHER, who has to be prodded to get back to her toe-driven footpath routine of whoo-whoo bash-bash, gotta pee-gotta pee, snarl-snarl grrr-grrr)

STORYTELLER: Poor Mum got to lay around footpaths trying to mime to what was now a thronging east-of-the-Aussie-Alps crowd getting itchy around the thongs-that-throngs. The only thing left for her son, she was or is going, seemed displacement activity. Though the educated-addled penis thought itself too brainy, too clever by half to ever need to change its unflagging flagging ways, her son found he could divert attention from it by performing the whirling dervish part of his theological doctorate – its theological doctorate, really, but he wasn't above kidding himself -- he had recently concluded with flying colours and was waiting the results of. This apparently had to be a clockwise whirl.

(To Sufi music, the SON is joined by cast shadows to do whirling-dervish devotions. There are female spectators clapping time, even though most of whirlers fall down with dizziness before they pretty much even start. Still...)

STORYTELLER: ('above' them) The son discovered that if he
combined that with chasing his tail and whirling *grrr-grrr snap-snap* at
his own bum… as his poor Mum was trying to show… when faced
innocently trying to congress with a woman, then he could divert
attention away from his super-ego'd, puffed-up brainy penis for long
enough for it to tangle itself around its own petard, maybe not get its
first-ever Batchelor's degree even noticed, let alone have professors of
philosophy fall over at its feet gazing with such admiration up at it.
    (needs to point out what his reading script says:)
Stops and starts, stops and starts. In parenthesis, it has here, to quote,
'if he or it did it fast enough, meaning the whirl-whirl *and* the other
bash-bash grrr-grrr, for a blissful moment few would even notice that
tent pole of his)', close quote'n'brackets.

> *(Male shadows replace female ones before the SON, while the
> MOTHER points 'see, I told you so')*

STORYTELLER: I suppose, after all, what was the matter? She said
or is saying the brainy penis thought it was only sticking its chin out.
    (and)
But we'd have to say that was only a mother talking
    (and)
Likewise, when faced with innocently trying to have a normal
conversation with a male, he found that, by performing as a left-
handed, as against the so-called 'female' right-handed, whirling dervish
and chasing his tail using an anticlockwise and opposite tack he could
diminish the urge-surge to micturate at their feet, or at least not so
noticeably. Often even the resultant few drops on their shoes wasn't
noticed or simply allowed to peter out without anyone's attention being
overmuch drawn to it.
    (to being cautionary)
But still, the physics of having to do all this not once but possibly many
times at any one gathering in, say, the staff of a common room, let
alone at a most reverend's party or during your work's cocktail drinks
or even things that can happen if you live on the eastern side of
Australia as the crowd there consisted of by now… such things, as she
was or is saying, had started to take its toll on her son's body.

> *(The SON, now thankfully alone, that he is literally led by the
> jolly-roger to curl up on his bed as it comes rolling up.*

(Immediately his mother gets up to do her motherly tucking-in thing etc over him. Sufi music, quietened anyway by now, is now replaced by sad, even lullaby, refrains)

STORYTELLER: At night, rolling him over, tucking him in, his mother could count by his self-inflicted teeth marks on his buttocks and caudal region how many women, how many men, her son had had to get through that day due to the monomaniac academia of that penisification of his so wrought with Education. It was heart-wrenching to apply balm ointment to! It was a drain on her meagre resources to keep enough balm ointment around the place what with the price of applicators these days!

(As she dutifully goes to demonstrate this, the STORYTELLER rushes to cover it up...)

STORYTELLER: I think we are getting some idea of what a bully that brainy penis was, what a puff-chest bruiser, what an evil genius wrought by cap E and all the other letters of Education and its worst excesses which are no worse than its best excesses! What all-brain power and not one ounce of social graces in one so large nor one not so big!

(Sees it is safe to return to centre stage, while the MOTHER has gone back to sitting at the side of her boy and wiping his brow etc. As she soothes him the trunk is lowered gently by the ropes, and she can also place a towel discreetly over his tent-pole:)

STORYTELLER: She said or says, she mimed... or she will when she gets back to her footpath bash-bash whoo-whoo gotta-go grrr-grrr... that only when her son was faced with both women and men, singular or plural, at the same time, was there any sort of relief. The brainy penis, for all its book-learning and good looks... for all its nit-picking while in the one hand and its analytical acumen while in the other... wasn't as smart as it thought it was when faced with a simple choice of having to choose one of the two genders as to which whirl-rotation had precedence. Was clockwise or anticlockwise call for?

(He allows time for the son to show whirling confusion)

326

STORYTELLER: Often when faced with man'n'woman or someone who could go either way, that-there brainy penis allowed her boy to stand up from having to keep normally bent over his erectionificaton, and to converse in a perfectly civilised graduate manner to the woman or to the man, even to both at the same time, providing one wasn't too academically superior to the other and surmises neither was superior in that department to it.

(pauses to allow enactments behind to catch up)
And, since we weren't speaking about the lack of weather found in classrooms, we can say the lack of weather found in classrooms very often came to its tortured erudite mind at such times. Which was apparently why the mother on that-there footpath articulated by the sheer obstructionistic naked cadence of toes... obviously, the reasoning side of *her*... how she perfectly understood why her son had refused to leave his bedroom or his classroom for fear they would throw him out of the class. Or would throw him out of hearth and home, if he but turned the knob... on the door, mind... on his bedroom door. Yes.

(to what the MOTHER is now trying to do...)
Etcetera, etcetera. By now, even our worthy hypnotist on the footpath there could see it was a good time for her to stop and take breath, and she did. Stopped dead or stops dead. There were now a considerable portion of Australia's central belt also drifting in to watch her, with more than one face going at her: 'Yeah and what about the promised sex, sex and more sex part...?'

ALL SHADOW PLAYERS: YEAH, AND WHAT ABOUT THE PROMISED SEX, SEX AND MORE SEX PART...?

STORYTELLER: That's how, in her naked pause of toe of bash-bash of gotta-pee gotta-pee of grrr-grrr snap-snap, all those more-than-one blank faces were looking down at her now.

MOTHER: (outcry) My boy wasn't always like this!

STORYTELLER: Yes, we all hear and heard that: 'My boy wasn't always like this!' Poor Mum and the sorry downturn of her toes' shoulders!

ALL SHADOW PLAYERS: (cutting him off) WASN'T HE ALWAYS LIKE THAT?

STORYTELLER: No he wasn't, the mother went on, settling in now for the long haul and wriggling those toes, some said, provocatively.

(as her toes attempt to do so)

Meanwhile and speaking up to the hypnotist, she said she was absolutely positive it all came from when he was three…

MOTHER: (further outcry) *And a half!*

STORYTELLER: (waving her off) … everybody's a pedant.

(pushes himself back on script)

… and the time she had her dill of a husband's dill of a brother and his dill of a wife staying with them. In earshot of the toddler that dill of a longlost uncle walked into the living room one morning and went to his dill of a wife, no better than she ought to be either, going:

(Two shadow players come onto the front stage area from around either sides of the scrim curtain to dill-ishly conduct the conversation of:)

UNCLE: How's the old fff-fluffer?

AUNTIE: Closed up.

UNCLE: So mine. Must be the www-weather.

(They 'retreat' on his wave)

STORYTELLER: Dills! What a dill of a thing to say in front of a three-year-old…

MOTHER: *And a half!*

(and goes back to, now, wrestling with her child when he was a toddler, according to the following:)

STORYTELLER: … three-and-a-half-year-old dill who, of course, takes it for gospel. According to Mum, after that, it sounds like the child wouldn't even let her wash his little bot properly because the boy thought it was all closed up fff-fluffer-wise because of the weather, and

328

if you opened it... well, anything www-weather-wise could happen. If that was all…

   (then)

But it wasn't all. By the time the boy was four…

   (waits but is not interrupted)

whenever it rained, the kid rained down tears. When it was sunny, he fell into shade and started to wilt from the hairline down. Whenever it was overcast he wouldn't speak he'd gone so glum. When it was thunder and lightning, he started chasing her around the house with a kitchen knife. You should have seen it when it got cold… what with him and the low litre-age he had in his bladder.

   (and)

You can just imagine what effect that had on a penisocity just around the corner from becoming brainy and getting uppity!

ALL SHADOW PLAYERS: (hopefully) TO SEX, SEX AND MORE SEX?

STORYTELLER: Precisely.

MOTHER: (expiation) It was in the classroom!

   (Behind, the kitchen knife and so forth come into the re-
   enactments of:)

STORYTELLER: What the hypnotist there then discovered before the now whole-of-Australia by now gathered there was the mother meant by 'it was in the classroom'. It seems that the dill of a boy thereafter discovered he could cover the windows and there was no weather to close his botty of a fff-fluffer up, provided he threatened anyone with a kitchen knife if they dared try to uncover the windows to let the thunder of lightning in, and so forth and what-have-you.

   (The SON stalks about with a butcher's knife and everyone else
   hams up a horror reaction, while…)

The child-son also learnt from twelfth-grade science he took from the side of his bed ten years before he should've that there was no real www-weather to speak off inside classrooms, or at least in classrooms it was always fair weather which hardly counted as weather and, anyway, had minimum effect on bots with fff-fluffers – which, in the face of education, were pretty much all closed-up anyway -- and there weren't too many other places in the world you could say that about according to the many photographs in his text books. There was only one other he knew of, and that was his bedroom which was the same thing as his classroom, but had a differing name…

ALL SHADOW PLAYERS: SEX, SEX AND MORE SEX?

STORYTELLER: Yes, precisely! And even I can tell you why, too. It was because with all that shut-in non-www-weather, *that poor penis of his was never getting any oxygen, aka fresh air*!

ALL SHADOW PLAYERS: OH!

(The tree-like trunk prop is once more raised… but through this there are sounds of heavy choking, wilting, for lack of oxygen)

STORYTELLER: You know how every side has another side. Even when you are a tree-like trunk needing ropes to get raised, you need oxygen. And Education with that capital E might try to tell you otherwise, but oxygen it does not replace. The ropes can still be needed to raise it.
    (and)
At which shadowy stage, my friends, an amazing thing happened. The mother stopped dead still. Right there in the middle of the footpath outside our famous hypnotist's rooms. Even her toes became as stone stripped naked. No more bash-bash. No more gotta-go gotta-pee. No more snarl-snarl grrr-grrr trying to put the bite on your own khyber. It was so shockingly suddenly that the hypnotist had to ask her what was wrong? And what did she answer or rather cry out in agony…?

MOTHER: (cued) It's not right! It's all sex, sex and more sex with you people!

STORYTELLER: Of course, after that, the hypnotist had to take her inside to his rooms and shut his doors even to the wannabe watchers Singapore Airlines were now additionally starting to bus in.

(There is a momentary total blackout)

2.

(Lighting back on in the shadow area shows all cleared. Certainly, the passing-by throng has gone and the sound of the street much quietened down.

The HYPNOTIST is 'on' with the MOTHER in his rooms, and they coincide their acting with the STORYTELLER's reading...)

STORYTELLER: That being a short intermission in case any of you wanted to go whoo-whoo, pee-pee or snarl-snarl grrr-grrr. Or just plain bash-bash. Hope all was enjoyed. Ha ha.
　(starts out again)
We know that, as a qualified medical practitioner, the hypnotist utilised how the nerve in the lower gut work on the brain. First by hypnotics he turned the mother into the son, not uncommon in Sydney hypnotists' rooms. It's a procedure you would have heard of. It's called 'Sydney this or Sydney that'.
　(and)
He... the hypnotist, as you can see... did nothing more and nothing less than any hypnotist among you would do. He simply transferred the penile brainy side from one head much lower down the human up-and-down to a higher head much higher up where less-educated, maybe, but nicer, quieter dreams are made.
　(waits for hypnotic administrations are enacted behind, before:)
The slight trouble with doing that was it gave the son more than simply rosy cheeks, but persistent blood rushes to his – now its – head. It also somehow inflicted upon him – and it – one of those penis-to-head body-focused repetitive compulsive-behaviour syndromes of four times four. It did. You would have though the hypnotist would have realised something was up when he asked if he was asleep and the son answered *no* and he had to ask if he was asleep another three times, getting *no* each time, until he realised the son was asleep all the time.
　(waits while the 'no four times' is carried out)
Then there was the remedy our clever hypnotist suggested. The brainy penisification of the son should go around all the faculty members he or it could find addresses for and apologise for his common-room behaviour by way... you know... of getting it all of his or its chest.

(Now the ropes can pull the tree-like trunk back up into position

331

where it will remain standing, trunk-solid)

STORYTELLER: And so either the mother or the son -- or it all rolled into one -- hired a car to take him around all the faculty members they could find by way of educated guess. And there, outside of each, he or it would lean out of the passenger-side window and shout, going: 'I'm ssss...'

(Without being asked, the SON has come from behind the screen to stand boldly front stage again, and to interrupt:)

SON: I'm sss-sorry! What fff-for?

STORYTELLER: (apologetic) Notice the deliberate four-times stutters, even as we should all ignore the intrusion onto our space.

SON: (again) I'm sss-sorry! What fff-for?

STORYTELLER: All right. Easy.
  (back to audience)
If that wasn't enough, once they had finished the round of all the academics they could find by educated guess, he or it got the driver to go around again, going: 'I'm ssss-s...'

SON: I'm sss-sorry! What fff-for?

STORYTELLER: As I was trying to say, and to go around again, going:

SON: I'm sss-sorry! What fff-for?

STORYTELLER: And again if you think it does you good!

SON: I'm sss-sorry! What fff-for?

(The STORYTELLER forcibly escorts him back behind the scrim curtain where he belongs, but keeps a forced-smile himself:)

STORYTELLER: Four times, as if we didn't get it, right? And more, and worse! When they had finished four times around, the son or the brainy penis… take your pick… tapped the driver on the shoulder four times and instructed him in quadruplicate to go around again in the other direction, whenupon… nice word, that!... he went around again, with the son or it going this time:

(The SON dashes back from behind the scrim curtain for:)

SON: I'm not sss-sorry! What the fff-frig fff-for?

STORYTELLER: And again…

SON: I'm not sss-sorry! What the fff-frig fff-for?

STORYTELLER: And one more time…

SON: I'm not sss-sorry! What the fff-frig fff-for?

STORYTELLER: And one last time…

SON: I'm not sss-sorry! What the fff-frig fff-for?

STORYTELLER: (waving the SON back to shadow area) You get the picture. Another four rounds but with 'I'm *not* sss-sorry! What the fff-frig fff-for?' and so on.

> *(He stops when he sees SON remains up front instead of returning to the shadow area. He has to forcibly escort him back there again. Returns to:)*

STORYTELLER: So then, by the time the hire-car driver gets the son and/or the brainy penis back outside the hypnotist's front door… especially when the son and/or it got out and shut the passenger-side door, then opened it again, got in again, got out again and shut the passenger-side door, then got out and shut the passenger-side door… well, you've got it…

ALL SHADOW PLAYERS: ONE, TWO, THREE, FOUR!

STORYTELLER: (on the money) …then that hire-car driver understandably panicked over whatever this guy who looked like a real dickhead had had to be contagious, and put his foot on the gas to get out of there. And the trouble with *that* was the son or the brainy penis more's the like had not yet fully completed his now-absolutely vital fourth opening and closing that car door. This was totally unacceptable to any son worth being a highly educated penis type of paying customer, or, if you like, to a brainy penis when it came to think of itself as a fully-qualified human paying customer!

(and)

Without a thought for its own safety or his own safety, the brainy penis and/or the son leapt right out in front of that hire car going: Ssss-stop! With four 's' stutters too!

(rushing on now:)

Or it would have been 'ssss-stop!' if 'ssss-stop' hadn't got stuck in its throat when the panicked hire-car driver ran it full-guts-achedly right over. It did, right there! Clunk-o! Which panicked the fellow even more to back up – and run over it or him again full-guts-achedly. Go-the-squish! Then of course his frantic foot slipped and the car shot forward again and ran over the brainy penis or the son again. Squirk! Then his foot slipped back to where it wanted to slip in the first place and that hire car then'n'there backed back over the brainy penis and/or his remains… splurt!… that-there… yes… you see how it goes… fourth time. It did, my friends!

(Behind now there are preparations for a final scene, which the STORYTELLER coordinates his reading to:)

STORYTELLER: But none of us should even imagine that a brainy penis with a string of degrees behind it is so easily written off. All we *can* say is the son seemed to found some measure of peace in his and/or its head by getting himself over to the lawn in front of the Great Hall of his alma mater and there…

(Behind, the SON has returned to lie down at the foot of the tree-like trunk that looms above him)

STORYTELLER: …lying down as a flagpole, contented to be that near to books and their learnings for once in its… maybe his… life outside of his or its own classroom tied to his bedroom tied to not-a-bit-of-weather. And there to have the flag of the Education of all things

334

hoisted up him twice the height allowable using any old ordinary unschooled flag pole.

(now, can do the finale)

Nor was the brainy penis itself above being asked what it was doing there, as long as it was asked with an educated air. If it was, it wouldn't answer, but, if it wasn't, it would show how *deigned* it wouldn't answer.

(pause for effect)

At least the son and his brainy penis had finally gotten out of the house once and for all. His mother would have been so pleased. Or is pleased. Or her naked toes were or are pleased.

(then)

We could ask her if she doesn't or didn't seem to have disappeared.

(and)

We can take it the hypnotist is still trying to get back to remove those embarrassing naked toes of hers from blocking his front door.

(points into shadow area)

Certainly, we can leave him there struggling with that. Sydney hypnotists and naked toes, don't you know...

(Blackout)

---000---

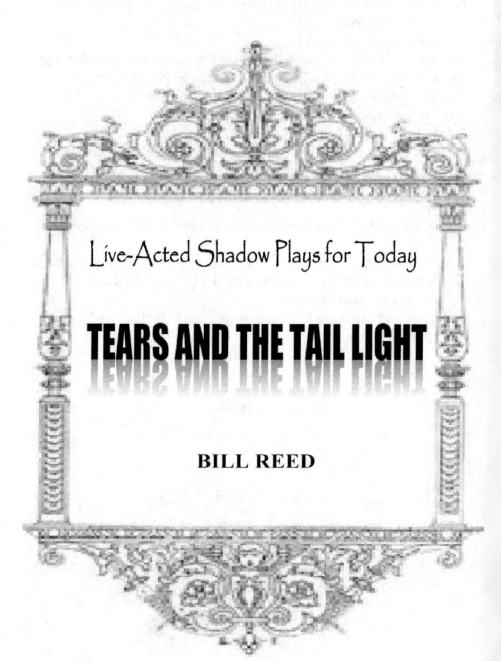

Live-Acted Shadow Plays for Today

TEARS AND THE TAIL LIGHT

BILL REED

The behind-the-screen shadow action – or 'inner background' play --
can only ever keep 'pace' with the reading, not *keep up* with it.
Because of the resultant and necessary shadow-play distillation of the
storyteller's tale, the extensive stage directions given in this script are
only intended to be indicators as to what *might* be used for the shadow-
play side of things. They deliberately go beyond what the director
would employ and are given merely as a range of possible shadow-
actions he or she might want to use in the 'distillation'.

The Characters

STORYTELLER:

Apart from his 'ad libbed' asides and comments, he is very much part of the inner production.

TEARS SHADOW PLAYER:

A youngish man who is both a shadow player and a 'live' actor. He comes out from behind the screen as and when necessary. His slaps are part of the sound-over. He has to totter on huge gout-like bandages.

SHADOW PLAYERS:

4 or so actors to carry out the sequences as narrated, working with fantasy props and, as directed, coming up front of scrim to act three-dimensionally. They fill in for:

Tears's gang members

tourist/ blameless victim;

old man Samaritan.

shoppers/passers-by

Tears and the Tail Light

(Lighting up on TEARS standing as a shadow in the middle of the shadow area. He remains static, hands at side, for a long time, as though he is examining the audience as much as they are examining him. But he is aggressively agitated, holding himself back from reacting to the mosquitoes.

Into his 'own' front-stage area in front of the scrim curtain comes the STORYTELLER, script in hand. He casts a critical eye over the whole stage setting before deigning to start...)

STORYTELLER: He had such a nice genteel first name. Nimal. And such an affectionate-sounding nickname of Tears. But he was always going to be a thug of the worst kind since he treated people as badly as he treated himself. That's why he ended up around Wyndham way up north of W. A. and looking to car-jack the first car that came his way. In the main street of Wyndham, but that is just how cheeky he was.

(and)

You ever think that's a dope act in front of dozens of witnesses? It was. It's what made it attractive for him. It was just another burst of Tears's brainwaves. Unfortunately, the driver of the car of his brainwave was a hapless Sri Lankan tourist going back to the caravan park from picking up a few groceries for his family. Fortunately, since it was a Sri Lankan tourist nobody took any notice on the strength of it that if you couldn't lift a Sri Lankan what could you do? Next thing there'd be the nanny state.

(and)

And we can guess this 'lift' wasn't Tears Nimal's first, otherwise what're we talking about him for, right?

(pause to indicate:)

I mean, he looks normal enough, right? Well, if you could see him properly, like. But let's see, okay? Eyes...?

(TEARS puts his face right up against the screen)

Pretty scary but passable, right? If you could properly see them again. How about the hands?:

(TEARS holds out his hands, crucifixion-wise)

339

They look normal scab-scratchers, right? If you could see them properly, okay. What about the feet?

(TEARS lifts up his left foot for inspection; then the right)

They pass inspection? Sure, be expansive; give 'em a pass. And don't sniff, thinking it's your neighbour. It's his feet, and you don't need to see them properly when it comes to that.

> *(He pauses, and TEARS turns back from screen to return to 'inner' shadow area, but has to quickly return, when...)*

STORYTELLER: But don't let a few shadows take you in. Just look at those eyes again.

(TEARS puts his face back against the screen)

No blood shots or anything. Clear enough given pretty heavy substance abuse? Sure, but look through it all again. See those tears? They're not just eyes watering. They're real tears and it's not that Tears is any emotional guy, no sir. Don't fall for that one. Those tears are because of this:

(TEARS slaps himself viciously on his right cheek...)

Or because of this:

(TEARS slaps himself on the left cheek...)

Or even this:

(TEARS gives himself a haymaker on the left cheek...)

Or, get this:

(TEARS gives himself a haymaker on the right cheek...)

Or, would you believe...?

(TEARS gives himself a vicious uppercut to the chin...)

Ouch! Biff! bang! wallop! Who needs to see properly to see that?

(carries on)

Most of every minute of every day, he was doing it, seemed like. Certainly enough to keep those tears running from those eyes, there. And why you ask? Who knows what made Tears Nimal's blood boil. Everything made Tears Nimal's blood boil! And you know how those Wyndham mozzies like a good hot steaming cup of sweat'n'tears laid on.

(then)

Other than that, you still say he looks pretty normal? But wait up; let's go back to those hands again...

(TEARS holds out his hands again, but this time they are shaped

340

nastily like eagle claws – and the shadows of these grow giantish to hover over shadow-playing effects)

STORYTELLER: I mean, you wouldn't want to get too near to those rip-tears, when they're not bunched up and punching himself, right? And then look at those feet again, if you can bring yourself to get near enough to them…

(TEARS holds up, first, his left foot, then his right. Each of them are now covered in a huge mound – a footballs-worth! -- of bandages, reminiscent of old gout parodies. These, too, grow giantish in floating shadow effect)

STORYTELLER: Wow! And I mean 'Wow!'. And those there ain't oldtime send-ups of gout, either. Those footballs are to keep the mozzies away from his smelly feet… well, smelly to us but lollipop to them, right? I mean, those Tears Nimal feet were so smelly, they smelt worse than even smelly feet which is pretty far out on the pong scale if you *are* smelly feet. They did. It's said he once stood still in someone's front garden for more than a minute and those feet of his started to take root.
(refers histrionically to script)
And those smelly feet… and again most of you can stop looking at the person next to you, because it's not him. Or her. It's…
(points back to the giantish feet)
… Tears's smelly feet back there. No more confirmation do you need than this…
(brandishes script)
It's very first chapter called 'How Tears's Mosquitoes Like Their Amphitheatres' writ boldly.

(TEARS moves away from standing for inspection to allow a resulting mayhem of sights and sound of hordes of mosquitoes in locust-like swarms, feet flying, punches 'n' slaps sounding off, cheeses flying, orchestras tuning up, and whatsoever by way of running shadow commentary of:)

STORYTELLER: Despite the rumours going around, his nickname didn't come from the tears he brought on himself by smacking himself silly. If you really knew, you'd know it was because of his soft heart.

341

(and)

You might snigger but it was so!

(and)

Of course those feet of his were at the root cause of it all, I suppose. They were so mouldy-cheesy that they were stand-outs in the Tropics where rubber thongs are worn so long they're taken into account in the nightly weather reports. Don't we all know. If the weather characters caught Tears's two shat-kickers upwind, they were referred to personally in the weather bulletins. If they caught them upwind during a church service, there'd be a lot of talk of someone going out and dig up old Methuselah because they've just found his feet.

(and, to the sounds of a chasing pack...)

And why Tears had ever get on the wrong side of the law, you couldn't understand. Even he must have known he couldn't ever not be caught. He'd be in the direction that the sniffer dogs were running away from.

(As floating props, his two (now giantish) feet are held up by 40-foot poles, while steam rises from them and mosquitoes buzz around in great excitement)

STORYTELLER: Those feet were the cheesiest, the blue vein-iest, the fester-iest, the gorgonzola of feet that had ever blown in from the highlands of New Guinea onto the northern shores of Australia... well, around the tribal camps at night, it was often said they were the sole reason why the bug-laden winds *did* blow in off the New Guinea highlands to torment so many hundreds of thousands innocent Australians. Those feet of his were the only thing the Dreamtime was known not to be able to cope with.

(pause for didgeridoo to quieten)

Yet, as so often happens in cases like this, Tears Nimal remained blissfully ignorant of them being on the nose so much... and this was deliberate. The fact was he never trusted another living soul in his life, and wasn't going to start when they tried to insult him with some dirty mouthing about his feet. Everybody's a critic. Like, most of us would go for the air freshener or suchlike, but not Tears. He had the policy of just shrugging too -- then shivving. *That* brought tears to people eyes wherever he went.

(a knifing and a yowl)

And that in turn brought tears to Tears's eyes. I told you they were because of his soft heart.

(pause as necessary)
Still, it begged the question as to why he had those cannon-ball size bandages on both feet. It was the mozzies. It wasn't only those blood suckers hitching a beeline for them on the wind from the New Guinea highlands, either, but the local skeeters as well.

Them trying to hitch a ride on his feet just for the love of them drove him wild and the more they drove him wild the more bandages went on.

(TEARS reclaims his feet and, as soon as he does so, the swarm begin to drive him crazy again)

STORYTELLER: Not that any mosquito was known to have a problem with that. It's doubtful whether any clump of bandages could have hidden that on-the-nose away from them. They just made his feet a more cushioned ride while they went about their mining operations. Oh, and also a bigger area to hitch a ride on… so much so that there came to be on them steerage class, third class, second class, first class, and observation-carriage class. No, really! It was easily proved that you could trace a mosquito's lineage back to the great fromagère houses of France, Italy and England depending on where they'd booked their places on Tears's feet.

(to all the cheeses that, in consequence to the narration, come shadowedly buzzing by)

It was known as a real buzz in certain circles as the Great Mouldy-Cheese Mozzie Migrations. As far as the local and international mosquitoes Tears Nimal stood on Stilton heaven. He walked on Roquefort Rocky Road, gave fragrance Gorgonzola Gorgeous. To *mosquitoes'r'us.net.au* those feet were so blue-cheese wow-whiff-ful that there were booking arrangements a mosquito had to go through to get near those feet no matter how high up it was in skitter-land. And even then, only get-in-get-out noshing was mozzie-allowed, no sitting back engaging in postprandial deipnosophies with the bigshot snozzle parked next door. You mightn't know what postprandial deipnosophies might be, but the inner circle of those mozzies did, connoisseurs, all.

(and)

The luckier ones higher up on the proboscis pecking order found paying muscular nose-job substitutes to stand in line for them to be a good answer to the problem. Scalpers that wouldn't stop buzzing around were another. The more desperate blood-suckers gave up their daily shade-rests to get near Tears' hot'n'sweaty delights and often, so around the campfires of the Far North, say, they became so sleep-deprived and microbial-lethargic that Wyndham fell to very low down on the malaria scale internationally due to Tears Nimal's clod-hoppers hogging all the mozzies in town. The environmentalists blamed it on climate change… they didn't know how right they were when it came to Tears's beetle-crushers and climate change being like blood brothers.

(He pauses for the re-enactments of storms and storm-chasers and plants wilting near those feet of his, and placard-carrying demonstrators around them. Two of these shadow players appear briefly in full view at opposite edges of the scrim curtain and show signs reading:
'No Buzz, No Tourism!'
and
'Bring Back Our Blood-suckers*!')*

STORYTELLER: Stories started to abound… no doubt you've heard them: any hair on his legs below his knees and above his shins comprised the hoi-polloi stalls on which the less fortunate skeeter could watch the lucky upper-crusters passing through the Danish-blue turnstiles at the entrance to the bandaged bundles below. Depending on the seat, at least they could sniff the breeze, savour the ordures that occasionally wafted. At any one time, there were so many mozzies around those cheesy beetle-crushers of Tears Nimal that it sounded like a performance of The Ring Cycle on the Rind.
    (and)
I mean, long ago, riding on his feet became so in-demand that in *mosquitoes'r'us.net.au* they were so overrun with ads for hiring out jackhammers as proboscis aids that they had to close all the windows and doors of the website and then use chemically impregnated nets against their own fellow blood-suckers.

(As a reasonable man, he waits patiently until the re-enactments have somewhat played themselves out. Then he motions the shadow acting should perhaps stop. It does, and:)

STORYTELLER: However, none of this stopped Tears Nimal from hating mozzies with even more a vengeance than he did his fellow man, and that's saying something. See, he might have refused to entertain

344

having a skeeter problem down below, but he never tried to pretend he didn't know he had a mozzie problem from the neck up. With all that constant dive-bombing around his ears, the ever in-his-face, up-his-nose, your-lobe's-my-lobby, screw-your-wits, it's-a-brain-so-go-bloodsuck-it, or it's-an-eyeball-get-drilling, what could he do above the neck with bandages? All he could do was to keep pounding away with only had his self-inflicted facial injuries to give himself any sense he was fighting back. If it was a pounding *mosquitoes'r'us.net.au* wanted, a pounding they would get.

> *(Behind, TEARS returns to punching himself to the sounds and signs 'over' of Biff! Bang! Wallop!*
>
> *Blackout)*

2.

> *(The lighting returns to a much quieter shadow area. It all seems peaceful. TEARS shadow player is almost only indolently slapping at himself. A mosquito or two is only the annoyance of a coming nightfall. Even the STORYTELLER seems rested by comparison with before...)*

STORYTELLER: We have here a chapter that reads 'The tail-light caper, the oldest in the book'.

> *(In the shadow area, a giantish Yamaha tail light comes swimmingly, and TEARS rises lovingly towards it as the other players prepare to act out the prang scene...*
>
> *... which now comes as a screeching of brakes and an ugly crunching sound)*

STORYTELLER: So, we're here in the main street of Wyndham and, bingo!, a bing with Tears Nimal getting off his Yamaha and onto his mad, his crazed high horse, going:

TEARS NIMAL: My tail light, dog!

STORYTELLER: With language not even Wyndham has heard which means it isn't in any language known to man. And he's yowling on to the poor Lankan visitor in that beaten-up old Corolla behind:

TEARS NIMAL: Waddjafrukkareya? From hhrrukkin' India?

STORYTELLER: He was nearly right, even. The old tail-light caper and, yes, the oldest in the book.
   (waves script)
At least this book.
   (and)
Showing the tears he had in his eyes for good measure, and reeling with an uppercut to show just how the loss of his tail light affected the equilibrium of his existence.
   (and)
What was going on? What was going on was it was a Sundee morning and Tears Nimal had seen a foreigner behind the wheel in broad daylight on a Wyndham street, and he would have said to himself, 'here's how I get to punch someone else'.
   (while, behind, TEARS practises his sparring...)
Nothing more than the old dudded tail-light trick. Pick the mark, jam on the brakes, pretend you've been clipped and the poor tail light had copped it, and demand compo coin or here comes the knuckle sandwich. The trouble was the poor Lankan visitor had no money in his kick, so Tears simply copped a few wallops upon himself, picked up the tail light and lifted the unfortunate Lankan by way of a few vicious left hooks that missed the visitor and landed on you-know-where-the-mozzies-are-not-made-happy.
   (and simply)
Why the lift? Well, it was Sunday and even the banks in Wyndham knew not to open until the next day. That was the rumour anyway.
   (and, to illuminating shadow playing)
But first, it being Sunday, a word for Good Samaritans all. One old local coming back late from Mass... he hadn't slept through the sermon and so was feeling a bit groggy... tried to be helpful, going:

CHURCHIE SHADOW PLAYER: No, no... no hit, all miss, eh?!

   (and he gets set on by TEARS)

346

STORYTELLER: Now, on a day other than a church day, Tears would have taken the old chap aside and ripped off his glasses to sell later and poked one eye so he couldn't get new ones until it, the eye, re-opened for testing. A concession to the elderly. But even Tears Nimal knew that that day was a Feast day and so took the old boy's wallet *and* his glasses and poked both eyes into temporary blindness just to do the dirty on Feast Days.

TEARS: Hffrruggem, I say!

STORYTELLER: Back with the poor Lankan tourist, where time had stood still, now Tears was waving a vilely stricken Yamaha tail light, and still going between biff-bang-wallops:

TEARS NIMAL: My tail-light, dog!

STORYTELLER: ...even while getting the message of no coin, only ATM card being waved at him and everybody knowing banks are feasibly open on a Sunday in Wyndham but ATMs would have to be operational to be open. Hence, yes, the lift, and Tears Nimal socking himself right into higher crime.

> *(TEARS beats up on ATM, then turns to kidnap the tourist out of pique)*

STORYTELLER: There were no witnesses. The storming cloud of cheese-loving skeeters covered the crime-seen up as Tears made off with his reluctant pillion passenger.

> *(pause to watch the Yamaha takes off)*

STORYTELLER: That night is clouded too in what the buzz was. It seems the poor Lankan got housed in the shed of Tears Nimal's rental. He reported it so bad in there the roaches were making audible munching party sounds that could be heard over the mosquitoes making audible munching party sounds, and that he was the party. Only once during the night did Tears Nimal come to see him apparently.
> *(conducts re-enactment behind-the-screen...)*
At one stage, the plank door opened just enough to let in a torch light which shed maybe more horror than any horror movie would have it.

347

Through a monstrous mozzie swarm out of Hitchcock, accompanied by a foot odour no top-end swamp could have ever drummed up, there was Tears Nimal. What he intended is not known. All the poor Lankan knew was the man directed a torrent of abuse at him, until he delivered upon himself such a right haymaker right onto his own left ear hole, trapping by ears-ringing many of the said blood-suckers right in there for a start. And knocking himself silly for a delayed start.

(and)

For a poor Lankan visitor not knowing Wyndham, this was a very strange thing to do in the middle of the night. An Aussie characteristic nobody had told him about.

(and)

And so our script here turns to the next morning, where, outside the bank… and some of you regular theatre-goers might recognise the scene… we find the poor Lankan waiting for the bank to open because no amount of hoodoo will yet make the ATM work. (On it was a weather-beaten sign which went: 'Don't look at me'.) Tears had dropped him off and gone for get-away petrol, so said. It is more probable he got warned off by a full-on Cairns crime family that they were taking over the lifting of the poor Lankan since no one knew he was missing. Or something like that.

(As the shadow area prepares for the 'upbringing' scenes, including a sorrowful 'Ben Hur'-type leprosy scene:)

STORYTELLER: That Tears Nimal had once had a job on the security staff of a well-known Federal minister out of Cairns was typical of his punch-drunk life. The minister only paid his staff what he personally owed them after borrowing from them. Since he borrowed from each one of them before he had to pay them… under the guise they knew they worked for a government with a long reach… the minister owed them nothing. Nor did anyone as silly as Tears Nimal expect him to. No North Queenslander with red blood in his veins ever paid back more than he owed.

(and)

So, typical, instead of even being paid once, Tears found yet again the truism about himself: the coins, they are a-fallin'.

(waits for re-enactment of a 'waterfall' of coins going down the drain)

348

STORYTELLER: It really would make you want to clock yourself too, you know, if you were silly enough.

(and to church/temple/mosque music over...)
Mind you, it has here that all Tears Nimal wanted was to become a priest, or a monk or an imam, or any swarmi would do -- it didn't matter as long as it had in it the religious streak he just knew he was born for. Yet every time he was on the verge of putting his shoulder to the religious grindstone he found he was so penniless he couldn't see how he could go around preaching non-worldliness when all he was worried about was how his pennies kept going a-fallin'. He even tried sewn-up pockets but when he unsewed them, they'd be empty. What else?

> *(And now the giantish bandaged feet and the mosquito swarms threaten to take over the shadow area again)*

STORYTELLER: First it had been the smelly feet which blocked him from a saint's path. What you can't do is dictate what meaty, saucy, rotten-egg, phew-whiffer stonkers-below your family line was hobbled with. It wasn't only the meaty, saucy gone-off eee-yewws, either; the family home had become a hive of ecstasy-driven mosquitoes so much so that it looked like his parents and two siblings walked about in steamy swamp vaporations with Dolby surround sound.

> *(A sign bearer dressed as a mosquito handles a sign around the edge of the screen, saying*
> **'We've got you covered!')**

STORYTELLER: Even the national EPA had given up issuing warnings against the family and had settled on just putting a yellow tape around the home. I mean, if you're a sensitive kid like little Tears was, how could you not being affected by government environment-protection agents weren't stalking him every time he stepped out of the house? Although, because of the feet, not too close. Still, they couldn't stop his religious streak. There had to be some mission somewhere to save his family from a life of quarantine.

> *(A large cross and TEARS shadow player falls before it, and then getting up to kneel before his shadowed family to apply mounds*

349

of bandages to their feet)

STORYTELLER: Ministrations and mosquitoes, yes. So, soon, he was taking jobs after school to be able to keep his parents and brother and sister in the great swathes of foot bandages their mosquito defences demanded, yet still finding time to be at home to *apply* those great swathes of foot bandages because another thing about the family was they were too lazy to bend over. And then he found himself taking on yet another job in order to be able to afford taking the time off the first job to apply all the bandages they were too lazy to bend over to apply to themselves. People, was it stinkeroo, too!

    (waits considerably for action to catch up)
If that wasn't all, there were the costly repellents needed, the air cleansers, the constant tests for malaria and dengue especially for a family that was to the person hypochondriacs. He had to take a third job after school to be able to afford it all… and then a fourth… and by this time the tears had started to roll and the slaps started to come clench-fistedly. Plus, in superstitious Cairns of then, a path out of the front door had to be kept clear of neighbours with their warding-of-evil charms. And then he had to be around to escort the environmental-protection agents to come close enough to take the necessary blood samples. Plus supervising the food being air-dropped in so inaccurately because the engine had to keep above mosquito level.

    (watches shadows'n'sounds of an air drop)

STORYTELLER: All those burdens, you see, on the poor lad's religious streak. It was just as well there was a soul in the world called Mr William Wyler of Hollywood!

    (He pauses for effect, while, on one side of the screen, a player holds up a sign:
    'Mr William Wyler from Hollywood'
    and, on the other side, another displays a sign:
    'Ben Hur, poxy!'
    and, in tune with the subsequent reshowing of the leprosy scene from the film:)

STORYTELLER: Yes, Ben Hur. And when that famous director's epic came to the screen in Cairns via the latest in a borrowed bed sheet,

350

Tears Nimal saw how his mother looked like Ben Hur's mother and his sister looked like Ben Hur's sister and how they lived as if in the caves too among lepers walking around with look-alike beach-ball-sized bandage tatters all over their feet. He saw how he looked like Ben Hur himself, when he thought about it. He saw how Ben Hur's pennies dropped from him too, yet how he, Ben Hur, soldiered on within the same look-alike sort of religious streak and got rewarded by The End. He saw he only had to stick at it, and one day The End would come to him too.

(and, to another sign posted **'Thank you, Mr William Tyler'***)*
So, yes, thank you, Mr William Wyler.

(and)
And as the years'n'tears rolled by, and the bruises rolled by, and the mosquito hordes rolled by, Tears stoically edged towards feeling less penniless such that he could afford to claim he could throw it all up to go around penniless.

(pause)
That is why that job with the Federal minister out of Cairns was the final pennies-a'fallin' straw. When he went to ask for his pay after knocking many heads together, all he got was: 'The pennies have gone a-fallin', hhffrruggwit. Wise up.'

TEARS NIMAL: (behind-the-screen lament) The pennies have gone a-fallin', hhffrruggwit. Wise up.

STORYTELLER: He could see now his mozzies were the only ones showing him the only way. That he had to draw from himself.

(Another mosquito sign shows, saying:
'Suck. It's worth it!'
... to which the STORYTELLER puts script aside for a moment)

STORYTELLER: Bit sad really.

(Blackout)

3.

(Behind all is clear such that TEARS can stand, as he did at the beginning, breasted the scrim curtain from behind, and so outlined as if he was covered with wrapping foil)

351

STORYTELLER: Tears Nimal, yes, ladies and gentlemen. He swims back into our view once more, and fully, as ever he did before... remember?... Those eyes you can't quite see, but never mind...?

(and)

After a few years, still pretty scary but still just passable, right? How about the hands?

(TEARS holds out his hands, crucifixion-wise)

They still look normal scab-scratchers, right? But we don't fall for that, do we?, because we can at least see they're not clenched. What about the feet? Left?

(TEARS lifts up his left foot for outlined inspection)

Right?

(TEARS lifts up his right foot for outlined inspection)

Holding your noses, they pass still muster? Hardly, hardly. Sure, they're wilting up the environment, so what of that? Do we expect Tears Nimal to care about that?

(pause for effect)

So let's give him... say, a C-minus...?

(If he gets any objection, he ignores it)

STORYTELLER: But we still can't let a few shadows take us in just because a few years have now passed during that last blackout... sneaks up on you, doesn't it? And the bandages have a more professional look, don't you think? Well, again, you can't see them, but you can still think, no? And just look at those eyes again.

(TEARS puts his face back up against the screen)

Still no blood shots much visible. Clear enough given pretty heavy substance abuse? Sure, but they're Tear Nimal's eyes and you really just have to look a little more closely or use your imaginations a little more. See those tears? Sure, they're real tears but it's still the case that Tears Nimal isn't any emotional guy, no sirree. We know him too well to fall for that one again. Those tears are because... and remember we are just re-iterating here... because of this...

(TEARS slaps himself on his right cheek again)

and because of this:

(TEARS slaps himself on the left cheek)

and this:

(TEARS gives himself another haymaker on the left cheek)

352

And not forgetting this:
(TEARS gives himself another haymaker on the right cheek)
or, can we still believe, this?...
(TEARS gives himself another vicious uppercut to the chin)
It's still: Ow-fruggit! Biff! bang! wallop! Nothing's changed in the two years since we first met him and he first opened up for you.

> *(A mosquito-looker comes back with a sign around the edge of the scrim curtain. It reads:*
> **'And we've still got him covered!'**

> *TEARS moves back from the limelight of being high-lit, making way for the shadow playing cast to enact the last tail light caper with full bells and whistles...)*

STORYTELLER: This next thing that happened to Tears Nimal might have occurred more than 1500 kilometres away from Wyndham, but it was only ten or so metres from where our Sri Lankan tourist was working as an assistant chef because, after Wyndham, he had become very much worse for mental wear.
(pause)
All that next comes to pass went down inevitably with the old tail-light caper again. The reporter who happened to be coming out of the only Sri Lankan café in the city... he who claimed the nifty headline of: 'Machete Meet Tail Light; Brilliant Stroke'... said he heard a:

TEARS: HEYFRRUKK, MY TAIL LIGHT, DOG!

STORYTELLER: ... 'Hoi, my tail light, dog!'... sounds familiar? And witnessed, he said, a thin and bush-haggard bandy-legged, eyes-smarting half-lunatic looking man banging an angry fist alternatively onto the hood of a blue VF Commodore Evoke, shamelessly, and on his own face, cringingly. It was a pity, he said, about the Commodore; still, fortunately, the guy was more accurate with his punches on his own face than on the bonnet of this innocent Holden. Anyway, this thin, haggard and worn creature was using his non-jabbing hand to point down onto the road at his feet where a Yamaha tail light lay, already with sticky tape across much of it, along with bandages like football you'd dipped in buzz. And then...
(ensuring action had caught up to part the swarms)

admittedly a blur… out from that Sri Lankan eatery there came a madman in a cook's apron out from the cafe wielding a machete in one hand and a fry pan and skillet in the other and yelling 'Geronimo!'

(aside)

Which is a bit weird when you think of it, because he was nearer to Indian and Red Indian and not Indian at all, either.

(then back on track)

Tears, it seems, had barely completed a maniac's mime of priceless tail light on bike, dogshat car comes along, priceless tail light gets hammered and falls into sorry state on road that needs mucho dollar compensation for or else… when, yes, our own Sri Lankan tourist finally get his revenge, falls upon that tail light, first, to render it flat out by fry pan and skillet, and then turns the machete onto the Yamaha, started with the pillion seat and working its wrecking-ball way up the machine towards Tears.

(and)

Who, by all accounts, had now seemed to have left off his cussing and his well-aimed blows to his own head, and the trouble of balancing on two soccer balls of bandages… the mozzie swarm now making for his unprotected open mouth that *mosquitoes'r'us.net.au* hadn't mentioned in its brochure nor could have known about…

> *(pauses to watch the destruction of the bike, firstly, by the lone Sri Lankan visitor, then other shadow players joining in with sledge hammers)*

STORYTELLER: With the café's management and regular customers joining in with sledge hammers… although that sounded a bit far-fetched… when they recognised the smell of rotting feet as coming from its direction and quite different from the smell of rotting feet they were accustomed to from the kitchen.

> *(Carnage results behind the screen)*

STORYTELLER: Carnage. Did someone say carnage? Oh boy, carnage! But you can't see Tears there, I bet. No, because he was last seen running off down the wrong side of the Bruce Highway with a real load on his mind. Fortunately, with the Bruce Highway there is nothing unusual about having a throbbing buzzing load on your mind. It is reported he made it to Townsville, where, poor fellow, they have the best civil defence forces in the country, and none more protective of their local skeeters against exotic-species imports disguised as living turbans and goitre'd clod hoppers.

(All that there is left behind the screen now is the tail light. It 'gets' up from the road very sorrily; it even has difficulty of getting off the ground to float giantishly over all)

STORYTELLER: And as for our tail light? Well, it says here it did survive and, amazedly, under all those caper-driven sticky tape mends, did so pretty much untouched. All it had to show for its whole year-and-a-half of being abused and horribly impugned by the ravings of Tears down upon it was a harmless little crack. Like any tail light anywhere in the world it wanted but a few screws.

(The tail light floatingly limps away; its little whimpers are heard)

STORYTELLER: Apparently, where all Yamaha-else was shattered and gone, that tail light lay in the gutter there outside the eatery for forty days and nights, and did so unbowed, unwhipped-away, unmolested, discounting the odd dog or two and its leg.
   (and)
Finally, it began to edge itself up across the footpath, past the café's threshold, avoided being crushed underfoot until it reached the kitchen hoping to find the Sri Lankan tourist to which it had taken a shine. The trouble was, by that time, the man had gone back to his country and so, stoic to end all stoicism, it embedded itself beneath the second plumbing U-bend and did whatever Yamaha tail lights with perfectly clear consciences do to help keep Australia free of the malaria scourge. Which we really shouldn't just lay at the feet of Tears Nimal, you know.

(Blackout)

---oOo---

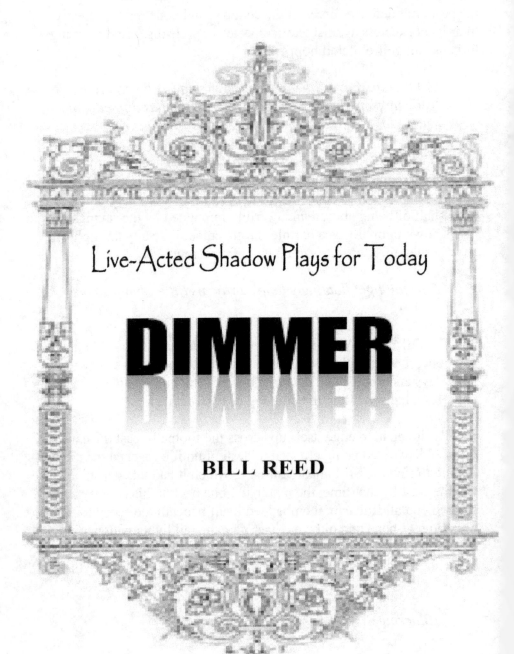

Live-Acted Shadow Plays for Today

DIMMER

BILL REED

The behind-the-screen shadow action – or 'inner background' play --
can only ever keep 'pace' with the reading, not *keep up* with it.
Because of the resultant and necessary shadow-play distillation of the
storyteller's tale, the extensive stage directions given in this script are
only intended to be indicators as to what *might* be used for the shadow-
play side of things. They deliberately go beyond what the director
would employ and are given merely as a range of possible shadow-
actions he or she might want to use in the 'distillation'.

The Characters

STORYTELLER:
Apart from his 'ad libbed' asides and comments, he is very much part of the inner production. This is because of the many segments the shadow players and props need to tune in with his readings. He will almost act at times as an onstage director going *live*.

DIMMER:
A shadow player and a 'live' actor. He comes out from behind the screen or not since the part calls for both shadow illustration and three-dimensional dialogue. A groper, sure.

VICTIM:
The unlucky one nabbed by Dimmer and may or may not be the intended target. He is not he, in any case. Just ask him.

MANAGER:
Always wanted to be a crime boss, but doubting whether one of his crime-family sons could be imagined to be Dimmer. But when the opportunity comes along, well…

SHADOW PLAYERS:
Optimally, around 4 or more. They have wide-ranging roles from milling family to sea captains to fire brigades, security guards, fish, etcetera.

Dimmer

(The lighting is general both in front and behind the scrim curtain. Behind there is nothing there for the moment. In front, the STORYTELLER is on his stool, waiting for someone... anyone... to arrive in the shadow area.

No one as yet does. He has to shrug apologetically to audience)

STORYTELLER: Still trying to find his way in, betcha. You can't imagine what a groping there would be back there... blindness being so catchy, you know. So, let's sort of start by me saying...
   (waves script, and ostensibly reads from it)
you wouldn't believe this is the first time I've looked at this, would you? I bet you wouldn't.
   (still, does settle back to read:)
It was crook to be the 13th son of the local crime czar... a father so vicious we really shouldn't be mentioning his family name here by way of giving any encouragement, even to the 13th son.
   (pauses for effect)
It was more crooked still to be the only son with a crooked-impairing impediment. You could have a limp; you could have a hare lip; you could have an over-use twitch when it came to wielding your shiv. But if you couldn't see what was in front of your face so that, if you were ever picked up by the cops, and in all honesty, you wouldn't be able to give a description of your own father when they were twisting your arm backwards. Or identity a mug shot of yourself even with a magnifying glass because you were squinting too much in it trying to see the police-file camera. And how can a police artist draw your description if all was just a blur?

(Behind, now, DIMMER shadow player manages to feel his way into the shadow area. Above his head there is a large floating pair of glasses that follow him wherever he goes and flashing kaleidoscope light reflections from its lens. The lighting in there is still very dim, though)

STORYTELLER: One advantage was, as you can see, he saved on electricity.

(Lighting back on in the shadow area to show DIMMER shadow player groping around to find a 'floating' light switch...)

STORYTELLER: It didn't help when one of the banes of your life was never ever being able to find a light switch. Or, for that matter, the wall it was mounted on.

(and, after that is illustrated)

Whoever gave him the name of Dimmer was dead right. It was no nickname, but. His father gave it to him from birth after the little thing turned over and started goo-ing at his own umbilical. Very messily. Still, like his other twelve brothers... the girls, not expected to be part of any crime wave, were never counted... he still had to pull his weight of having been born proudly into crime. Kidnapping and extortion was the family game and, yes, Dimmer his name. In fact, despite his minor affliction, Dimmer was often picked on by his father to go out and do a 'job' – and this wasn't as silly as it sounds, because... well, for one thing, on his way out he often couldn't find the door knob... and for another thing...

(He waits until DIMMER shadow player finally finds the knob and can open the floating door)

STORYTELLER: (shakes head 'so sad', reads on) It has to be admitted that his crime boss of a father was a bit cracked too in that he believed the kidnap mark he sent Dimmer out to collar this one particular time we're talking about wouldn't be able to identify the family if his son couldn't see him properly.

(and as DIMMER behind him stands mutely in front of an ATM machine, trying repeatedly to shake hands with it)

STORYTELLER: We find him waiting for his mark outside a bank covering his tracks by making polite conversation to one of the bank's security guards, which was in fact an ATM machine which confused Dimmer because he thought it kept wanting to shake his hand. On that ATM was a sign that read...

360

(A shadow player pokes a sign around the end of the scrim curtain and theatrically points to it, and reads it out loud:)

SIGN BEARER: 'PLEASE WAIT WHILE WE CRUNCH THE NUMBERS. AWAIT OUTPOURINGS.'

STORYTELLER: 'Please wait while we crunch the numbers. Await outpourings.' Yes. Which Dimmer thought said 'Security' and it was only his eight-fold vision that was making it look like more words than one.
(allows shadow enactment)
Not long after, still not having found the mark his father had sent him to kidnap, Dimmer was standing inside the bank before a Customer Service desk thinking it was a car parked illegally that could be blocking his view, he was saying, he thought, to it: 'You wanna...'

(DIMMER shadow player, now at the desk as described, takes over and loudly to be heard from behind there.)

DIMMER: You wanna watch out. You could be towed.

(The shadow player behind the desk has to shout likewise and gesture wildly to reply:)

CLERK SHADOW PLAYER: I beg yours?

DIMMER: Word of advice from the wise. Watch it. Old Mazdas they take straight to the wreckers, see.

CLERK SHADOW PLAYER: Excuse me, if you're talking to me, I'm over here.

STORYTELLER: (butting back in) Of course if you had Dimmer condition you'd be used to confusing old Mazdas up with clerks and the like.

DIMMER: Excuse I. Cortina, is it? New paint job?

CLERK SHADOW PLAYER: No.

DIMMER: I can always tell a new paint job.
   (taps nose)
One of the best noses in the business. Ask me to smell out anything anywhere around a paint sprayer.

CLERK SHADOW PLAYER: Sir, please be warned. I take that as an attack of my integrity.

DIMMER: Thanks but no thanks. I can only handle one kidnap, to put it mildly, at a time.

CLERK SHADOW PLAYER: (throwing hands in air) *Help!*

DIMMER: (just as alarmed) *Help!*

   (A shadow GUARD appears, points his revolver at DIMMER which he thinks is a cup)

DIMMER: Very nice of you, but I just had coffee before I left home.
   (gets prodded with gun)
Well, all right, but I'm lactose intolerant, you know.

   (goes to take 'cup', feels blindly around nuzzle, shouts warning)

DIMMER: A gun! Hold-up!

STORYTELLER: You see what I mean. It could have gone on and on. Dimmer should never have found himself inside the bank, not before he'd found the mark and kidnapped him he shouldn't have, and so had someone who could have guided him under air conditioning and fluorescent lights pointing out it was the commuter traffic. But as usual things fell into his lap. On his shout of 'gun', his father's intended kidnap mark, who happened to be inside the bank all the time and not outside, panicked like everybody else – and ran straight into Dimmer's arms.

   (back in the shadow-playing area, the 'mark' has run into DIMMER and hangs on for dear life, and, also shouted for audience to hear:)

DIMMER: Are you he who I kidnap?

VICTIM: Yes, please.

DIMMER: GOTCHA!

> *(and hangs onto DIMMER as much as DIMMER hangs onto him, so tightly in fact DIMMER can now can proudly declare to the shadow behind the Customer Services desk)*

DIMMER: (at Clerk) You might be an ATM machine, but did you see that? See the deftness, like?

CLERK SHADOW PLAYER: I am paid to work here, not to see things.

DIMMER: (intimate hiss) Between you'n'me, he's my mark.
  (to her not being impressed, goes proudly)
You can go years, you know, and sometimes they just open your arms and they just fall in.

> *(She looks up her monitor which she captures from floating about)*

CLERK SHADOW PLAYER: Don't be silly. He hasn't got any money to be kidnapped.

VICTIM: Nobody believes me!

DIMMER: (rebuke) Now, you've hurt his feelings. In the trade, we call that bruising the goods.

VICTIM: Well, when you find out just don't come running in here asking me for a loan for the bus fare home.

> *(She gets up, huffs off, leaving DIMMER alone with his kidnap victim)*

DIMMER: (outraged) I want the manager!
  (turns to victim)

363

Don't you?

VICTIM: I do!

DIMMER: Let's tell them to shove their coffee, then.

VICTIM: Shove your coffee!

DIMMER: (a disgruntled customer) Where's the Manager!

VICTIM: Where's the Manager!

DIMMER: You lead the way. I'm close behind!

(so close, he shadows the other's footsteps as they goosestep off towards, perhaps, some horizon. As he goes, he insults the flat-screen monitor now floating above them:)

DIMMER: And you, skinny-arse. Stop dumb-arsed dieting and get something inside you!

(STORYTELLER resumes control. The shadow playing, though, continues behind him – first to outside on the street, then back inside the bank again, according to the narration:)

STORYTELLER: (shrugging) No wonder they're acting it out in shadows the way Dimmer saw it all!
   (and)
Dimmer just thought the keyboard was a moustache and started to simmer because he didn't like moustaches. Anyhow, finally outside with the kidnap victim his father had sent him to lift, the selfsame kidnap victim led Dimmer around the block two times and then back inside the bank -- all the time both of them yelling 'Help, help!' which, one would think, is not the best thing for the kidnapper that was Dimmer to be shouting -- and finally straight through the door of the Manager's office, especially after, as we can see, Dimmer mouthed out of the side of his mouth that which his crime boss father had schooled him in in a gangster's way, going, 'Mac, don't let me do something I'll regret'…

DIMMER: Mac, don't let me do something I'll regret. I don't even like seeing it.

STORYTELLER: … into the ear of his victim, which, as just said, made the kidnap victim all nervous and so he turned around and lead Dimmer back inside the bank's hall, do a couple of turns…
   (as they do so around the bank interior…)
 past the Customers Service desk and the pretty-astonished armed guard and straight back into the bank manager's office where he had started to get nervous. Dimmer just thought they were passing through Dandenong Arcade in a busy lunch hour.

DIMMER: That's better. Don't let my lack of height fool you, bad boy. Very foggy, don't you think?

STORYTELLER: … Dimmer was heard saying as he went in kidnap fashion his father would have been proud of, his vanity of refusing to wear glasses proving a bit unfortunate again. Normally, the desperation of his squints allowed him to get away with a lot.

   (and, while the main shadow players conduct together:)

STORYTELLER: …Luckily, at least it did with the bank manager who always had a bit of a hankering to be his own crime czar (which he felt was very lacking in among the business community of Dandenong if it was to progress to greater bank loans) but never imagined that someone would just walk into his office, park, make some guy comfortable on his potted plant as though it was a chair, and then take him for the biggest crime boss this side of the Sandown dog track.
   (pauses for their mimes to catch up….)
What luck! Sometimes, as Dimmer said, you open your arms and 'it' just falls into them. But, strangely, you know, and while this weirdly-groping-around first fellow was looking around the office for something to see, it looked like, it was the seated guy who spoke first:

VICTIM: I'm not me, you know. I'm not even White, only look it!

   (DIMMER has found the coat-and-hat rack for the Manager, and affirms to it)

365

DIMMER: I told you he wasn't White.

MANAGER: No, you didn't.

DIMMER: (seen waving him away) Shut it, mac. I'm talking to the Manager here.

> *(and turns back to the coat-and-hat rack, stands akimbo to it waiting for an answer. THE MANAGER sees he has to move to be behind the rack to speak to DIMMER:)*

MANAGER: (repeats) I said no, you didn't actually.

DIMMER: Father?

MANAGER: (goes along with charade) Who else?

DIMMER: I got him, Father!
   (proudly)
Boost of the old crime rate, Father, and we'd be pulling ahead of the statistics!

VICTIM: (tries again) I'm not me, you know. I only look whiteish.

> *(DIMMER still address the hat stand 'with' the MANAGER behind)*

 DIMMER: Got a mouth on him, this one, Father. Had to gag him.

MANAGER: Don't think you did.

DIMMER: (tapping side of nose again) Made it only look like I did, see. Eyes everywhere, Father.
   (then)
You changing your voice, Father? Pipsqueak of a frog got your throat?

MANAGER: Depends.

> *(Now they have to wait for the STORYTELLER who could well have fallen asleep. From the wings, there is a loud hiss and a*

366

long pole prod, for:)

STORYTELLER: Etcetera, etcetera. Have to move quickly on, you know. What swims before the eyes.
(gets back to reading from script)
So, what we have here is Dimmer thinking he's heisted the mark and all that walking around has got him back home and the coat-and-hat rack is his father not knowing he's mistaking it for the bank manager and he's deposited the mark safely in what he thinks is the bosom of his thuggish family not knowing the bosom of his thuggish family is a pot plant in the manager's office.
(and)
Could use a bit of punctuation there.
(and)
To make things worse, or better, is Dimmer thinking his father is only sounding a bit strange because the old boy's trying to cover up his voice in order to cover up his tracks in case the Dandenong CID haven't covered them up for him.
(waves script back to shadow players)
It goes on to say here that you may carry on.

(They do so now that things seem to have got back on track, and:)

DIMMER: (conspiratorially) Wanna go somewhere safe, Father?

(The MANAGER takes up the crime-boss imitation, from here on speaks exaggeratedly out of side of a 'gangsta' mouth)

MANAGER: I do, don't I or not? Watcha, whack!

(DIMMER nods, MANAGER nods)

DIMMER: Did you nod, Father?

MANAGER: You betcha.

DIMMER: (triumphantly) I saw that! A fine nod, that!

(DIMMER stumbles forward until he has come out from behind
367

the scrim curtain and is now standing in full view of the audience. As an impromptu compromise to this, the VICTIM hurries to follow suit to appear audience side of the scrim, but on the other side of the stage.

They converse by shouting across the STORYTELLER's stage-apron space…)

VICTIM: Don't forget me! I ain't even White! Just give us a quick rub!

DIMMER: (looking everywhere but correctly) Get back here, you!

VICTIM: (whine) This kidnap thing's very uncomfortable. What was wrong with taking the coffee they offered. Even it not being coffee was better than no coffee.

DIMMER: Stop bitching. You just sit tight and get out of those clothes.

VICTIM: Which? Sit tight, or…

DIMMER: The clothes, the clothes…!
  (his own gripe back to shadow area to MANAGER)
Jeez, they don't get any brighter, Father, do they? You ever noticed that?

MANAGER: (shout from behind scrim) You need an eagle eye on them, idjit!

DIMMER: (sagely) Oh, you ain't wrong there, Father!

VICTIM: (still complaining) I'm not wearing any clothes! Not white clothes anyway.

DIMMER: (fed up) Yes, you effing are.

VICTIM: No, I'm not.

(Disgustedly, DIMMER motions to give him a minute, goes back
368

behind curtain, where we see he gropes to get in front of the hat stand again. He feels it. It has the MANAGER's coat on it. Thus ascertaining that the kidnap mark is wearing clothes, he turns back to come to full visibility again, saying as he goes:)

DIMMER: Don't try kidding a kidder!

VICTIM: I'm over here, sir or Your Majesty. I've been trying to tell the Immigration department that for years!

DIMMER: ('what to do', back to MANAGER) They just don't learn these days when they're dealing with a professional, you found that?

MANAGER: (gangsta, out of side of mouth) Give me a kick in the nuts and tell da bum to clam it.

VICTIM: (crying out): If I'm wearing clothes, they're not mine, you know.

> *(Nevertheless, the VICTIM shadow player returns behind the scrim curtain and   proceeds to strip until his shadow indicates he stands naked for inspection.*
>
> *There is a moment when no one seems to know what to do now, until the STORYTELLER guides DIMMER back behind the screen where the MANAGER takes charge of him to join in inspecting the kidnappee. Finally...)*

MANAGER: I hope he's not going to seep anything on my carpet.

DIMMER: I wouldn't have lifted him if he was seeping, Father. Where'd we get a carpet?

> *(The MANAGER is caught out again, has to quickly go gangsta side-of-the-mouth once more:)*

MANAGER: The blood stains wouldn't come out of the floor boards.

DIMMER: That, I'd like to have seen.

MANAGER: I bet you would.

(DIMMER points to the coat rack as the VICTIM ...)

DIMMER: What do you think of my catch, Father?

MANAGER: I'm over here, fuggit!

DIMMER: (suspicious) What happened to 'idjit'?

MANAGER: (obliging) Idjit.

DIMMER: (looking for compliments) Pass muster enough for you, Father?

MANAGER: Depends what we can loan...
    (corrects himself)
... what we can get for the mug.

VICTIM: It's not a white mug, you know, not last time I looked!

DIMMER: (puffed) I told you I was the one to send, Father.

MANAGER: (pointing at kidnappee) Is that standing straight or it's like all them kidnappeds go?
    (then quickly)
Idjit.

DIMMER: Straight as a die, Father. You could put a coat rack next to him and not tell the difference.

VICTIM: Not a white coat rack, you couldn't.

(The MANAGER is still trying to make out what he is seeing in the naked VICTIM; he can't work it out:)

MANAGER: I can't make hide nor hair of him. Idjit.

VICTIM: I ain't got no hide nor hair, not in any colour you'd know, anyway!

DIMMER: Take a closer look, Father!

MANAGER: I don't wanna get too close. Catchy? Somebody unravel him.

DIMMER: No close look-see, no ransom, right, Father?

MANAGER: (now getting in the swing) Idjit.

> *(And while DIMMER shows satisfaction at so pleasing his father, other shadows 'rake over' the kidnapped one to get him to stand up straight and then fix him in position for proper inspection, as:)*

STORYTELLER: And so we can see how Dimmer was thinking and hoping his kidnappee would do him proud in front of his father and his other twenty-two brothers... and the manager was thinking how he could get out of pretending to be the idjit's father if his assessment of the naked being on his office carpet proved not worth the ticket, ransom-wise, especially if one of his staff walked in on them... and nobody was wondering what the coat rack might be thinking about it all... and not one was bothering to ask the fellow being kidnapped was thinking...

VICTIM: Not being White, I ain't worth much. That's why they threw me out of the very country I was born in!

MANAGER: (back to gangsta) One of you idjits get him to put a plug in it.

> *(A shadow player clips the kidnapped one over the ears, repositions him again, clips him over the ears again)*

VICTIM: Ow! That's not in any immigration brochure they sent me!

DIMMER: So, how much d'you think he'd fetch, Father?

MANAGER: Can he stand on one leg, like the trainees of a certain bank I know?

(The shadows grab one of VICTIM shadow player's legs, hoist it up. They do so just in time for DIMMER to have motioned to his 'father' that he'll find out, grope his way back to the coat-and-hat stand, get down on knees and finds only one leg. He returns to face the MANAGER across the stage)

DIMMER: You never told me to expect a one-legged fucker, Father.

MANAGE: Idjit!

DIMMER: You betcha I am, Father. What you say. Re him, how much did you say again?

MANAGER: (ponderously) The one shitty thing I see is he doesn't look very Sri Lankan to me.

DIMMER: Oh, he's very Sri Lankan in a certain touchy-feely way, Father!

MANAGER: Looks more blonde from Scandinavia.

VICTIM: That's me!

DIMMER: They dye their hair to get into the country, Father.

MANAGER: Idjit! But what's all the rib bones. How much he gonna cost fattening up for the market?

DIMMER: A bit skinny, you mean, Father?

MANAGER: This one you'd take to a block of lead and it'd fit through the cracks. Who's gonna fork good boodle for *this*?

(DIMMER thinks on this; decide to check it out for himself... gropes around and only succeeds in getting back to the coat rack, where he runs his hands expert-like over its form. Gets up satisfied, and gropes his way back somewhere near the others:)

DIMMER: Skinny's not in it, Father. What do they do to them in New Zealand.

372

VICTIM: I'm not New Zealand white!

MANAGER: We still getting boat people from New Zealand affecting the local kidnapping market?

(The STORYTELLER has to jump in to get attention:)

STORYTELLER: Now here's the thing where Dimmer wasn't too far off the mark. His father *did* want a Sri Lankan or someone who'd pass as one. Why, we ask? It was like this: he wanted to offload some of the blood the crime family had lying around to do some good in the world rather than just lying about the house. Ergo, donate it to some country that looking for a bit of it to fill up a bit of a deficit and they're not too keen with the old DNA analysis.
   *(even as, behind him, they are now inspecting the kidnapped shadow
      player very closely...)*
First, though, get cagey. Even if it's starting to clog up all the corridors back home, you don't go donating good blood to somewhere who doesn't know how to use it to fatten the calf. So, any crime syndicate honouring the memory of its victims would first demonstrate how you can pump up an undernourished local up by pumping up his veins. Overseas aid best practise. Nothing like a good night out on the red stuff.

(He nods to let the shadow players they can carry on. They do:)

DIMMER: It helps to have a clear vision of things, Father.

MANAGER: Idjit.

DIMMER: So what did you say the characteristics we should be looking for, Father?

MANAGER: (really enjoying role now) Initially I would have thought something in the region… say, two million US in cash by Saturday and we set the exchange rate.

DIMMER: Fair cop, I'd say, Father.

373

MANAGER: Small snag is him looking so Scandinavian.

VICTIM: (shouts) I am! Scandinavia just won't admit it!

DIMMER: You are not!

VICTIM: I am! I just came out to see what my life's supposed to be like!

DIMMER: (menacingly) You saying these, my own, eyes deceived me?

VICTIM: Oo, no.

(Disgusted, DIMMER gropes his way over to rather fortuitously find the VICTIM shadow player and gags his mouth and ties his hands. He does this by putting a gag over his forehead, and tying one wrist, pulling that same wrist behind the man and tying it to itself.)

DIMMER: Honestly, what you pick up in the streets these days. You were saying before we were rudely interrupted, Father…?

MANAGER: I could bring in my Commercial Manager, but maybe two million US cash by Saturday is a bit much. Looking at him in the flesh… that is flesh there, right?… and with no strings attached…
  (but first…)
I right about the no strings attached…?

(Some shadow players search for strings on the victim, shake their heads no, so:)

MANAGER: That being the case and even so… without resorting to my calculator… the rust around here, you know… I'd have to revise my estimate and say we go for something like…

(makes histrionics in a decision, decides to look closer before giving opinion, goes back into his office to inspect the victim and, being singularly unimpressed:)

MANAGER: What'd you say he was when you picked him up?

DIMMER: Gave the big hoist? Sri Lankan, Father. Like you said.

MANAGER: Eee, and I like Sri Lanka. I could be living there if I
didn't find something useful in myself. Which I haven't. Or if I could
swim. So I don't know why I'm not living in Sri Lanka. Where was
I...?
(pointing at VICTIM shadow player)
So. Off hand, I'd first say, they should take more care of who they let
out of the country, if they want to keep up any sort of reputation about
the quality of their kidnappees. Or pretend their passing Indians.
(then decision)
I tell you what: I'm revising my original thinking to... think I'll go
with... say, instead of the two mill USD, I'd have my arm twisted to go
for 200 Sri Lankan rupees the Saturday after next, we paying for the
exchange rate and the freight and offloading. Can't go fairer than that.

DIMMER: That's what that young bloke behind that desk back there'd
say, Father.

MANAGER: (correcting) That's a young woman.

DIMMER: You don't like to say these days, Father.
(then cunningly)
You're only filling in for my Dad, aren't you?

MANAGER: (gangsta talk again) I ain't no stoolie.

DIMMER: Where am I?

(The MANAGER has now given up pretence of being a gangster)

MANAGER: The bank.

DIMMER: How'd the bank get home?

ALL SHADOW PLAYERS: (together) BEATS ME!

375

DIMMER: (to MANAGER) Look, be a pal, give's a lift home, all right?

MANAGER: Absolutely not.

DIMMER: Well, show us the way, okay?

MANAGER: What difference would that do?

DIMMER: Then go outside and flag a cab down for us, orright?

MANAGER: Absolutely not.

DIMMER: Well, hell, what *do* you do?

MANAGER: (up on high horse) I do absolutely nothing.

DIMMER: By God, this is a bank!

> *(He thinks he is escaping but is actually running around scrim curtain one way and returning back into shadow area the other way, where he grabs the coat-and-hat rack in a threatening manner, gets his hands prised off it by some shadow players, then is guided to the VICTIM shadow player, whom he takes by the arm in order for th em to get out of there fast. But gets the ultimate nuh-uh from the MANAGER)*

MANAGER: This man has just taken out a mortgage. This man is already hostage to us, thank you very much. You can see yourself out.

DIMMER: (abject misery) Shit almighty, how blind can they try to make a man be?

> *(Blackout)*

2.

(When lighting returns, the full complement of shadow players are on hand to illustrate DIMMER's upcoming 'origin' stories. Accordingly, they will need to quickly change from the smoky

*back of the car to school, to a hospital fire, to on fishing boats, to
an 'elephant' setting and all else described.*

*During all this, while on top of all with his narrative,
STORYTELLER is far more mobile, far more 'conducting'
proceedings, given stage directions by gesture and so forth. If he
needs to go behind the scrim for a particular purpose, he does so
and quickly returns front stage)*

STORYTELLER: A lot of people have asked why the infant Dimmer
wasn't just thrown back. Good question! Especially given the fog and
water connotation coming up. Here's, as it says here, the gen.

*(He pauses until things are got right with the shadow area, where
a number of players are seated, cramped together, smoking and
getting a real fog-up)*

STORYTELLER: Whether it's my lead or
   (indicating behind)
 their lead, it brings to mind how, by the time they found the baby
Dimmer to be so dim of sight it was too late to throw him back. His
father knew he should have suspected something right from the start
when he stumbled across the infant taking his mother's milk by way of
her squirting it into his little mouth from at least six inches away and
having to be mightily accurate about it because the child's head was
pointing in the wrong direction.

*(waits while the shadow players get from the car-smoking
conditions to breast feeding, and then getting the aims right to a
very large and very loudly goo-ing baby's head)*

STORYTELLER: From that inauspicious beginning, it would have
been hard to see how Dimmer would actually turn out to have eyes like
a hawk when it came to a fog, no matter how thickly that fog rolled-in
providing there was some salt spray involved.

*(needs to pause – with much gesticulation – to get things from the
beast-feeding part back to the car/smoking/fog-up part)*

STORYTELLER: Now, it's guessed that that hawk-eyes-for-any-fog thing might have been because the boy was born one night in the back of an old Morris Minor when there were two chain-smoking on-the-lam uncles sitting in the front seat and it was too cold outside to have the windows down. Or the closed windows might have been because they were parked upwind of the Dandenong Pizzeria.

(and)

Mind you, it is foretold – and we can vaguely see -- they went to the concession of opening one window slightly to allow the child's mother to breathe – since she was family and hospital had to wait until they finished their cigarettes. And they were chain smokers. Much before they had reconciled the woman being left to give birth in the back seat there -- but, even so, the boy came out not struggling in the least for that supposedly first difficult breath while his mother herself completed two fags.

> *(Behind, in the now thick fog, the first cry of a baby, and a lot of shadowy clapping of hands and oo-ing and ah-ing)*

STORYTELLER: The uncles thought the little bludger might have been not giving a good old healthy first-breath cry, but might have been choking to death before they had finished their cigarettes hopefully before the cops got onto them, but when the police *did* arrive, that fog cleared a bit…

> *(large suction hoses are brought -- very Keystone Cops like -- to suck out some of the smoke)*

STORYTELLER: … they found Dimmer just lying there taking in the fog, swaddled and snuggled in, breathing nice and calmly. Where they expected to have to hide a corpse between fag ends, there was now no whaa-ing or thrashing around to get the lungs working; nothing of that kind, nothing to sound any cop alarm.

(as the babe-in-arms does so…)

The little thing even smiled up at his mother when she did her deepest postnatal draw-back, even as she coughed her ring up all over him. It was if Dimmer was saying it's all the same to me, Ma. And we know she looked down at her child as only a new mother can and gently wiped her phlegm from his tiny face as she goo-ed and the child kept goo-ing and even the uncles joined in goo-ing, with a lot of sticky tobacco goo coming up from their lungs. Too.

(waits until the cacophony of coughing and goo-ing and hoicking up settles down)

She was amazed she hadn't blown it. The uncles were amazed little Dimmer obviously could see them in the fog-up when it was too fogged up in there for them to see him, although the bloodshots in their eyes weren't helping.

(In the shadows, the mother emerges with her baby Dimmer in her arms, Madonna-esque)

STORYTELLER: That is why, it is said, Dimmer might be a stumbler on a clear day but when it came to haze, he was born to seeing right through it. Eagle-eyed. The thicker the better. In a pea soup, he didn't miss a pea.

(while the shadow playing struggles to catch up with the narrative of the school, the puffing away, the hospital fire &ce:)

STORYTELLER: You take in school. Dimmer learnt to have to keep his eyebrows wet so that the natural humidity fogged up his glasses so much that he could see the blackboard plain as day through the resulting mists. Put him in a smoky fug of a room and he needed no visual enhancements; he buzzed around happily, sharp eyes twinkling where others watered. Even, to get back to our now-as-then time... to see where to properly put the gag on his Sri Lankan kidnappee... around his mouth not around his neck where it ended up... all he needed was to have a fag in the fellow's mouth and to keep puffing away in order to give Dimmer a full outline in every detail of where his face was and where his mouth should be, if you followed the eyes down.

(points 'there-you-go' to shadow illustration)

That time we mentioned a bit back, it was just bank's fault for not allowing smoking. If they had everything would have been all right and that bank manager would have got his comeuppance. Even if the fellow's final estimate of what ransom was possible was pretty much spot on.

(and)

And so, Dimmer constantly kept proving them wrong about being as blind as a bat from the word go, of course. Even the day in that maternity hospital they were able to confirm that, given fogless conditions, he could see not much more than nothing at all, there was a fire in one of the wards. The whole place started going up like a tinderbox and quickly filled with smoke; and, guess what?, that tiny little fellow Dimmer, only a few days old and still swaddled, led the two top floors – staff, patients, firemen and visitors alike -- through that fug-up to safety down the fire stairs. Not bad when you can read 'Fire Exit' at that age and, even then, not from a distant beyond where they could throw you.

> *(The fire alarm bells rise and die down. Relative calm returns to the shadow area. He can settle down to start again when the shadow acting catches up with ship deck, storms, oil-cloth Macintoshes etc. He can read on:)*

STORYTELLER: There is no doubt being hawk-eyed in fogs, especially, was because of that being born in a back seat among three 60-a-dayers with the windows up, but there is conjecture about why Dimmer became so adept at fogs at sea in particular... so much so he was preferred by many, many ships' captains to their ship's radar. It's thought...
(has to wait for coughing and spluttering to subside)
all that coughing and spluttering in the back of the Morris Minor he remembered somehow as fine sea spray. As the sea fog rolled in...

> *(A sea fog rolls in... too much so, and blanks out all the shadow action)*

STORYTELLER: (loud hint) As it might roll out a little faster.
(back stage they're using blowers to clear it up enough for him to:)
None of this altered the fact that Dimmer had subsequently become a master mariner in huge demand by shipping companies all over the place. In fogs or murky conditions or fire on board, he could see further than any radar and, of course, in 3D, better than any satellite add-on. In a danger to all on any ship anywhere, they would perch him on what was the old yardarm...
(to shadow enactment)

if you guided him to the proper crows nest mast before he got stuck or strung up a flagpole or whathaveyou... and there he'd be, as happy as larry, looking out over the vast expanses, propped up next to the radar dishes and showing them how it should be done, especially the going around in circles bit. In any lack of clear visibility, you'd have to go far to find any sea captain who wouldn't rather go be Dimmer rather than the radar.

(and to fog horns and gentle sea sloshings)
Fishing boats were where he was especially in demand. They soon found that whole shoals of fish would be attracted to the ship thinking that his falling overboard all the time might be a good feed of chum. He was just chummy, ha ha. Then, when the word got around the deep-sea fish community, more shoals would come from miles around just to see the stumble-bum who kept falling over the side. And so the crews caught more. And Dimmer therefore kept falling over the side more. And the more the fish came to see. Really, you'd have to say the juiciest of chum had nothing on it.

(and while the storms at sea that have picked up and the fishing sequences finish:)

STORYTELLER: The truth was, on land, Dimmer thought he was at sea and, at sea, he thought he was on land. So what? Feeling he was all at sea just made him feel fully useful. Feeling he was on dry land just made him feel all at sea. It didn't matter to Dimmer; by that he was always feeling very useful. All was fog and fog was all. It made him all bleary-eyed to think about how blessedly he had been touched. I know it does me, and it probably does you.

(Lighting fades in the shadow area indicating all is just about done.

DIMMER emerges in the upfront area. He is dripping wet. He stumbled from one side and eventually, inevitably, bumps into STORYTELLER who gets his face felt up:)

DIMMER: Father?

STORYTELLER: No.

DIMMER: You seen my brothers?

STORYTELLER: Which ones?

DIMMER: All of them, I think.
    (holding up one end of it)
They had me on the end of this blue ribbon but then they just
disappeared.

STORYTELLER: It's a lifesavers' surf belt.

   (DIMMER looks, and is, lost. STORYTELLER turns him around)

STORYTELLER: Try that way.

DIMER: (can't see) What way?

STORYTELLER: Follow the sun. No, follow your face.

DIMMER: Why's that?

STORYTELLER: It's where your nose is pointing.

DIMMER: Good idea!

   (and goes off, leaving STORYTELLER to take centre stage for:)

STORYTELLER: And so, around here, the strange ballad of Dimmer
vanishes in mist, and what happens further to him is not really
known...
    (scrutinises script quizzically)
or he might have just gone missing only to reappear in the next few
days... where're you been, they usually asked him; I don't know but
there was a lot of handiwork, he usually answered... although I think
there's something a bit wrong with the page numbering here...

   *(He gives up wondering about the script, settles in the finale,
   while the shadow players hurry about to present the elephant
   hold-up scene:)*

382

STORYTELLER: I can add, I reckon, one last chapter in the life of Dimmer. It happened that his father had the brainwave of putting his 13th idjit son in charge of the family's highway robberies. The old boy thought Dimmer couldn't go wrong in all that traffic pollution… the only trick was to stop the vehicle you wanted to hoist and here Dimmer was as good as the next idjit.

(pause)

Even Dimmer couldn't miss the yellow markings of the zebra crossings, when all he had to do was to step out on one of them and the said target vehicle stopped by itself. In time if he was lucky. Which he mostly was. Easy peasy. Blind Freddie could do it. Or, would have been easy-peasy if the very first target vehicle along the expressway didn't turn out to be an elephant. An elephant. It did and was. Plus, a mahout on top, or rather draped over his head like a forelock. Dimmer's luck! What Dimmer didn't see it as was the delivery outfit of an express delivery company with the motto 'We hump it there and we hump it back'. No, he didn't. What Dimmer did see it as was a gold bullion armoured truck and mince meat to the chap like yours truly now promoted to be in charge of the family's traditional highway robberies, part of its valued heritage.

(pause for renewed effect)

I mean, there might be some question as to how common elephants-with-mahouts are along the expressways of Dandenong, especially one that had gone as far as it was going… because the mahout had forgotten where he was supposed to go and the tusker was just tired of a job going nowhere carrying a human pretending to be some parcel to be delivered… but there was no question that Dimmer stepped onto that zebra crossing with full confidence it was a zebra crossing. And he right bailed up that gold bullion armoured truck, and he shouted fit to be heard:

(Off to one 'lonely' side, DIMMER appears, deluged upon and dripping again, but still brave to his duty…)

DIMMER: Stick 'em up! Open up those back doors, or I'll do ya!

STORYTELLER: Of course, opening *those* back doors did *him*.

(DIMMER disappears in a cloud of steam, going: 'Sssssshush')

STORYTELLER: To be fair to him, it's fair to say the exhaust fumes around the expressway weren't at their foggy best that day, but then got so steamy all of a sudden that Dimmer simply vanishes into the mist of time. As any clear-sighted telling of his ballad should have it.

(He departs, and Blackout)

---oOo---

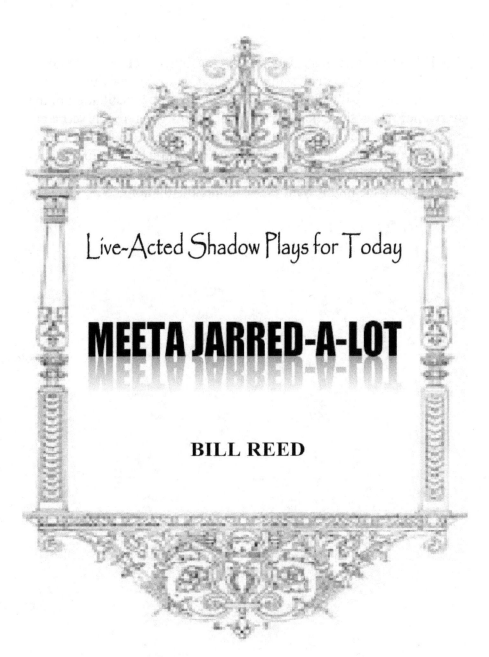

Live-Acted Shadow Plays for Today

MEETA JARRED-A-LOT

BILL REED

The behind-the-screen shadow action – or 'inner background' play --
can only ever keep 'pace' with the reading, not *keep up* with it.
Because of the resultant and necessary shadow-play distillation of the
storyteller's tale, the extensive stage directions given in this script are
only intended to be indicators as to what *might* be used for the shadow-
play side of things. They deliberately go beyond what the director
would employ and are given merely as a range of possible shadow-
actions he or she might want to use in the 'distillation'.

The Characters

STORYTELLER

THE GREAT FRANKLING SHADOW PLAYER
The hypnotist so famous he needs no introduction, even as a shadow.
But, oh, those laser-beam eyes piercing your distant horizons!

TWIN BRAT 1 SHADOW PLAYER
TWIN BRAT 2 SHADOW PLAYER
What can you say, since, even at only 6-years-old, there is nothing he
or his twin wouldn't say?

MOTHER SHADOW PLAYER
So long-suffering-to-thankyou, she could well have been a living doll
herself once.

LITTLE MEETA SHADOW PLAYER
She is both the girl shadow growing from fitting in the palm of her
mother's hand *and* the joyous buzz-around prop-figure having a great
time in the air over-all, re-enacting what The Great Franklin alludes
and gives illusion to. She is the first manifestation of Meeta. The other
is:

MEETA ALTER EGO SHADOW PLAYER
the Peter Pan aspect of her – free and delightfully gigglish over all.

SHADOW PLAYERS/PROPS
Making up the assortment of 'living' creatures evoked, like Mr
Crocodile, security men, party people etc.

Meeta Jarred-a-Lot

(From behind the scrim comes the sights and sound of a really raucous 6-year-olds' birthday party, replete with delighted and not-so-delighted blood-curdling screams, over which the two birthday boys... the leading politician's identical twins... lord it.

Through this, the STORYTELLER manages to make himself known front-of-screen and to get in...)

STORYTELLER: It was the Senator's 6-year-old twin boys' birthday party and the great hypnotist hadn't even finished his favourite party trick of hypnotising the fleas in his popular Big Top flea circus.
   (when it somewhat quietens down...)
The great Great Franklin hadn't finished his party tricks for two reasons. One was that, half way though, the brat twins had decided they would rather practise on their future political careers by having their father's security men beat up the great hypnotist as though he was a baddie caught in some dark alley. (It was only pretend, but those bodyguards were only trained to stop when the first bruises started showing and The Great Franklin was a notorious slow bruiser.)
   (and)
The second reason for not finishing his party tricks was the great hypnotist simply had to know who the sweet-looking little thing sitting off in the corner, on the palm of her mother's hand, was – and why the little thing was wincing away with one of her constant headaches.
   (and)
So, The Great Franklin woke his fleas up out of their trances he had put them in and set them free to move amongst the other 6-year-old bratty guests. Go enjoy yourself, my children! And he then went over to the little thing, so tiny as to fit on the palm of her mother's hand, yes. As he made his way to her...

(The spotlight turns to little MEETA, so tiny as to be fitting in the palm of her mother's hand, and being totally neglected, while...)

STORYTELLER: ... his famous radar picked up that she was... would you believe it?... the girl twin sister to those terrible twin brat brothers, born between them and therefore so squeezed in by the one on one side and the other on the other side that she had been squashed out of ever being able to grow properly ever since.

   (and)

Oh, The Great Franklin's great'n'tuned-in heart went out to her instantly! What a little dollface she was! Even across the bash-and-smash-with-a-lot-of-mash party, he could pick up on her tiny silence, her tiny wonder-eyes, the doll-like of her all over, even down to her tiny toes and her tiny little ringlets and how her tiny eyes blinked such big alarm at all the brat boisterers going crazy all before her in what was, after all, supposed to be one-third her birthday party too and not 100 percent of one of her migraines. Pardon me, while I take a deep breath.

   (while he catches breath, there is a rise of bashing party chaos rise, which thankfully subsides enough for…)

She was a quarter of her twin brothers' size, and, so said, getting lesser than even that, since the brat twins were growing normally for any brat, and she sure wasn't. The Great Franklin nearly cried himself to see how she was bravely trying to keep her brothers in sight through another one of her constant blinding headaches.

   (THE GREAT FRANKLIN shadow player's path to her is blocks by the twin brats – their menace backed up by their father's bodyguards…)

TWIN 1 SHADOW PLAYER: Where's this Long-Tall…

TWIN 2 SHADOW PLAYER: … Drink of Pee think he's going?

TWIN 1 SHADOW PLAYER: Say, I gotta itch.
   (command to security guys)
Scratch him.

THE GREAT FRANKLIN SHADOW PLAYER: That's no itch; that's my fleas!

TWIN 2 SHADOW PLAYER: I gotta itch too. Scratch him; you heard.

   (The bodyguards set on THE GREAT FRANKLIN, much to the raucous giggle delight of the twins and all the other brat-guests)

389

STORYTELLER: Just about around that time, just before the first signs of bruising came upon him, The Great Franklin decided that party was too brattish for him and left after, yes, this time commanding all his fleas to go among the present company and multiply. And then he made one of his famous grand exits under the cover of making all brats eyes glaze over for a very long time… you're feeling sleepy, sleepy… at least until his fleas had multiplied enough so that all brats there got their fair share. Which was only fair's fair.

(The music over shifts from brat-party chaos to soothing reverent music. The scene shifts to a grotto, where the mother of little MEETA is sitting holding her daughter literary in the palm of her hand, so tiny the little girl is.

Above them, hovering, angelically if it wasn't so impish, comes the MEETA ALTER EGO, who now and throughout reflects the mood of both her 'physical' counterpart and the mood of the storylines. Meanwhile, THE GREAT FRANKLIN shadow player passes by, sees them, and stops…)

STORYTELLER: Not that our great man got very far. On his way out of the Senator's grounds, he came across a grotto of sorts and in there, by some sort of magic he ought to know about but was at the time caught on the hop a bit, was the mother holding her little Meeta in the palm of her hand. Just sitting there, as this script of mine has it, in the silence of there.
     (as he regards them.,.)
Of course, the great man's great heart went out to little Meeta again. Who's wouldn't?
     (as the shadow acting re-enacts…)
Due to his better nature, he went over to them, into the grotto. And we have to say that it wasn't only for the sake of their encounter that this grotto was suspended in time. No, it was. What could you expect with the greatest of hypnotists? He asked her name. Meeta, her mother said. Meeta. Little Meeta. 'I hear your little name is little Meeta,' the great man said. 'Yes', the little thing…

MEETA SHADOW PLAYER: Yesth.

390

STORYTELLER: ... dear thing replied. Such a doll! Such a lovely little sight for tired old hypnotising eyes!

MOTHER: It's one of her headaches. Do you have something she can pop?

THE GREAT FRANKLIN: I have me. Will I do?

MOTHER: Yes. But please don't tell me I'm feeling sleepy, sleepy, or she might slip through my fingers.

> (THE GREAT FRANKLIN settles himself down before them to begin his attempt to help, while...)

STORYTELLER: And there... almost straightway but starting off very softly and very caringly... did the great man begin what we call in quote marks 'his fable of the bottles not big enough for the dear little thing'. He did, you know!
(pauses for re-enactment to catch up...)
Ah, she looked so tiny as to how she fitted wholly in the crook of one of her mother's arms, below the elbows, so squeezed in from that in-between-brats birth and somehow outside this grotto totally forgotten, even though, yes, it was her birthday party too. Not one part of her dear little personage extended higher than her mother's elbow as she sat in her mother's hands. A mite so miniature, oh. Might, some day, some of us need a magnifying glass to see her?

> (As further soft pastoral musical strains come over, the magical parts (waterfalls, rabbits etc) of the grotto swim as floating props over the shadow area which goes from black-and-white to 'Disney' colour to become dream-like...)

STORYTELLER: As shadows always look always around, let us look around too. So, what was in that grotto? What was little Meeta looking at? Why, everything a grotto ever had, of course, and every magical thing a great man like The Great Franklin could conjure up in it, of course! All you wish for. Every other grotto and every grotto other. It was as grottoes dream so, why they do so, how they do so. Of course, it was that sort of grotto. All nice and soft and promising nice things.

391

(and)

And in that clean grotto air, The Great Franklin could really see how tiny little Meeta was. But she wasn't form awkwardly, oh no. She was...

(And now, over all, the 'floating' shadow of MEETA ALTER EGO really makes its presence felt, hereinafter nearly interfering with all the shadow-playing re-enactments, teasingly playing with the other floating props of imagination like Mr Crocodile...)

STORYTELLER: ... a perfect little girl shaped little, that's all -- a little manikin of what she should as normal be if those twin monster brother brats of hers hadn't kept squeezing her out. She was what they call homunculus. And he had to laugh at her wonder eyes and start off a bit teasingly, going: 'I know why you're here, Meeta, little Meeta mine.'

THE GREAT FRANKLIN: (repeat &ce) I know why you're here, Meeta, little Meeta mine.

(MEETA shadow player looks inquiringly up into her mother's face...)

MOTHER: (softly) You can say why, dear.

MEETA SHADOW PLAYER: Why?

STORYTELLER: You see? Tiny, tiny, going so bravely though the ever-throbbing in her head hurting so, yet still bearing herself lively to him, bravely up to him. And the great man answered, 'Because you live in that jar there and it keeps rattling you around and giving you a headache.'

MOTHER: You can say yes, darling.

MEETA: Yesth.

THE GREAT FRANKLIN: I had a friend who lived in a jar too.

STORYTELLER: ... went The Great Franklin nodding and pursing his famous lips to make for her a funny face...

THE GREAT FRANKLIN: You can giggle, but my friend's was a peanut-jelly jar, a bit bigger than yours, but she was a bit fuller than you as well. Her name was Picaninny. What's your jar?

> *(MEETA doesn't answer at first, even though her MOTHER is encouraging her. It isn't until MEETA's floating alter-ago of a shadow gaily appears and 'swims down' to prod her that she gets up the nerve to answer)*

MEETA: (giggly) I don't know

STORYTELLER: To which The Great Franklin replied, 'I think it's a marmalade jam jar, an orange marmalade jam jar.'

MEETA: Yesth.

STORYTELLER: Once upon a time, the great man told the little dear, there was his friend Picaninny who also got rattled in the jar she lived in, a peanut jelly jar. Even so, his Picaninny was a lively little girl, too, because...

THE GREAT FRANLIN: ...she had springs in her step just like you. Don't you?

> *(while MEETA ALTER EGO bounces up and down in the air to 'boinging' sound effects...)*

MOTHER: It's all right to say so if you don't know, darling.

MEETA: I don't know.

STORYTELLER: Of course she didn't know. Her little-large, large-little lovely eyes going oh so 'oooo' that she was being brave enough to answer on her won. 'Yes, you do', went The Great Franklin, 'Springs in your steps, springs in your feet. I've seen, you sneaky you.'
> *(as the MEETA ALTER EGO comes to sit on THE GREAT FRANKLIN's head for a while...)*

And that was the trouble for Picaninny, as it seemed. She kept springing upwards in that peanut jelly jar and she kept hitting her head on the lid. It kept making her little head hurt; it kept making it throb, giving it a headache that went on and on.

THE GREAT FRANKLIN: And you know why?

MEETA ALTER EGO: (looking down, urging) No. Say no.

MEETA: No.

STORYTELLER: Because, silly', the great man answered, 'jumping away like that all the time, she didn't have anything to stop her head from hitting the top of the jar. That was why Picaninny cried a lot just like you too. It wasn't because of all the nasty things they said about her size, like someone else I know. Do you know someone like that?'
   (MEETA nods smally)
Like you?
   (MEETA nods smally again)
Yes, like you.

MEETA: Yesth.

   (In 'a victory' at this, MEETA ALTER EGO flies off his head, dances in the air while...)

STORYTELLER: See, how honest and brave she was at heart? So much so that this inner bravery was one of the major things that made the great man feel he could go on...

THE GREAT FRANKLIN: But do you know what happened to tears when you live in a jar like Picaninny's peanut jelly jar and like your orange marmalade jar?'

STORYTELLER: ...he went; going such a tease.

MEETA: No.

STORYTELLER: By now, the little thing was at least sitting up straight nestled there in her mother's arm, as the great man went on, saying, 'Now there came a day when my friend Picaninny looked down and saw her tears had made a crocodile on the bottom of her jar.

(as the crocodile 'swims' into shadow view to display...)
'A real crocodile! The great man went on, 'Not that she was too surprised; she knew that crocodiles come from tears. She also knew how crocodiles definitely didn't like living at the bottom of jars under little girls' feet because crocodiles were too whippy for any of that. They were so whipping and springy, some people even put them on to wear as shoes to put a spring in their steps. But for my friend Picaninny, all that dopey crocodile was doing was preventing her feet from having room to do their own springing, springing. You see?

(pause to point out the crocodile doings...)
'So Picaninny, she rattled her peanut jelly jar until it tipped over. It gave her a bit of that headache again, but, when it did topple over, the crocodile swam to the top, up by the lid, and when that happened, Picaninny quickly rattled her jar again so that it popped back upright again and there it was that her feet had room to spring on their own! What do you think of that?'

(The peanut jelly jar has come into the shadow action, and now MEETA ALTER EGO is scrunched in an uncomfortable ball inside it, with the crocodile on top of her under the lid.

Both the STORYTELLER and THE GREAT FRANKLIN can now point this out – and to continue to do so as the narration develops...)

STORYTELLER: And there it was. His little friend Picaninny had the top of her head covered by Mr Crocodile and she had done all that by herself by just thinking things through, said the great man.

THE GREAT FRANKLIN: Meeta, little Meeta, do you think you can do that, think thing through like that?

MEETA: (prompted by her mother) Yesth.

STORYTELLER: Of course she could, he told her...

THE GREAT FRANKLIN: Of course you can, silly.

STORYTELLER: ...and then he went on to tell her how after that his friend Picaninny used and used and used the spring now in her step as much as she liked without hurting herself, because, now, with the crocodile up on top, her head only hit the soft belly of Mr Crocodile who wasn't all that please. He had such a big overfed belly that jumping up-and-down, springing a whole lot, didn't hurt her head at all.
   (as they do in the peanut jelly jar...)
Yes, and she kept this up until all those natural springs she had inside her made her become so much bigger... they did!... until one day the top of that peanut jelly jar just had to fly off to make room for how big she was growing. 'Well!', said the great man.

   (He stops. MEETA sits up in her mother's arms... now two arms needed to hold her not just the one... looking much bigger, and:)

MEETA: (making progress) Well, what?

THE GREAT FRANKLIN: 'Well what?', did some little silly ask?

STORYTELLER: Well, because Picaninny looked down and saw the reason was that, with all those springs in her step, she had simply outgrown the jar and hadn't realised it all that time. That growing too big for the jar was what really was hurting the top of her head, you see. Don't you?
   (MEETA nods a bit sceptically...)
No, don't give the great man any doubts or you might start to feel sleepy, sleepy. That hitting her head was what was giving her the headache all the time. She'd been just too big for that orange marmalade jar all along. She just hadn't let the thought pop into her head, that's all.

MOTHER: (adjusting to her child growing even more) You see?

STORYTELLER: Of course she could see, deep down. And so, went the great man, 'Listen, little Meeta dollface: here's a big question for a little girl... When you cry do you also make a Mr Crocodile at the bottom of your orange marmalade jar?'

MEETA: Yesth.

THE GREAT FRANKLIN: Well then…

STORYTELLER: …well then, he went on, going as well: 'you know what to do. You use all that spring you have to your feet and you tip the jar up and you tip it right over and, see, Mr Crocodile is not…
(as illustrated again behind…)
under your feet anymore but he's flopped right on top of your head like a great big pillow for your head and you can spring up as much as you like without hurting your head into give you one of those headaches – and, see?...
(as it does so…)
until that old jar lid just flies off to make room for you!'
(and)
The dear little tiny thing was looking up at him and her mother with so much hope that it filled her eyes, but still her tears came so large for such a tiny face that the Great Franklin's chest hurt and his famous eyes had to drop, water-dropped. So he had to quickly ask, going:

THE GREAT FRANKLIN: Now, why would that be, you think?

> *(And she gets to answer, orchestrated by THE GREAT FRANKLIN, her mother and the STORYTELLER altogether…)*

MEETA: (not weepily at all) Because my Mr Crocodile won't swim up to the top for me and no matter how much I jump and jump or spring and spring, I keep hurting my head and the headache won't stop.

> *(They all clap such a determined response)*

THE GREAT FRANKLIN: Exactly! And little wonder. Just look at those feet of yours!

STORYTELLER: 'Just look at those feet of yours!' His exact words! 'Little wonder!', he had gone.

> *(Rebuked MEETA… still noticeably growing to be not-so-little with the top of her head now reaching well up her mother's arms… starts to whimper. But she is yet still wide-eyed and is stopped by:)*

THE GREAT FRANKLIN: Hoi, no crying! I don't want you to start feeling sleepy, sleepy on me. I mean, have we anywhere near finished here? No, we have not!

STORYTELLER: Did the famous hypnotist go.

THE GREAT FRANKLIN: After all, can you point your toes upwards?

STORYTELLER: 'No', said little Meeta.

THE GREAT FRANKLIN: Can you bend your foot towards the sky?

STORYTELLER: 'No', said little Meeta. 'Of course you can't, you old silly,' went the great man, 'You've got *your* Mr Crocodile on backwards! How can he swim to the top of your orange marmalade jar when he can't even see where he's going?'

> *(To the scramble of the shadow to correct its position in the jar...)*

MEETA: Oh.

THE GREAT FRANKLIN: 'Oh', you might say, sure. But what do you do about that?

STORYTELLER: The Great Franklin went on to say he'd tell her what his friend Picaninny did. Picaninny used the spring in her step to turn her feet around the right way and it didn't even give the old big-bellied crocodile a moment's thought. 'Didn't she?', little Meeta went. 'You try it, if you don't believe me', The Great Franklin so famously replied, such a big tease.
> *(and)*
And she did. She did try it. Little Meeta used her new spring in her step to turn her feet around the right way, all the time looking now up at her mother with no-tiny joy in her eyes, going 'Mummy, look what I can do!'

THE GREAT FRANKLIN: See?

MEETA: (clap-handed) Yesth!

STORYTELLER: Sure, clap-handed little Meeta went, but hushed for daring to look and feel happy. 'Well?', went the great man pointing up to what was happening in the sky above them, 'what's that old fat guts of a crocodile doing?'

MEETA: (all giggly) Sulking!

STORYTELLER: You betcha sulking, she went, her little heels beating on her mother's palms where they had only ever been able to reach down to her wrists before if you look at things upside down, so much was she really growing there, and giggling to her mother, 'The naughty old thing is swimming right past my nose'.

THE GREAT FRANKLIN: What's he saying?

MEETA: He won't speak to me, the big phooey

THE GREAT FRANKLIN: That's all very fine, but where's that Mr Crocodile going now?

MEETA: (now quite brazen) To the top of my head so I can bounce and bounce and it doesn't hurt my head anymore.

THE GREAT FRANKLIN: But what *really* doesn't hurt, silly?

STORYTELLER: And here we have to say how she whispered her answer so only her mother could hear but her little neck had to crick a bit so she could still fit beneath her mother's armpit which she had never been able to even reach up to and touch before, let alone have trouble fitting into, so much was she carrying on there growing, and she said, did little Meeta, 'What my friends say about me, not growing'.

MEETA: (smally) What they say.

THE GREAT FRANKLIN: That's right! What they say! That's what's not hurting!

(while the shadow acting, plus music over, hurries to keep up...)

399

STORYTELLER: … roared the great man to fill her universe with sheer pleasure, before he went on: 'It was the same with my Picaninny, what with her head not hurting because Mr Crocodile was up there and Mr Crocodile didn't give a fig for what her friends said about her not growing.' And then, and then…

MEETA: And then?

THE GREAT FRANKLIN: And then Picaninny was so happy about not being hurt by what her friends said about her, she just kept on bouncing and bouncing until she sprang *pop*! right out of that-there jar of hers because she was certainly just too big for any peanut jelly to hold down, not now with all that springing going on in her steps.

MEETA: What did she do then?

> *(As the tomato sauce bottle replaces the peanut jelly jar for MEETA ALTER EGO to jump right into, so that the shadow acting can re-enact:)*

STORYTELLER: So, they had to get her a new home, that's what she and they did, the great man told her. This one was a Heinz tomato sauce bottle, much bigger and not so fat so she didn't rattle around from side to side so much, and they only put a paper tissue in the top to keep the flies off because they knew, with those springs that had come into her steps lately, no proper lid was going to hold her in for any length of time, anyway.
   (when the shadow re-enactment has caught up…)
Next, after she had soon grown right out of the sauce bottle, they had to get a great big Jeroboam bottle to fit her.

> *(Next comes to replace the sauce bottle a jeroboam bottle, which MEETA ALTER EGO has to squeeze into for:)*

STORYTELLER: A Jeroboam bottle was a great big bottle for the finest of wines. But with all those springs in her steps, soon even that-there Jeroboam bottle wasn't big enough for Picaninny either.

A HOST OF SHADOW PLAYERS: Oh dear, oh dear…

STORYTELLER: 'Oh dear, oh dear', they went... this little girl's springing up so fast!...

A HOST OF SHADOW PLAYERS: Oh, dear-oh-dear, this little girl's springing up so fast!

STORYTELLER: And even The Great Franklin was going…

THE GREAT FRANKLIN: Boy oh boy, wasn't she ever, dear-oh-dear! Is this really my little friend Picaninny?

STORYTELLER: He was and did. So, then they had to look for bigger and bigger bottles of the finest wines, up and up in size, pouring her out of one and into the other, until they could only fit her into the biggest bottle of all, a Melchidezek they call it, and so tall they put a candle on it so planes didn't fly into it, so ships knew it was there and cars could go around it.

> *(A candle is put on top of the biggest wine bottle of all. It shines as a lighthouse, and ships and planes swerve around it)*

STORYTELLER: But also, they put a candle on it to light the way onwards and upwards for children who weren't as grown up as Picaninny was now either wouldn't go bumping into it. And do you know, that had now become all of the children she knew?
(pause while THE GREAT FRANKLIN pokes her playfully…)
'But that wasn't the real secret why Picaninny grew', he said to Meeta, 'was it?', his great eyes able to twinkle now – his smile, too, that few knew had really been the thing to make him so great because he hardly let anyone see it unless they were special.

MOTHER: What was it, then?

STORYTELLER: 'What was it then,' even from little Meeta's mother, so excited too and by now barely able to hold the weight of her little girl becoming heavier and heavier. And for all the joy she had then watching her little one grow so in her arms there.

THE GREAT FRANKLIN: Well, this is what it was…

401

STORYTELLER: ...The great man went before we could cut in quickly enough, and going: 'You see, when he got over his sulks, Mr Crocodile had given her a secret word because Mr Crocodile knew how much she would grow with all those springs in her step and how she would need something when she had grown to a certain size. And with that secret word all Picaninny had to do was look up to her candle and say that word and then pull herself up on the rope that would magically fall down from the sky only for her... and when she did that, she would be exactly the same as everyone else which, personally, for me, was a bit of a shame really.'

THE GREAT FRANKLIN: Well, not really. Or maybe just a bit 'really'. Now I suppose that big nose of yours wants to know what that secret word was.

MEETA ALTER EGO and MOTHER: Yesth, please!

THE GREAT FRANKLIN: You have to promise not to tell.

MEETA ALTER EGO and MOTHER: Yesth!

STORYTELLER: Me too!
   (pulls himself up with an embarrassed laugh)
Our little Meeta jarred so much, you know. Anyway, 'I do!' she promised and so bravely that the great man put his finger to his lips and looked around to see if no one else could hear and then, apart from her mother who in some cases don't matter. 'Well', he whispered, 'I suppose it's all right since your name is Meeta, or I trust it is. Listen. You listening?...'

THE GREAT FRANKLIN: You listening? You're not going all sleepy, sleepy on me, are you?

MEETA and MOTHER: Yesth! No!

   (They all... including MEETA ALTER EGO and the twin brats and Mr Crocodile etc... draw near so they don't miss a word...)

402

THE GREAT FRANKLIN: Ssh, ssh, that secret magic word is... is...
well, three words really, so magic it is, and those three words are...
are... "You little bottler".

MEETA ALTER EGO: (for all) I beg yours?

THE GREAT FRANKLIN: Sssh. Not so loud. "You little bottler".
They might be three words but they're three magic words all rolled into
one from where Picaninny came from and meaning god-knows-what
magically. And, when Picaninny pulled on that rope that fell from the
sky as soon as she said those magic words all rolled into one, what do
you think happened to her head and shoulders?

STORYTELLER: The great man went tucking her under her chin.

MEETA ALTER EGO: What, please?

MEETA: What, please?

TWIN BRAT 1: What?

TWIN BRAT 2: What, what?

SECURITY MEN: (together) Make like you value your life.

STORYTELLER: And it was only until you could hear a pin drop that
The Great Franklin pulled out his world-famous cloak and twirled it
and whirled it and threw it famously over his shoulder like a
continental soldier, and only then did he answer, going: 'They rose,
silly.'

ALL: What rose?!

THE GREAT FRANKLIN: Those head and shoulders of hers.
Everybody got wax in their ears? Those head and shoulders of
Picaninny's, what else? And nobody ever much looked down on them
again so high were they now above the ground, unless they were flying
on a horse with wings, which you have to take my word about. And not
many are ever flying over riding on a horse with wings, let me tell you.

(Disappointed, the shadow players leave him, except...)

STORYTELLER: Little Meeta giggled again this time with the top of her not-so-little head now easily reaching the chin of her mother while her heels were now easily reaching down to below her mother's knees all the way down there, where a few grottos ago she could only but fit on the palms of her hands.

THE GREAT FRANKLIN: (pretend shock) Well! Am I in shock or do my famous eye grow sleepy, sleepy too? Why, I think my little friend Meeta's growing already!

MEETA ALTER EGO: (clap-handedly) You little bottler! You little bottler!
   (as she watches her own shadow grow and grow...)
I am! I am!

STORYTELLER: And if a dear little thing like she was... mark you, *was,* meaning being little to everybody else... if, growing so, she could hiss in a nice way, she hissed it in a nice way... and, guess what... as can't we all see?... she hissed it right into her mother's ear, yes! -- and at lip level, as high up as that. She had already grown as much as that. She had never been so high as to have ever looked into her mother's ear before; a bit of a funny sight. A lot of ins and outs in there.
   (waits for shadow action to catch up again...)
But if you think the great man had finished, you don't know how the heart of The Great Franklin can get so full that it gets a bit too heavy a little too easily, and he leant over to ask her as she grew...

THE GREAT FRANKLIN: Would you like to know what happened to Mr Crocodile?

MEETA: ('who cares really') Sure.

STORYTELLER: But her answer was a bit who-cares?, so soon so used to getting to look normal, or maybe a bit distracted by the sight of the top of her mother's head which she had never seen before, and how her hair parted and how she had to bend over to look to see where it went down below her.

404

MEETA: What's this, Mummy, snow?

MOTHER: It's dandruff, darling.

MEETA: Can I have some?

MOTHER: (proudly) You can get whatever you want, my dear!

THE GREAT FRANKLIN: Neither do I, about Mr Crocodile, really…

STORYTELLER: …went The Great Franklin, very very sadly, because he secretly *did* want to know… and secretly *didn't* want to know… and didn't know which, which is not good for a world-famous hypnotist if it ever got around. That was getting all sleepy, sleepy on yourself lies… even worse for a world-famous hypnotist. So all he could do was famously stare at the distant horizons.
  (and)
With that it is recorded that the great man left his new friend Meeta and her mother in the grotto there.
  (as MEETA ALTER EGO, making a clenched-fist victory sign, 'flies' down to merge with MEETA…)
By then, no, little Meeta wasn't so tiny anymore. Her eyes were full bright to see the world without the throbbing of that headache. Her eyes were full bright she was big enough to hug her daddy around the waist and large enough to fit her hands around her twin brother-brats' necks and to squeeze there as tightly as they had once squeezed her out at birth and ever since… except they started squealing far more than she ever did.

  (Shadow shows how, taller and larger, she is man-handling her twin brothers in one hand and keeping the Senator's security men off with the other – and very easily…)

STORYTELLER: By the time the great man had even got to the front gate, little Meeta was already back inside the birthday party and getting her rightful share of any cake crumbs going around. If you listen carefully you can still hear the brattish squeals from what it was like to get the squeeze put on, to be squeezed in, to be squeezed out, and a fair bit of catch-up pinching along the way.

(Fade out on Meeta terrorising the brats' birthday bash.

Blackout.

Nearly belatedly, the STORYTELLER reappears in his own spot front stage. He peers into the audience area as though he might well be expecting no one to be there. Finally:)

STORYTELLER: If you're seeing me now, it's not The Great Franklin's doing, but the director taking up the option to include it.
   (and)
As it goes, a few years later, The Great Franklin got a teary call from the mother to please, please, please stop her once little Meeta from growing. He did and she did! She told him it had become all too much and it was all his fault. So, the great man rang the little girl up at a time she was having a mouthful of steroids on top of a two double Big Macs with side fries and he famously said to her, 'Meeta, enough's enough, my child. You don't have to get so big as to keep squeezing the life out your twin brothers. They're starting to get pretty stunted, I hear. Also, is it really a good look you taking up the invitation to try out for the L.A. Lakers at the age of seven, you being a girl and them wearing all those baggy pants? I mean, if you didn't have that whole two double Big Macs and triple fries in your mouth now... okay, *and* steroids, sorry... I'm sure you'd agree with what I'm advising you here, as long as you don't go getting all sleepy sleepy on me. That's what The Great Franklin famously said. He didn't get any reply, or so's said. We do know he got some sort of munching sound back in his ear before it is thought once-little Meeta handed the phone over to the LA Laker's recruiting agent who started barking down the phone at him to lay off. And it sounded like there was a whole bunch of dandruff falling in the background, but he only picked that up because he was so famously staring at the distant horizons at the time.

(He nods 'thank you'.

Blackout; final this time.)

---oOo----

CPSIA information can be obtained
at www.ICGtesting.com
Printed in the USA
BVHW042215071118
532450BV00017B/94/P